Gothic forms
of feminine fictions

Gothic forms
of feminine fictions

Susanne Becker

Manchester University Press
Manchester and New York

Distributed exclusively in the USA by St. Martin's Press

Published by
Manchester University Press,
Oxford Road, Manchester M13 9NR, UK
and Room 400, 175 Fifth Avenue, New York, NY 10010, USA
http://www.man.ac.uk/mup

Distributed exclusively in the USA by
St. Martin's Press, Inc., 175 Fifth Avenue, New York,
NY 10010, USA

Distributed exclusively in Canada by
UBC Press, University of British Columbia, 6344 Memorial Road,
Vancouver, BC, Canada V6T 1Z2

British Library Cataloguing-in-Publication Data
A catalogue record for this book is available from the British Library

Library of Congress Cataloging-in-Publication Data applied for

ISBN   0 7190 5330 7 *hardback*
        0 7190 5331 5 *paperback*

First published 1999

05 04 03 02 01 00 99   10 9 8 7 6 5 4 3 2 1

Designed and typeset by Lucy Morton & Robin Gable, Grosmont

Printed in Great Britain by Redwood Books, Trowbridge

Contents

List of illustrations

Acknowledgements

Gothic novels have long fascinated me: because of their emotional powers, their provocative and pleasurable plots and their feminine form. Mary Shelley's *Frankenstein* sparked my readings of gothic classics and my sensibility of contemporary gothica. Thus, I have come to propose this culture-critical study on the powers of gothic in the late twentieth century.

The gothic has shaped and sharpened my literary studies and numerous stimulating exchanges: in Munich, with Sibylle Kastl and Elisabeth Bronfen, who shared with me their sense of the absurdities in literature and life; in Mainz, with Professor Wolfgang Riedel, who has always both challenged and supported my academic endeavours; and in Toronto, with Professor Barbara Godard and Carmen Cáliz, who unfolded my first, rough ideas into the realm of theory – often through dark and stormy winter nights! The Government of Canada Award brought me to Toronto's York University from the fall of 1988 to the spring of 1990: there, the 'Canadian connections' of this study emerged.

At the English Department of Columbia University, New York, where I taught as Adjunct Assistant Professor in 1991/92, I wrote the first outline, and, as a Visiting Scholar in the fall of 1997, I conceptualised Part III. I thank my inspiring students there, as well as those at Mainz University, where I have been teaching since 1990. I thank the Johannes Gutenberg University for awarding the University Prize of 1996 to my dissertation. Carmen Birkle in the American Studies Department has been supportive throughout. Cyrus Patel has genially formatted the manuscript. My editor at Manchester University Press, Matthew Frost, has proven both clairvoyant and practical. I am thankful to him and everybody involved in transforming the disk into this book.

In Toronto I studied with Professor Linda Hutcheon: to her spiritedness, her professional guidance and intellectual sensibility I owe so much more than I can here express. Her work on postmodernism, as well as her open and suggestive discussions of my evolving ideas, reverberate throughout this book. Professor Alfred Hornung courageously accepted my hopeful fragments as a dissertation when I returned to Mainz. I am grateful for his clear views of my project, for his amazing sense of structure and for important and inspiring discussions. His work on postmodernism and autobiography influenced my readings, and he has patiently overseen the final drafts of the manuscript. I thank Linda Hutcheon and Alfred Hornung for their continuing interest and confidence in my ideas and project.

Special thanks go to Margaret Atwood. In the last years, she has been very generous and supportive and has met me for several intense talks about gothic appearances – her own as well as those of today's culture. Our meetings at her kitchen counter in Toronto as well as at public events like the book fair in Frankfurt are unforgettable.

Finally, I thank my parents for their persistent support, my brothers for their encouraging sense of humour, and my sister for many gothic ideas and images. And Bernhard, for everything.

'We live in Gothic times.'
Angela Carter

Introduction

The gothic romance is one of the most popular literary forms ever. Since its origins two hundred years ago, it has attracted mass audiences and intellectuals alike. Having emerged with the novel and the earliest forms of modern mass entertainment in the last decades of the eighteenth century, the gothic exhibits unchanged vitality in the present media age, obsessed with incessant stimulation and excitement. Today's globalised entertainment culture – relying on daily soaps, tabloids, confession shows like Oprah Winfrey's and media icons like the late Princess Diana – is reflected in the emotional trajectory of the gothic's violence, eroticism and sentimental excess.

Gothic fiction, I think, is closely connected to these cultural developments. In the last decades, it has experienced a revival that is related to the two most powerful political and aesthetic movements of the time: feminism and postmodernism. This might be because it shares with them a radical scepticism concerning the universalising humanist assumptions of modern thought and of classic realism. In its both sensationalist and provocative form, the gothic functions like pulp fiction, as Clive Bloom has recently defined and historicised it, as 'a refusal of bourgeois consciousness and bourgeois forms of realism' (1996, 14). The gothic, of course, has from the first proudly celebrated its anti-realism. One of its most effective narrative strategies, both for its popularity and for its attack on classic realism, has always been what I will call excess: excess in moral terms, excess of realism into the supernatural, but also formal excess. Of course, in the gothic world anything might happen, and its excessive emotional experiences of desire, terror and pleasure become reading-experiences of liberation. Thus, this study will be a culture-critical reading of classic and post-modern gothic with the aim of working out the persistent powers of gothic for literary forms and cultural shifts of the late twentieth century.

Neil Cornwell has linked the gothic era to postmodernism in his literary history of the fantastic (1990, esp. xii–xv), and more recently various essay collections have discussed historical and contemporary gothic from a postmodern perspective (Sage and Smith 1996; Tinkler-Villani and Davidson 1995; see also Botting 1996). These academic explorations of the connectedness of postmodern culture and gothic literature are extended into more popular explorations that happen on a variety of Internet websites with their continuous communication and inscription of gothica. Approaches range from neo-Romantic nostalgia to the sense of apocalypse that also opens the collection of contemporary *New Gothic* short fiction (Morrow and McGrath 1991, xiv). The 1990s exhibit the ongoing dynamics of the gothic, which from the first has always reflected 'what is most active, developing and changing in the literary, social and cultural developments of the times in which it is written' (Tinkler-Villani and Davidson 1995, 5). It is my argument that gothicism – or rather *neo-gothicism* – will signal the emancipatory possibilities of postmodern culture: we live again in times that are sensible to gothic forms of emotion and representation. And it is my conviction that one of the secrets of the gothic's persistent success is gender-related: it is so powerful because it is so feminine.

Because of its instant popularity with women both as writers and as readers, the gothic was early on seen as part of female culture and as a 'women's genre'. This recognition points to its importance in the contemporary literary scene, where 'gender writing' has been one of the most exciting recent developments. Feminist and masculinist texts – texts that are aware of and productive in the constructions of gender in a specific cultural-historical context (see Moi 1989, 117–32) – have become increasingly influential since the 1960s and the birth of the feminist movement, and have used new forms of writing that trans-cend the established critical categories for prose. While it seems that masculine texts often consider gender constructions in a dialogue with feminist theory and practice (for example, read Martin Amis, *Informa-tion* [1995]), feminine fictions are interwoven with a web of writing that has long been exploring and inscribing gender. In the contemporary cultural context of growing gender awareness – and awareness of race, class, ethnicity, nationality, sexual preference and other aspects of difference – a new generation of feminine writing has arisen that redefines the established notions – mostly from the 1970s – of 'women's literature' as confessional, didactic and highly serious; it also reminds us that there is not one feminism but many feminisms, in art just as in criticism. Moreover, this writing resists the conservative backlash that in the early 1990s managed to domesticate the emancipatory discussion of gender and difference into its reverse – another reactionary ideology. Political correctness unites liberal intellectuals and ultra-conservative politicians (see Marcovits 1992) – especially, it seems, as part of the backlash against (multi-)cultural politics and feminism.

In the face of these recent developments, the new feminine writing presents itself as a strong, rebellious force, a dynamic challenge to the traps of such institutionalised liberalism. This writing comes from writers as diverse as Toni Morrison and Margaret Atwood, Angela Carter and Siri Hustvedt. It evokes and reveals established images of femininity, but does not propose new role models; it evokes and re-writes familiar narrative forms, but undermines their established effects; it evokes and repeats ideological constructions of established power structures, but defamiliarises their 'natural' existence. The terminology here suggests postmodern strategies, and particularly Linda Hutcheon's concept of a 'paradoxical postmodernism of complicity and critique ... that at once inscribes and subverts the conventions and ideologies of the dominant cultural and social forces of the twentieth-century western world' (1989, 11). If the subversive potential of the postmodern thus shapes the narrative strategies, its playful dimension marks the characteristic tone of the new feminine fictions: their lightness of voice. This voice is full of irony and humour, which ensures entertainment – and certainly much of their unquestionable popularity – but also produces a challenging effect, and, sometimes, a biting feminist critique. Feminist 'practice' and the work of postcolonial writers have contributed to the 'emancipatory turn' of postmodernism in the 1980s (Hoffmann and Hornung 1996); and the politicised dimension of the new feminine writing is shaped, I think, by its formal and inter-textual connectedness to that long-established women's genre, the gothic. After all, the gothic has for two hundred years played an important role in female culture despite dramatic cultural changes; it worked early on to feminise established literary forms and has, throughout its history, strongly challenged established notions of femininity. Thus, postmodern feminine fictions are politicised by their recourse to the gothic form and work to attack the often misogynist complacencies of the contemporary cultural establishment.

In the era of sampling and mixing, of quoting and rewriting, a new form of gendered writing has thereby emerged, a form that I call *neo-gothic*. It spans the time between the politicised 1970s, the conservative 1980s and the millennium-ridden 1990s. What connects these decades is a lack of orientation especially relating to everyday life, as the traditional separation of the spheres of production and reproduction along gender lines is radically shaken: images of career women and new fathers, alternative modes of family organisation and single parenting, mark the way towards a new – post-feminist? post-patriarchal? – culture. Neo-gothicism reflects the feminine dimensions of the ongoing cultural and literary change: after all, gothic horror is domestic horror, family horror, and addresses precisely these obviously 'gendered' problems of everyday life.

However, while neo-gothic fictions poignantly address and evoke the contemporary cultural as well as personal crisis, they do not pretend to supply solutions, an effect that connects them to the provocative politics of postmodernism. Rather, they adopt a somewhat paradoxical position: gothicism has always been provocation and rebellion against order, control and the powers of restrictive ideologies. At the time of postmodern ambivalence, however, it does offer a certain orientation-effect in the recognition of the familiar textual form that has constituted the feminine gothic and its exploration of domestic horror throughout the last two centuries. This form, as I hope to show, highlights gender-constructions and the related constructions of culture, but it also evokes the constructions of experience and writing. Thus, it addresses not only the cultural but also the specifically literary 'death-of-the-novel' crisis; and it does so by being both creative, postmodernly *neo*, and by being familiarly *gothic*. Thus, this sceptical time seems to need the most provocative, rebellious – and for some even nihilistic – narrative form to provide reassurance and orientation without enforcing what is both dreaded and desired: order and stability.

Let us look at the range of writing that works through this neo-gothic paradox in postmodern culture. It is especially prominent in anglophone cultures: Fay Weldon's comic-ironic bestsellers and Angela

Carter's erotic gothic fairy tales in England might be the best-known examples. In the USA, it seems, there is often more seriousness in the ironic tone of postmodern gothicism, as in Joyce Carol Oates' postmodern gothic novels about WASP myths and culture. Oates has characterised her complex novel *Bellefleur* (1980) as 'a Gothic novel' that is also 'a diary of my own life, and the lives of people that I have known', as well as 'a critique of America' (Oates 1988, 371). She emphasises the personal and political powers of the feminine gothic that also work in ethnic texts like Toni Morrison's *Beloved* (1987), with its black orality and its gothic ghost baby–woman; or Maxine Hong Kingston's interweaving of Chinese and (to the Western reader) gothic ghosts in the mother–daughter story *The Woman Warrior* (1976). Similarly, New Zealand writer Keri Hulme, in *The Bone People* (1985) mixes Maori ghosts with gothic ones, which in her radical family drama of violence, punishment and redemption heightens the humanism of a horrific tale.

In this study, I will focus on English-Canadian texts that have played an important if not always acknowledged role in shaping 'gendered' writing over the last twenty years. Ontario writer Alice Munro's work is well-known for its realism; however, her early *Lives of Girls and Women* (1971) explores the gothicising of female life-writing: it self-consciously introduces gothic features and highlights their possibilities and dangers, and is thus a text that overtly establishes gothicism as an adequate and indeed appropriate feminine form of writing, also at the time of radical feminism. Margaret Atwood, an international star of Canadian literature, has been famous for her gothic poetry since the 1970s; her third novel *Lady Oracle* (1976) powerfully rewrites various dimensions of gothic form, from the popular, conservative 'gothics' to the provocative feminist ones. And Aritha van Herk from the Canadian West, critically established as 'postmodern' but not at all as 'gothic', exposes the strength of a radical feminist gothicism in the conservative 1980s in her third novel *No Fixed Address* (1986). These examples from the Canadian postmodern context show, as we shall see, not only the variety, but also a progressive development of the gothic forms of feminine fictions towards the 1990s. Two centuries after Ann Radcliffe, important novels like A. S. Byatt's *Possession* (1990) and Margaret Atwood's *Alias Grace* (1996) use the possibilities of the neo-gothic form to disclose the epistemological urge, the emotionalised sense of (global) culture and sensationalist media industry on the threshold of the millennium. Throughout, my reading also involves a recentring: although the power and international impact of women writers in Canada have long been recognised, criticism have tended to marginalise them or else to subsume them as American. Thus, in this study, Anglophone intertexts will be discussed around core examples from the Canadian postmodern.

My discussion of neo-gothicism takes place at the intersection of different strands of both theory and fiction. The intersection of feminism and postmodernism seems a good place to start. That they are not mutually exclusive still seems to surprise some critics; others have pondered the advantages of 'annexation of feminist art' (Bertens 1996, 104), although feminist activism has anticipated the more philosophical postmodern scepticism and criticism of liberal-humanist assumptions. For example, what ironically has become a definite 'master narrative' of postmodernism, namely Jean-François Lyotard's *La Condition postmoderne* (1979), with his criticism of the 'master narratives' of Western Enlightenment thought – Knowledge, Subjectivity, History, Meaning, Truth – reads like the philosophical version of feminist practice. Consciousness-raising has been the feminist attack on the patriarchal 'master narrative' of a coherent and unified subjectivity, with its related prescribed ideal feminine. Moreover, the narrative strategies related to these challenges – for example irony, but also a complex subjectivity and contradictory textual structures – are used by both postmodern and feminist writers. Linda Hutcheon has shown that '"de-doxification" is as inherently a part of feminist as it is of postmodern discourse' (1989, 20) and that what distinguishes the two is postmodernism's political ambivalence (1989, 168). In contrast to the 'high' postmodern phase of narcissistic playfulness – as in Raymond Federman's *Surfiction* (1975), or in Richard Brautigan's genre play *The Hawkline Monster: A Gothic Western* (1974) – feminisms have an agenda; they insist on practice – and, by extension, on profound cultural change (see, e.g., Fraser and Nicholson 1990, esp. 26; Flax 1990, esp. 52; Hutcheon 1989, 141ff). In some ways, the new feminine texts point to such a change: the idea of *Woman* – the 'natural' or ideal feminine – is being shifted to *women* – in all their historical difference. The gothic here foregrounds the hidden horrors of a unifying, universalising image of Woman – after all, some of the most striking literary figures of madwomen, daemonic women or of the monstrous-feminine come from gothic texts. In this sense, feminine gothic writing partakes in the more general postmodern challenges to the master narrative of the Subject.

This suggests the next intersection in this study: that of the gothic and the postmodern. The close affinities of gothicism and postmodernism have been evoked best in Angela Carter's postulate that 'we live in Gothic times' in the Afterword to *Fireworks* (1974, 1987). According to her, gothicism

> grandly ignores the value systems of our institutions; it deals entirely with the profane ... Character and events are exaggerated beyond reality, to become symbols, ideas, passions. Its style will tend to be ornate, unnatural – and thus operate against the perennial human desire to believe the word as fact ... It retains a singular moral function – that of provoking unease. (1974, 133)

Such unease is shared by postmodern and gothic art. Carter implies that 'the marginalized subgenres of former times have necessarily become the appropriate and dominant modes of our present discourse' (Neumeier 1996, 141). This situation marks art and criticism after 'the Great Divide' between mass culture and high modernism (Huyssen 1986, viii); a divide that, like all binary oppositions, has also been gender-coded (Huyssen 1986, 44; McGowan 1991, 20). Accordingly, the popular genre of the gothic appears positioned with 'mass culture as woman' (Huyssen 1986, 44). The challenges of contemporary thought to such binary oppositions and their exclusions suggest *difference* by 'multiplicity, heterogeneity, plurality' (Hutcheon 1988a, 61; see also Flax 1990, 56), with the emancipatory postmodern and feminist emphasis on situating and contextualising. The postmodern insistence on difference supports a critical interest in formerly marginalised genres like the gothic. Most recent readings emphasise the parallels, best summarised in Allan Lloyd-Smith's view that 'what underlyingly links the Gothic with the postmodern is an aesthetic of anxiety and perplexity, as similar responses to the confusing new order' (1996, 18). Theo D'haen, in his essay 'Postmodern Gothic', has revalued the possibilities of the gothic 'unreal' and argued 'for the fantastic in postmodern literature as the counter-axial counterpart of present-day forms of (social) realism in opposition to poststructuralist/aesthetic postmodernism' (1995, 289). As we shall see, this relationship to realism will be of major concern to a gendered reading of the gothic.

I would like to emphasise that, where postmodernism becomes an almost all-male affair, gothicism is again placed in the margins – or reduced to a matter of setting. For example, Brian McHale (1987) postulates that postmodernist fiction offers different and intruding 'worlds'. Here the gothic is reduced to

> the recurrence ... of that hoary gothic locale, the haunted house: nothing is more domestic, more normal, than a middle-class house, so nothing is more disruptive than other-worldly agents penetrating and 'taking over' a house. (1987, 77)

However, the middle-class house's normality as well as the normality of domesticity are decidedly a matter of perspective. In the 'normal' middle-class organisation of family life, this perspective does differ along gender lines. Of course, a hero must typically leave the house; a heroine, however, more often than not remains in the house which is 'her place' and her enclosure. And to her, McHale's 'disruption' need not be that 'outerwordly' to be horrific! This is clearly shown in Randi Gunzenhäuser's study of the gothic sublime, with the programmatic title *Horror at Home* (1993). She shows that the house as most important (inner) space in the 'Female Gothic romance' repeats the gendered external power structures and thus becomes the *Bewährungsraum* – the space of probation or trial and success – for a female subject (Gunzenhäuser 1993, 22). As the house or inner space constitutes the realm of the *beautiful*, this distinguishes the 'Female Gothic' romance's spatial trajectory from the Burkean as well as recent American theory's *sublime* where the external, male world offers that space of proving oneself. Horror at Home! Aliens voluntary!

This excursion leads to another intersection I wish to discuss here: that of gothicism and gender. Ellen Moers famously coined the term 'Female Gothic', the gothic written by women, in her female literary history (1978), which connects Ann Radcliffe with Mary Shelley with Emily Brontë with Sylvia Plath. Moers's work is still legendary, mainly for its assumption that the gothic is a (physically) affective genre; for its reading of Mary Shelley's *Frankenstein* as 'birth myth' (Moers 1978, 92); and for its original celebration of the attractions of the excesses of gothic romance for women writers and readers:

> In the power of villains, [Ann Radcliffe's] heroines are forced to do what they could never do alone, whatever their ambitions: scurry up to the top of pasteboard Alps, spy out exotic vistas, penetrate bandit-infested forests.

And indoors, inside Mrs. Radcliffe's castles, her heroines can scuttle miles along corridors, descend into dungeons, and explore secret chambers without a chaperone, because the Gothic castle, however much in ruins, is still an indoor and therefore freely female space. (Moers 1978, 126)

A variety of studies of female gothic are grounded in Moers's reading: Juliann Fleenor's critical collection *The Female Gothic* (1983), with its inclusion of popular with classic gothics and its reading of the gothic as metaphor for female experience (27); but also essays on the female gothic as 'discourse of the other' or as giving 'voice to the female condition' (van Leeuwen 1982, 33); as liberating revision of Leslie Fiedler's well-established, all too seductive and completely homocentric reading of literary forces like *love* and *death* (Restuccia 1986, esp. 245–8); and as perfect starting-point for a reconsideration of contemporary American culture (Showalter 1989). In the early 1990s, critics have asked the question 'what's female about gothic' as interest shifts from the female writing tradition to psychoanalytic readings, for example of 'women, masochism and the gothic' (Massé 1992), or towards more poststructuralist approaches to gender and genre. For example, Susan Wolstenholme proposes gothic texts (from novels to film) as 'establishing "woman" as a textual position' – especially by assuming an implied spectator – and thus as establishing 'a pattern that becomes a recognisable symbolic code' (1993, xi). What connects most of these readings is their assumption of the gothic's potential subversion of patriarchal culture, mostly through its anti-realism. Rosemary Jackson's reading of fantasy's subversion has established non-realist forms as 'countercultural'; unfortunately, it mentions their feminist potential only in a footnote: 'Non-realist narrative forms are increasingly important in feminist writing: no breakthrough of cultural structures seems possible until linear narrative (realism, illusionism, transparent representation) is broken or dissolved' (Jackson 1981, 186 n. 10, see also 104). All of these approaches to gender and genre have influenced this study.

As my title indicates, I will focus on form: on the narrative and ideological components that shape gothic fictions as feminine forms. What I would like to pursue is the extension of gendered gothic criticism into the realm of feminist semiotic thinking and contemporary culture criticism. One of the most important metaphors for me will be that of the house. The implications here are threefold: the well-known gothic stock device, the haunted house; its extension into Henry James's famous critical term, the house of fiction; and its gendered ideological connotation, the house as woman's place. In this sense, the house will structure my reading: the haunted house in the text just as much as the house as form of gothic fiction. This focus on form shifts the (traditional) critical interest from the gender of the author (female gothic) to that of the speaking subject in the text (feminine gothic). Accordingly, the (haunted) house as narrative structure is seen as constructing the gender of the subject just as much as the generic horror and the other narrative conventions. In this sense, the 'break-through of cultural structures' of Jackson's fantastic can be gothically reformulated: the fictional house signifies the containment within traditional power structures; gothicism is used then not only to expose but, as we shall see, to *exceed* these homocentric structures and their control.

In a conversation with Joyce Carol Oates, Margaret Atwood has asked: 'What about that "Madwife" left over from *Jane Eyre*? Are these our secret plots?' (1977, 7). This idea has sparked and framed my readings for this study: Atwood links contemporary writing to the dark and dangerous figure of Charlotte Brontë's Bertha Mason, the most famous 'madwoman in the attic' of women's literary history, as outlined by Gilbert and Gubar (1979). This has surprising implications for contemporary female culture. First, it emphasises the presence of gothicism in the context of a dominant feminist criticism that has privileged two different modes as representative of today's women's literary culture: that of autobiographical confession and that of ex-perimental feminine writing (see Weigel 1987; Felski 1989). Second, it evokes the contemporary intertextualisation around the nineteenth-century figure of the 'madwoman in the attic': most notably in Jean Rhys's *Wide Sargasso Sea* (1966), which tells Bertha Mason's story, but also, as we shall see, in much neo-gothic fiction. The resonant 'madwoman in the attic' is a clue to the attractions of gothic form for feminine fictions. As the female figure enclosed not only by the house but moreover by its most marginal part, she dramatically signifies women's assigned place of enclosure and constraint; of domestic horror with no escape. I will investigate the narrative effects of this mad-woman figure who, in the 'house of the text', always plays a central part, as well as her textual construction as representation of the 'monstrous-feminine'. The persistence of this gothic madwoman, as suggested by Atwood, might be the most dramatic reminder of the gothic's attack on traditional power structures.

Moreover, Atwood's allusion to women's 'secret plots' suggests a complex narrative, and recalls the idea of hyperbole that Angela Carter has defined as essential to gothicism: such hyperbole not only marks characters, events and style, but also narrative structures and form. My term for this gothic feature, *excess*, is one of the terms of gothic criticism that has been used pejoratively to marginalise the gothic as a 'feminine form'. I hope to show that it indicates a potential liberation from constraining – both cultural and narrative – structures. The idea of a secret plot from the past that structures a contemporary narrative, for example, suggests an excess in narrative, a level of narration that doubles or contests – and thus problematises – the conventions of a surface narrative pattern: for example, the pattern of the traditional 'heroine's text' – the text that ends in marriage or death (see Miller 1980).

Such questions of gender and narrative will shape the following readings. Part I offers a theoretical and historical background and explores the classic texts of two hundred years of gothicism on three levels: first, their contextualising of the specific cultural-historical situation that they both come from and address; second, their narrative texture, marked by a complex subjectivity; and third, the intertextualisation of feminine gothic writing that continues but also challenges historical feminine gothicism. These three levels offer a web of connections rather than a linear 'red thread', and a reading of anticipations and recollections between gothic classics and neo-gothicism, gender-culture and the excesses of the 1990s.

The readings of the neo-gothic texts then take up and continue these terms. They lead us to a twofold view of gothic effects in contemporary female culture. First, continuity, an ongoing elaboration of women's gothic intertextualisations; and second, deconstruction, a challenge to the limits of gothic form and to the myths of the feminine that shape both that form and the larger order of traditional power structures. For example, Alice Munro's *Lives of Girls and Women* uses gothic contextualising to tell a gothic story of growing up, but also of the process of telling it. This was written at a time – the early 1970s – when confessional life-writing seemed the appropriate feminist genre, and when feminist criticism espoused traditional humanist values. The

transformation of these values into more difference-oriented thinking
was anticipated by neo-gothic texts, like Munro's, that already mock
the trust in classic realism.

In a further development, Margaret Atwood's *Lady Oracle* parodically incorporates gothic *texture*: enforcing its persistence and scruti-
nising its potential conservatism. This novel's comic irony points us to
another gothic source, besides the feminine gothic classics: it also
alludes to the 'gothic boom', the explosion in the paperback romance
market that strangely coincided with the women's movement of the
late 1960s and early 1970s. In a postmodern recognition of popular
culture, Atwood's self-consciously gothic fiction deals with this important phenomenon of contemporary female culture, and explores
the attractions of these pulp romances.

Such popular gothic romances also have their traces in other new
feminine fictions. For example, in Aritha van Herk's *No Fixed Address*
(1986), the stereotypical love plot of the popular romance is ironically
evoked, only to be radically rejected. This is a text of the 1980s'
emancipatory thinking in difference, of critical theory and fiction. Van
Herk's novel continues feminine gothic intertextualisation and extends
the gothic's 'unfixing' processes even further, towards incessant motion beyond the narrative's ending and beyond the (both geographical
and metaphorical) Canadian frontier.

The gothicism of *No Fixed Address* also relies very much on the
Canadian landscape. It points us to the intersection of neo-gothicism
and Canadian culture. 'Canadian Postmodern' as defined by Linda
Hutcheon (1988b) and D'haen and Bertens (1992), offers two important characteristics for our discussion: one is the specific persistence
of literary realism in Canadian fiction and criticism that becomes the
'defining base' for not only postmodern (Hutcheon 1988b, 21) but also
gothic challenges. The other is the perception of Canadian culture as
ex-centric – a position that Hutcheon shows to be, like the frontier,
'the place of possibility' (1988b, 3). It describes the international, postcolonial position between British and American dominance, but also
the more internal Canadian multicultural mosaic with its 'firm suspicion of centralising tendencies' (1988b, 3). Both gothic and feminine
writing have been perceived as ex-centric in similar ways – in fact, the
power of Canadian women writers has often been linked with their
'doubly colonised' status (see Kamboureli and Neumann 1988, Irvine
1986). The possibilities of such a position in the Canadian context

offer the frame for my own exploration of the dynamics of neo-gothic ex-centricities.

These dynamics have accelerated throughout the past decades. The role of gothicism has changed in art and criticism, and my chosen texts from the Canadian postmodern reflect the parallel development of neo-gothic writing. My metaphor of 'stripping the gothic' for *No Fixed Address* announces the recognition of an exciting formal shift towards the end of the 1980s. The house of gothic fiction still forms Munro's novel; Atwood's later narrative 'excess' effects the more complex form of the maze – still an enclosure but an elaborate one from which a female figure can lead the way. Then, van Herk's multi-levelled story defies the constraints of enclosing structures altogether, with a travelling heroine in the Canadian West: her only enclosure left is that of dress. In the 1990s, then, complex novels like Byatt's *Possession* and Atwood's *Alias Grace* exhibit the powers of neo-gothic textures for the disclosures of emotional and epistemological urges. From houses of fiction to textures of dress: neo-gothicism – the feminine excess in postmodern times – promises new, exciting dynamics for the textures of gender and culture.

PART I

Gothic forms – feminine texts

But what, then, is *feminine* about the gothic? Addressing the question of the 'feminine text' still means stepping on shifting ground. The terms of discussion were first laid out in the 1970s between the author-centred model that excludes male artists, but also many differences between female artists (e.g., Moers 1978, Gilbert and Gubar 1979; for an overview see Eagleton 1986, 88–148), and the avant-garde model that celebrates differences, includes male artists (in fact, even privileges them) and rejects the perpetuation of narrative conventions (e.g., Cixous 1981; Kristeva 1974). Two aspects of this ongoing discussion are central to this study: the theorisation of feminine style – often convincingly emphasising its powers and subversive potential through 'plurality', 'diffuseness', 'multiplicities of meaning' (e.g., Kuhn 1982, 11; Felski 1989, 30) – and the theorisation of gender culture – emphasising gender as designating 'the very apparatus of production whereby the sexes themselves are established' (Butler 1990, 7; Laqueur 1990). These ideas and the recent recourse to reflections on corpo-reality and 'bodies that matter' (Butler 1993) lead the gender-oriented pursuit of gothicism to new dimensions.

This study, as has been suggested, will shift the focus from novels written by women – female gothic – to women-centred novels – feminine gothic. This shift indicates a focus on the, necessarily gendered, subjectivity *in* the text. Subjectivity will be a central point of departure for the discussion of texts from the gothic tradition as well as from the Canadian postmodern; and the focus on a female subject rather than author allows for discussing a text like Henry James's *The*

Turn of the Screw (1897) alongside Charlotte Perkins Gilman's *The Yellow Wallpaper* (1892). Moreover, this takes into account the cultural constructions of literary forms – genre – but also the cultural coding of sex – gender. The old question of the gothic's attractions for women is then rephrased as one of how narrative form can be feminine – bearing in mind that gender, too, is a cultural construct: 'The construction of gender is both the product and the process of its representations' (De Lauretis 1987a, 5). Gothic representations of gender are a case in point – after all, the gothic has long been seen as feminine because it was considered the genre that best represents female *experience* (e.g., Fleenor 1983; Miner 1984). These views of a feminine genre need further discussion.

In the era of mixing and sampling, genre is no longer a safe category (as it might still have been for Northrop Frye). Most notably, it plays a role in the commodification of literature by providing marketable labels and recognisable signals to the reader-consumer. According to Fredric Jameson, '[g]enres are essentially literary *institutions*, or social contracts between a writer and a specific public' (1981, 106) where 'the older generic specifications have been transformed into the brand-name system' (107). And the brand-name 'gothic' sells well to female readers in today's airports and drugstores, just as it did through the Minerva Press two hundred years ago. Like Jameson's Marxist criticism, the feminist discussion of genre has a pragmatic, political dimension, and is thus able to historicise and contextualise. Contextualisation emphasises such extra-textual dimensions, especially with regard to the readership: the receiver and the context of reception. It also implies the analysis of narrative gestures within gothic texts that address the authors' and readers' world(s) of experience.

Formally speaking, the ongoing blurring of boundaries and obfuscation of discrete genre categories does not mean that narrative conventions become invisible. Rather, they are 'played off against each other; there is no simple, unproblematic merging' (Hutcheon 1988a, 9). And this 'playing off' is a postmodern strategy that draws attention to the traditional expectations, uses and effects of form. These will be discussed as *gothic texture*, with examples from gothic classics of the eighteenth and nineteenth centuries. Finally, *gothic intertextualisation* outlines the processes that Barbara Godard calls *filliation* (1983) and the further connectedness with Canadian gothicism and the history of pulp gothic. This section thus provides a historical but also conceptual background to the subsequent discussion of neo-gothicism.

What, then, is *gothic* about it? Let us approach this by looking at a 'master narrative' of structuralism (when genres were still genres, and women were...): 'The definition of genres', writes Todorov, 'will ... be a continued oscillation between the description of phenomena and abstract theory' (1975, 21). His chosen genre, the *fantastic*, has as its core phenomenon a radical doubt, a hesitation in the face of an inexplicable event: 'In a world which is indeed our world, the one we know, a world without devils, sylphides, or vampires, there occurs an event which cannot be explained by the laws of this same familiar world' (25). This definition of the fantastic includes the gothic, which Todorov's model acknowledges as 'the uncanny and the marvellous' and thus as a 'neighbouring genre' to the fantastic. In the gothic, of course, the unfamiliar event can be further classified as one of horror, or terror, or – in Kristeva's term – 'abjection' (1982). This is not only a matter of subjectivity and perception but also, as we shall see, closely related to the female body.

And so to the 'madwoman in the attic'. Since its origins, gothic horror has been situated not only in 'our world', but in the home. Here, then, continues our approach to gothic form: Kate Ferguson Ellis's analysis of the early gothic novels underlines their subversion of a domestic ideology that has sanctified the home since the late eighteenth century. The female middle-class readers of the time, a significant part of the reading public precisely because of their separation from the world of work and their position within the home (the 'woman's place'), were, according to Ellis, 'a major market not simply for novels but for novels about haunted houses and their haunters' (1989, x). These houses represent 'the failed home ... the place from which some (usually "fallen" men) are locked out, and others (usually "innocent" women) are locked in' (ix). Ellis's reading exposes the idea – and *ideology* – of the home as place of protection that turns into a prison.[1] Thus, domestic horror draws attention both to the horrors of enclosure for a female subject within 'her place', and to her desire to leave it.

Chapter 1 unfolds the gothic contextualisation of 'experience' related to this female space. Two more important terms from traditional gothic criticism address the trajectory of gothic horror and female space: 'excess' and 'escape'. They characterise the challenges with which gothicism has always confronted forms of enclosure: gothicists early noted the generic provocations of boundaries – the real and natural; the home or prison; property and propriety. These thematic challenges will here be extended to the boundaries of fiction and of ideological containment: experience, excess and escape characterise not only the *thematic* enclosure of the female subject within the house – or mansion, or castle – but also the *formal* enclosure of the text. Textual and linguistic constructions constitute a third form of enclosure: the *ideological* enclosure of femininity in a culture that might best be described in the feminist reading of Lacan's Symbolic Order: the order of language by the Law of the Father, abstracted by his *nom* (name) and *non* (prohibition). Like language, like any signifying system, the law is arbitrary, abstract and fictional – the task for women is to enter the symbolic in order to position themselves as subjects (see Cixous and Clément 1986). The dynamics and provocations of domestic horror gothically relate to all of these levels: what is suggested in this threefold perspective and especially in the idea of 'excess' is the liberating effect of gothic horror: a trace of its feminist potential.

At this point, the metaphor of the text as house comes in. Henry James's famous image of the *house of fiction* from the beginning of the century (in the preface to *The Portrait of a Lady* (1881, written for the New York edition 1907–18) achieves new dimensions when transformed into the haunted house of feminine gothic fiction. First, James's 'watcher' – the artist at the windows – can be related to the reader as part of the creative process and to the representation of what is outside the house; thus, the *house of fiction* is not only marked by the openings to its surroundings but also by its separation from them and becomes, in this sense, a metaphor for containment. For a female subject, this house's 'ghosts from the past' offer both the recognition of this containment and their challenge. They also contribute to the complex female subjectivity with which, as we shall see, gothic texture becomes a multi-layered construction, an *interrogative text*. The other 'ghost' that haunts the gothic house of fiction is the intertextualisation of the feminine gothic, challenging not only the boundaries of fiction but also traditional theories of origin.

The metaphor of the house offers a further dimension in a gendered reading: feminist criticism and feminine art have long linked the woman's sphere to her body. American writer Lynne Tillman's novel *Haunted Houses* (1987) is a perfect example. It is a fictional braid of three gothic life stories of girls growing up in contemporary Brooklyn; the 'haunted houses' of the title are their bodies that are, in de Beauvoir's sense, not born but *becoming women*. Feminine gothic classics as well as neo-gothic texts circle around such processes: they foreground the gothic emphasis on the body and emotion – sex, desire, fear, horror, abjection. They also draw attention to the processes of gender construction, of idealised femininity, of the *femme fatale*. And gothic heroines, caught in the web of femininity, spin their threads to *exceed* or *escape* the attics and 'secret plots' in Atwood's sense that reverberate in the gothic houses of fiction. Lorna Sage's feminist extension of James emphasises that '"the house of fiction" isn't ... only a metaphor for containment. It is a reminder that fiction isn't placeless' (1992, ix). She contradicts Roland Barthes's postulate for the pleasure of the 'atopic text' (Barthes 1975); her insistence that '[w]omen's writing "comes from some place"' (ix) foregrounds the pragmatic dimension to the haunted houses of feminine gothic fiction in the sense in which I will relate them to their cultural-historical context. These houses also signify cultural changes, especially the desire and possibility for mobility that has always been at the core of feminine gothic writing. And the postmodern gothic texts, as we shall see in Part II, recognise and continue the liberating and challenging powers of gothic within modern female culture.

Note

1   The problem of the home recalls Freud's *das Unheimliche*, which he identified with revenants which are 'in reality nothing new or alien, but something which is familiar and old-established in the mind and which has
   become alienated from it only through the process of repression' (1919,
   241). This concept has been central to the feminist psychoanalytic discussions of the gothic (e.g. Massé 1992, esp. 29–39), to recent theories of the
   sublime (see Mishra 1994, 46f), and to Kristeva's *Étrangers à nous-mêmes*
   (1991). I am not addressing these implications here as my interest is a
   more formal one.

Chapter 1
Gothic contextualisation

Experience

Contextualising, the process of culturally situating a text, has been essential to culture critics in general and to feminist critics in particular. Many feminist gothicists are so interested in the gothic, because they see it as the genre that best 'expresses female experience' (e.g. Fleenor 1983; Miner 1984). As I have indicated, I would like to extend the discussion beyond the realism this implies, and to include gender theory and ideas of corpo-realism in the late 1990s, a development that is both reflected and extended in neo-gothic texts. It seems that it is the gothic's specific *anti-realism* that accounts for its popularity, for its representative and rebellious power; thus this section will explore its relationship to experience with regard to its thematic, formal and more theoretical dimensions in gothic form.

Experience has long been a key term in gender criticism; it has been important in the pursuit of a feminine aesthetics (Bovenschen 1979, 91) and feminist practice (Weedon 1987, 85), and it has been theoretically formulated as cultural construct (see Modleski 1986, 132–53). The most illuminating reading experience in this context for me has been Teresa de Lauretis's definition of 'experience' via C. S. Peirce as 'the process by which, for all social beings, subjectivity is constructed' (de Lauretis 1984, 159). She emphasises subjectivity as process: 'For each person ... subjectivity is an ongoing construction, not a fixed point of departure or arrival from which one then interacts with the world' (159); it both *is* an effect, of the interaction with the world, and it *has* an effect: on how one places oneself within that world or cultural historical reality.

In Virginia Woolf's *A Room of One's Own* (1929) there is the unforgettable moment when certain visual and verbal signs – the Oxbridge beadle's arrogant interdiction against stepping on the grass – produce the recognition: 'I was a woman' (1985, 6). De Lauretis reads this decisive 'experience' in terms of Peirce's notion of 'habit', which presupposes the physical presence of an interpreter but also a self-awareness of the 'habit' which can result in a 'habit change' (1984, 182f). The attribution of 'self-awareness' to 'habit' relates the concept to de Lauretis's feminist insistence on 'action'; she shows how feminist consciousness-raising, a practice towards self-awareness of habits, has resulted in 'a habit-change in readers, spectators, speakers etc. And with that habit-change it has produced a new social subject, *women*' (1984, 186).

This liberating idea of 'women' has in different ways always been important to feminine gothic form, especially to its complex subjectivity. It also draws attention to literary texts as – in de Lauretis's term – 'technologies' of gender and thus of 'the experience of gender, the meaning effects and self-representations produced in the subject by the sociocultural practices, discourses, and institutions devoted to the production of women and men' (1987a, 19). In that sense, cinema, narrative and theory, de Lauretis's chosen 'texts', are germane because they can produce a 'habit change'. So can the gothic.

Like other 'technologies of gender', the gothic has developed specific narrative processes of contextualising experience; however, they have so far been marginal in both feminist and gothic criticisms.[1] This might be because the gothic is the genre of negativities, of the *un*-real, the *anti*-rational, the *im*moral. It thus presents a sharp contrast to the feminist politics of realism, to the confessional life-writing of the 1960s or the super-realism of the 1970s. However, it seems that these typical negativities of gothic contextualising suggest the potential for another 'habit change' that I hope to show in the transition to neo-gothic writing. In terms of 'experience', Alice Munro's texts maybe show most strongly the shift from confessional realism to the powers of gothic representation.

The gothic's traditionally anti-realist mode of representation and contextualisation has come to be seen in new ways after the 'death of the novel' crisis, which left the ideal of realism behind (Todorov 1975;

Brooke-Rose 1981; Kosofsky Sedgwick 1986; Haggarty 1989). Since its origins in the late eighteenth century, the gothic – 'that old literature of unreason and terror' (Jackson 1981, 3) – had been marginalised by a critical establishment that valued the novel as a 'full and authentic report of human experience' (Watt 1957, 11) and privileged rational and realist forms.[2] Hence the gothic's positioning as Other, and even as 'feminine' Other to the dominant discourse. Andreas Huyssen has shown how theories of modernism have coded 'mass culture as woman' (1986, esp. 47–58), and gendered readings of the gothic have revealed similar classifications of the gothic in 'pejorative feminine characteristics' (Huyssen 1986, 49). For example, Juliann Fleenor:

> From the first [the gothic] has been seen as a 'feminine' form, outside the mainstream of literature. Its authors have been criticised as dealing in trivialities or as being too emotional, charges frequently characterised as feminine. Since the Gothic has been and continues to be written by both women and men, both sexes have been accused of these Gothic excesses. (1983, 8)

As these critics suggest, the traditional critical coding of the non-real, the popular and the emotional as feminine has perpetuated the thinking in binary oppositions, with all the hierarchies this entails. However, I think that the gothic as feminine form uses these 'excesses' precisely to question this binary, and by definition androcentric (Cixous 1986, 63), system of thought – which might offer a first step towards the suggested 'habit change'.

The idea of the emotional in gothic anti-realism – which I see as key to the gothic's survival in an era of postmodernism – is also essential to the gothic's complex system of addressing and connecting with the readers: its 'excessive' narratives work 'to *involve* the reader in a new way' (Hume 1969, 284), and thus to create the genre's celebrated combination of terror and delight. Ellen Moers has emphasised the physical effect of the gothic, which distinguishes it from pity and terror of the tragedy (1978, 90); George Haggarty more recently wrote that: 'Gothic form ... is affective form' (1989, 8). This affective aspect of gothicism has been emphasised by generic narrative gestures that draw attention to the importance of a 'you' in gothic form; the need for a narratee or an addressee who will sympathetically read, and paradoxically believe, an unbelievable story on its own terms. Mary Shelley's *Frankenstein* (1818) is a good example of how such contextualising of an incredible experience works (see Johnson 1987, 146). Each narrator's – Walton's, Frankenstein's and the creature's – 'auto-biography' is prefaced by the plea 'hear my tale' to the implied listener (Mrs Saville, Walton, Frankenstein). In the beginning as well as at the end of the story, this implied listener is a woman who – like the reader – reads Walton's letter in the 'safety' of her home in England. The gothic involvement of its (female) addressee here marks a deeply seri-ous connection between a text that can be read as a radical attack on English family life (the De Laceys' false idyll, the destruction of Frankenstein's family), but that is in fact read precisely and physically within these attacked structures. Family horror, the horror of the home: the gothic seems to be especially 'affective' in this typically feminine context.

This active involvement of the readers emphasises how the anti-realist gothic's 'affective form' depends on the textual recognition both of 'experience' in a specific cultural-historical situation and of the narrative techniques of realist representation. I would like to distin-guish three gothic ways of contextualising experience that have marked early gothicism and that strongly shape neo-gothic texts. Each of the Canadian examples emphasises one of the three, and thus recalls gothic classics. I am thinking of *defamiliarisation* and *refamiliarisation* of the supernatural and the *displacement of the radical doubt* outside the text.

Ann Radcliffe's *The Mysteries of Udolpho* perfectly exemplifies the strategy of *defamiliarising* a recognised experience, as we shall see in the next section. When Alice Munro takes up this strategy in *Lives of Girls and Women*, the familiar domesticity of 'woman's place' becomes radically *unheimlich*: neo-gothic defamiliarising often means enforcing the familiar, the domestic, everyday experience, to an excess. By con-trast, *Frankenstein* has early used the contextual experience of encoun-tering strangers or 'Others', as well as the narrative conventions of placing central figures in an elaborate familial web, and first-person narration, successfully to *refamiliarise* the supernatural: at the plot level, there is no space for doubting the existence of Frankenstein's creature. Margaret Atwood's *Lady Oracle* is similarly marked by gothic refamiliarisation of the supernatural – for example when the mother's astral body follows the narrator, or when the 'Fat Lady' interrupts a television hockey game. As we shall see, in Atwood's neo-gothic this way of contextualising experience can be both comic and horrific, but it always questions the easy acceptance of what we consider to be the real – gender roles included.

Henry James's *The Turn of the Screw* similarly uses recognisable constructions of experience (social isolation and the interdiction of asking questions) and narration (the framing story that is not taken up again; the open ending) to create the radical doubt that suggests the fantastic or supernatural, before *displacing* that doubt into the realm of the reader. Similarly, Aritha van Herk's *No Fixed Address* constructs a radical doubt concerning Arachne's encounters with a *Doppelgänger* and various ghosts in the last section of her travels; a doubt that is left with the readers and enforced by the 'Notebook on a Missing Person' that frames the text. Here again, as we shall see, gender is not fixed by experience, but is itself subject to doubt and pursuit. Needless to say, the three gothic ways of contextualising experience are not exclusive to, but only more pronounced in, the different texts. Their 'affect' is a challenge to assumptions about reality and gender; they draw attention to the workings of experience. And what their treatment of the anti-real and the supernatural shares is their formal hyperbole – or excess.

Excess!

'Excess' is one of the terms most frequently, and mostly pejoratively, used in established gothic criticism: 'excess' in moral, but also in formal, terms. I hope to show 'excess' as a pleasurable but also subversive gothic strategy, the emotionalising centre of the gothic's provocation as well as of its ongoing intertextualisation.[3] *Lady Oracle*'s self-conscious postmodern play with gothicism especially highlights these possibilities of excess. It seems that excess can play such an important role in feminist gothic art, as well as criticism, because it offers not only the well-known moral provocations but also a formal provocation of well-established narrative and cultural structures – for example, the house and its ideological order. The following section will explore the background to neo-gothic excess by working out its traditional contextualising strategies in thematic, formal and cultural dimensions: in recent gothic criticism and in two early classics, Ann Radcliffe's *The Mysteries of Udolpho* (1794) and Mary Wollstonecraft's *The Wrongs of Woman: or, Maria* (1798).

In the age of poststructuralism, classic gothic excesses that produce gaps in the story – like 'the unspeakable' – have achieved much critical attention. Eve Kosofsky Sedgwick has explored 'the difficulty the story has in getting itself told' through an illuminating litany of lost letters, indecipherable manuscripts, unintelligible housekeepers' tales, and of 'live-burials' of letters and communication (1986, 37). These narrative 'excesses' seem to mock both readers' expectations and conventional narrative. At the same time, a whole apparatus of just as typical narrative gestures attempts to reconcile the reader with such gothic eccentricities, and especially with its anti-realism: extensive footnotes that 'explain' the outrageous as foreign (for example, as 'Irish' in Maria Edgeworth's novels); elaborate prefaces and introductions that pretend to assert the 'truth' of the incredible tale, and so on. Horace Walpole's elaborate preface and translation-games opening *The Castle of Otranto* (1764) have been shown only recently to be an *ironic* treatment of neo-classical traditions (Mohr 1990, 11) of the realist novel, then in the ascendant.

Mockery, irony, reconciliation: the terminology strongly evokes the workings of parody. Contemporary gothic criticism has emphasised the parodic implications of gothic excess, and reformulated the established, mostly New Critical, view of the gothic as allegorical form. For example, William Patrick Day writes: 'The relationship of the Gothic to the conventional world, and to the literary forms from which it derives, can best be described as parodic' (1985, 59). In his definition, 'the Gothic parody creates a state of metaphysical uncertainty and anxiety: through its distorted lens, we see the whole world' (60).

The implications of a metaphysics of being are problematic from a feminist perspective; the image of the distorted lens for the whole world, as well as the view that the 'system of the gothic fantasy' has 'no form or shape of its own' (Day 1985, 14), perpetuate the humanist critique of established gothic criticism (see Kiely 1972, 17; Napier 1987, 7). However, the notion of parodic representation is useful: I think it *provokes* this desire for metaphysical wholeness, only to contest strongly just such a secure and comfortable position by its narrative 'excess'. Thus it seems that parody offers the recognition of the familiar in the gothic world of the unreal – and that this treatment of the familiar is one aspect of the gothic's potential for feminist challenge. Linda Hutcheon's theory of parody as *repetition with a critical difference* (1985, esp. 101) of both art and life is the background to my exploration of gothic excess: Chapter 5, on Margaret Atwood, will show the neo-gothics' parodic relationship to feminine gothic classics. These classics' own parodic excesses are the focus of the present section.

Feminine gothic classics use parody's methods of 'excess' – mockery, irony, allusion – to repeat with a critical difference specific instances of both their cultural-historical and literary context. 'Female experience' is a central aspect of this. For example, sensibility, a strong motif in the gothic novels of both Ann Radcliffe and Mary Wollstonecraft, was a familiar concept to their female contemporaries, and readers, as a gender ideal constructing 'Woman'. In Radcliffe's *The Mysteries of Udolpho*, the family horror that structures Emily St Aubert's story is confronted with, and in some ways produced by, her 'sensibility'. The early gothic critic Edith Birkhead has shown the implications of the Rousseauian concept in the eighteenth-century cultural and literary context:

> Like 'sentiment', 'sensibility' came from France, where it was cultivated as a fine art about half a century before it became fashionable in England ... During the latter half of the eighteenth century it came to be regarded as essential to emotional respectability. It led to a form of spiritual snobbery. The moralists of the period were keenly alive to its dangers, if it were allowed to run riot, uncontrolled by the will and judgement, and the satirists attempted to laugh its affectations out of countenance. (1925, 97)

Radcliffe's well-educated heroines are contextualised as prime examples of such 'emotional respectability'; the much-quoted deathbed scene of the father in *Udolpho* (80), strongly represents a moralist warning that typically avoids naming the real 'dangers' of 'sensibility' for women: 'physical sensations' (Birkhead 1925, 97). However, female sexuality reverberates in Emily's story, not only because of her containment in the villain's power but also because of her confrontation with Laurentini di Udolpho: a murderess for love and one of the first 'sexual woman' figures in the gothic. Laurentini repeats on her own deathbed the father's advice in more explicit terms: 'Sister! beware of the first indulgence of the passions; beware of the first! Their course, if not checked then, is rapid – their force uncontrollable – they lead us we know not whither' (646). The dictum of constraint, uttered by both the father and the 'fallen sister', enforces the ideology of sensibility – the symbolic order's control of women's bodies (see Ballaster 1996, 61).

However, this explicit 'message' contrasts dramatically with Radcliffe's own version of gothic excess: her elaborate style that suggests indulgence, pleasure, bliss! (see Howells's Barthesian reading, 1989). Her excessive style challenges the ideology of containment; and so does her specific concept of terror: 'Terror and horror are so far opposite, that the first expands the soul and awakens the faculties to a high degree of life; the other contracts, freezes, nearly annihilates them' (1802; Sage 1990, 72). While recalling Burke's view of terror as source of the sublime and 'productive of the strongest emotion which the mind is capable of feeling' (Burke 1987 [1757], 39), Radcliffe's language clearly links the emotional experience of terror to the physical, sexual 'dangers' of 'sensibility'. In this sense, her heroines' gothic experiences become experiences of excess – and their terror is liberating.

Restrictive gender culture on the one side and gothic excess on the other: in between there is the gothic heroine; and she is much less a victimised 'maiden-in-flight' than a subject-in-process of 'becoming a woman' in de Beauvoir's sense. The domestic terrors that structure Emily's story from the idyllic La Vallée through the horrific Udolpho and back to harmony, happen at the clash of *propriety* – the dictum of constraint – and *property* that necessitates active self-defence: both submit her to Montoni's power and to the conflict between obedience and desire. These typical processes of subjectivity and gender-construction will be further explored in the following chapter on gothic texture. Here, I would like to pursue the feminist possibilities of gothic excess when further contextualising such mainly economic power structures.

Terror is liberating – and 'produces delight' in the Burkean scheme 'when it does not press too close' (Burke 1987, 45). Further examples of gothic 'excess' are its distancing strategies, which recontextualise the contemporary as well as the supernatural into faraway, isolated, or enclosed spaces, or else into earlier – preferably medieval and thus more superstitious or mystic – times. For example, the first American gothic novel, Charles Brockden Brown's *Wieland, or, The Transformation* (1798), uses such strategies to expose the threats of European anarchy to a naive American family at the time of the French Revolution (see Ringe 1982). Thus, as different gothicists have emphasised, the gothic's anti-realism did comment on the contemporary, but made it mockingly both more 'plausible' and more 'pleasurable'.[4] *Udolpho*, for example, with its explorations of the late-eighteenth-century ideology of sensibility, is set in a very vague historical version of the late sixteenth century, and in a fantasy Italy derived by Radcliffe from paintings and travelogues. The gothic as 'armchair travelling' for female writers as well as readers, bound to woman's place, anticipates that other gothic effect: 'escape'. Whether seen as journey, quest, flight or escape, the heroine's travelling in the feminine gothic occurs in a weird world. But this fantasy world is not a 'chaotic Gothic world', as some critics have suggested (e.g., Day 1985, 31). Rather, it is structured according to the patterns of power familiar to female readers and writers in (and since) Radcliffe's cultural historical context. Therefore, gothic anti-realism addresses the very real ideology of woman's place – the home.

Which brings us back to the metaphor of the house and to the related excess-effect of defamiliarisation. The castle of Udolpho itself is the perfect example of the gothic romance's attack on the reigning power structures. Located beyond Radcliffe's fantasy Alps, it is a typical villain's space: far away from social community and civilisation (Thompson 1974, 45; Radway 1977, 213). Thus isolated, it is the perfect world for the supernatural and the horrific. However, as feminist gothic criticism has suggested, Udolpho – like other gothic castles, mansions and houses – is also a grotesque version of the English middle-class home, where women are not only expected to perform as touchstones of sanctity but also to feel safe in a protected place.[5] Most readings of the important scene where Emily first encounters Udolpho display the classic views on Emily's 'distortion of perception caused by excessive sensibility … [and] social isolation' (Punter 1980, 62, 77; see also Radway 1977, 213) or her 'vision of various sex organs' (Ronald 1983, 179). However, Emily perceives the castle as threatening personification of masculine power: 'it seemed to stand sovereign of the scene and to frown defiance on all, who dared to invade its solitary reign' (227). The accurate recognition of the threats of that masculine version of female space is suggestive; after all, Emily looks at the house from the *outside*, moving into it makes it 'a prison' (227). It also makes it into the gothic space where anything might happen.

And indeed, Emily does encounter the *unspeakable*: the mystery behind the veil – with its perfectly Radcliffean excessive deferral of an explanation, the *supernatural*: in the shape of Laurentini's 'ghost', and other gothic excesses that are subsequently conveniently 'explained away'. Radcliffe's famous conjunction of realism and gothicism brought her admirers as diverse as Sir Walter Scott, who coined the term 'supernatural explained' for her, and Tzvetan Todorov, who included her in his category of the 'fantastic/uncanny' (see also Heller 1987, 13). However, she does not explain away the male aggressions and demands that Emily encounters with Montoni. The whole contextualisation of the castle works to ridicule the ideology of woman's place: the gothic's hyperbolic 'repetition' of domestic structure constructs it as space entirely in male control and as prison with (almost) no escape. The elevating role of the woman in the house is also attacked: Montoni, the owner and master of the house, is only interested in Emily's property and continually provokes her by alluding to her performance of this feminine role (270). Radcliffe's narrative excesses – hyperbole, reversal, displacement in time and in space – defamiliarise the common power structures and open up a critical perspective. The gothic attack is here directed at woman's place – the home – and by extension at the symbolic order's constructions.

Her heroine's happy ending, finally, displays yet another unsuspected dimension of Radcliffean excess. Emily escapes from Udolpho, she is not rescued by her lover; she is then safely restored into another – her father's – house, with a husband of her own and her father's choice. However, her restoration to the symbolic order is not complete: the lengthy 'explanations' of the formerly 'unspeakable' goings-on in Udolpho are even more implausible, with their highly constructed and fairytale qualities. *Udolpho*'s happy ending, too, is told by Emily's maid Annette in a non-realistic discourse: she clearly relates it in the conventions of a fairy-tale. Radcliffe, it seems, mocks the formal demands of closure – and her heroine's narrative exceeds the related order.

Radcliffe's gothic excess – pleasurable, liberated, popular – is the source of endless imitations and intertextualisations, from the pulp fiction of her own times, via Jane Austen, to the current wave of neo-gothicism. Just as excessive but much less popular is the early feminist gothicism, with its very different contextualising strategies. Although both types treat family horror, repeat domestic structures with the difference of gothic excess and thus re-contextualise female experience, whereas (Radcliffean) gothic romances emphasise the liberating aspects of exceeding the real, the natural, the moral, the expected, early feminist gothic novels use gothic excess radically to expose the limitations – and the constructions – of the real, from which no escape seems possible. In the feminist gothic, horror, the 'supernatural', the radical doubt, is closer to *home*; not the creation of a weird world, but a very specific background composed of aspects of the contemporary and familiar domestic life. The notions of isolation and enclosure remain. Radcliffe's delightful encounters with the sublime and the 'supernatural explained' give way to inescapable horror of powerlessness and oppression.

The feminist gothic, like the feminine gothic romance, emerged in the 1790s. Like Radcliffe, Mary Wollstonecraft addresses the implications of the Rousseauian ideal of 'sensibility', especially its implications for women. Female miseducation is one of the most important issues in all her texts – her famous *Vindication of the Rights of Woman* (1792) is above all a vindication of women's education. Critics emphasise her shifts in style: 'masculine' in her political writing; 'feminine' in her gothic writings (see Jacobus 1986, 120). However, her gothic voice is radically different from Radcliffe's. Especially the unfinished *The Wrongs of Woman: or, Maria* (1798) shows how she uses gothic excess to provoke the recognition of women's inescapable containment within an order that reduces her to powerlessness.

Maria is a prime example of a gothic form that still reverberates in contemporary gothic – for example, in Sylvia Plath's *The Bell Jar* and, as we shall see, in *Lady Oracle* – a form that might be called 'the madwoman's story'. The opening sets the gothic tone, reverberates with literary allusions, and evokes the gothic house:

> Abodes of horror have frequently been described, and castles, filled with spectres and chimeras, conjured up by the magic spell of genius to harrow the soul and absorb the wandering mind. But, formed of such stuff as dreams are made of, what were they to the mansion of despair, in one corner of which Maria sat, endeavouring to recall her scattered thoughts! (85)

Maria is imprisoned in an insane asylum, in which her husband has quite legally placed her, in order to get control of her property. She also has been forcibly separated from her baby daughter; one of her greatest anxieties during her imprisonment as 'madwoman' is thus for the little girl's fate. Despite its self-conscious construction of a gothic scenery, this opening announces a major departure from Radcliffean gothic romance: Maria's dark gothic story starts *after* the 'happy ending' – within a prison that is a direct effect of marriage. This narrative reversal radically discards the ideology of happy endings and romantic love: the feminist gothic becomes a horrific study of marriage.[6]

Gothic excesses adopt different dimensions in this context. Adultery – in the gothic romance another vice of the Montonis and Laurentinis – is justified for a heroine mistreated by a loveless, brutal husband. As we shall see, the interconnection of the sexual woman and her treatment as 'mad' or 'monstrous' is thus redefined. In terms of form, the longest section is Maria's autobiographical letter about her life before becoming a mother and subsequently being 'buried alive' (170) in the asylum. This letter is gothic not because of any supernatural horrors – after all, it is her real life-story – but because of the very real horrors of a woman's life, outlined with gothic sentimentalism and excess. It is addressed to her daughter, but is read by her friend in the asylum, Darnford, who subsequently becomes her lover. This is only the beginning of a multitude of female life-stories told to ever-changing listeners. When Maria's jailor Jemima tells her own life-story to Maria and Darnford, the narrator herself becomes a narratee, and the reader connected to her reaction – the recognition of what Wollstonecraft calls in her fragmentary preface 'the misery and oppression, peculiar to women, that arise out of the partial laws and customs of society' (83).

In this early feminist fiction, gothic 'excess' marks the form with its multiple female stories and with the gothic emotions of horror and fear, only to heighten its realism. Feminist critics have seen it as a 'fictionalised documentary':

> It succeeds in cataloguing wider social grievances as *The Rights of Woman* did not, by illustrating that women have few work opportunities, and those few ill-paid; that they suffer sexual harassment and exploitation; that their own sexuality is denied by 'a false morality … which makes the virtue of women consist in chastity, submission and the forgiveness of injuries'; … that marriage and property laws effectively make the wife the husband's chattel. (Todd and Butler 1985, 25)

The different contextualisation of 'woman's place' marks the shift from the gothic romance to feminist gothic: the house's sublime impression from the outside – 'formed of such stuff as dreams are made of' – is from the beginning excluded by the voice from inside 'the abode of horror'. Tania Modleski, comparing *Maria* to the popular gothics after Radcliffe, emphasises that the asylum 'is not simply a physical embodiment of [Maria's] fears of entrapment; it is also a real insane asylum' (1982, 83). When Maria reflects: 'Was not the world a vast prison', as Radcliffe's Emily might have done, she adds, 'and women

born slaves?' (see Todd and Butler 1989, 25). Birgitta Berglund summarises: 'Wollstonecraft in fact spells out what Radcliffe only indicates' (1993, 79). Where in Radcliffe's romances gothic excess magnifies
'woman's sphere', Wollstonecraft's feminist gothic dramatically re-
visions the world as one large prison for women.

Wollstonecraft's feminist gothic contextualises in documentary style;
excess does not evoke the supernatural but rather the very real horrors
of female (marital) experience and entrapment. It reverses the theme
of love triumphant – which still has a redeeming function in the gothic
romance – by showing its violent side in private life and its public
horrors. The gothic plot includes multiple stories of female lives; it
becomes life writing, or rather life *telling*: a narrative excess with
universalising tendencies. It also suggests an extension of the 'house of
fiction': the madwoman's story anticipates the attics of *Jane Eyre*'s
Thornfield and of other haunted houses in feminist gothic fictions.
Here, gothic excess is used to demonstrate the extent of women's
containment. Maria's escape is her death.

Escape?

Escape – a metaphor central to feminist criticism, but also to the
analysis of popular fiction – is crucial to this study: as a central theme
in feminine gothic texts, as a formal aspect in the sense of 'escape
literature', and as a more theoretical notion of escape from cultural
containment. French theorists of *écriture féminine* start from women's
escape from the discourses of men (e.g., Cixous's 'Sorties', in Cixous
and Clément 1986), and so does Lindsey Tucker's reading of contemporary women's fiction that links escape, subversion and mobility:

> [W]hen women do write subversive texts, when they do manage escapes
> from imprisoning, male-identified narrative models, from genre, even from
> mimesis itself, their discourses often have as a central concern the problem
> of movement. (1994, 4)

Of course, the history of gothicism is also the history of modernity,
with its hitherto unknown mobility. Feminist critics have emphasised
the attractions of the feminine gothic's 'travelling heroinism' (Moers)
and of the 'armchair travelling' for Radcliffe and her readers (Porrmann 1985, 167). Critics of popular culture see popular horror fiction

as escape literature – characterised by delightful fear. For example, Kathryn Hume outlines popular horror as a 'literature of illusion', which means 'the enjoyment of vivid sensations [and] the delicious pleasure of freedom from responsibility' (1984, 55) with the reading-effect of 'contentment' (57). By contrast, feminine gothic 'excess' – especially excess of formal closure – works to unsettle and defy contentment, and it seems that a gendered reading opens up new dimensions to the notion of 'escape literature'.

At the end of the twentieth century, with its obsession with mobility, a 'travelling heroine' like Aritha van Herk's Arachne in *No Fixed Address* redefines escape in the context of neo-gothicism. 'Escapism' then means dealing with cultural constraints by drawing attention to their existence and ideological construction rather than just running away. However, as van Herk's neo-gothicism will show, it also means self-consciously to explore alternate spaces, forms or texts. I would like to show how gothic escape is concerned with dungeons, prison, and houses, but also with the idea of 'Woman' and its cultural containment.

The classic gothic narrative when thinking about escape, subversion and mobility is Charlotte Brontë's *Jane Eyre* (1847): a 'cult text of feminism' (Spivak 1989, 176) and, I would say, the heartbeat of much feminine gothic intertextualising. *Jane Eyre* gestures to realism in its subtitle, *An Autobiography*, but it is a romance in form. Like Wollstone-craft, Brontë uses gothicism to contextualise the contemporary. Because of its gothic romance 'appeal' mixed with social realism, *Jane Eyre* is seen as marking 'the change from "old Gothic" to "new Gothic"' (Heilman 1981, 171; see also Ohmann 1977, 757–78). However, the emotional appeal seems to be utterly different, too. Noel Carroll writes on the appeal of horror:

> The argument has been that if horror is, in large measure, identified with the manifestation of categorically impossible beings, works of horror, all things being equal, will command our attention, curiosity and fascination ... [T]hat fascination with the impossible being outweighs the distress it engenders can be rendered intelligible by what I call the thought theory of our emotional response to fiction, which maintains that audiences know horrific beings are not in their presence, and, indeed, that they do not exist, and, therefore, their description or depiction in horror fictions may be a cause for interest rather than either flight or any other prophylactic enter-prise. (1990, 206)

By contrast, it seems that the reading-effect of *Jane Eyre* is less that of a fascination with the impossible and more that of the recognition of the limitations of the possible; the horror of the real. This goes beyond a sheer delight in terror – or any simplistic escape-effect – into a feminist critique of the contemporary.

Let us start by looking at aspects of 'escape literature' – in the sense of both Kathryn Hume and Noel Carroll – that do structure *Jane Eyre*. The opening recalls Radcliffe's gothic moment – Emily facing 'Udolpho' and the reader in front of *Udolpho* – with its direct involvement of the presumably English, middle-class, female reader. Jane withdraws from her oppressive foster family into the window seat with her book, and the reader becomes, in Gayatri Spivak's words, Jane's 'accomplice: the reader and Jane are united – both are reading' (Spivak 1989, 180). What links reader and heroine is a moment of 'isolation' or 'withdrawal' from her common surroundings – the family, the home – despite the famous recognition of the impossibility of leaving: 'There was no possibility of taking a walk that day' (9). This is the form of 'escape' that has been seen as one clue to the popularity of the female gothic at especially conservative times: the escape into the haunted house of the gothic text, which repeats but exceeds such daily structures.

Jane Eyre contextualises early Victorian women's lives: whether genteel but poor governess Jane Eyre, or passionate and rich wife Bertha Mason, or beautiful heiress Blanche Ingram, these female figures suffer from the specifically female experience of limited mobility. For Jane, a paradigmatic poor orphan, this includes the problem of social mobility; however, Bertha and Blanche, although rich, are even more 'fixed' in the house. *Jane Eyre*'s famous fantasies of escape are legendary with gothicists and feminists: Jane at an open window in Lowood, after the loss of her teacher and friend, desiring 'liberty' – and then deciding on a 'new servitude' (88); Jane in the attic of Thornfield, unknowingly next to Bertha's prison, looking out over the landscape to the far horizon:

> I longed for a power of vision which might overpass that limit; which might reach the busy world ... I desired more of practical experience than I possessed; more of intercourse with my kind ... Women are supposed to be very calm generally: but women feel just as men feel; they need exercise for their faculties, and a field for their efforts as much as their brothers do; they suffer from too rigid a constraint, too absolute a stagnation, precisely

as men would suffer, and it is narrow-minded in their more privileged fellow-creatures to say that they ought to confine themselves. (112–13)

Confinement becomes Jane Eyre's domestic horror. Her outspoken rebellion against it also means rebellion against the Victorian 'Angel in the House' – that feminine ideal that Virginia Woolf famously wanted killed, so that women could develop their creative potential (1979). Accordingly, confinement is the fate of Bertha Mason, and the sign of Rochester's – perfectly legal – violence against women. Bertha, like Wollstonecraft's Maria, effects a redefinition of 'madness'. Sensibility in the late eighteenth century, hysteria in the nineteenth – the power of ideology remains. For these female figures, escape into liberty is not possible, but neither is the return to the social order.

Gothic form underlines this conflict by suggesting escape on the level of the narrative itself. Brontë's genre mix – autobiography, romance, *Bildungsroman* – suggests gothic excess on that formal level. Moreover, exceeding realism offers escape from the horrors of confinement and immobility. Jane literally addresses the idea of escape from her enclosure within the female condition in woman's place:

> [T]he restlessness was in my nature; it agitated me to pain sometimes. Then my sole relief was ... to open my inward ear to a tale that was never ended – a tale my imagination created, and narrated continuously; quickened with all of incident, life, fire, feeling, that I desired and had not in my actual existence. (112)

This reflection corresponds to Rosemary Jackson's view of fantasy. She sees fantasy as 'produced within, and determined by, its social context' and adds: 'fantasy characteristically attempts to compensate for a lack resulting from cultural constraints: it is a literature of desire which seeks that which is experienced as absence and loss' (1981, 3). This view of escape into the realm of fantasy – as practised by Jane Eyre as well as by the readers – on the one hand points to that social context and its problems or lack for a specific group of readers; on the other it represents and enforces a desire for the unreal. The supernatural in Jane's gothic life-story comprises two significant narrative events: Jane's mysterious encounter with the mother-moon who tells her to 'flee temptation' before leaving Thornfield, and Rochester's magic 'call' that brings her back. This version of the supernatural is strikingly different from Radcliffe's 'supernatural explained': it calls for action, emphasises the need for a strong vision and a voice. In this

Travelling companions   Exceeding woman's place! Radcliffe's heroines travelled in the power of villains; Brontës longed for it all their lives – the feminine gothic is motivated by the desire for travelling. Egg's picture is also a study in sense and sensibility.

sense, feminist gothicism redefines gothic escape as platform for change.

At the same time, Bertha Mason's fate radically points to the impossibilities of change. Gilbert and Gubar read the 'madwoman in the attic' as the woman writer's double, as a figure for female rage, for the woman writer's escape: 'it is … through the violence of the double that the female author enacts her own raging desire to escape male houses and male texts' (1979, 85). This reflection equates escape with violence and rage, two emotions that definitely structure the feminist gothic. It also recalls the formal implications of the house as male textual structure in which the attic might function as gothic version of Virginia Woolf's famous 'room of one's own': a starting point for the escape into art. *Jane Eyre* discursively takes up this idea through Jane's art: her paintings are created at a point of depression, and display imagery of death – the ultimate escape. And Bertha dies when she burns down the house – the construction that has imprisoned her for most of her adult life.

Bertha's escape into death means Jane's happy ending, and yet another escape: into social isolation, in which equality of the sexes and mature love are possible. The archetypal Cinderella plot, which Jane's story has also been read as (e.g., Moretti 1987, 185–9), is effectively discarded by gothic excess and this version of escape. Her female success story relies on a strong vision of gender equality, which ultimately requires the destruction of Thornfield, Rochester's dependency and Jane's emotional and social empowerment. This equality appears to be both realistic and surreal, just like Ferndean, far away from Victorian culture, and the setting for *Jane Eyre*'s 'happy ending'.

Escape into death is the ending of Bertha Mason, the 'sexual woman' figure in *Jane Eyre*; and it is one of the two possible endings that Wollstonecraft's notes suggest for the unfinished *Maria*. In both versions her lover leaves her: in one, she decides to live for her daughter; while in the other she commits suicide. Feminist readings of Kate Chopin's *The Awakening* (1899) have shown such a suicide as a 'happy ending', a liberation from otherwise inescapable misogynist structures. Less didactic, but just as radical as Wollstonecraft's gothicism, Charlotte Perkins Gilman's *The Yellow Wallpaper* (1892) posits escape into madness. Its horrors contextualise contemporary women's concerns and fears, and once again the structure of the house becomes an important thematic as well as formal metaphor of confinement. The reasons for this horror – the suppression of a creative and dynamic female figure – become quite clear, in part because of the form of the text. It is a diary-in-progress, told by a young mother and writer: she has been placed into a nursery-attic for a 'rest cure' by her doctor-husband and brother, because of 'a slight hysterical tendency' (1148) – despite her plea for mobility. This gothic story contextualises important publications on hysteria:[7] first, through an autobiographic trace – Gilman herself experienced a 'rest cure' (then a popular treatment for postpartum depression) when she became a mother; second, there appears, as a major threat in the story, the American nerve specialist Silas Weir Mitchell (1829–1914), 'the major proponent of the "rest cure"' of the time (see Gilbert and Gubar 1985, 1146). Such contextualising 'repetitions' are confronted with gothic horror: the narrator's imprisonment, the patriarchal 'order' of the family home that subjects her life and body entirely to her husband's power. This situation is told in an almost antithetical discourse of understatement and reasoned logic: the narrator does not allow herself to speak in an overly emotional language, for fear of not being taken seriously. However, she uses the 'excess' of gothicism for her attempt to present convincingly the fatal situation of women in a male economy: the wallpaper of the title insists metaphorically on the inescapable persistence of established patterns, but it also offers a material barrier and a realm for escape – from the enclosure in the house's attic into the virtual realm of the 'madwoman'. —

Thus, the idea of gothic escape has different versions and effects: the pleasures of Radcliffe's playful defamiliarising on the one hand and the more disturbing refamiliarising of alternate worlds and radical attacks on the familiar on the other. The recognition of the parallel development of feminist uses of gothicism and the gothic romance offers a different angle at the escape-effect of gothic excess, one that brings us back to the notion of 'transgression'. In the context of postmodern gothic criticism, Noel Carroll writes: 'in general, works of horror represent transgressions of the standing conceptual categories of the culture. Within horror fictions, standing classificatory norms are dislodged; the culture's criteria for *what is* problematised' (1990, 210). This suggests a twofold notion of 'transgression'. On the one hand, it refers to going beyond the norm – thus drawing attention to its limitations. On the other, it refers to an unknown world beyond these limitations, often referred to in (pejorative) 'feminine' terms like chaos, fantasy and dream. However, it can be seen as an alternate world that does not function according to the laws of the symbolic order and in which the strange becomes possible – which is horrific but also liberating. For the feminist gothic this notion of 'transgression' works in the sense of the escape effect of gothic excess: it will not only address the order of confinement, but also the relationship of experience and language: the space of the female subject.

Notes

1 Gothicists as well as feminist critics have discussed gothic politics (e.g. Punter 1980; Radway 1984), its origins in terms of production (Mohr

1990) and its reception (Tompkins 1980). See also Felski's general 're-contextualising women's writing' (1989, 50).

2 Critical appreciation of the gothic's anti-realism began after World War I in the mostly thematic studies by Birkhead (1921), Railo (1927), Tompkins (1976 [1932]) and Summers (1964 [1938]). For overviews of gothic criticism see Just 1997, 14–22; and Botting 1996, 17–20.

3 I see *excess* as feminised extension of two well-established terms for gothic effects: the debate about *transcendence* (see Hume 1969; Hume and Platzner 1971; Day 1985, 61; Heller 1987, 189f; Fleenor 1983, 16), and, more recently, the concept of transgression (esp. Graham 1989, x). Botting (1996, 1–12) uses both *excess* and *transgression* in his introductory definition.

4 Most gothicists revel in this manifold gothic potential to be 'anti-bourgeois' (Fiedler 1960), or 'subversive' (Punter 1976), to offer pleasurable terror (Trautwein 1980, 229), to introduce evil into eighteenth-century middle-class consciouness (Poenicke 1971, 10; Klein 1975) – and even to be 'essentially philanthropic' (Just 1997, 28). Their emotional response goes back to contemporaries: De Sade saw the gothic as 'a partly unconscious response to the revolutionary upheavals in Europe', Coleridge called it a crime – 'blasphemous' – in 1797 (see Sage 1990 for both).

5 Moers (1978) has emphasised feminine mobility in the castle; Mussell (1981, 54) sees the heroine as 'doubly victimized' in the villain's castle; Porrmann (1985, 169) shows how the castle's structure repeats the social order; Gunzenhäuser (1993, 21) emphasises its gendered power structures; Weißmann-Orzlowski (1997, 68f) its reflection of Emily's soul. On many eighteenth-century women writers' 'ambivalence' about the house, and 'the tension ... between the images of confinement ... and exposure', see Berglund (1993, esp. 14ff).

6 Michelle Massé coins the term 'Marital Gothic', but locates its origins in the nineteenth century (1992, 20).

7 Freud and Breuer's 'Preliminary Communication' appeared in January 1893 in *Neurologisches Zentralblatt* with Freud's classic line: 'Hysterics suffer mainly from reminiscences.' *Studies on Hysteria* was published in 1895.

Chapter 2

Gothic texture

Subjectivity

A necessarily gendered subjectivity structures the gothic as feminine form in three ways: as a split subject it feminises the romance into an 'interrogative text'; as a subject-in-process it turns the gothic into the story of gender construction; and as subject-in-relation with a gothic figure like the 'monstrous-feminine' it posits a radical attack on the constraints of 'Woman': the feminine ideal in a specific cultural historical context. Like the metaphors of experience, excess and escape, and in relation to them, female subjectivity becomes a strong thematic and formal, as well as more theoretical, challenge to textual and ideological orders. Neo-gothic texts self-reflexively highlight these processes and effects of subjectivity – Atwood, especially, turns the subject-in-process into a 'subject-in-excess'. This section presents an excursion into feminist and poststructuralist thinking about the subject.

Gothic subjectivity has early shaken the belief in a competent and controlling narrative centre: narration – and/or focalisation – occurs through one or several characters whose identity is disrupted[1] and whose limited perception effects the typical gothic distortions and 'excesses'. Two critical positions are interesting here: Barbara Godard uses the term 'decomposition of the persona' to characterise this complicated gothic subject, because it 'places the emphasis on decon-struction, rather than on madness' (1983, 41 n. 23). This idea opens up the view that gothic excess of traditional logic in feminine texts is subversive (rather than pathological) – an aspect that I will treat in narratological (rather than psychoanalytic) terms. Second, recent gothicists emphasise the unreliability of the narrator (Day 1985, 27), which has been narratologically defined with a powerful example from gothic writing in these terms:

> the main sources of unreliability are the narrator's limited knowledge, his personal involvement, and his problematic value-scheme ... The governess in James's 'The Turn of the Screw' ... can be seen as a reliable narrator telling the story of two haunted children, but she can also be considered an unreliable, neurotic narrator, unwittingly reporting her own hallucinations. (Kennan 1983, 100–103)

Such an unreliable narrative voice and 'decomposed' or 'excessive' subjectivity have drawn attention to the problematics of a single unified vision, not only as locus of identification, but also as the centre of consciousness.

These terms strongly suggest contemporary thought; here the subject has become a fashionable as well as tricky subject, since the belief in a Cartesian cogito as source of truth – a belief that had ruled the liberal humanist tradition – has come to be questioned and attacked. 'Crisis' is the key term: a 'crisis in legitimation of the master (European) narratives – history, philosophy, religion' as Alice Jardine characterises the situation in Lyotard's terminology; subjectivity here is one of the 'major topics of (Western) philosophy: Man, the Subject, Truth, History, Meaning' (1985, 25). In this crisis, structuralism, post-structuralism and deconstruction, all have posited challenges that are epitomised in the proclamation of 'the death of the subject' (on the range of positions see Hutcheon 1988a, 158–60). And the necessity for such challenges is not gender-neutral: these are 'crises in the narratives invented by men' (Jardine 1985, 24). The contemporary critique of this crisis in legitimation mostly starts with the complexities of subjectivity; perspectives range from a politicised psychoanalytical/semiotic position (Kristeva 1986, 27), to a more pragmatic 'social' position (Felski 1989, 51). In gender studies, positions oscillate between two extremes: on the one hand, the – mainly American radical feminist – celebration of the 'female voice' as the 'expression of the Other' that had been silenced or ignored in patriarchal discourse; on the other hand, the sceptical rejection of its very existence within the economy of the symbolic order: 'Any theory of the "Subject" has always been appropriated by the masculine' (Irigaray 1985, 133; on the range of positions see Weedon 1987, 74–106; Felski 1989, 51–5). I will offer a brief overview of the theoretical positions behind the subject processes that mark feminine gothic texture.

The feminist–semiotic discourse on subjectivity relies on Émile Benveniste's definition of the 'speaking subject': 'It is through language that man positions himself as a subject, because language alone establishes the concept of "ego" in reality, in *its* reality' (1971, 224). Subjectivity comes into play through difference – by separating the 'you' and the 'I' – and is therefore relational: 'not an essence but a set of relationships ... it can only be induced by discourse, by the activation of a signifying system which pre-exists the individual, and which determines his or her cultural identity (Silverman 1983, 52). Furthermore, this signifying system – itself a process within cultural historical dynamics of a specific context – determines the gendered aspects of that cultural identity. Hélène Cixous contextualises:

> The political economy of the masculine and the feminine is organised by different demands and constraints, which, as they become socialised and metaphorised, produce signs, relations of power, relationships of production and reproduction, a whole huge system of cultural inscription that is legible as masculine and feminine. (1981, 81)

The emphasis on cultural inscription and gender construction recalls the break with common-sense equations of sex and gender, a disjunction first voiced by Simone de Beauvoir in the well-known opening to the second book of her classic *The Second Sex* (1949):

> One is not born, but rather becomes, a woman. No biological, psychological, or economic fate determines the figure that the human female presents in society; it is civilisation as a whole that produces this creature, intermediate between male and eunuch, which is described as feminine. Only the intervention of someone else can establish an individual as an *Other*. (1989, 267)

What distinguishes de Beauvoir's idea of the 'Other' from that of contemporary feminisms is her inclusion of 'the second sex' in the representations of transcendent and immanent constructions. By contrast, Luce Irigaray sees women as 'this sex which is not one' – as being both multiple and unrepresentable (see Butler 1990, 9–12). However, this idea is important to two aspects of subjectivity as it is discussed today. The feminist conceptualisation of civilisation's constructions has already been mentioned; accordingly, discussing how

the subject of the feminine gothic is engendered means drawing attention to the discourses of her time – that is, any time between the 1790s
and the 1990s. And these cultural inscriptions, albeit varying in time
and space and system – between the (English) 'Age of Dr Johnson',
the (Canadian, German, American) 'Dark Romanticism', the (American and Canadian) time of the New Woman, the (Western) dynamics
of the world wars and Feminine Mystique of the 1950s – these varying
inscriptions share an ideological norm of what is 'naturally' feminine.

This brings us back to the female experience or Peircean habit
change from Woman to women (de Lauretis 1984, 5). To the ideology
of 'Woman', any subjectivity of 'women' is always-already put 'in-
relation'. This is precisely the process that structures feminine gothic
form, and not only those that, like *Jane Eyre*, obviously have the pattern of a *Bildungsroman*. As we shall see, a range of texts deal with the
feminine ideal by putting the female subject in relation to what has
become the most famous female figure of the gothic tradition: the
monstrous-feminine. This way gothicism highlights the devastating
effects of the Woman/women opposition that Toril Moi has outlined
in these terms:

> Patriarchal oppression consists of imposing certain standards of feminine
> on all biological women, in order precisely to make believe that the chosen
> standards for 'femininity' are *natural*. Thus a woman who refuses to con-
> form can be labelled both *unfeminine* and *unnatural*. (1989, 123)

Feminine gothic horror is often structured through the implications of
this 'unfeminine': gothic texture is shaped by this opposition.

Binary structures are always power structures (same/other, subject/
object, presence/absence, being/nothingness, identity/difference) in
which the one, privileged, pole positions itself as subject and defines,
and devalues, the other as object or Other. This system is gendered
and strongly contested by contemporary thought (for example, Cixous
1981, 63). In de Beauvoir's terms, the relationship between the sexes
is one of oppression that even lacks the reciprocity of the Hegelian
master–slave relationship. Both drawing on and contradicting this in-
sight, Irigaray exposes the objectification of women as an act essential
to the (self-)institution of the male subject:

> Woman, for her part, remains an unrealised potentiality – unrealisable, at
> least, for/by herself. *Is she, by nature, a being that exists for/by another?* ...
> Is she unnecessary in and of herself, but essential as the non-subjective

subjectum? As that which can never achieve the status of subject, at least for/by herself ... [T]his 'lack of qualities' that makes the female truly female ensures that the male can achieve his qualifications ... Theoretically, there would be no such thing as woman. She would not exist. The best that can be said is that she does *not exist yet*. (1985, 165–6).

Such recognitions have shaped the idea of a female speaking subject. Barbara Godard relates Irigaray's position to the linguistic construction of subjectivity: 'I' indicates the subject of speech that represents the subject of the enunciation, the speaking subject, in the text (Benveniste). This position would be unattainable to the Other/the Woman/the nothingness:

> [T]here remains a problem for, if Man as subject undertakes the work of civilisation, creating languages, cultures, machines while assigning to the non-I the terms of woman, the emotions, the body principle, the 'nothingness' that must be overcome when he embarks on any significant enterprise, how can woman speak or write? Not I, she is not the subject of the enunciation, but its object. (Godard 1983, 14)

This is where the poststructuralist/feminist idea of the subject-in-process comes in. Women's position of negativity or absence is precisely the locus for change or 'renewal' in Julia Kristeva's discussion of the speaking subject: a 'subject of a heterogeneous [signifying] process' (1986, 30) – a 'subject on trial' that represents itself in the text. Her 'semanalysis' between 'bio-physical processes' and 'social constraints' features a 'divided subject' in a way that will, as we shall see, be important to feminine gothic texture: it produces a split subject that works to feminise the gothic romance and to transform it into an 'interrogative text'.

Kristeva's positioning of the speaking subject – also in terms of gender – occurs through an analysis of a text's 'semiotic disposition' that centres around a transgression: 'of systematicity, e.g., a transgression of the unity proper to the *transcendental ego*' (1986, 29). This version of transgression refers us back to *excess*: here the formal excess of 'systematicity' through unreliable narrators; gothic excess that has early and persistently challenged a unified transcendent ego.

Kristeva's call for an analysis of the moment of the enunciation emphasises once more the contextual dimension. Like Cixous and Irigaray, she assumes 'a certain bisexuality' of the speaking subject. This assumption has two effects for neo-gothic writing. One is its refusal to present new role models or any fixed image of femininity; in

Kristeva's terms, the most revolutionary position for women in this context is that of 'assuming a *negative* function: reject everything finite, definite, structured, loaded with meaning, in the existing state of society' (in Marks and de Courtivron 1981, 166). The other is the possibility of change suggested by such a subject-in-process; Kristeva suggests the *present* as that moment for a female subjectivity:

> The avant-garde has always had ties to the underground [that which is 'beneath' the symbolic order]. Only today, it is a woman who makes this connection. This is important. Because in social, sexual, and symbolic experiences, being a woman has always provided a means to another end, to becoming something else: a subject-in-the-making, a subject on trial. (in Marks and de Courtivron 1981, 167)

There is a metaphor from feminist semiotics that aptly summarises the related potential of the neo-gothic subject: the idea of 'the transformation of woman and the feminine into verbs at the interior of those [Master] narratives that are today experiencing a crisis in legitimation' (Jardine 1985, 25). Women-as-verbs suggests mobility, a textual dynamics from within: a characteristic move of feminist neo-gothicism, as we shall see in the following readings, especially of *No Fixed Address*. One of the implications of women-as-verbs in gothic texts is a change in texture: from romance to 'interrogative text'.

Interrogativity: romantic love and female desire

Gothic texture relies on romance conventions concerning flamboyant villains, harmless lovers and wildly distressed heroines. The 'maiden-in-flight' has long been called *the* gothic feature, but mostly in readings that position her as function in a plot that gravitates around the villain rather than as subject of the story. This view can best be demonstrated in the semiotic terms of the syntactic, the semantic and the pragmatic. On the syntactic level, the heroine – her body, her money, and so on – presents an object of value for the villain's desire and quest for power. On the semantic level, the heroine personifies values that contrast the villain's moral corruption, his evil and his power; she thus both highlights that evil and balances its effects in a plot that ends in the restoration of order. Accordingly, on the pragmatic level, the gothic heroine represents, in perfect incorporation, the 'ideal feminine' of her cultural-historical context.

While such a reading would aptly characterise some masculine gothic texts like Walpole's *The Castle of Otranto*, it would not fit the feminine gothic like Radcliffe's *Mysteries of Udolpho*. A structural outline of Walpole's gothic story could be: 'a lonely, self-divided hero [embarks] on an insane pursuit of the Absolute' (Thompson 1974, 45); thereafter, one could continue, he persecutes the maiden-in-flight and is himself destroyed, rather than attaining his immoral aims. An outline of Radcliffe's story indicates a difference already: the heroine's pursuit of self-fulfilment through marriage is interrupted by the villain's intervention, which – ironically – enables her to solve a mystery related to her mother and to position herself with a much stronger sense of – psychological, social, linguistic – identity before attaining her original goal. This outline might seem surprising in the face of much gothic criticism that sees Radcliffe's gothics as romances, motivated by romantic love for the good hero and by escape from the villain.[2] However, a reading that considers the mother-figure and the related emotional complex of female desire and creativity will show the excess of the romance in gothic texture.

The recognition of gothic mothers started with Moers's well-known reading of *Frankenstein* as a birth myth (1978, 93); Fleenor reads the 'quest-for-mother motif' as structuring the female gothic's exploration of female sexuality (1983, 15); Kahane's reading focuses on the mother-figure as 'spectral presence, ... a ghost signifying the problematics of femininity which the heroine must confront' (1980, 336). Such readings often use the physical dimension of the house metaphor: 'The heroine's exploration of entrapment in a Gothic house ... can be read as an exploration of her relation to the maternal body which she too shares ... with all its connotations of power over and vulnerability to forces within and without' (Kahane 1980, 338). I hope to extend this thematic discussion into the more formal and theoretical dimensions that gothic texture offers: questions of how maternity, creativity, the female body, relationships between women are related to the pleasures and horrors of the gothic; questions for the (female) body in the text as much as the (feminine) body of the text. Such a reading extends the (mainly psychoanalytic) feminist critical positions in which mother-figures have largely been discussed as representations of the Freudian 'uncanny' or as horrific functions in the heroine's social development. By contrast, I want to make a case *for* the mother-figures, as gothic texture foregrounds the mother's demise as horrific

sign of cultural containment and her potential as liberating force of
female desire.

As my outline of the plot in Radcliffe's *Mysteries of Udolpho* suggests,
Emily's romance is rivalled by a 'mother–daughter plot' – the solution
of her mother's mystery. This suggests a complex subjectivity:
Catherine Belsey has shown, using Lacanian insights, that a contradiction in the subject, 'between the conscious self, which is conscious in
so far as it is able to feature in discourse, and the self which is only
partially represented here ... constitutes the source of possible change'
(1980, 85). The suppression of such contradictions works to *enforce*
ideology, as in 'classic realist texts' – however, addressing these contradictions works to *subvert* ideology. Moreover, Belsey connects Lacan's
split subject and Benveniste's three modalities of the sentence – de-
clarative, imperative and interrogative – and defines an 'interrogative
text':

> The interrogative text ... may well be fictional, but the narrative does not
> lead to that form of closure which in classic realism is also disclosure ... [It]
> invites an answer or answers to the questions it poses. Further, if the inter-
> rogative text is illusionist it also tends to employ devices to undermine the
> illusion, to draw attention to its own textuality. The reader is distanced, at
> least from time to time, rather than wholly interpolated into a fictional
> world. Above all, the interrogative text differs from the classic realist text
> in the absence of a single privileged discourse which contains and places all
> the others. (1980, 92)

The gothic romance plot – with all its ideological, affirming, perpetuating qualities – has long been seen as such a privileged discourse.
However, a gendered reading highlights the contradictions in gothic
texture. It seems that the mother–daughter plot functions, in Belsey's
sense, as alternative discourse and even as challenge to the romance
plot. This means that it shifts the subject/object positions between
heroine and villain, and sheds a different light on the heroine's 'happy
ending'.

Radcliffe's *Udolpho* exemplifies such feminine gothic texture. Emily
performs a multiple quest, she motivates and mainly focuses the story.
By the end of the first chapter, her mother dies, and soon she is in the
typical position of the gothic heroine: a poor orphan, whose lack of
financial security as well as emotional comfort shapes her quest for

romantic love and marriage. It is significant that her dying father lays out these 'objects of value' for Emily: his warning about sensibility, his order to marry Valencourt and never to sell his house, La Vallée, of course also enforce the ideology of the cultural-historical context. The prescribed romance is disrupted by the villain, Montoni, who (with aunt Cheron) effects a separation from Valencourt, prompts a journey to Italy and threatens to take her property, La Vallée, from her; he introduces the typical gothicism of domestic horror, the supernatural and extensive travelling.

As we have seen, Radcliffe's stylistic excess undercuts the formal closure and affirmation of Emily's 'happy ending'; her excess in narrative extends this unsettling effect into gothic texture. The romance is only one discourse, the 'manifest' story, motivated by the female subject's desire for security and romantic love. By the end of the second chapter of *Udolpho*, Emily also desires 'knowledge': a decisive event throws her into doubt about her mother's – and thus about her own – identity. She observes her father without his knowledge, and sees him looking at the miniature picture 'of a lady, but not of her mother'. The scene continues:

> St. Aubert gazed earnestly and tenderly upon this portrait, put it to his lips, and then to his heart, and sighed with a convulsive force. *Emily could scarcely believe what she saw to be real.* She never knew till now that he had a picture of any other lady than her mother, much less that he had one which he evidently valued so highly; but having looked repeatedly, to be certain that it was not the resemblance of Madame St. Aubert, she became entirely convinced that it was designed for that of some other person. (26, emphasis added)

This initiates a typical Radcliffean deferral of explanation, a mystery that has interested critics much less than that of the supernatural or unspeakable events of Udolpho and that therefore will be briefly outlined here. The event is not mentioned further, until Emily dutifully burns her father's papers after his death, seemingly ending all hopes of further knowledge about her mother, the picture, and the other woman. The thread of this mystery is taken up again much later in the shape of three pictures: one at Udolpho (278), one in Villeroi that betrays 'a conspicuous likeness' to herself, and lastly another miniature that Laurentini gives to her, only enhancing Emily's doubts about 'a mystery of her birth dishonorable to her parents' (645). The mystery is finally solved by Laurentini's tale (655–62), which reveals the mysterious lady to be St Aubert's sister, the victim of Laurentini's murderous 'passions'. This identification, with all its reassurance for Emily, significantly occurs only one chapter before her final reunion with Valencourt; faith in Emily's mother is thus restored, and Emily positioned with a stronger sense of self before her marriage.

This reading reveals a second discourse, with a second quest concerning the mystery of her origins. It can thus be seen as a 'mirror-text', developed 'underneath' the romance plot and challenging its dominance. Initiated by the heroine's curious transgression of her father's privacy, she desires knowledge about her mother, her origin, her self. The father, refusing to share his knowledge with her and instead commanding her to burn the papers, complicates this quest; whereas Montoni, by taking her to Italy, ironically helps her to solve the mystery.

This mirror-text is crucial to feminine gothic texture and changes the reading of its politics. Emily, the first heroine of the feminine gothic, can be seen as a 'split subject' – with her desire for security and love, as offered by the good hero, on the one hand; her desire for a more complicated personal identity, as offered by the mother, on the other. The mother-plot is mostly absent from the narration but functions as her 'latent story'. The female subject's split is between the 'conscious' romance-heroine – 'conscious in so far as [she] is able to feature in discourse' – and the questing daughter-figure – 'the self which is only partially represented' – to use once again Catherine Belsey's terms (1980, 85). She goes on to show that 'it is this contradiction in the subject ... which constitutes the source of possible change' (85): the values of the manifest story are questioned, subverted, contradicted – and, I would add, gothically exceeded – by the latent story. And this version of gothic excess works – like the supernatural, like domestic horror – to expose ideological presuppositions and containment. In this sense, the interrogative text is an effect of the gothic's formal excess.

It is in this reading as 'interrogative text' that the gothic texture's feminist potential is recognisable. While the romance plot virtually reaffirms the 'law of the father', the latent mother–daughter story is motivated through the transgression of that very law and exceeds it. This also changes the implications of the happy ending. Although it suggests narrative closure, this is often undermined: the fairy-tale quality of Emily's and Blanche's wedding in *Udolpho* has already been shown. Similarly, Charlotte Brontë's 'happy endings' are famous for their implicit critique: shifted into ambiguity (the hero's questionable return in *Villette*), a surreal setting (Ferndean in *Jane Eyre*), a questionable achievement (voiced by Rose York in *Shirley*). In neo-gothic texts, as we shall see, such scepticism is foregrounded, especially in van Herk's *No Fixed Address*, the text that most self-consciously exceeds and escapes closure ... and enclosure.

Generic gothic 'excesses' like horror and the supernatural interact with this formal excess of feminine gothic texture in surprising ways: the encounters of the unreal (as in Emily's reaction to her father's reverence of a strange woman), of the supernatural, or the realm of dream and nightmare (as in the magnified domestic situation in Udolpho), are connected to the mirror-plot. This coding of the mother–daughter plot as 'unreal' works not only to further disrupt the 'normality' and acceptance of the romance plot, but also to disrupt and comment on the development of the romance itself.

Jane Eyre is a good example of how the interrogative texture of the feminine gothic works with regard to the supernatural. Jane's story – although a paradigmatic romance in form – has early been read as the story of a 'motherless woman' (Gilbert 1976; Rich 1976); or as an example of much nineteenth-century women's writing that revolves around the absence of mother-figures (Spacks 1975) or their replacement by cruel surrogate mothers (Modleski 1982, 68). Jane's refusal to compromise, her departure from Rochester and Thornfield after the encounter with Bertha, is virtually initiated by the mother as ghost, in a beautiful gothic scene:

> I dreamt I lay in the red-room at Gateshead; ... the gleam was such as the moon imparts to vapours she is about to sever. I watched her come – watched with the strangest anticipation; as though some word of doom were to be written on her disc. She broke forth as never moon yet burst from cloud: a hand first penetrated the sable folds and waved them away; then, not a moon, but a white human form shone in the azure, inclining a glorious brow earthward. *It gazed and gazed on me.* It spoke to my spirit: immeasurably distant was the tone, yet so near it whispered in my heart – 'My daughter, flee temptation.' 'Mother, I will.' (346)

In this supernatural, nocturnal encounter, the moon returns the 'daughter'-figure's gaze. The ghost-mother's call initiates Jane's journey, which enables her to find her family as well as her inheritance and, of course, the wrong man, St John Rivers: narrative events that produce 'equality' with the hero – a precondition for a Brontëan happy end. There is no radical break between the level of the 'real' and that of the 'supernatural'; the 'ghosts' do not function metaphorically. Rather, their connection is one of combination and contiguity, it is *metonymic* (Jakobson 1960) – another aspect that is often seen as characteristic of feminine writing. Such immediate interference of the supernatural – as well as of the mother–daughter story – with the manifest romance plot underlines the contradictory texture of gothic feminism.

Jane Eyre shows the emotional dimension of the gothic interrogative texture: the feminine mirror-text, I think, can also be seen as narrative of female desire – desire for another woman or for a female community. The metonymic relationship of the two plots exposes the classic heroine's desire for the hero that Rosalind Coward has characterised in these terms:

> The qualities which make these men so desirable are, actually, the qualities which feminists have chosen to ridicule: power (the desire to dominate others); privilege (the exploitation of others); emotional distance (the inability to communicate); and singular love for the heroine (the inability to relate to anyone other than the sexual partner). (1986, 146)

Similarly, Kaja Silverman sees desire 'as culturally instigated, and hence collective', and as questioning 'the notions of both the private and of a self synonymous with consciousness' (1983, 130). She paraphrases the Lacanian notion of desire as 'that permanent condition of alienation from a mythically "good" object which results from self-recognition and access to language' (1983, 56). The dynamics of lack and alienation in the generic gothic isolation and in the motherless situation of the gothic heroine constitute a typical ground for desire – in unexpected directions. In *Jane Eyre*, it reveals the connectedness of Bertha and Jane, first and second wives of Rochester. Jane's narration of the horrific encounter in the attic, and especially of the subsequent conversation with Rochester, reveals her empathy with the otherwise hated and imprisoned wife:

> I interrupted him, 'you are inexorable for that unfortunate lady: you speak of her with hate – with vindictive antipathy. It is cruel – she cannot help being mad.' 'Jane, my little darling ... you misjudge me again: it is not because she is mad I hate her. If you were mad, do you think I should hate you?' 'I do indeed, sir.' (303)

Jane Eyre   In the recent film adaptation of Brontë's classic, Anna Paquin self-confidently dramatises young Jane's rebellious spirit.

This is the recognition of a likeness: in relation to both Rochester's love and his power, Jane and Bertha have something in common rather than acting as rivals. Bertha, herself approaching Jane whenever she can – for example, warning her by slashing the veil before the wedding – has been seen as acting as Jane's 'agent' (Gilbert 1976, 797). The dynamics of desire between these and other female figures in women's gothic writing 'feminises' Jackson's (un-gendered) notion of gothic fantasy as 'literature of desire ... which seeks that which is experienced as absence and loss' (1981). In *Jane Eyre*, as in other feminist gothic texts, female desire liberates the female figures from being narratively constructed only in relation to men.

These dynamics of female desire are anticipated in Wollstonecraft's gothicism. Maria's desire is for her child; this mother–daughter relationship structures all others: for example, the origin of the sexual relationship with Darnford marks the moment when Maria is convinced that her husband has murdered her daughter. It is based on the dark recognition of the oppression that will inevitably contain the daughter as well (*Maria*, 85). In terms of gothic texture, the exchange of the multiple female life-stories works to obfuscate the ideology of romantic love and modern marriage – even the romance in her prison. Her own autobiography as told to her lover is metonymically interwoven with the autobiography of her jailor and rescuer Jemima; and the similarly gothic life-stories of the upper-class prisoner and her working-class jailor connect the two female figures in '[t]he novel's central relationship, which … would symbolically have substituted woman for man as woman's natural ally and protector' (Todd and Butler 1989, 25). The mirror-plot of female desire thus also early suggests difference in similarity: *women* instead of *Woman*.

In the feminist gothic, desire connects outsiders, and by forming a mirror-text it challenges and critiques the accepted plots. In this way gothic texture – similarly to gothic contextualisation – suggests the construction of an alternate world, though one without any fixed or fixing shape. No text is more clearly structured through desire in this sense than Mary Shelley's *Frankenstein* (1818), a feminist gothic in that it explores gendered similarity and difference in such an alternate world. The nameless creature in *Frankenstein* demands from Victor Frankenstein a partner 'like himself', a figure to share his otherness in a world outside society's acceptance.[3] Desire arises (in Silverman's Lacanian paraphrase) at the point of 'self-recognition and access to language': in the creature's development at the point of observing and imitating family life and language at the De Laceys'. Their domestic idyll is then attacked in a radical gothic critique of their violent and unjust treatment of the creature. The creature's well-known plea to his maker emphasises the desire for similarity in difference:

> I am alone and miserable; man will not associate with me; but one as deformed and horrible as myself would not deny herself to me. My companion must be of the same species and have the same defects. This being you must create. (137)

This language constructs a sense of self as Other. The subject's self-recognition as 'deformed', 'horrible', 'defective' – monstrous! – suggests the reference to a value system that is structured according to binary oppositions and thus excludes otherness and difference. However, although the voice is that of the Other, it is also (at this point) that of the speaking subject. Frederike van Leeuwen (1982) has called women's gothic 'the discourse of the Other'; Frankenstein's creature is an early and most striking example of such a speaking subject that has become one strong feature of neo-gothic intertextualisation. For example, in Atwood's *Lady Oracle*, Joan Foster continuously engages in a play with herself as Other, as we shall see. This Other in the feminine gothic often participates in the specific gothic construction of subjectivity as female – and, in some ways, as 'monstrous'.

Gothic texture constructs this subjectivity first and foremost through a clear narrative event: the mirror-text of female desire is typically motivated through a violent separation – from mother through death (*Udolpho*), from daughter through imprisonment (*Maria*), from the creator through abandonment (*Frankenstein*), from the family through exclusion (*Jane Eyre*). For Eve Kosofsky Sedgwick, 'separation' is one of the most characteristic gothic conventions:

> when an individual fictional 'self' is the subject of one of these conventions, that self is spatialized in the following way. It is the position of the self to be massively blocked off from something to which it ought normally to have access. (1986, 12)

Kosofsky Sedgwick's focus is on the continuation of two lives on each side of the separation, and on the 'most characteristic energies of the Gothic novel' – their reintegration: 'only violence or magic, and both of a singularly threatening kind, can ever succeed in joining them again' (13). What occurs in the process is one or the other version of 'violated separation' (as Catherine's hand at Lockwood's shattered window in the opening of *Wuthering Heights*), but also the opening of an alternate world – a world of the supernatural and of terror, but a terror that, as we have seen, can mean liberation.

In terms of female subjectivity, 'separation' is also importantly separation from the mother – explored mostly by feminist psychoanalytic gothicists.[4] In this sense, Kristeva's notion of 'abjection' will be suggestive to my reading of gothic form. Feminine gothic texture, with its complex subject processes, might be seen as dramatisation of gender construction; van Leeuwen writes: 'All the novelists I have discussed in this paper use the Gothic mode to reveal, in an indirect and grotesque way, the female condition. Their works read like *The Second Sex* in novel form' (1982, 43). However, I would emphasise that they recall de Beauvoir's postulate less by the recognition of a condition than by representing the process of becoming a woman.

Separation often means punishment, performed by those in power to demonstrate the Other's failure of the norm: suggesting for example that these female figures are somehow neither 'good girls' nor 'good women' or 'good mothers'; and that a correction of their femininity is required before they can be reunited or included again. This inclusion then is deferred: it even becomes a threat to the heroine, who discovers alternate desires and needs, but as we have seen, sometimes neither escape nor return is possible. This whole process is a dramatisation of de Lauretis's Woman/women distinction, and it is structured by gothic excess. It participates in the processes that engender the gothic subject as female and that make the 'I' realise herself as 'a woman' – or, more often in gothic texts, as 'a monster'.

Monstrosity: creation and seduction

'All human societies have a conception of the monstrous-feminine, of what it is about woman that is shocking, terrifying, horrific, abject' writes Barbara Creed (1986, 44). She enumerates impressive examples from different well-established disciplines, particularly psychoanalysis: Freud's uncanny; Campbell's phallic mother of primitive mythology; and the Medusa of classical mythology. What all of these figures share is their allusion to the maternal body. Creed shows how 'Freud linked the sight of the Medusa to the equally horrifying sight of the mother's genitals' (that is, the encounter with *das Unheimliche*) and concludes: 'the concept of the monstrous-feminine, as constructed within/by patriarchal and phallocentric ideology, is intimately related to the problem of sexual difference and castration' (1986, 44). The horror at the encounter of this 'monstrous-feminine' is one of the effects that horror narratives – from the contemporary popular gothic, to the Hollywood horror film (which is Creed's focus), to the whole gothic tradition – have traditionally relied on. And many of these narratives do construct a figure for the monstrous-feminine that enhances the horror of the story. In the feminine gothic, such a figure is particularly suggestive. First, it is here encountered by a female subject – a subject that is, as we have seen, split, 'in process', and in different ways challenging to patriarchal ideology. Second, the 'monsters' of the feminine gothic are among the most powerful female figures of literary history, representing forces which are among the most challenging to the structures both of the house of fiction and of the symbolic order. Not surprisingly, they still haunt the new feminist texts – Arachne Manteia in van Herk's *No Fixed Address* appears in some ways as a direct late-twentieth-century descendant of 'the madwoman in the attic'.

The figure of the monstrous feminine is one of the strongest connecting forces within the web of gothic writing. What all these texts share is a specific participation of the monstrous-feminine in the processes of gender construction. The narrative event of separation, initiating the mirror-text of female desire, offers a place to start; it also initiates those subject-processes that Julia Kristeva has called 'abjection' and discussed in relation to the mother-figure. I will briefly outline this concept, as it frames my reading of gender construction in the gothic 'classics', as well as its intertextualisation up to today's 'monstrous-feminine'. The 'powers of horror' explored by Kristeva are also the horrific powers of containment for the feminine within the symbolic order – that is, the target of gothic excess.

In terms of subjectivity formation, 'abjection' is the stage of necessary but painful separation from the mother and from the pleasures of the dyadic unity with her in the realm of the semiotic (Lacan's Imaginary) – a realm controlled by the ('double-faced') mother who is in turn controlled and contained by the symbolic order. Leaving this realm for the symbolic order means entering a process between borderlessness and border-construction, on the 'borderline' between an identity in flux and a subjectivity reached by separation. In this process, abjection, 'the twisted braid of affects and thoughts' (Kristeva 1982, 1), is related to the subject through opposition, like the object – however, unlike the object, the abject does not produce meaning through this opposition but 'draws ... toward the place where meaning collapses' (2). This is, once again, the frightening – but also potentially liberating – aspect of horror, in the physical sense. What causes abjection 'disturbs identity, system, order. What does not respect borders, positions, rules. The in-between, the ambiguous, the composite' (4). The ambiguity lies between the emotional and physical sensations of repulsion and desire for the mother – but also the desire for meaning that 'makes' the subject – and evokes the emotions of terror and desire. 'We may call it a border, for "abjection" is above all ambiguity' (9).

This notion of the border is central to the construction of the monstrous in horror narratives. Creed's discussion of horror film is also relevant to the discussion of the feminine gothic: she shows how the monstrous can be produced at the border between 'the normal and the supernatural, good and evil (*Carrie* ...); or ... at the border which separates those who take up their proper gender roles from those who do not (*Psycho* ...)' (1986, 49). Such border-types also structure feminine gothic texts which constitute the female subject according to a specific understanding of the 'normal' and the 'proper'. It has already been suggested that this female gothic subject typically somehow exceeds her 'proper' gender role, as symbolised most clearly by woman's place – the house. Seen in this sense, her extensive travelling puts a late-eighteenth-century heroine in a 'border position' that can make her feel 'monstrous' and then connects her to her seeming opposite, the monster. This recognition suggests the liberating dimension of the monstrous. At the same time, the border, as violent but not complete separation, partakes in constructing the other woman (in the gothic not necessarily a maternal figure) as *abject* in this sense of gender-role ambiguity and is thus also central to the construction of that monstrous-feminine.

However, it is not only a gender-role ambiguity that produces a monstrous-feminine. In Kristeva's scheme, the encounter with the feminine is mostly abjective – only in rare cases ecstatic (1986, 59), but not uncanny (57):

> What we designate as 'feminine', far from being a primeval essence, will be seen as an 'other' without a name, which subjective experience confronts when it does not stop at the appearance of its identity ..., what will be dealt with here ... is a coming face to face with an unnameable otherness – the solid rock of jouissance and writing as well. (59)

This encounter is also with the mother as other, and abjection in this situation means (phobic) fear and (physical) repulsion. The fear of evil involved turns out to be fear of the other, fear of evil-the-feminine. Kristeva's studies of different societies show a common handling of sexual difference which is based on the view of the feminine as threat to power:

> whether it be within the highly hierarchical society of India or the Lele in Africa it is always to be noticed that the attempt to establish a male, phallic power is vigorously threatened by the no less virulent power of the other

sex, which is oppressed. That other sex, the feminine, becomes synonymous with a radical evil that is to be suppressed. (1986, 70)

The female body becomes a target for this suppression. Three aspects
of this phenomenon can here be named and briefly shown in their
gothicised dimensions: female sexuality, the power of procreation, and
the 'two-faced mother'.

Female sexuality is feared as 'evil' – an age-old recognition (see
Beauvoir 1989, 167; Dinnerstein 1976; Daleski 1984; Gay 1984, esp.
169); represented early in gothic texts, where imprisoned female
'monsters' have traditionally been 'sexual women' like Laurentini and
Bertha Mason. Arachne Manteia in *No Fixed Address*, already introduced as their contemporary descendant, will show the neo-gothic
version of that female type. What the postmodern gothic texts especially recall is the whole signifying system for female sexuality as developed throughout the feminine gothic classics. Most characteristic is
the visualisation of a dangerous beauty: in *Udolpho*, 'her features were
handsome and noble, full of strong expression' (278) – Laurentini; or,
in *Jane Eyre*, 'she was a big woman, in stature almost equalling her
husband, and corpulent besides: she showed virile force' (296) –
Bertha. The danger clearly results from another border-confusion of
gender. It is enforced by structural oppositions and evocations of feminine ideals: the image of the late-eighteenth-century ideal as (Burkean)
'beauty in distress' (1987, 110), or the whole array of Victorian
'passionlessness' (see Cott 1978, 219; Gay 1984, 169; Vicinus 1972) –
the bodiless 'angel in the house' (Woolf 1979, 59); the 'sexless' governess (see Peterson 1972, 15). Of course, the typical feminist gothic
treatment of this imagery means a reversal: the heroine experiences
the 'passionless' ideal as 'monstrous'.

For example, Jane Eyre's horrific encounter with herself as bodiless spirit in the mirror of the 'Red Room' prefigures the horror of
Rochester's verbal negation of her body and sexuality during their
courtship: 'you little elfish [thing]' (288), 'a very angel' (288), 'ma-
demoiselle is a fairy' (296). Her explicit rejection of this bodilessness
in her outspoken monologues to him – such as 'you must neither
expect nor exact anything celestial of me – for you will not get it,
anymore than I shall get it from you' (288) – is offered as the only
way out of a misery that finds expression in Jane's most explicit evocation of the border of femininity: 'Why! – am I a monster?' (267).
Strikingly, the term is later used by Rochester for Bertha – coded

throughout as excitingly and dangerously sexual: 'a fearful voyage with such a monster in the vessel' (311). Jane experiences and fights the spatial and ideological containment of the female body, the violence of which is fully demonstrated by Bertha's fate. Both women are pejoratively labelled 'wild', 'animalistic' and 'mad'. That all female figures share the 'suppression' resulting from male fear of their sexuality is thus gothically suggested. This recognition undercuts the seeming separation of Jane and Bertha, as in Rochester's comparison of his wife and his bride in the attic scene. This 'official' separation is also shown in the highly symbolic division of his house into the forbidden, sexual sphere – Bertha's attic – and the proper, public realm – Jane's drawing room. That neither of the women in Thornfield is allowed to inhabit the whole house is another sign of male control; both female figures continually exceed the boundaries of that forcible separation, into each other's realms. In *Jane Eyre*, the 'monstrous-feminine' is gothically presented as masculine construction of what Peter Gay calls 'offensive women' (1984, 169) – women who leave their assigned sphere and make men ask uncomfortable questions about their own roles. Accordingly, the figure of Rochester – but also those of Brockle-hurst and St John Rivers – represent 'defensive men' in this Victorian context. Brontë's gothicism highlights the violence this defence does to women, their lives and their bodies. As we shall see, postmodern gothicism recalls these dynamics of the monstrous-feminine and explores their implications for the late-twentieth-century context – which does not seem that different, despite the sexual revolution. Margaret Atwood asks with characteristic provocation: 'What will happen to the heroine once she is the hero's wife? Will she also go mad?' (Becker: interview).

Besides female sexuality, the power of procreation is also shown as 'a dreaded one, that patrilineal filiation has the burden of subduing' (Kristeva 1982, 77). Here the gothic core text of criticism and inter-textualisation is Shelley's *Frankenstein*, suggesting themes like trans-gression of gender roles, but also postpartum depression, and the autobiography of a female artist.[5] Charlotte Perkins Gilman's *The Yellow Wallpaper* (1892) intertextualises *Frankenstein* in these ways. A story of complete isolation and interdiction of mobility, communication as well as creativity, it presents a typical feminist gothic reversal: an image of the monstrosity of male control rather than that of the supposedly mad woman. The narrator 'creates' another woman in the wallpaper, who is both her double and her Other, reflecting like a gothic mirror the 'monstrous' state of the heroine and playing the roles of ally and agent. Gothic excess 'multiplies' this figure into the image of the 'creeping women' of the ambiguous ending, an ending in incessant motion with the narrator herself 'creeping' over her husband's body (1161). Whether read as escape into madness or into the suicide suggested by the first encounter with a strangled woman in the wallpaper (1152), the ending refuses to restore the female subject to the symbolic order. This story, like *Maria*, is told by the figure of the monstrous-feminine – a narrative move to be further explored by neo-gothicism. The processes of controlling procreation have been delineated in Margaret Atwood's neo-gothic dystopia, *The Handmaid's Tale* (1985).

The dreaded power of procreation also shows the mother as 'two-faced'. She gives birth to life that is finite and will end in death. In twentieth-century literature, therefore, Kristeva sees the 'theme of the two-faced mother' that 'is perhaps the representation of the baleful power of women to bestow mortal life' (1982, 157). This theme, also representing the maternal body as a site of conflicting desires, can be a construction of the mother as monstrous. Mothers have been, as has been mentioned, largely absent in the gothic tradition: their physical appearance is one of the most important developments in twentieth-century feminine gothic writing. It is a theme that structures all of the texts chosen from the Canadian postmodern and that could be seen as culminating in the striking role of the mother in *Lady Oracle* and the young daughter's early recognition that 'My mother was a monster' (70). I hope to show how such statements in neo-gothic texts refer to an age-old attitude and how gothicism is used to reveal – and exceed – the ideological construction of both such a statement and the mother's 'monstrosity'.

Two more aspects of horror in Kristeva's concept of abjection are productive for a reading of horror in gothic gender construction. One is her emphasis on placing subject and abject within specific cultural discourses of rites but also of language. The link to language is important because it again underlines the power of horror for liberation or change:

> In abjection, revolt is completely within being, within the being of language. Contrary to hysteria, which brings about, ignores, or seduces the symbolic but does not produce it, the subject of abjection is eminently productive of

culture. Its symptom is the rejection and reconstruction of language. (Kristeva 1982, 45)

Here might be one of the greatest potentials for a feminist reading of 'abjection' which is, in Kristeva's essay, not gendered. The potential productivity of culture then becomes one aspect of the feminist, pragmatic potential of horror for a female subject of abjection. The constructions of language offer a place to start: 'there is nothing "loathsome" in itself; the loathsome is that which disobeys classification rules peculiar to the given symbolic system' (92). Once again, there is a suggestion of the potentially liberating act of disobedience – challenge, transgression, excess – that is then excluded. On the other side of the 'border' – the side of the obedient or 'normal' – is another cultural and linguistic construct: the notion of the 'proper'.

In feminist theory, the 'proper' has become a strong concept, especially since Hélène Cixous and Catherine Clément have conceptualised what they call *le propre* as constitutive to subjectivity and gender construction in the symbolic order – or, in their terms, in 'the economy of the Selfsame' (1986). This economy presupposes a bisexuality in every human being: not in the sense of sexual preference but in the sense that everyone has aspects of the Other within themselves. As this Other within the male subject is that very feminine he has always devalued/negated/killed, he cannot embrace that difference within himself and goes on to externalise/negate/kill this Other in favour of the Selfsame. Externalising can be done by labelling it, and by thus putting it in relation to *le propre* – that which fits the Selfsame, the 'ownself' (167). Obviously, both the 'Selfsame' and *le propre* carry Marxist as well as psychoanalytical (and even erotic) overtones. These associations, as well as the function of *le propre* in that 'economy' become clear when its various connotations are looked at separately: the (Marxist) one of 'property and appropriation' – the (cultural) one of 'the proper and appropriate' and the (physical, erotic) one of 'the clean'. These terms come to strongly connote the female body: 'Since woman must care for bodily needs and instil the cultural values of cleanliness and propriety, she is deeply involved in what is *propre*, yet she is always somehow suspect, never quite *propre* herself' (Cixous and Clément 1986, 167). This is the recognition of the gap between ideological norm, the responsibility assigned to women and their – ironically similarly 'assigned' – non-fulfilment of this norm (see Kristeva's similar conclusions on *le corps propre* or 'the clean and proper body' 1982, 101–10). This gap, defined in terms of *le propre* in its various connotations, is central to gender construction in the feminine gothic.

Of course, notions of what is 'proper' are culturally specific and have changed in the Western European context over the two hundred years of the gothic's existence. However, language betrays a surprising continuity. One related metaphor abounds in the feminine gothic with striking emphasis; in its centrality to female subjectivity in the gothic it connects Radcliffe's Emily St Aubert even with van Herk's Arachne Manteia: 'respectability'. 'Respectability' characterises the early gothic heroines, despite the narrative challenges to their gender roles: travelling women are 'chaperoned' by villains (see Moers 1978, 129); an adulterous woman like Wollstonecraft's Maria is 'respected' and 'esteemed' (*Maria*, 172), and her love relationship develops in the enclosure of the prison that also means removal from culture's pressures and the ideology of *le propre*. Both of these examples suggest a self-conscious and even ironic redefinition of 'respectability'.

Moreover, in the feminine gothic, the *construction* of respectability has been early suggested by linking it with specific signs of a 'proper' femininity. The role of beauty is deeply connected to the myth of a 'natural' femininity which dominated Victorian thinking especially and today again influences radical feminist groups. This myth is discarded repeatedly throughout feminine gothic texts. For example, when Jane Eyre sketches her own portrait in charcoal as 'Portrait of a Governess, disconnected, poor, and plain' (163), and Blanche Ingram as a coloured miniature of 'an accomplished lady of rank' (163), to discipline her own desire for Rochester by an imaginary imitation of his gaze, both the material and the titles of her art draw attention to the construction of female beauty. The treatment of food is another sign not only for a proper femininity but also for the control of women's bodies – as the scenes of near-starvation at Brocklehurst's Lowood as training for a proper womanhood, in juxtaposition to Jane's liberated love expressed in her care and cooking for Rochester at Ferndean, suggest. Third, one of the most important signs of respectability is dress, as documented in memorable scenes in *Udolpho* of Emily, always appropriately dressed, even for gothic elopements or nightly intrusions into her chamber (261); or of Jane Eyre, who feels completely estranged from her image as bride in the mirror: 'a robed and veiled figure ... unlike my usual self' (289).

All of these signs of a proper femininity are taken up by post-modern feminine texts, and their gothicism exposes how they work towards a unified, controllable subjectivity of Woman. In this sense, food separates the 'proper' femininity from the 'monstrous feminine' both for fat Joan Foster in *Lady Oracle* and for chunky Arachne in *No Fixed Address*. And dress, a classic feminine gothic sign for both propriety and property is shown in the postmodern context not only as thematic enclosure of the body but also as formal enclosure of the story. Gothic textures: from houses of fiction to text/ures of dress.

Notes

1 See Kosofsky Sedgwick (1986, 9–11) for an overview of gothic criticism in these terms; she emphasises its 'privileging the spatial metaphor of depth ... to represent a model of the human self, and reading the other gothic conventions in terms of that one' (11). Such gothic representations of the 'human self' have mostly been studied with attention to the ego's psychological split (Miyoshi 1969, Rigney 1978).

2 An influential outline of the basic Radcliffean plot has been Fiedler's (1982, 127), with an emphasis on the dream landscape, on the duplication of the girl's escapes and on the ending when she 'is married to the virtuous lover who has all along worked (and suffered equally with her) to save her'. By contrast, I think that the Radcliffean lover, Valencourt for example, has all along waited passively and, instead of suffering, collected experiences of the world – mainly in Paris. 'In the end', Fiedler continues, 'all the ghosts that have terrorized her are explained as wax-works or living men in disguise' – however, as we shall see, the ghost that has haunted her most, namely that of the mystery concerning her mother, turns out to be very real.

3 Various critics have seen the creature as inhabiting the realm of the feminine; van Leeuwen's reading is exemplary:

> Because of his ugliness this male monster is an outsider to society in the same sense in which women, because of their sex, are outsiders to it. Like women, he is not responsible for his situation, yet can in no way alter it. Nothing can make him a human being, just as women can never be men. He tries to find his way into the dominant culture in the same way women try to fight their way into it: by imitation. He is deprived of male privileges, speech and education, in the same way women are deprived of them. He is thus very much the kind of monster a woman would create ... It seems ... that the author identified with Frankenstein's monster, his own creation, but an outsider to culture, like herself. (1982, 42–3)

4 Feminist psychoanalysis focuses the pre-Oedipal phase, controlled by the both all-powerful and oppressed mother, and explores the difference for daughters and sons in the separation from the mother at entering the symbolic order; separation is presented as especially painful for daughters (and mothers) because of the gender similarity, but as necessary for life in patriarchal culture. Pragmatic/social studies on the perpetuation of the patriarchal model of mothering are Chodorow (1978), Friday (1977), Dinnerstein (1976) and Rich (1976a); more culture-critical are, e.g., Mitchell (1974), Flax (1978), Gallop (1982) and Rose (1987); post-structuralist studies are Irigaray (1981) and Kristeva (1982). For gothic criticism that uses these approaches on separation and female identity see Johnson's suggestive reading of *Frankenstein* (1987b), Dinnerstein's *The Mermaid and the Minotaur* (1976), and Friday's *My Mother/My Self* as female life-writing (1977). Kahane is illuminating on the gothic's metaphoric mirroring of similarity and difference with the maternal body; she writes: 'For women, then, the struggle for a separate identity is not more tenuous ... but is fundamentally ambivalent, an ongoing battle with a mirror image who is both me and not me' (1980, 56). Holland and Sherman write: 'To the two of us, other people or objects never seem in gothic to be quite other. Rather, they are intimately connected to, part of, dependent upon, and controlled by the heroine or the parent-figures around her' (1977, 290). An influential pre-feminist reading of the gothic as dramatisation of the Oedipal conflict in terms of separation and identity is Fiedler's, with his well-known image of gothic maternity: 'Beneath the haunted castle lies the dungeon keep: the womb from whose darkness the ego first emerged, the tomb to which it must return at last. Beneath the crumbling shell of paternal authority, lies the maternal blackness, imagined by the gothic writer as a prison' (1982, 132).

5 *Frankenstein* has become a core text for the discussion of the monstrous. Its theme of creation is basically seen in two related ways: as 'horror story of maternity' that makes it into 'a version of the gothic created by women authors to explore formerly unspeakable "monstrous" aspects of female lives' (Stein 1983, 126); aspects that in different ways contradict the feminine ideal of 'the moral mother' of the time (see Bloch 1987, Rich 1976a). Related is the reading as autobiography of a female artist: represented by both Frankenstein, the creator as imitator (Stein 1983, 126) and transgressor of gender roles but also by the creature in its isolation and 'Otherness' (see Poovey 1980, Johnson 1982b or Tillotson: 'The world has no more use for a loving monster than it has for a thinking woman' (1983, 168)).

Chapter 3
Gothic intertextuality

Filliation

The web of feminine gothic writing has prompted contemporary critics to revise traditional concepts of literary influence: this new thinking about a feminine intertextualisation, which Barbara Godard calls 'filliation', and some core examples from historical gothicism are the focus of this section. Second, neo-gothicism also reflects, in a post-modern move towards popular culture, what has been an important phenomenon of women's culture in the early 1970s: the so-called 'gothic boom' – an explosion in the production and consumption of gothic romances. This phenomenon will be the focus of the second section of this chapter. Third, there is the specific version of Canadian gothicism in its fictional tradition, its current critical discussion, and its ongoing intertextualisation, which is the focus of the third section. All of these aspects will recur, with a development from feminine gothic connected-ness (Munro), to a parodic interaction with popular gothicism (Atwood), to an escape into the haunted Canadian 'langscape' (van Herk).

The remarkable topography of interrelated feminine gothic traces has first been recognised through Moers's 'experiential model' along themes like the 'savageries of girlhood' or a specifically female 'fearful visualisation of the self' (1978, 107), which connects Emily Brontë's novel to Sylvia Plath's poetry. Susan Wolstenholme's *Gothic (Re)visions* (1993), relying on a proliferation of perspective that gothically de-centres the authority of the gaze, connects writers as diverse as Ann Radcliffe, Harriet Beecher Stowe, George Eliot and Edith Wharton in a 'symbolic exchange' among 'women writers [and] readers textually coded as "women"' (Wolstenholme 1993, xiii) that suggests new, more formal models for feminine intertextualisation. Wolstenholme's playful question 'Why would a textual mother haunt a house like this?' recalls Atwood's allusion to 'secret plots' of women's gothic (1977); and the metaphor of the house of fiction: feminine gothics are haunted houses, not only in the contextual sense of 'experience' but also in the intertextual sense of continuation and deconstruction of feminine textuality. In this sense, Barbara Godard's concept of *filliation* provides a useful matrix, based on the idea of a 'web of women's writing' – as women share, in open, communal phenomenological readings and collective writing, 'topoi, images, allusions, weaving a web of mutual quotations in their writing' (Godard 1987b, ix). Filliation 'exceeds' and decentres the idea of linear development and opens up different interdependencies of texts. It is a new theory of origins that revises and feminises Harold Bloom's influential theory of the 'anxiety of influence' (Godard 1984, 50).

One aspect of such a feminist poetics is the liberation from male models for the writer as well as for the text (such as Showalter's female tradition from *imitation* via *rejection* to *liberation* (1977, 35)). The first step might be a subversive, parodic 'misuse of common male traditions or genres' (Godard 1984, 50) – the sort of 'swerve' that Godard sees in the gothic's feminising of the picaresque. The parodic interrelatedness of the masculine picaresque and the feminine gothic is still powerful in the postmodern context, as we shall see in the chapter on *No Fixed Address*. However, in terms of filliation, the feminist uses of parody go beyond a reaction to the male tradition: as defined by Linda Hutcheon (1985), parody in its 'reverential' version – without its effect of ridicule – has been a strong connecting thread in the web of feminine gothic writing. In a postmodern context, parody recurs as a self-conscious model – as *Lady Oracle* in particular will show – and as opposed to 'stylisation' as defined, with exclusively masculine examples, by Christine Brooke-Rose: 'Parodic dramatisation of a theme works on the principle of expansion. Stylisation, on that of reduction' (1980, 171). As in gothic contextualising, filliation is marked – in Hutcheon's terms – by parodic 'repetitions' that continue and extend the literary gothic web.

Thus, feminine gothicism is marked not by an anxiety of but by a *desire for* influence by literary 'foremothers' or -sisters. Godard does not exclude 'the spirit of the fathers' (52) from these dynamics: 'not creation by elimination or subtraction, as the male Oedipal configuration implies, but creation by addition, creation as paradox, both identity and difference' (51). Wolstenholme, similarly feminising Bloom, further highlights the related paradox of (feminine) creation in the symbolic order:

> Since both her [the woman writer's] own writing and that of other women writers must inevitably fall under the sign of the father, her use of these writers is especially problematic. I wish to suggest how these writers reread one another's texts, almost as a special code which conveyed a message about writing. (1993, xii)

Her own model of a symbolic textual mother–daughter connection comes to emphasise a desire for sameness and identification which distinguishes it from the Oedipal model (Wolstenholme 1993, 151). Such a desire for similarity has, as we have seen, worked to challenge patriarchal structures in gothic texture. It also seems to be (re)productive – especially in gothic intertextuality:

> As linguistic structures, novels are always inscribed in paternal law; in one sense (a strictly psychoanalytic one), no text can really have a 'mother' because inscription in language implies differentiation from the maternal. But ... Gothic-marked narratives always point to the space where the absent mother might be. (Wolstenholme 1993, 151)

Pointing to the absent mother and to the 'lost foremothers' (Godard), gothicism does play an important role throughout the almost two centuries of modern female culture: there has been a vigorous exchange of allusions and re-visions, and even of provocations and answers, a dynamic – and self-conscious – writing and rewriting of feminine texts haunting one another: around the interrogative texture of romantic love and female desire, of gender construction between le propre and the monstrous-feminine, of the (contextualising) dynamics of domestic horror. Gothic form in this sense has anticipated the textual and ideological liberation of the new feminist texts.

In the earliest well-known literary response to the gothic Ur-texts, Jane Austen's *Northanger Abbey* (begun in 1798; published posthumously in 1818), filliation is almost self-consciously suggested in the narrator's defence of the novel, and of the novel as an aspect of female culture:

I will not adopt that ungenerous and impolitic custom, so common with novel writers, of degrading, by their contemptuous censure, the very performances to the number of which they are themselves adding: joining with their greatest enemies in bestowing the harshest epithets on such works, and scarcely ever permitting them to be read by their own heroine, who, if she accidentally take up a novel, is sure to turn over its insipid pages with disgust ... Let us not desert one another; we are an injured body. (35)

This affirmation of feminine novelistic connectedness – even in the emphasis on a physical unity – is both underlined by and itself underlines the emotional connectedness of female friends in the text: Catherine Morland and Isabella Thorpe share the pleasures of reading 'horrid' novels together. This shared reading has a twofold effect in terms of filliation: first, it evokes a whole range of gothic texts, not only their favourite *Udolpho*, which recalls Radcliffe and other 'serious' gothic writers around her (see Spender 1986, 230), but also the numerous pulp gothics of the time – thus ensuring the survival of some of them as so-called 'Northanger Novels' (see Sadleir 1969, 20). Moreover, the two young women's readings of gothic romances quickly develop into a shared discourse that shapes and romanticises – and ultimately even gothicises – their everyday experience. This process, the gothicising of everyday life becomes a self-conscious, neo-gothic structuring principle, as Munro's *Lives of Girls and Women* will show.

In Austen's response to the literary gothicism of her time, the desire for influence is not only a matter of allusion but also of faithful 'repetition' of form. Catherine's friendship with another woman motivates the plot and challenges her romantic relationship: there is the feminine gothic's characteristic, interrogative texture. However, it is repeated with a self-reflexive twist: in an inversion of Radcliffe's pattern, where female desire for the mother questions the ideology and containment of the love plot, in *Northanger Abbey* the mirror-text challenges, ironically and self-reflexively, by asking for the romance story, not by escaping from it. Formally speaking, in this way *Northanger Abbey* mocks gothic conventions and effects. The mockery plays on the typical hyperbolic gothic contextualisation, but again with a decisive – and demystifying – twist: the generic romantic fantasies are shown to idealise a bare social necessity (marriage); and the domestic horrors are shown to romanticise very real female fears. However, gothic horrors are not only ridiculed – as in Catherine's famous gothicising of a laundry-list – but also revised, as in the suspicion of

General Tilney. And here, in another reversal of Radcliffe's formula, they are not explained away, but reconfirmed with a difference: General Tilney does become a villain-figure, not because of the crimes that Catherine suspects him of, but because he tries to prevent her marriage to his son because of class difference (see also Fleenor 1983, 5).

Repeating and reversing: thus parodically incorporating the gothic's interrogative structure, Austen's novel in one sense further reaffirms gothic texture. *Northanger Abbey* works as a 'reverential parody' in Linda Hutcheon's sense (1985), as *critique* of the potentially damaging effects of the romance, but also *complicit* with gothic texture and its feminist challenges to the myths of romantic love and a proper femininity. The parodic incorporation of gothic structure, with its – at first sight perhaps paradoxical – move *for* romance within the mirror-text highlights not only the impact of marriage as social necessity (a well-known Austen theme), but also the devastating effect of women's lack of education. This is where Austen's parody also 'repeats' Wollstonecraft's feminist gothic. Austen contextualises what Wollstonecraft elsewhere has radically discarded as the source of 'The State of Degradation to Which Woman is Reduced' (1986 [1792]). Catherine's education consists in accepted, non-novelistic Literature that proves utterly useless to her; quotations from Shakespeare, Pope or Thomson mock the late-eighteenth-century education in sensibility for girls and ironically echo St Aubert's deathbed scene in *Udolpho*. On another level, they re-affirm the gothicism that with pointed irony prepares women for the dangers of being defined through their position on the marriage market. Accordingly, Austen's parody unromantically and ironically concludes Catherine's 'horrific' story with a wedding that appears both as social and as intertextual necessity (347, 8).

Thus, as early as in the 1790s, gothic form has taken a range of different shapes – from the interrogative romance and the radical feminist story to their ironic, feminist parody – a range that demonstrates the dynamic uses of gothic form for a critique of patriarchal constraints. This early feminine gothicism demonstrates the desire for connectedness through haunting allusions, 'repetition with difference', re-vision. Neo-gothicism self-consciously returns to these forms of filliation; *Lady Oracle*, as we shall see, even 'exceeds' it. Not surprisingly, it also returns to the well-known figure that has strongly haunted the house/s of gothic fiction: the 'mad wife' with her (monstrous) excess of whatever constitutes *le propre* of her time. That the archetypal madwoman, Bertha Mason, also has a direct predecessor in Radcliffe's *A Sicilian Romance* was early pointed out by Ellis (1923, 194). However the 'madwoman' and her sisters like tragic heroine Maria have formed filliation in various ways. Three texts will show the range: Charlotte Perkins Gilman's American story, *The Yellow Wallpaper*; Henry James's *The Turn of the Screw*, written in England in the same context; and the contemporary *Wide Sargasso Sea* (maybe the best-known direct literary answer to a feminist gothic classic).

James's important gothic story *The Turn of the Screw* (1898) playfully recalls a whole range of gothic conventions: the obfuscation of the story's origin; its 'live-burial' and the process of making it accessible; the need for an audience and the insistence on truth; the deferral of explanations – 'hanging fire' becomes a key phrase. It thus introduces a ghost story read by the fire: a governess's story. Her tale is motivated by the interdiction of communication with her far-away master – which is an aspect of her generic isolation but more importantly a great example of the live-burial of language that is 'exceeded' by the tale itself. The supernatural events of her story – encounters with ghosts from the past that lead her to fear that she is faced with either persecuted or daemonic children – are all the more horrific, as she is (as a surrogate mother) responsible for the children. The radical doubt, whether these appearances are fantasies or signs of a secret plan, is displaced, by the open ending, into the realm of the reader: a typical gothic effect that has been critically related to the unreliability of the narrator (Rimmon Kennan 1983). However, it seems crucial (especially in comparison with Poe's and Lovecraft's similarly open endings) to realise that this unreliability both constructs and is constructed by the narrator's gender. This happens in two ways. On the level of structure, the prologue establishes an all-male audience (the women leave when the ghost story of a governess and two children is announced)[1] that constructs the governess' tale into an utter Other; if the male audience is established as rational and reasonable, the female speaking subject can be read as opposite – irrational, unreasonable, nervous, unreliable. Moreover, the governess-figure contextualises – like the likewise unnamed narrator of Gilman's story – the popular notions of 'hysteria' that at the time turned every woman into a potential madwoman – as which the figure of the governess indeed has been 'analysed' (by Edmund Wilson; see also Varma 1966, 38). In such a reading, the gothic story becomes the construction of a feminine discourse that is, by extension, somehow 'mad'.

One gothic effect here could be – as in Kathryn Hume's 'literature of disillusion' – the general recognition that 'reality is unknowable' (Hume 1984, 56). For James, the flirtation with gothic anti-realism as aesthetic principle in this story signals a shift away from the psychological realism of his fiction towards modernist writing – especially, if one sees the gothic novel in England and the United States as anticipating the modern novel (with the realist novel as 'interlude'). Therefore, a gendered reading of the story shows how James uses the feminine gothic form for a haunting anti-realist story – but without the pragmatic challenges of gothic excess and interrogative texture. What is specifically lacking in James's text is female desire: the governess's predecessor Miss Jessel, presented as a weird 'sexual woman' figure, is constituted as a threat to the governess, rather than as a 'sister' who anticipates her problems within the male control of the house. One aspect that would clearly link the two female figures – and also to a whole range of female figures from gothic filliation – is early distanced by mockery: Miss Jessel's mysterious death 'of so much respectability' (8).

The direct intertextual allusions in *The Turn of the Screw* that evoke feminine gothic classics work similarly: 'was there a "secret" at Bly – a mystery of Udolpho or an insane, an unmentionable relative kept in unsuspected confinement?' (21). They support the link of the feminine to the 'mad' discourse; the governess's reading of gothic fiction seems to heighten her imagination and to prevent rational thought, and her language does nothing to challenge this supposition. Such references underline the governess's unreliability and enforce the thrill of her story. In gothic filliation, it seems, such a reference would have a strengthening rather than weakening impact, by once again constructing a similarity, for example of the discursive experience of enclosure, and a protest against this situation. And the transtextual connectedness, I think, would then work to construct another aspect of gothic excess – excess of textual enclosure.

In Charlotte Perkins Gilman's *The Yellow Wallpaper* (1892) such references to the same texts seem to work in this sense of filliation. The narrator's familiarity with gothicism is seen as a danger by her husband (1151) and is thus always discursively juxtaposed with a reasonable argument that might demonstrate her clear judgement in his eyes. But it helps her to realise her own entrapment. The house itself provides a good example; it makes her 'think of English places that you read about' (1149) – in gothic stories – and it has 'something queer about it' (1148). Despite all reasoning that this is because it has been long untenanted (1149), gothic filliation suggests that she is right. For her fantasy that the house is haunted (1148) does suggest a dark past – possibly another 'mad wife' behind the attic room's barred windows – and a present secret – the narrator herself, hidden away in the yellow-papered attic, separated not only from friends and family but also from her child. But her enclosure through house and text is also haunted intertextually by the various 'abodes of horror' and attics that have housed and contained figures of the monstrous-feminine, in this sense the creatrix-figure of the mother and artist. The ending – open like James's – is intertextually suggested, in a typical move of gothic filliation: through another feminine gothic classic. 'I've got out at last' are the last words of Gilman's narrator directed at her husband, 'in spite of you and Jane. And I've pulled off most of the paper, so you can't put me back!' (1161). There has been no 'Jane' in the house before, but a 'Janet' – Rochester's own name for Jane Eyre at times of courtship (248, 438). The names, like the narrative situation, read like an indirect response to Brontë's feminist gothic. The interrogative structure of *Jane Eyre* not only has clear reverberations in Gilman's story but also adds an extra level: it anticipates an inevitable ending – of a 'mad wife' – that the new text does not spell out. And it further emphasises the actual threat of domestic horror.

The extra level also opens another effect of gothic filliation: exceeding the house of the text itself. The contemporary textual answer to *Jane Eyre* is Jean Rhys's *Wide Sargasso Sea* (1966). Recentring its story on the 'mother' text's marginalised and muted female figure, Rhys's novel anticipates the (Atwoodian) 'secret plots' of contemporary women's texts around the unresolved figure of the mad wife. It suggests a further reflection on the narrative constructions of relationships among women, a reading that shifts the Woman/women dynamics (of the symbolic order) into a feminine realm (albeit within that order). Molly Hite, reading Bertha's life as 'the other side of the story', characterises the resulting shift in these terms:

> By recentering the story on the character who is in many ways the most necessary accessory to the action – most necessary and most necessary

accessory – Rhys demonstrates how both social and narrative conventions mandate that certain categories of women must be devalued if other categories of women are to assume importance. (1989, 33)

Similarly, Gayatri Spivak has brought out the imperialism in the women's relationship, in which the white Creole woman eliminates herself 'so that Jane Eyre can become the feminist individualist heroine of British fiction' (Spivak 1989, 184). She concludes: 'At least Rhys sees to it that the woman from the colonies is not sacrificed as an insane animal for her sister's consolidation' (185). While there are indeed power relations (and other hierarchical relations) between these female figures, the intertextual relationship of Brontë's and Rhys's texts works to radically stress what they have in common: the enclosure in male structures. Hite pessimistically writes that Rhys's revised version of Bertha's story reveals 'how narrative conventions that confine and finally eradicate Bertha are at the same time ways of bringing a rebellious female protagonist [Jane Eyre] back into the patriarchal fold' (Hite 1989, 39). However, as we have seen, gothic texture – and even its 'happy ending' – is also rebellious. And such a 'sister text' not only stresses but also 'exceeds' the enclosures of patriarchal structures and the separation and substitution of narratives.

Such responsive intertextualisation also demonstrates the power of a muted and marginalised female figure to exceed her various enclosures and thus to persist. As a motif this kind of excess of structures and boundaries has marked the feminine gothic ever since the various elopements and flights from castles and abbeys. In *Wide Sargasso Sea* this is taken up in a more radical way when Antoinette virtually 'exceeds' her body – also a 'house' in male control. The presence of her disembodied voice disrupts Rochester's narration of her – and his – story. This gothic moment happens when his treatment of his wife – of her body and her emotions – is challenged by Christophine, the figure of surrogate mother, female friend, wise woman. Antoinette's relationship with and desire for her initiate the mirror-plot of *Wide Sargasso Sea*. This plot culminates in Christophine's and Rochester's confrontation with the mysterious and uncanny presence of Antoinette's voice. It first echoes the female friend's proud judgements – that could be a reverberation in Rochester's mind, but subsequently forms a statement of her own, detached from Christophine. This separation happens at the moment when her name comes up – and with it the problem of her identity, which has been brutally damaged both by Rochester's renaming her Bertha. Antoinette's gothic appearance as a speaking but bodiless subject is also noteworthy, as the 'you' that constitutes her subjectivity is not her husband but her female friend: 'And I came to you. Oh Christophine' (154). There is continuity (as Christophine voices Antoinette's reproaches) as well as difference (as Antoinette's I/you shift indicates) between the two female figures; one has helped the other to find a form of communication and self-inscription out of the isolation and imprisonment that has contained them.

This important scene in one way indicates the twist of this gothic motif since Radcliffe, where such an escape from physical enclosure from male houses needed the figure of a rescuing knight (even an ironic one, as in Emily's escape from Udolpho). In this sense it is not only a modern answer but also prefigures the postmodern twist that parodically replaces this male figure by a female one: for example, in Angela Carter's story 'The Bloody Chamber' the mother saves the daughter from her husband in the impressive shape of such a knight (1979, 40).

Gothic interconnectedness in this sense suggests not only the idea of re-vision but also that of anticipation, which brings us to another aspect of filliation: simultaneity. Godard speaks of '"Croneology", youth and age contained within a cyclical whole' (1984, 51). 'Croneology' further underlines the changed view of connectedness through time that in filliation replaces the idea of a linear development from generation to generation. The term 'generation' itself is thus revised, in the sense outlined by Julia Kristeva in her influential essay 'Women's Time': 'My usage of the word "generation" implies less a chronology than a *signifying space*, a both corporeal and desiring mental space' (1986, 209). This space allows for recognising the parallel existence of feminist movements and developments and of the ways in which they are interwoven (209). In this sense, two hundred years of gothicism are interwoven with the uses of parody, pastiche, collage and plagiarism (Godard) that postmodern feminist fictions self-consciously take up. This is not to say that these techniques are specifically feminist or postmodern strategies; Kristeva (among others) has throughout her work emphasised that each text is 'constructed like a mosaic of quotations' and defined the use of 'intertextuality' in the Barthesian way that relies on the reader's powers of recognition. However, both postmodernism and feminism have used intertextuality in new, self-conscious ways, as the discussion of neo-gothicism will show.

One aspect of this postmodern interweaving that particularly relies on the reader's power of recognition is the recourse to popular forms of gothic writing, the 'formulae' (see Cawelti 1976) which are familiar to a large international readership. The phenomenon of popular horror with its specific set of narrative conventions and cultural effects is the subject of the next section. One version of filliation 'points to the textual mother' by rewriting both her text and the woman writer's life in gothic form. Godard mentions Margaret Atwood's rewriting of Susanna Moodie: *The Journals of Susanna Moodie: Poems by Margaret Atwood* (1970) continues Moodie's gothic autobiography *Roughing it in the Bush* (1848) and connects Moodie's voice to Atwood's vision. This re-vision ensues in a multiple subjectivity that 'exceeds' even the split subject of the feminine gothic in its inclusion of life-writing – and live writing. Similarly, Liz Lochhead's play *Blood and Ice* (1982) not only gothically re-presents *Frankenstein* on the contemporary stage, but also, in Beate Neumeier's terms, 're-constructs the links between Mary Shelley's life and her novel' by reconstructing Shelley's own (gothic) reconstructions before rewriting her novel for the second edition (Neumeier 1991, 189). A further Canadian example is Jane Urquhart's novel *Changing Heaven* (1990), which gothically connects a contemporary Canadian literary scholar to the ghost of Emily Brontë haunting the moors of Haworth. These texts 'exceed' (and feminise) traditional concepts of time and further dynamise subjectivity in process. Another homage to Emily Brontë, a different medium: in 1978 the haunting and romantic song 'Wuthering Heights' made the 19-year-old Kate Bush into a star. Composed under Brontëan inspiration, it points to the many forms and unbroken force of contemporary popular gothica.

Pulp – Horror – Romance

'Last night I dreamt I went to Manderley again.' Thus opens one of the most popular books ever: *Rebecca* (1938). Daphne du Maurier's romance circles around a house named Manderley, haunted by one of the most terrifying and fatal female figures of literary history – Rebecca. The story is told by the young mistress of Manderley, Mrs de Winter. This otherwise unnamed narrator has much in common

Rebecca   Their love is haunted: the classic couple of the gothic romance, with Joan Fontaine as young, terrified Mrs de Winter and Laurence Olivier as a rich but troubled man of the world.

with Jane Eyre, but shares neither her outspokenness nor her independence; her husband, Maxim de Winter, has much in common with
Rochester, especially as far as the treatment of first wives is concerned
– Rochester's live-burial of Bertha in the attic is even overtaken by de
Winter's murder of Rebecca in the boathouse. And Manderley, a virtual personification of Rebecca and almost a protagonist of the plot (as
houses often are in du Maurier's fiction, see 1982, 128f), burns even
better than Thornfield ...

   I do not want to overemphasise the parallels, for the reading-effect
is much different. Du Maurier's first draft of *Rebecca* ends with a car
accident and an epilogue that recalls much of the 'maimed Byronic
hero' situation of Ferndean: set on the French Riviera, the invalid de
Winter and the first-person narrator lead a static life, full of the
pervasive horror of their routine, the pain of longing for England, and
a strange 'glow of contentment' (see 1982, 44). However, this rather
unsettling ending is replaced in the finally published version by the
narrator's recognition that Manderley is burning – and that the horrors
and crimes that happened there will disappear with it, like the nightmare that the opening suggests. The reading-effect is thus in more
than one sense what Tania Modleski has called 'a disappearing act':
the escape from everyday life into a fantasy world with a happy – or
pacifying – ending that nevertheless does explore 'very real problems
and tensions in women's lives' (Modleski 1982, 14). Here, Modleski
sees the 'transformational' value of romance plots and suggests that an
understanding of their narrative pleasures 'can be useful for
constructing more radical feminist narrative strategies' (Spigel 1985,
215).

   In this sense, the emotional trajectory of *Rebecca*, with its narrator-
protagonist's fear of failure in her role as Mrs de Winter, her fear of
punishment or loss of her husband's love, with the horror of and
desire for the 'other' – sexual as well as monstrous – woman, evokes a
set of responses between rebellion, rage and relief. These might be
vicariously experienced by the reader, as well as the pleasure of the
moment when the plot offers for the narrator the possibility to prove
capable and intelligent, even a superior saviour figure for the erring
hero in the end.

   This sketch of the emotional dynamics between provoking and pacifying of a popular romance assumes a further cultural dimension in
Clive Bloom's recent definition of pulp fiction:

Pulp is public expression lived out privately. If human nature is at once private and historical (that is, subject to change) pulp may have more than art to tell us about ourselves. Pulp is the child of capitalism and is tied to the appearance of the masses and the urban mediums of the nineteenth and twentieth centuries. As such it is the embodiment of capitalism aestheticized, consumerized and *internalized*. Hence it is both oppressive and liberating, both mass manipulation and anarchic individualistic destiny. Pulp is our daily, natural heightened experience: a product and channel for a moment in human self-consciousness and its aspirations lived in the banal and in the now. (1996, 14)

This twofold effect of oppression and liberation that Bloom's 'Marxian' (10) reading explores, from the penny press to today's comics and tabloids, also characterises much of women's romance fiction that Bloom self-consciously excludes from his book, because he sees it as an overly discussed '"cause" among feminist critics and social historians' (9). I think that present studies of pulp like his owe a lot to the early recovering of romance culture, which I will here review with regard to socio-economic context, culture-critical potential, relations to other 'cult fictions' like pornography and to the intertextual background that romance offers for neo-gothic writing.

The popularity of horror narratives must be realised as deeply connected to the dynamics of feminism. This can be seen in the context of the 1960s' women's movement and the simultaneous change and expansion of bestselling mass horror forms. Gothic horror is, as we have seen, family horror; it often relies on a specific contextual and intertextual construction of feminine monsters. This is also true for contemporary popular horror, from Stephen King's international bestsellers to the epitome of the American entertainment industry: Hollywood cinema. According to Robin Wood, popular cinema recognised 'horror as both American and familial' in 1960, when Alfred Hitchcock's *Psycho*[2] marked the transition from the family or marital comedy of the 1950s to the family horror film (Wood 1986, 87) – and when American society had to realise the shift from the 'feminine mystique' to women's power.

This contemporary context of popular horror recalls a specific circumstance from the socio-historical context of the rise of the gothic – which was also the rise of modern feminism – around 1800. This was a time during which the population of England and Wales expanded tremendously; in the first half of the nineteenth century it almost doubled from 8.9 million to 17 million (see Altick 1957, 45). Similarly in the 1950s, the decade that anticipated the contemporary explosion of bestselling mass horror, 'the American population increased from 151 million to 180 million people. This was the largest growth in any decade of American history (before or since)' (Patterson 1983, 345). As a consequence, the 1960s faced a kind of 'aftershock of the baby boom' which (in Western countries) clashed with the political and counter-cultural movements of the time. Ann Douglas has contextualised the popular horror texts of the time in these terms:

> In these thrillers, parental characters, like many of the authors who create them, are baby-boomers, creatures of the sixties, dramatised and imagined as they begin families in the seventies and eighties: in other words, they are protagonists of pressing, intricate and culturally telling contradictions. (1980, 293)

She concludes that 'family horror fiction is a collective autobiography of a generation's psyche' (1980, 293). Once again, gothic form seems to successfully represent a culture's obsession with family and the home: the American 1950s' 'cult of domesticity' (Patterson 1983, 344) recalls the English eighteenth-century sanctification of the home. The generation involved has been characterised by George Stade with regard to Stephen King's success:

> The collective psyche of Stephen King's generation came of age when American politics turned psychopathic, or at least paranoid, when a sexual revolution overturned the life-denying decencies of the 1950s. The venerable prejudices that governed relations between men and women, husbands and wives, parents and children, were all shook up, while the literate middle-class stroked itself with a reverse racism that turned every Afro-American into the unlikely combination of sexual saviour and saint. All the while, the divorce rate rose. (Stade 1987, 260)

Read in this context, Stephen King's characters' male fantasies to leave the family and to be free like a boy again – as in the opening of *Pet Semetary* (1983) where Louis daydreams of escaping to Disneyworld while he is moving his family into a new house – definitely seem to represent the repressed desires of a whole generation of men.

However, I think that contemporary horror narratives also represent repressed fears of a related contemporary development: the feminist movement. Once again, Stephen King's success is a good example: the story of his first bestseller, *Carrie* (1974), links the

destructive potential of telekinesis explicitly to female powers left un-
controlled: they virtually explode in the young girl's act of revenge
against oppression and eradicate a whole city. The horror of the story
is specifically tied to the female body: Carrie's supernatural powers
are directly related to her body's natural functions, such as menstrua-
tion. Carrie becomes a figure of the monstrous-feminine that gothically
'repeats' early 1970s' fears of the uncontrollable effects of 'women's
power'. And the popularity of *Carrie* – which became a major Hollywood film (directed by Brian de Palma) two years after its success as
bestseller – allows for the maybe surprising recognition of the extent
of that fear. Popular horror: a signifier for culture's hidden fear of
female power?

Criticism has mainly emphasised the conservative effects of popular
horror as a phenomenon of contemporary mass culture. Wood characterises the horror genre's 'true subject' as

> the struggle for recognition of all that our civilisation represses and op-
> presses, its re-emergence dramatised, as in our nightmares, as an object of
> horror, a matter for terror, and the happy ending (when it exists) typically
> signifying the restoration of repression. (1986, 75)

Terry Heller, too, 'hypothesises' that the horror thriller functions as
're-enactment of repression'. His reading emphasises even more
strongly the reader's involvement as well as the conservative, affirming
function of the horrific for the above-described context:

> By bringing readers into carefully controlled contact with symbolic repre-
> sentations of the culturally forbidden and affirming that control, the horror
> thriller becomes one of a culture's instruments of repression. (1987, 72)

Heller relates this conservative effect back to gothic form:

> The horror thriller ... presents the implied reader with ideas and images of
> terror screened by various conventional and special techniques so that the
> real reader can experience power over these images and ideas. This is what
> we mean by safe thrills. (72)

'Safe thrills' might also mean that 'women's power' is played out in
the narrative, to then be safely restored to the control of patriarchy.
Films like *Psycho* and *Carrie* are cases in point as far as a general
public of that generation is concerned. In this context, a look at the
explosion of popular horror fictions for women, namely super-selling

mass-market 'gothics', offers insights into female culture, and its own repressed desires and fears: between baby-boom and bra-burning, between ultra-conservative femininity and radical feminism.

The 'safe thrills' of women's romance reading are often critically linked to their erotic effects: 'housewives are getting their kicks in the afternoon from pornographic love stories' (for an overview see Radway 1984, 103–4). Anne Barr Snitow has shown how Harlequin romances sexualise everyday activities and how their heroines are 'in a constant state of potential sexuality' (1979, 145). Similarly, Alison Assiter writes:

> Such novels are pornographic, not because they encourage women to play the part of the hustler or the dude ... [but] because they paint a picture of the woman wanting nothing so much as to be desired; they present an image of woman as passive, responding, just like the woman in the pages of *Penthouse* and *Playboy*. (1988, 106)

Such positions emphasise the reactionary effects of romance-reading. Assiter concludes that 'in reading [romantic fiction], women are reproducing their oppression' (108). Why, then, have romances always been so popular at times of outspoken feminism? The origins of popular gothic romances coincide with the origins of modern feminism – and those of modern pornography (Vinken 1997, 7); and the earliest depictions of the romance reader emphasise the obsession and loss of reality to the point of cliché, as Kate Flint has shown (1996, 269). However, maybe the most memorable depictions of romance readers of the time are Jane Austen's Catherine Morland and her friend Isabelle in *Northanger Abbey* (written around 1800; published in 1818). And while most critics have emphasised Catherine's 'gullibility' (Flint 1996, 269) and her seduction by sensationalism, Austen also suggests certain mimetic functions of her horrors, especially in her recognitions of patriarchal oppression (as personified in General Tilney) and in the demystification of romance.

Austen's early parody revises the traditional cliché of the romance reader and becomes suggestive when we turn to the contemporary phenomenon of parallel explosions of feminism and romance reading. The late 1960s to early 1970s was a time when representations of sex were liberated, and so were feminist activities against any form of patriarchal oppression. Romance reading, sexual liberation, and feminist activism are related, and a striking sign for this is the 'gothic boom' – the explosion in romance production and consumption during the peak of the women's movement. Gothic form, as I have shown it so far, is never just one thing or the other: never just conservative, and like other forms of pulp – or even porn (see Strossen 1995; Vinken 1997) – it suggests more complex implications of representation, formula and effect.

As has been suggested, the gothic has a subversive edge in the sense of a 'literature of desire' (see Jackson 1981). At the same time, it offers what Kathryn Hume – without explicitly treating gothicism – calls mimetic escape: 'It accepts our stereotypes – such as the high value we place on good looks, or our cultural sex-role stereotypes – but insinuates that the reader can beat the system, whether through talent or through such loopholes as luck or socially advantageous marriage' (1984, 80). Richardsonian romance – rather than Radcliffe's feminine gothic – sets this pattern for the majority of criticism (see Russ 1983, 666) that has emphasised the superficiality and sensationalism of mimetic escape (Hume 1984, 81) while excluding the consideration that it might point to the absences producing fear and desire in the lives of women.

Postmodern gothicism, of course, responds to these complexities, intertextualising the successful 'formula' but also the publishing phenomenon of popular romances. The 'gothic boom' is product and effect of the international entertainment industry: related to (and synonymous with) specialised publishing houses such as Mills & Boon in London, Harlequin in Ottawa and Fawcett in New York, it was capable of selling 800,000 copies for a first edition by its bestselling authors; and over thirty-five titles per month (or more than four hundred a year) between 1969 and 1972. This 'true cultural phenomenon' (Radway 1984, 33) has been critically discussed mostly in its dimensions for women's culture (e.g. Modleski 1982; Russ 1983; Mussell 1981, 1984). It seems interesting to realise that the erotic 'bodice-rippers' of the 1970s superseded the gothic (Mussell 1984, 31), until the 1980s saw a revival of gothic romances in the Harlequin series 'To Have and To Hold' (1984–88) with plots reflecting the rising divorce rate in Western culture.

In one sense, the 'gothic boom' is a marketing product: the term 'gothic' was a label for selling paperbacks addressed to the mainly white middle-class women who were perceived to be the majority market by the publishing industry. Harlequin claimed to have 'a

regular readership of over 16 million women in North America alone'
(Radway 1984, 40), and these readers have been analysed both by the
publisher's consumer research and by feminist critics (see Mussell
1984, 13). Obviously, the very heterogeneous reading group 'women'
shared as an essential aspect of female life the care for house and
family – other changes in the modern division of labour and re/pro-
duction between the sexes notwithstanding. Janice Radway's extensive interviews with romance readers suggest the close interrelatedness
between the 'meaning of the romance-reading experience' and female
everyday life in 'the way the story itself addresses anxieties, fears and
psychological needs resulting from [women's] social and familial
position' (1984, 44).

The question of this close relationship between the gothic and women's everyday lives brings us back to Modleski's concept of the 'disappearing act': the gothic's popularity might seem out of step at a
time when feminism attacked exactly the idea of 'woman's place' and
the patriarchal ideology that produces it. A look at the successful
gothic 'formula' (see Cawelti 1976, 5) and its contextualising strategies
is illuminating. The label 'gothic' was first used of a modern novel in
1960 for Victoria Holt's *Mistress of Mellyn* – 'a crossbreed of *Jane Eyre*
and Daphne du Maurier's *Rebecca*' (Russ 1983, 666) – and thus a
prime example of gothic intertextualisation. It is a governess story, set
in the nineteenth century, and in a strange house haunted by another
woman, with a mystery that the heroine, by her courage and incessant
activity,[3] is able to solve and thus 'earn' her happy ending with the –
unsympathetic, violent and brooding – hero.[4]

Three narrative aspects of this successful pattern will be looked at
here: the 'domestic test', the 'love' relationship, and the construction
of the 'monstrous-feminine'. These are, as we shall see, favourite points
of neo-gothic intertextualising – which is all the more illuminating as
all of them can be put in relation to the ideal feminine both of the
popular gothics' context and of the contemporary. For again, both are
times when gender roles and family structures are in flux and conservatism is on the rise, armed with a conservative feminine ideal.
Janeway's observation of the 'promotion campaign for Happy-Wife-
and-Motherdom' (1972, 151) in 1950s' America concludes: 'Society, in
fact, had been frightened by the woman militants' (see also Chafe
1972, 109). What follows is the well-known feminine ideal that Betty

Friedan called the 'feminine mystique': the background to much feminine horror, within and outside of the fiction of the time.

Friedan's study takes off from the postwar phenomenon of a female
identity crisis that she realises as collective: 'There was a strange
discrepancy between the reality of our lives as women and the image
to which we were trying to conform, the image that I came to call the
feminine mystique' (1963, 9). Friedan's language anticipates de
Lauretis's Woman/women model: it reveals both the violence of the
artificial image and the psychological consequences of a whole public
discourse about the failure of conforming (see Chessler 1972, esp.
42–3 on 'female diseases' and 50f on 'sex-role rejection'). Moreover,
she sees the ideal as concerning mostly white middle-class women: like
the earlier ideals of sensibility and the Angel in the House, this feminine
mystique is mainly conceptualised on the female body and sexuality
and aimed at containment and control (Friedan 1963, 43). And like
these earlier ideals it produces a gap between the 'norm' and the possibilities for its fulfilment – a gap that is experienced as painful, coded
as pathological, and productive of revolt or escape. Gothics offer a
world to go to.

As Kay Mussell has shown, what qualifies the modern heroine for
her 'happy ending' is the *domestic test*: her typical activities as governess, nurse or, in a more contemporary context, (child) therapist, are all
linked to 'the three traditional and interrelated roles of female
socialisation: wife, mother, and homemaker' (1984, 91, 95). These are
the discourses that engender subjectivity in the popular gothics. The
popular heroine's perfection in these terms is underlined by her strong
sense of justice; contradictory discourses that could shape a 'mirror-
plot' are not to be found. This perfection recalls but simultaneously
avoids the implications of what Elizabeth Janeway has shown as the
specific 'pluralism' and 'multiplex functions' of the female role (1972,
169). That role is further complicated by 'woman's place': a very isolated one in suburban nuclear family life of the 1950s – paradoxically
persisting while the world all around changes rapidly – that inevitably
produces a sense of inadequacy (Janeway 1972, 86). Janeway emphasises the related function of money as social valorisation in capitalist
societies or, as in the case of the housewife–mother, the lack thereof
(173). The popular gothic's representation of these complexities uses
generic hyperbole to dramatise, sexualise and glamorise – most importantly by the presence, gaze and love of the hero.

'He treats her brusquely, derogates her, scolds her and otherwise shows contempt and anger for her' – such is Joanna Russ's mocking characterisation of the 'supermale' in popular romances (1983, 677). Minudri relates gothic heroes to the 'great stereotypes of male chauvinism' (1973, 658); and Radway contextualises provocatively: 'The gothic aristocrat does not differ substantially from the typical male stereotype of twentieth-century America; as such, he is the perfect antagonist for the uncommon heroine' (1981, 148). In this structural and emotional antagonism, the gothic romance – in which love transforms into fear – differs from the Harlequin romance – in which fear transforms into love, as Tania Modleski has convincingly shown (1982, 60): Modleski distinguishes 'cores of truth' that mark the mimetic dynamics of the gothic plot of romantic love, most importantly the heroine's rage at the hero's injustice and arrogance. Untamed, uncivilised, wild: these Byronic heroes, modelled after Rochester and Max de Winter, are easily recognisable as products of a culture that degrades women. Importantly, the clever heroines' recognition and rage at this phenomenon are pumped into wild soliloquies and clear articulations, in a lonely chamber. Unlike Jane Eyre's passionate debates for equality with Rochester, modern heroines live out a mute protest – one that becomes a vicariously lived out protest for the reader. The narrative conflict is solved through love, a love that comes as surprise: unlike Jane Eyre's powerful striving for a marriage on her terms, modern heroines follow their fate by a shady vision.

Accordingly, love quickly becomes suspicious: the power relations between the married hero and heroine are unchanged, their spheres of action remain separated and his 'untamed' manner suggests both distance and violence. Suspicion follows rage; Russ's title's ironic paraphrase of gothic emotions 'someone is trying to kill me and I think it's my husband' (1983) adequately characterises the typical version as well as suggests the extent of marital distrust in the popular gothic (see Russ 1983, 668). And mute fearful lethargy follows the heroine's early activism. This typical gothic conflict, too, is resolved through love – and a miraculous change of the hero. Here, Modleski's 'core of truth' concerns 'the letdown women feel as their dreams of romance and marital bliss ... inevitably conflict with harsh reality' (1982, 64): any problem of marriage is both articulated and obliterated in the happy ending. Furthermore, this ending comes out of the blue, has fairytale overtones and shows the hero's innocence and love; it suggests the heroine's own responsibility for the problem – a figment of the imagination like Emily's *unspeakable*. Not the supernatural but very real misogyny is thus explained away.

Marital horror indeed becomes 'the unspeakable' in popular gothics. Articulated only in soliloquies but not communicated to anybody, it remains a private and somehow unreal problem. This is an important recognition in the context of the feminist practice of consciousness-raising – the articulation of private problems and their recognition as collective – and a politicised society that propagated the slogan 'the personal is political'. Sharing protest with the fictional heroine rather than a real friend means escape instead of change. It also means a vicarious feminism – which Modleski has stressed as utopian value in her reading of women's popular culture as *Loving with a Vengeance* (1982).

The last aspect of the gothic formula to be discussed here is its specific use of *le propre*. In the popular romance, just as in the feminine gothic, (the lack of) property and (the possession of) propriety construct both the female subject and the monstrous-feminine. The heroine is usually in the state of abjection caused by the separation from her past through marriage; she here also experiences a complete separation from the 'other woman' who may haunt and otherwise torment the heroine but who is not an object of desire. The 'other woman' is, in terms of *le propre*, the heroine's opposite: rich, beautiful and sexual. Kay Mussell (1975) has discussed the female foil in popular gothics as 'sexual woman' (and rival for the hero's love) – a figure intertextually related to Blanche Ingram in *Jane Eyre* and to Daphne du Maurier's Rebecca. This figure shows how beauty and sexuality are both inseparably linked and defeated. The pattern Mussell explores in numerous gothics is this: beautiful women are attractive to men; they are passionate and therefore dependent on and corrupted by their sexual nature; hence they either lack 'natural feminine instincts' (bad mothers) or they become cruel and criminal (possibly guilty of murder) – in both cases they are similarly unnatural, unfeminine, 'monstrous'.[5] Therefore, they do not qualify for a 'happy ending'. The romance relationship dominates story and structure; all other relationships are defined through their relation to it and to the highest prize: the hero's love.

Love in the popular gothic must thus be realised as a complex emotion, connoted by passionate rage but certainly not (yet) by passionate sex. The heterosexual romantic relationship is strikingly different from the 'soft porn' by which Ann Douglas characterises the Harlequin romances, although they do respond to the 'female emotionality' she outlines.[6] For in the popular gothic, love responds to the pains of separation and the horrors of abjection by restoring the heroine to the position of a self-in-relation. The separation from the mother – who is also an important other-woman figure – leads to the new connection with the hero: the heroine as child-bride. Accordingly, heterosexual love is not erotic or sexual, it is nurturing, as Jane Flax defines:

> By nurturance, I mean the expression of love that conveys a deep concern for the well-being of the person receiving it, without requiring that the person prove herself worthy or fulfil the nurturer's own needs, fantasies and so forth as the condition of receiving such care. Nurturance has a sensual aspect as well because the care extends to the recipient's body as well as to her psyche. The model for nurturance in our society is the love a mother gives her child. (1978, 187–8)

It is not only abjection that is taken care of with this kind of heterosexual mother love; female desire also loses the challenging function that structures, as we have seen, feminine gothic texture as interrogative text. While dreams, fantasies and uncanny similarities in mirrors and miniatures suggest the potential for a contradictory female subject, these challenging discourses are reconciled by the romantic-love theme. And one further narrative move prevents the challenges of the feminine gothic texture: the impossibility of desire for the other woman.

It is important to note that the catalogue of feminine deficiencies of the other, the beautiful, the sexual woman includes her independence. Rebecca might still be the most prominent example of how hero and plot show her as inappropriate because she is financially and emotionally independent – and effect 'a sort of warning about what happens to a woman who does not admit her need for dependence on a man' (Radway 1977, 251). Independence is part of this figure's cruelty and villainy, but it is also her doom and, as for Rebecca, her death. As attractive and desirable as she might appear, the heroine must keep her distance; thus, in structural as well as emotional terms the romance plot remains uncontested. And the gothics' conservatism seems to be explicitly directed against one of the ideals of feminism: independence.

If the gothic formula here functions as mimetic escape with a reconciling effect, at the same time it highlights the necessity for such escape. It points to painful containment in the gap between the ideal of the feminine mystique and the reality of the housewife–mother in the suburban family. And this gap connects white middle-class romance readers to white middle-class feminists (see Mitchell 1986, 52). Romance readers have been seen as 'the underside of the women's movement' (Mussell 1984, xv) – Atwood carefully speaks of 'slightly prefeminist women' (Becker: interview) – women facing the very problems that sparked radical feminism but avoiding the movement's confrontation with these issues. Moreover, feminism has initiated a new ideal feminine: the independent feminist woman, an image that produces 'culture's now doubled capacity to belittle the intelligence and activities of the "ordinary housewife"' (Radway 1984, 78). Hence, another painful gap is suggested: another space for romance?

Popular horror's 'mimetic escape', 'vicarious feminism' and 'disappearing acts' emphasise emotions of rage, revenge and relief as the main reading-effects. All these effects are sources of critical parody and playful reference in neo-gothic intertextualisation. Re-reading popular horror fiction through these later texts brings us back to a larger picture of discontent: the oppression of women's lives between the feminine mystique and feminist rebellion; the gothic formula with its domestic test, its devious love plot and its 'monstrous-feminine' that all point to that oppression. After all, it is a real rage that provokes the production and consumption of the vicarious one – and the gothic highlights that 'symptom' of contemporary culture. In this sense, I would like to recall the pleasures of gothic excess and to conclude this section with Alison Light's recognitions of the ravenous appetite for it:

> Romance reading ... becomes less a political sin [as Marxist critics see it] or moral betrayal [as feminist critics would] than a kind of 'literary anorexia' which functions as a protest against, as well as a restatement of, oppression. Their compulsive reading makes visible an insistent search on the part of readers for more than what is on offer. This is not, of course, any kind of argument for romance fictions being somehow progressive. Within the realities of women's lives, however, they may well be *transgressive*. Consumerist, yes; a hopeless rebellion, yes; but still, in our society, a forbidden pleasure – like cream cakes. (1986, 143)

Canadian connections

Canada's own Harlequins – named after the publishing house in
Toronto that is just the centre of a global distribution machinery – are
still so popular that they have become synonymous with 'gothics'. They
are of strong intertextual interest for much contemporary writing, and
of course especially so for Canadian neo-gothicism. However, there are
further aspects of Canadian culture and Canada's own gothic writing
that come together in neo-gothicism here. I would like to start with a
striking and typical 'national' connection: Margaret Atwood's *The
Journals of Susanna Moodie* (1970) points us to one of the core texts of
Canadian gothic filliation, Susanna Moodie's gothic autobiography of
frontier life, *Roughing it in the Bush: or, Forest Life in Canada* (1852).
Both this central text and its contemporary re-reading have been revised again in Atwood's novel *Alias Grace* (1996), which I will discuss
in Chapter 9. They lead us to an important metaphor of Canadian
criticism: the garrison mentality. Northrop Frye's metaphor (1971) and
Heather Murray's feminist re-reading of it (1986) delineate a central
trace of Canadian gothicism, setting up a dichotomy (Frye) or a cline
(Murray) between fort and forest, civilisation and wilderness – a
dynamics that connects the English-Canadian tradition, as represented
by Moodie, with the Québécois tradition of Canadian gothic. In the
(English-Canadian) neo-gothic texts, the garrison mentality also constitutes a central tension: the scenery of a 'domesticated wilderness'
(Murray) with its own, grotesque familial horrors in Munro's *Lives of
Girls and Women*; the 'ordered' strictures of the provincial yet urban
life in 1970s' Toronto from which Joan Foster escapes in Atwood's
Lady Oracle; and the wide open wilderness of the haunted – and haunting – Canadian West in Aritha van Herk's *No Fixed Address*.[7]
    First of all, discussing Canadian gothic means confronting the
ghosts of Canadian realism so pervasive in critical views of the
Canadian tradition: 'It's only by our lack of ghosts/ we're haunted' –
Earle Birney's famous line from his poem 'Can. Lit' (1947) – is still
the best metaphor for this view of Canadian culture as voiced by writers (like Cohen 1981, 65)[8] as well as critics (like Keith 1985).[9] This
exclusive position has been revised, mainly from postmodern and postcolonial positions. The strand of 'magic realism' in world literature
and in the Canadian tradition has been emphasised by critics like
Geoff Hancock and writers like Michael Ondaatje (for an overview see

Delbaere 1992). Of course, Ondaatje's own work magically exceeds realism and his fictions and poetry rewrite the history of our century into new recognitions of poetic narrative and international connections and possibilities. The success of Ondaatje's Booker prizewinning *The English Patient* (1993) and that of the subsequent Oscar-winning film by Anthony Minghella (1996) led, as one effect, to a virulent debate about the adequacy of representation of Count Almasy and his historical context ('The Real Count was no "English Patient"': *International Herald Tribune*). These questions are transcultural, of course, and they might voice a desire for knowledge beyond postmodern deferrals that I want to discuss in the last part of this study. However, they can be answered by relating Ondaatje's writing to the postmodern genre that Linda Hutcheon calls 'historiographic metafiction' (1988, esp. 61f, 86f), and to the specifically Canadian postmodern. This (English) Canadian postmodernism, as first defined by Hutcheon, has a decisive relationship to realist representation:

> What is striking and particular about Canadian postmodernist fiction is that the very real challenge to the conventions of realism has always come from within these conventions themselves. Unlike the more radical American 'surfiction' or the Québécois linguistic play, English Canadian novels have self-consciously milked realism for all its power, even while parodying and subverting its conventions. (1988, 20)

This postmodern paradox vis-à-vis the realist tradition is not that different from the neo-gothic narrative strategies, as especially the 'hyper-realism' of Munro's gothic will show. Just like a postmodernist reading of contemporary Canadian culture, a gothicist revision of realism's dominance might start with a look at the time which – following the beginnings of nationalist and feminist movements – has seen the most powerful critical and artistic pursuit of a Canadian postcolonial identity: the 1970s.

This important decade following the 1967 centenary and national celebration still haunts Canadian neo-gothic texts. Atwood, powerful as both artist and critic in the politicised context of the time, voices with characteristic irony two interrelated ideas that especially illuminate the postmodern/gothic connection and that relate literary realism to the 'unique Canadian experience' with colonialism:

> The first [reason] is that the Canadian fiction tradition developed largely in the twentieth century, not the romantic nineteenth. The second is that in a

cultural colony a lot of effort must go into simply naming and describing observed realities, into making the visible real even for those who actually live there. Not much energy is left over for exploring other, invisible realms. (1977, 98)

Atwood's ironic view of Canadian realism anticipates today's post-colonial perspective. Canada's perceived peripheral position, facing and fighting a stubborn persistence of British heritage and American imperialism, becomes a typically postmodern position in Hutcheon's concept of the 'ex-centric'. As has been suggested, this position of the periphery has two implications: it is 'also the frontier, the place of possibility'; and it posits a challenge to 'borders as limits' (Hutcheon 1988b, 3, 4). Both of these ideas return in neo-gothic fiction (especially van Herk's), in terms of space but also of playful explorations of realist and anti-realist genres and narrative traditions. And clearly the awareness of an international readership, possibly signified in the history of Booker Prizes since Salman Rushdie's 1981 success with *Midnight's Children*, has pointed to new powers of the periphery, to the new makers of world fiction – 'the empire writes back'. Canada with Atwood, Ondaatje, Carol Shields, Rohinton Mistry and other important writers is part of that movement.

One of the most important ex-centricities within Canada is the North, not only because it signifies the periphery of the (perceived) periphery, but also because it represents the Canadian frontier and is thus a mythic place.

> In the Canadian North of popular image, the Mounties with their barking dog teams relentlessly pursue madmen through the snow, prospectors stumble raving out of the bush clutching their little bags of gold-dust, jolly voyagers rollick in their canoes, Indians rescue hapless whites who get endlessly lost in the woods, wolves devour lone hunters, or not, as the case may be; Eskimos ... well, you get the picture. (Atwood 1995b, 9)

This picture, of course, is an ironic one of popular Canadian myth by Margaret Atwood. Her 1995 essay on 'The Malevolent North in Canadian Literature' is entitled *Strange Things* and recalls earlier views on the Canadian wilderness, the frontier, the North as 'a symbol for the world of the unexplored, the unconscious, the romantic, the mysterious and the magical' (Atwood 1977, 100). This idea of the wilderness not only exceeds realism, it also extends the concept of Canadianness as it represents the realm of Native cultures. Accordingly, Atwood has related figures like 'the fearsome and many-faceted Wendigo' (see 1995b, esp. 64) to the oral traditions of Native myths to assert that 'there is, indeed, a mass of dark intimations in the Canadian soul' (1977, 121). Such specifically Canadian 'monsters' can be traced in modern novels like Sheila Watson's *The Double Hook* (1966) with its uncanny coyote figure or P. K. Page's *The Sun and the Moon* (1973) with its feminine supernatural powers that manipulate nature. In neo-gothic texts the ghosts might be different ones, but the 'wilderness' recurs in Munro's Southern Ontario just as much as in van Herk's wild West.

The idea of the wilderness presents a first trace of gothicism in the Canadian criticism of the 1970s. Atwood's telling phrase 'Nature the monster' structures *Survival* (1972), her own thematic study of Canadian literature, and focuses on the encounter of alien surroundings that has marked – and 'gothicised' – Canadian culture since the first days of settlement. For Atwood, these alien surroundings have a broader scope and a powerful political dimension, especially cultural colonialism. Much Canadian gothicism has focused more on nature, the frontier and the wilderness. For example, the only book-length study of Canadian gothic, Margot Northey's *The Haunted Wilderness* (1976)[10] uses the binary oppositions of nature and culture, of wilderness and civilisation and the idea of the frontier to conceptualise the connection between gothicism and Canadian culture (1976, 110). The core metaphor is Frye's image of the garrison mentality (1971). Starting from historical but also 'cultural' maps of Canada, where forts are the only inhabited centres, he juxtaposes the garrison – 'a closely knit and beleaguered society … its moral and social questions are unquestionable' – to nature, looked at with terror from the safety of the fort, and subject to a conquest that 'has its own perils for the imagination' (1971, 225f). Frye's well-known image of 'a terror of the soul' in the face of 'the vast unconsciousness of nature' (225) echoes the eighteenth-century sublime and transhistoricises it into modern Canadian culture, where the wilderness still needs to be separate from the fort to protect humanity – from what?

> The real terror comes when the individual feels himself becoming an individual, pulling away from the group, losing the sense of driving power that the group gives him, aware of a conflict within himself far subtler than the struggle of morality against evil. (Frye 1971, 226)

This type of terror recalls overtones of the pains of separation in Kristeva's abjection and characterises well the gothic hero in traditional gothic criticism. The first Canadian novel, John Richardson's gothic *Wacousta* (1833), has been discussed in these terms; Northey introduces it as a prototype of this Canadian type of terror, with its 'feeling of menace from within civilised society as well as from without' (1976, 24). This might recall readings of American nineteenth-century frontier writing; however, the 'garrison mentality' forgoes the American possibility of staying in the wilderness. Although the fort can be left for exploration and annexation, return – a move back into the safety of the garrison – is a decisive move in Canadian gothic, even if it is a vain effort, as in *Wacousta*: Richardson's generic treatment of the Faustian gothic man means death in the abyss that separates forest and fort. Gaile McGregor has discussed *Wacousta* in terms that extend Frye's implied binary oppositions: as 'border fiction', at the 'interface between the civilisation and the wilderness ... in terms of both setting and moral/emotional co-ordinates' (1985, 3). McGregor, like Frye and Northey, emphasises the terror of the wild. However, as she explores the implications of the abyss that separates fort and forest in *Wacousta*, 'the gothic mood' for her 'is not merely a function of particular circumstances that may be confronted and overcome by human courage and will; instead it becomes an inseparable part of the human condition' (1985, 7). This specific inclusion of the Other, the wild and non-human, is for her the type of gothicism that she calls the Wacousta Syndrome characterising the 'Canadian Langscape' of the nineteenth and twentieth centuries, from popular art like Harlequin romances to canonic fiction.[11] This view recalls the Canadian connectedness of ex-centric space and haunted wilderness, and points to another connectedness: that of postmodern and gothic voices, both speaking from a liminal space and thus challenging not only narrative realism but also the binary oppositions from which it springs.

However, the oppositions tied to the 'garrison mentality' have also dominated the critical view of what has long been considered *the* Canadian gothic: Québécois gothicism. Feminine gothic writing, especially that of Marie Claire Blais and Anne Hébèrt, is a strong marker of French-Canadian literature and has mostly been discussed in terms of Frye's forest–fort dichotomy (e.g. Davidson and Davidson 1981, esp. 254). For example:

Anne Hébèrt moves through the rooms of her 'Vie de châteaux' which are empty except for the mirrors from which spectres of the past emerge to embrace her in a barren shiver imitating love. The garrison mentality leads her from a closed garden to a closed room to the narrow world of the grave, where the only communion is the communion of saints, or of shades. (Jones 1970, 10)

In this gothic enclosure, the dangers of the outside become saviours; not surprisingly, this critic answers Frye's frame by proposing to 'let the wilderness in' (Jones 1970, 8). The imagery here evokes the containment, not only protection, through houses/texts that the feminine gothic has continually challenged and exceeded. Hébèrt's heroines, like Mme Rolland in *Kamouraska* (1970), in this trajectory are deeply connected to the sexual women figures of the classic gothic, as Mme Rolland's worst nightmare shows: after a long live-burial underground, a woman is let free to a world that fears her desire for life so much that it forces her to die (249). For a freed 'madwoman' there is no life: this pessimistic, almost cynical statement dramatically undercuts the image of marital love at the end of the novel. It is all the more haunting as it implies the metaphoric view of marriage as live-burial – Mme Rolland's husband is dying and the nightmare is also a vision of her own future. In this sense, the 'madwoman' figures from Brontë, Gilman and Rhys are *affilliated* with those of Hébèrt.

Another intertextual connection of Québec gothic that can only be suggested here is one that links the feminine gothic texts from Québec to those of the American South. One of the cultural parallels elaborated by gothicists is the power of religion, related to a specific sense of evil and spiritual anxiety (Northey 1976, 50). Québec and Southern gothic in such readings appear as representations of a specific kind of garrison mentality: the confining terrors of small towns in a bleak landscape (see Lennox 1984, 103). However, as we shall see, this kind of paradigm also works for Southern Ontario gothic, and its haunting atmosphere must be recognised as a strong marker of Canadian neo-gothicism.

'Wilderness in Canada is where you make it, or where you imagine it to be' writes Heather Murray (1986, 75), extending Frye's metaphor and offering an outline for postmodern inscriptions of this Canadian *locus classicus*. Murray's reading beyond binary oppositions is especially useful for a gendered look at Canadian literature. Related to her reading, gothic filliation since Susanna Moodie – Frye's 'one-woman garrison' (Frye 1971, 351) – inscribes a 'domesticated wilderness' or 'pseudo-wilderness' between fort and forest, civilisation and wilderness, culture and nature. This pseudo-wilderness is seen as a feminised space in women's 'wilderness writing' from Susanna Moodie to Sheila Watson to Alice Munro. Nineteenth-century immigrant women's life-writing displays this feminised space in different fictionalised versions; in the case of Susanna Moodie in a gothicised discourse that anticipates a specific contemporary Canadian feminine gothic.

I would like to relate important contemporary texts of the Canadian pseudo-wilderness to the formal house metaphor by a gothic paraphrase: 'the madwoman in the cabin'. Examples are Margaret Atwood's *Surfacing* (1972), Marian Engel's *Bear* (1976) and Joan Barfoot's *Abra* (1978). In all of these texts, the heroine constructs a space for herself in the wilderness, to live by means that she determines herself. Murray emphasises that such a construction of a domesticated, feminised place goes hand in hand with the construction of a similarly feminised language representing that change towards (in 1970s' terms) a self-determined life. The shape of the gothic house has always shaped the gothic text as feminine form: from elaborate Udolpho in Alpine sublime, to impressive Thornfield in its lonely estate, to the old house in the small town in the bleak landscape, to the simplicity of the wooden cabin in the wilderness. Ironically, here the simple cabin means gothic excess: of a life of enforced containment and constraints. In *Surfacing*, the cabin initiates a return to a more meaningful time with a more meaningful community (the family rather than superficial city friends); in *Bear*, it allows for a sensuous escape from a live-burial in a city office with an obnoxious boss; and in *Abra*, it opens 'a room of one's own' for a housewife–mother's virtual disappearing act. Each of the stories has a romance structure – most explicitly *Bear*, in which the bear, in a mockery of Harlequin soft porn, takes the part of the Byronic hero. Each of them has a mirror-text of female desire – most explicitly *Abra*, in which the central temptation is the visit of the daughter after her long search for the mother. And what all of them explore is the construction of a female subject when separated – or, in *Surfacing*, in the process of separating – from cultural constraints and totalising discourses. From the outside, they look like the 'madwomen' in the attics of English houses and texts; however, they speak the language of reason. They are subjects-in-process with a very serious voice that distinguishes them from the ironies of neo-gothicism. Refusal marks their happy endings – the programmatic refusal to be victim (*Surfacing*), to be perfectly adapted (*Bear*), to return (*Abra*). These texts anticipate another refusal that they share with the neo-gothic texts: the refusal to present a new model heroine by replacing the conservative role model by a feminist role model. Just as these texts are structured by the process of improvising alternative worlds to the ones we know, the related process of forming alternative structures of narration cannot have traditional closure.

One of the ways of exceeding such textual (en)closure is filliation. 'Cabin novels' contextualise the feminist movement as well as the 'gothic boom', and intertextually rewrite the discourses of both – for example in the satiric puns by which the sad figure of Anna in *Surfacing* is shown to adapt to her husband's idea of femininity. They link the Canadian tradition of women's wilderness-writing to its postmodern dimensions. Audrey Thomas's *Intertidal Life* (1984) – a 'cabin novel' of the 1980s with its clapboard house on Vancouver Island – is a good example. The story of a marriage breaking up, it rewrites a romance in reverse – the pains of separation and of abjection included. At the same time, romances, particularly Harlequin romances, become a frame of reference, as Alice and her daughter Flora read them together, full of cynicism. In *Intertidal Life*, romances mean a real danger: the danger of accepting endless humiliation 'in the name of love' (see Massé 1992). The emphasis is not on the readers' vicarious utterance of female rage through the heroine's 'mute feminisms', but on the vicarious acceptance of male cruelty or violence. Thomas has discussed romances as harmful in contemporary women's culture in an ironic essay: 'It worries me that millions of women are buying the violence and abuse, the *humiliation*, along with the happy ending' (1986, 11). Humiliation is much of the horror in Alice's story. However, a mirror-plot of female desire, between Alice and her daughters, frames and interrupts the sad love plot. And a metaphoric web of seeing and perceiving suggests that Alice moves from her static position, contained in the fog of the opening, and from the later '[i]t was hard for Alice to see. Things kept getting in the way' (*Intertidal Life*, 26) towards a recognition of events before they actually happen: '"You see so clearly Alice." "Do I?"' (240).

Intertidal Life is a good example of intertextual connections in Canadian women's writing. Its serious, at times almost didactic, tone of voice distinguishes it from the neo-gothic texts to be discussed in Part II. But its ways of gender construction connect it to them: the female subject here is constructed as not only between contradictory positions – mother and artist, lover and wife, city and island, cabin and wilderness – but also, once again, through other heroines of romance. Such heroines have an energetic history in Canadian realism as well as in feminist criticism – a history that neo-gothic texts take up. As early as 1885, the ironic voice of Sarah Jeanette Duncan called for 'the death of the old-time heroine' – who, as an object in a male novel plot, typically 'vanished with the last page, ceased utterly with the sound of her wedding-bells'. Now – at the time of the *New Woman* – Duncan celebrates the advent of a realistic treatment of women in fiction:

> The woman of to-day understands herself, and is understood in her present and possible worth. The novel of to-day is a reflection of our present social state. The women who enter into its composition are but intelligent agents in this reflection and show themselves as they are, not as a false ideal would have them. (quoted in Ross 1979, 80)

Duncan's statement still reverberates in Canadian feminine fictions, as seemingly 'realistic' heroines enter romance plots, thus exposing 'the difference between their own mixed and often painful lives and the simple life of a romantic heroine in an Arcadian world' (Ross 1979, 49). It is illuminating to note that the writers in question – Montgomery, Atwood, Lawrence and Munro – also invariably employ gothic conventions – like mirrors – to reveal the gap between romance and reality. At the same time, novels like Atwood's *Bodily Harm* (1981) and Thomas's *Mrs. Blood* (1970) – two texts that use gothicism to show the female body in sickness and objected to male technology – suggest the reconstitution of the heroines by recourse to such old-time-romance heroines, as Lorna Irvine's aptly gothicised terms show:

> Isobel and Rennie are stripped, peeled layer by layer, turned inside out. This uncanny opening up of the character is announced by the various ghosts that fade in and out of the central characters' purview like so many repetitions of former selves, the stereotypes of conventional female characters. (1986, 39)

The ghost of the romance heroine of old times becomes a sign of gothic excess in filliation: she haunts Susanna Moodie's gothic life-writing from the 'domesticated wilderness' just as much as the complex subjectivity of neo-gothic heroines, with their moves beyond the containment of the house, of the gothic text – and even of the female body, as we shall see in the following chapters.

Notes

1 I am aware of the fact that the first-person narrator of the prologue is not explicitly gendered as male; however, passages such as the following lead me to conclude that there is a strong link with the men, an emphasis on sameness instead of difference: 'The departing ladies who had said they would stay didn't of course, thank heaven, stay: they departed, in consequence of arrangements made, in a rage of curiosity, as they professed, produced by the touches with which [Douglas] had already worked us up. But that only made his little final auditory more compact and select, kept it, around the hearth, subject to a common thrill' (1988, 6).

2 *Psycho* is noteworthy for its violence against 'un-respectable' women. Marion is set up as a typical sexual woman figure, from the first intrusion of the camera into the hotel window behind which she has sex with her married lover. In Hollywood cinema, such extra-marital 'transgressions' have remained a death-sentence for women – a good example is Adrian Lyne's *Fatal Attraction* (1991).

3 On the heroine's activity, I agree with Mussell and disagree with Russ, Greer and Weibel, who see her as completely passive.

4 Tip sheets of the publishers ensured the perpetuation of successful aspects of the formula. I would like to draw attention to a most suggestive – and very serious – summary: Phyllis Whitney's 'Writing the Gothic Novel' (1967). Whitney has been the most successful American writer of gothics; her *Thunder Heights* appeared in 1960, and, in 1998, her *Amethyst Dreams* is forthcoming: her seventy-sixth novel at the age of 93!

5 Mussell argues that with the sexual-woman figure, popular gothics 'support in fictional form some of the ideas about sexuality that give rise to current alarms about corrupted morals in America' (1975, 84). She concludes: 'The formula "proves" that if women fulfill traditional roles, the family can be a viable institution' (1975, 89); significantly this was written at the time of unrest and change following the feminist movement. The paradox is evident: the family as horror and solution.

6 Douglas writes: 'Harlequins focus on one aspect of female experience, courtship: not courtship in the Jane Austen style with its intricate processes of choice, but coupling in the wary primitive modes of animal mating … The Harlequins are porn softened to fit the needs of female emotionality. They are located inside the female consciousness, but so are most hard-porn (heterosexual) stories and magazines' (1980, 25, 29).

7 Two of the already-mentioned book-length studies on Canadian women's writing suggest the impact of gothicism, although neither of them devotes

a chapter to it. I find one reason for this very interesting, namely the dynamics between French Canadian and English Canadian feminisms: the former deal with post-structuralist views, which often find genre limiting, and focus on linguistic aspects; the latter explore narrative themes and forms that relate to the dominant wilderness metaphor (e.g., the archetypal female quest) in terms of the 'feminist nature = female *vs* culture = male' model. Of course, this is only a rough picture; for a critical overview of Canadian feminism see Godard 1984 and 1976.

8 Nevertheless, Matt Cohen's own novel *Flowers of Darkness* (1981), plays out domestic horror before the background of the stifling puritanism of a Southern Ontario small town, with the heroine's eyeball in the bathroom as culmination of a very gothic plot!

9 Keith's *History of English Canadian Literature* (1985) is a good example of this position. He sees early Canadian romances as immature national writing that made nineteenth-century novelists look for English models, and as inferior to genres like that '"native Canadian art form" – the realist animal story' (46). Looking at more recent writing, Keith praises writers who (like Hugh MacLennan in the 1950s) 'realized that a Canadian fiction, to be recognized as such, must be firmly rooted in Canadian soil, that a novelist must provide real places for his settings and describe them in terms verging, if necessary, on the documentary' (133).

10 Relying on the psychoanalytic/social gothic criticism of Varma (1966) and Fiedler (1960), she defines the gothic as 'a subjective view of the dark side of life, seen through the distorting mirror of the self, with its submerged levels of psychic and spiritual experiences' (1976, 6). Her focus on genre anticipated a much-discussed alternative to the dominant thematic criticism in Canadian studies (see Davey 1986, Blodgett 1982).

11 McGregor – like Northey – compares Canadian and American frontier writing and stresses Canadian fears of both protagonist and writer when 'confronting ... the gothic face of nature' and lack of a 'promise of renewal' (1985, 6) that structures American gothic, e.g., J. F. Cooper's mythic quest journeys.

PART II

Neo-gothicism:
from houses of fiction
to textures of dress

Chapter 4

Exploring gothic contextualisation: Alice Munro and Lives of Girls and Women

Gothicising experience

'In the beginning, in the very beginning of everything, there was that house.' When Del Jordan in *Lives of Girls and Women* (1971) tells her mother's story, she starts from her image of the house where the mother grew up.

> The house which I had never seen in a photograph – perhaps none had ever been taken – and which I had never heard my mother describe except in an impatient, matter-of-fact way ('It was just an old frame house – it never had been painted'), nevertheless appeared in my mind as plainly as if I had seen it in a newspaper – the barest, darkest, tallest of all old frame houses, simple and familiar yet with something terrible about it, enclosing evil, like a house where a murder has been committed. (62–3)

This short paragraph reads like a compressed image of Munro's neo-gothicism. It shows well how Del's creative processes as writer work; thus it points to a textual self-reflexivity that highlights the processes of (as we shall see, gothic) writing. *Lives* is Del's story of becoming an artist, but it is also her personal history of the small town and rural area in Southern Ontario in which she grows up. Her retrospective narration is pieced together from numerous episodic tales of her surroundings, many of them starting from photographs. In this case, it is the absence of such a pre-produced visual image that proves productive. Telling about something she has never seen, either in reality or in any visual document, Del relies on the mother's verbal document, as she transforms that 'matter-of-fact' account into her own – in the end, not so matter-of-fact – narrative. What is at first announced as an ordinary documentary report in plain newspaper style – that is, as realist representation – is subsequently transformed into the image of a structure/house that is not only extraordinary but also endowed with a terrible, violent past – that is, as gothic representation. The process of this transformation, a transformation that gothicises experience, is explored here. Moreover, this introductory image presents a specific connectedness: between the house as both place of experience and text; the mother as related to both female desire and female stories; and the idea of origin, in cycles of both (narrative) traditions and their (recollective) transformations – the texture of Munro's self-reflexive neo-gothicism.

I would like to start with the processes of gothicising experience. In gothic contextualisation, the 'simple and familiar' – especially when it concerns domestic situations – is never unproblematic, as we have seen, since Radcliffe magnified – and defamiliarised – 'woman's place' into the sublime castle. Munro's neo-gothicism recalls (and the example cited above is typical with its deferral of origin) these feminine gothic defamiliarising strategies that magnify the home. However, her textual exploration of this gothic effect has a paradoxical consequence, as Magdalene Redekop has shown:

> This is Munro's territory: familiar, domestic actions are elevated to serve as a powerful means of resistance. Rejecting the [postmodern, playful] defamiliarising techniques common to many contemporary writers, Munro opts instead for a domestication so radical that we move through the homely to the *unheimlich* to the uncanny. (1992, 12)

I think that this radical domestication is a neo-gothic strategy – one that connects with but also transforms the traces of gothicism in the web of feminine writing. And it does so around the threefold dynamics of the house/text: a structure containing domestic horror (thematically) as well as the processes of a female subject (formally) and the related image of the ideal feminine (ideologically). This way, a new type of gothic excess arises: excessive domestication, excessive realism.

That the haunted house – the image that also ends the introductory sequence – is a fitting metaphor for this specific gothicising of (female) everyday experience can be shown by a look at the process of contextualisation that Munro neo-gothically includes in the story. The processes of 'conversion' (Hornung 1985, 70) – or maybe, in Del's case, 'translation' (Godard 1984, 70) – not only from one (the mother's)

Dream 1   Doubled, mirrored, multiplied: dreams of girls and women. Gothic form celebrates excess beyond one love, one life, one body, into feminine abundance.

story into another (the daughter's) story, but also from life into art, from experience into language, are cast, as we shall see, throughout Del's narrative in a gothic paradigm (of which this opening is typical). The familiar becomes both estranged and ultra-domesticated; emotions like mother love and romantic love are 'x-rayed' (in Kristeva's sense, 1982, 209, 210) into layers that range from the idyllic to the violent; the reader is both involved in and 'affected' by the scenes and story. These are all aspects of this 'gothicising' of experience. However, as has been indicated, the unreal, anti-real, 'meta-real' (Redekop 1992, 7) or 'super-real' (Munro in Gibson 1973a, 256) in *Lives* is never unproblematic: it is always played off against the expectations of realism or documentary. As we have seen, throughout the web of feminine gothic writing, such connections to literary realism range from the playful allusion to its conventions to the serious uses of its possibilities for feminist representation. Munro rewrites this aspect of the gothic tradition, and she does so at a time which strongly emphasises the importance of realist texts for representing, and even for documenting, women's lives and experience.

The late 1960s and early 1970s produced the feminist movement and a literary culture strongly influenced by the feminist practice of consciousness-raising: with the emphasis of telling about women 'as they really are', both to destroy traditional patriarchal images of women and to produce new female role models and contemporary liberated feminist heroines – prominent examples are Erica Jong's *Fear of Flying* (1973) and Marilyn French's *The Women's Room* (1977). Munro's 'excessive realism' contextualises these and other phenomena of contemporary literary culture: the practices of feminism, the related practices of 'life-writing' (as we shall see in the following section on texture), the strategies of the (Canadian) postmodern with its own characteristic treatment of realism, and (as suggested through the introductory image) the discourse of photography, again evoking questions of realist representation. These points of contextualisation then suggest another aspect of Munro's neo-gothicism: the exploration of gothic excess and its possibilities in the context of contemporary feminist culture and texts and their own strong representations of 'lives of girls and women'.

The corpus of established criticism offers a place to start discussing the notion of 'realism' here. Alice Munro's writing has been discussed

in influential studies under headings like 'Probable Fictions' (Mac-
Kendrick 1983), 'Saying the Unsayable' (Miller 1984), 'Controlling
the Uncontrollable' (Papp Carrington 1989), 'The Tumble of Reason'
(Heble 1994) – titles that address aspects of realist representation. She
has mainly been praised for her artful treatment of real life – real
female life, one should add – with critical emphasis on her sophisticated 'verisimilitude', privileging her 'realism' but not without addressing the complicated artistic process of its achievement.[1] Related
is another strand of Munro criticism that treats her work as realist in
the sense of being autobiographical.[2] It seems that the reason for all
this critical attention to Munro's treatment of the 'real' is precisely
that disturbing playing off of realist and gothic representation against
each other and the possibilities this strategy highlights for the gothic
contextualising processes in women's life-writing. This life-writing, I
think, relates both to the contemporary literary phenomenon that
Alfred Hornung has called the 'autobiographic mode' (1985) and to
the practice of feminist life-writing of the time that problematises, in
Barbara Godard's terms, the gap between experience and language
(1984). And while there are traces of gothicism throughout Munro's
work, it is explored not only most clearly but also most self-reflexively
in the three texts I want to focus on here: her second book, the short-
story novel *Lives of Girls and Women* – a central, complex and much
discussed text of contemporary Canadian writing – as well as the two
unanthologised fictions: the early story 'Home' (1974) and the long
narrative 'The Ferguson Girls Must Never Marry' (1982).

Significantly, according to Munro, the working title of *Lives* was 'Real
Life' (Struthers 1983, 28), and tracing these words in the text refers
us to the specific form of Del's story – a form that relates its gothicism
to the Canadian postmodern (see e.g., Heble 1994, esp. 17). The words
'real life' conclude the last full chapter in *Lives*, emphasising at this
point Del's decision to break away from her romantic desires and
imagination (tied to her first lover, Garnet) and to start what is here
emphasised as just this: 'real life' (*Lives*, 201). The following epilogue
reveals that this 'real life' for Del is that of a writer. Although Del's
story-making processes have structured her tale, it is the epilogue that
most clearly – and retrospectively – opens up the self-referential dimension that indicates the postmodernist context of both realistic and
gothic representation here. First, the epilogue shows Del's story of

growing up to be a *Künstlerroman*: it emphasises her quest not only for an identity as a female artist in rural – and gothic – Southern Ontario,[3] but also for appropriate forms of language and writing. Second, the novel about Jubilee that she is in the process of writing here is also the one we have just read: *Lives* is metafictional in Linda Hutcheon's sense of a 'narcissistic narrative'. This form of narrative auto-representation both thematises creation and includes the reader in the process (Hutcheon 1980, 27f); in that sense, the texture of *Lives* folds back upon itself at the recognition of these processes in the epilogue. Del's reflections on the writing of her novel in those last pages thus relates *Lives* to the postmodern paradoxes of creative processes and aesthetic product, but also to the specifically Canadian postmodern, with its characteristic persistence of literary realism. Magdalene Redekop – who argues that 'Munro's "magic realism" is a kind of meta-realism' (1992, 7) – documents that Munro's stories are 'examples of a typically Canadian product: the realistic work that is not realistic' (7). The epilogue's self-conscious presentation of Del's processes of novel-writing in *Lives* displays this Canadian attitude.

But the epilogue also highlights the processes of Del's 'changing' the real Jubilee into that of her novel as a gothicising of the 'lives of girls and women' there – and thus functions as self-conscious commentary on the questions of representation. Most obvious among the artistic decisions Del makes, after the choice of a Jubilee family with a tragic destiny, are the changes of names (into more romantic ones); and of professions (into, ironically, more 'likely' ones): 'I knew from my reading that in families of judges, as of great landowners, degeneracies and madness were things to be counted on' (203). This is where we find the introduction of both a gothic house (203) and the transformation of Jubilee – by 'pick[ing] out some features of it and ignor[ing] others' (205) – into a gothic town: most clearly operative is the characteristic excess with which people are transformed into types and through which the gothic atmosphere is created (206). Significantly, Mrs Sherriff, the mother, can remain 'just as she was' (203): if this implies that she is 'gothic enough', it also recalls the absence of mothers in nineteenth-century women's texts and suggests their neo-gothic reappearance. That gothicising is indeed a paradoxical process also becomes clear: some of Del's changes to the Sherriff family highlight the point that reality might be more dramatic/gothic than its fictional representation: 'In my novel I had got rid of the older brother, the alcoholic; three tragic destinies were too much even for a book' (204) – such reflections point us to the irony with which the conventions of realism are also treated here. Another example is the 'contamination' of this 'black fable' (206) with Del's 'real life' which is itself suddenly told in gothic terms: 'I had been *sabotaged by love*, and it was not likely I would get the scholarship' (207, emphasis added). Self-reflexive gothicising processes juxtapose real life's effects with – in this case – romanticised dramatisation.

But the epilogue – subtitled 'The Photographer' – evokes, as has been suggested, yet another mode of contextualisation: photography. This visual discourse and its relations to the real are explored, first, through the photographer of the title – a major figure in Del's gothic novel, which she here paraphrases in extracts – and, second, through the phenomenon of many of the episodic tales forming Del's story starting from photographic images. However, as we have seen in the introductory quotation, photography in *Lives* does not stand for realist representation in any simplistic way. Rather, it evokes contemporary culture criticism's problematising of photography's representation. 'Photography has the unappealing reputation of being the most realistic, therefore facile, of the mimetic arts' writes Susan Sontag (1977, 51), only to assert the contrary: 'In fact, it is the one art that has managed to carry out the grandiose, century-old threats of a Surrealist takeover of the modern sensibility.' In the postmodern context, this paradoxical conjunction of realism and surrealism is further extended; Linda Hutcheon writes: 'the subject-framing eye of the photographer is difficult to reconcile with the objectivity of the camera's technology, its seemingly transparent realism of recording' (1990, 121). The aspect of *construction* of the image through subjective choice (rather than natural, transparent repetition) is further underlined by another choice: that of the photographed object itself. '[W]hy choose (why photograph) this object, this moment, rather than some other?' asks Roland Barthes, (subjectively) approaching 'the disorder' of photography (1991, 6); what is considered worthy of being (documented or aestheticised by being) photographed?

These paradoxes of photography seem to be more apparent in *Lives* than the photographic realism that has often been ascribed to Munro's texts.[4] They are suggestive of the relationship of gothicism and postmodernism that is one focus of this chapter. Sontag's idea of the 'surrealist takeover' leaves a decisive trace in Del's novel's photographic acts: the Photographer's products don't show their objects as they are, but as they will be:

> Middle-aged people saw in their own faces the terrible, growing, inescapable likeness of their dead parents; young fresh girls and men showed what gaunt and dulled or stupid faces they would have when they were fifty. Brides looked pregnant, children adenoidal. (205)

This points to another neo-gothic twist. The uncanny presence of the past that has haunted the house of gothic fiction here is extended into a reversal: Del's story is haunted by the presence of a gothic future, the glimpses of which are grotesque and dark – an impression that defies the pacifying and reconciling potential of narrative closure (or of a traditional 'happy ending' that implies a 'happy' future) and instead provokes unease and critical caution. It thus anticipates change: a change in family life (or even its absence); a trace of neo-gothic excess, both in structural terms (beyond the ending), and in ideological terms (beyond the established notions of a female life).

Moreover, 'The Photographer' himself is characterised as a villain in Del's gothic novel: threatening to everyone, but attractive to Caroline the heroine – a 'sexual and doomed' figure with long black hair – who becomes his lover, gets pregnant, is abandoned and drowns herself. As if this was not gothic enough a female life/love-story, its horror continues post-mortem: when after her death her brother looks at the photograph of her taken by the lover, her *'eyes were white'* (205). Not returning the gaze, she has become a complete object of his presentation. This episode might be seen as a *mise-en-abyme* for Del's own story in which, as we shall see, the objects of her presentations gothically reflect back on the writer/narrator – at the same time darkly drawing attention to the processes of the female speaking subject herself.

Moreover, the uncanny photographic transformations become a metaphor for her own literary gothicising that is not only self-reflexively foregrounded but also explicitly *rejected* in the epilogue. Del's ambiguous attitude, her seeming rejection and abandonment of her novel, can be read in Christine Brooke-Rose's sense: 'Rejection is always interesting. Even early rhetoricians, and Hamlet, knew that protesting much could mean the opposite. And just as Chaucer's protestations that he knows nothing of rhetoric are themselves rhetoric' (Brooke-Rose 1981, 291), Del's protestations against the gothic, the romantic and the melodramatic may suggest that we can assume the contrary. And Del's story *is* gothic, not only in retrospect.[5]

A similar instance of an only apparent rejection of the gothic occurs in 'The Ferguson Girls Must Never Marry', where, as in *Lives*, there is a manuscript of a gothic novel that Bonnie, the writer, rejects:

> she came to realise that what seemed to her an extraordinary and sinister story, the story of a family in mysterious decline, was the most common-place story in novels. Even the grand decaying house was a commonplace, often seen on paperback covers. (37)

However, this is precisely the story we read: the story of the remains of a family haunted by early deaths, due to hereditary heart problems, which comes together at the occasion of the funeral of the oldest sister in her disturbing, brand-new house – disturbing because it eradicates the shared past and the emotional connections. Rejection becomes another self-reflexive device of neo-gothicism. And the transformations of the paradoxical photographic process include a shift in gender, from the traditional 'male gaze' (as defined by Kaplan 1983a) to a feminine-coded perspective and thus to another aspect of feminine gothicising: once more, it is the female subject's gaze at the family community that brings out its gothic patterns.

Munro's earlier story 'Home' similarly thematises the processes of artistic creation by the self-conscious negotiation of gothicising. In one way, it thus highlights another (Canadian) postmodern paradox: 'the paradox of concern for dynamic process (reading/writing) being unavoidably articulated in the form of a static product (the thing read and written)' (Hutcheon 1988b, 138). But furthermore, this story shows well how gothicism and the self-reflexive treatment – or rejection – thereof become markers for the specific dynamics of postmodern feminist narrative. In 'Home', the plot of a daughter's visit to her heart-sick father for a sad week-end at home is disrupted by the female narrator/writer's reflections on the possibilities of how to tell it differently. Her first comment criticises precisely the strong feminine gothic traces that mark the opening:

> Too slow as usual … too much house with the wallpaper and plastic chair-cushion kind of thing, hardly anything yet about the people in it. Also the bit about the Mother, who probably doesn't belong in this at all but I can't come within reach of her without being invaded by her, then trying to say

too much too fast to get her finished with. Even now I am tempted to put in my dream about her. (137)

Once again: the powerful connectedness of the house/text and its structure with the absent/present mother-figure. Feminine gothic form is recalled, rejected, rewritten.

The mother–daughter relationship is evoked here in its neo-gothic dimensions (on the postmodern dimension see Irvine 1983, 101). As we have seen, this relationship is central to the complex subjectivity and interrogative texture of the feminine gothic; and it is self-consciously revised in Munro's neo-gothic narratives. Rejection plays an important role again. In 'Home', the denial of the dead mother's importance to the text works to emphasise her presence that haunts the daughter's subjectivity and the story's structure. Magdalene Redekop has shown 'the uncanny presence of the absent mother' – one version of what she calls 'mock mothers' – as a central feature of Munro's plots (1992, 8–11) that revises the convention of the absent mother in narrative and language (8). Drawing on Derrida's notion of erasure, Redekop unfolds what I think is another typical feminine gothic dimension: the challenge to idealised mother-figures:

> Dancing in front of the erasure, the conspicuous mock-maternal figures do not affirm something inexpressible or sacred. Munro achieves, instead, what Bakhtin has termed a destruction of 'epic distance'. The entertainments of her mock mothers enable us to walk 'disrespectfully' around our idealised images of maternity. (1992, 8)

This recalls Ellen Moers's connection of the monstrous and the maternal and shows Munro's self-reflexive revision of the typical feminine gothic texture where female desire – for the absent mother – forms a mirror-text that challenges those (romance) relationships that construct the surface plot. Furthermore, in 'Home', the dead mother haunts precisely through her traces in the house, the changes to which – performed by stepmother Irmla – have hurt the narrator from the beginning. In this way, house and mother constitute and open up to the reader yet another relationship: the underlying – but only indirectly articulated – connectedness between the narrator and her father.

The feminine gothic women–house connection also intertextually recalls Del's version of her mother's story that starts with her house and suggests the characteristic form of feminine gothic fiction. Both *Lives* and 'Home' explore this connection self-reflexively. The paradoxes of photographic representation highlight a further parallel, this time with respect to the Barthesian choice of the object. The introductory quotation once again offers a good example: the mother's house is typically absent from any document, at a time – Del's year of birth can be situated in the mid-to-late 1930s – when photography's function is comparable to documentary historiography. This is suggested both by the ceremonial visitation of the photographer to Del's school (as well as in Del's novel) and by the textual relating of photographs to Uncle Craig, the local history writer. Del's interest in her mother's house suggests her own choice of object that is absent from the historiographic realm of photography: the private realm of *everyday life*.

Some Munro criticism maintains that she writes everyday stories because her own life is seen as 'uneventful' (e.g. Thacker 1988, 155); however, the recent theoretical interest in everyday life sheds new light on such narratives. Agnes Heller, for example, emphasises their culture-critical potential; her section 'Everyday contact' recalls much feminine writing:

> It is clear that the personal contact relations of one man or of a group of men [sic] do not, cannot, even when summed up, adequately reflect social relations as a whole. At the same time, every personal contact relation expresses something appertaining to the essence of the social aggregate. (1984, 219)

This idea provides a larger theoretical dimension for themes of everyday fiction, such as Munro's: the treatment of unmarried women by the community, the treatment of a young girl by a pious and lecherous man, the treatment of adolescent daughters by their pragmatic mothers in a 1940s' small town, and so on. All these illuminate the *gendered* 'order' of everyday life, especially from the perspective of the late 1960s/early 1970s with their disruption of gender-oriented spheres. In this sense, Munro's neo-gothicism highlights the anticipation of this dis-order by the discontent within the everyday lives of girls and women after the war.

Moreover, Heller's idea of everyday 'contentment' would aptly explain the dynamics of Del's desire to do something remarkable (by writing):

> Satisfaction in everyday life is an amalgam of two main components – pleasure and usefulness ... The emotion felt in major achievement, the

successful conclusion of a non-everyday enterprise, is either not pleasure or
more than pleasure. (251–2)

Reading the pleasures of everyday life in gendered terms is illuminating. Franco Moretti puts the 'classic' *Bildungsroman* in the context of
everyday life and sees as one of its tasks 'to show how pleasing life can
be in what Goethe called "the small world"' (1987, 36). Significantly,
as in Moretti's whole argument, this works well for the male (artist)
hero who can always leave this small world for the larger one with the
mobility that marks modernity. The female subject in the same context, by contrast, rather seems to realise how horrific life can be in the
small world which is, in fact, her (assigned and only) place.

Thus, in Munro's neo-gothic fiction, the everyday lives of girls and
women between pleasure and horror are metaphorically and formally
contained in the gothic image and structure of the – magnified but
familiar – house. Furthermore, her fiction multiplies into the stories
of girls and women, in whose lives houses play an important role: as
women's (internal) place, as space of their domestic power – or oppression, as locus of containment that is exceeded. These dynamics
are explored in *Lives* (and other Munro stories) in terms of gothic
texture. Del's own gothic novel, too, starts with a house – that of the
Sherriff family – as she reflects in the epilogue: 'But now I remembered with surprise how I had made it, the whole mysterious and, as
it turned out, unreliable structure risen from this house, the Sherriffs,
a few poor facts, and everything that was not told' (208). The relationship of the house's and the novel's structure, self-reflexively proposed
here, recalls Munro's reflections on the relationship of fact and fiction,
reality and art that point to the relationship of realism and gothicism
in her fiction. In her short essay 'What is real?' she links reading/
writing a story to entering a house:

> It's more like a house. Everybody knows what a house does, how it encloses
> space and makes connections between one enclosed space and another and
> presents what is outside in a new way. This is the nearest I can come to
> explaining what a story does for me and what I want my stories to do for
> other people.
>
> So when I write a story I want to make a certain kind of structure, and
> I know the feeling I want to get from being inside that structure. (1982b,
> 224)

The story as structured house, with the connectedness of enclosing
spaces, with separation from the outside, and strong emotions on the

inside: the image recalls gothic texture and its domestic horror, its plot of abjection and its affective form. Munro's fiction self-consciously rewrites that complicated structure of the gothic house with its un- canny centre that different critics (Fiedler, Kahane) relate to the present/absent mother-figure. In the complicated structure of *Lives*, it is the abandoned gothic novel of the epilogue that forms such a cen- tre, as it is linked structurally to the 'Princess Ida' chapter (see Tautsky 1986, xiv) and thematically to the notions of creativity and mothering. Magdalene Redekop writes, alluding to Del's own much-quoted meta- phor of the depth beneath the domestic surface:

> The parodic anti-structure of this book demands that we see the blind spot in the centre ... The heart of this 'abandoned novel' [of the epilogue] becomes like the abandoned wing of the typical Gothic structure. The dark centre of this womb and of the house is the place that cannot be seen or represented, the place of origins that ... repeatedly shows us the surface of our own constructions – the kitchen linoleums with which we pave our deep caves. (1992, 65)

The abandoned gothic novel in this sense also recalls Frankenstein's abandoned creature and highlights the – feminine gothic – interweaving of maternal and aesthetic creative processes that is central to Munro's narratives (see Irvine 1983, 102). But Redekop's notion of 'the place of origins' is another key phrase: in *Lives* the mother's house (with the mother's mother inside) becomes for Del the locus for situating origin – 'the beginning of everything' – and, while that in itself is already a typical feminine gothic connection, the matrilinear relationship is re- inforced through Del's retelling – and fictionalising – of the mother's 'oral report'. Both deferring origin and rewriting the mother's story in this sense recall Godard's 'filliation' and the specific intertextualisation of the feminine gothic that is here thematised. As we shall see, Del's fiction writing is not completely separate from her mother's letter writing. Moreover, re-telling the mother's life has become an impor- tant aspect of female life-writing. In *Lives*, Addie Jordan's story is told in the longest section, under the title of her Tennysonian pen-name, 'Princess Ida'. This section, as well as the whole mother–daughter relationship with its related themes, here points us to an important contemporary strategy: inscribing female desire in the form of femi- nine gothic (life-)writing.

◆

Before discussing this form in the next section, I would like to draw attention to an important effect of Munro's particular self-reflexive neo-gothicism. The mother's oral tales have a further role in Del's writing: as in the opening example, they can replace a photograph that would normally be the stimulus for the telling of an episode. In these instances of verbal and visual accounts as frames and as provocations to Del's story-telling, the deferral of origin obtains a particular quality: there is a conscious act of separation of narrative from reality, a deliberate removal of the story from the direct experience, through these intermediate discourses. This strategy not only questions the validity of 'realism' but also points to 'experience' as a complicated concept. This is all the more remarkable in a cultural context that relies on an epistemological interest in women's experience and on the possibilities of literary realism to adequately represent it for its definitions as well as demands of a feminist text: the late 1960s and early 1970s are the time of a powerful feminist humanism, especially in the Anglo-American critical and cultural context in which, and in response to which, Munro's writing can be situated (see Belsey 1980, 7–14; Robinson 1985, esp. 110–12; Donovan 1985, 141–69; Kristeva 1981, 13–35). Thus contextualised, Munro's neo-gothicism seems to anticipate post-structuralist and semiotic challenges to feminist liberal humanism and more aesthetic explorations towards feminine writing and feminine form.

In Munro's fiction, the deferral of origin and the rejection of gothic contextualising draw attention to the processes that *construc*t experience; refusing to take experience as a natural given implies a feminist challenge to dominant ideology. In a second – and equally feminist – step, it also draws attention to the gap between the construct of (feminine) experience and the conventions of (masculine) language. This recognition leads to what, according to Barbara Godard, is the underlying question of Del's story (and, I would add, of her subjectivity): 'How to write as a woman?' (1984, 43). With characteristic sense for sensibility, Godard unfolds the implications:

> For language here, as in much women's writing, has become problematic, turned back on itself, a system of signs divorced from experience ...
>
> How to write as a woman? Double talk. Speak with a forked tongue. Lived experience as a woman plus the conventions of language and literature. Two separate worlds which combined result in difference challenging established meaning. (1984, 43)

Godard's own poetic criticism shows how Del and other Munro characters 'test out' language to find their voice – for example by 'sounding' words, as in the dead-cow scene: '"Day-ud cow, day-ud cow." Sound out the word to see it with the ear, to hear it with the eye' (1984, 43). Such sensorial defamiliarising processes are important to gothic representation. Munro's neo-gothicism thus comes to highlight that underlying question that structures Del's subject processes as a woman writer, exploring the conventions of language, but also those of literature – most notably, as we shall see in the following section, the forms of autobiography and historiography. Godard's question, it seems, in terms of form is treated throughout in gothic terms. *Lives*, as well as other Munro stories, self-reflexively explore the possibilities of gothic form for narrating lives of girls and women, and for inscribing what has come to be seen as a complicated concept: the female subject-in-the-making.

The subject-in-the-making: writing her stories

One of the narrative strategies by which Del tests the gap between experience and language, is that of a retrospective voice. Accordingly, as has been suggested, one of the narrative conventions explored is autobiography. Del's own story, especially through the self-reflexivity of the epilogue, can be seen as autobiographic, telling her childhood and adolescence in rural Southern Ontario. In a way the generic retrospective voice comes to act as yet another instance of distancing from the 'real thing', as Del – the mature speaking subject – comments, with temporal and experiential distance, on her disposition and development as the younger subject of speech in her own life-story (see Warwick 1984, 205; Papp Carrington 1989, 8; Thacker 1983, esp. 38–46). This double voice accounts for much of the humour and many of the comic twists in *Lives*, also for the typically grotesque tone that often marks contemporary feminine gothic texts. The story is that of becoming this maturer woman and speaking subject, told with an emphasis on the processes of representation and subjectivity-formation. Gothic form connects with autobiographic discourse.

Formally speaking, *Lives* seems to be a self-conscious example of what Alfred Hornung has shown to be an important form in contemporary (American) fiction, where the autobiographic mode 'as foil

comes to the aid of fiction' (1985, 71).[6] This is how the epilogue
teaches us to read Del's story. The related process of 'conversion' –
'[t]he transference of the experience of life into the structures of
language' (Hornung 1985, 70) – is self-consciously (and gothically)
explored in Munro's narrative.

When Hornung details this process in Hegelian/Lacanian terms,
the possibilities for the (gendered) exploration of life-writing becomes
clear:

> The formerly stored abstract images of the past are recollected and form
> together with the power of imagination a mental presentation, recognisable
> for the intelligence, which is then converted into language by way of mem-
> ory. Although Lacan attributes to the unconscious the structure of language
> … it cannot be immediately understood. In the same sense in which the
> psychiatrist has to transfer the recollected images presented to him by the
> patient, and combine the recollected signifiers with his memorised code of
> language, the autobiographical writer converts his [sic] mental presentation
> into the narrative of the text. The emancipatory power implicit in this act
> of conversion is impaired by the mechanical aspects of a memory which
> adheres to the conventionalised patterns of language. (Hornung 1985, 73)

It is precisely these 'conventionalised patterns of language' that – as
Godard has shown – constitute the underlying conflict in *Lives* as
female *Künstlerroman* and as writing (of) the self. *Lives* self-consciously
thematises this process of conversion in the epilogue (and in traces
throughout the story); this conflict is thus brought to the foreground,
in its gendered dimension. Again, the rejected gothicism intrudes:
memory connects with dreams and creativity – and thus with the
gothic realm, as has been outlined for Day's gothic 'dream world'
(1985). The excessive codes of this other, chaotic, gothic world thus
come to structure the space of memory between 'mental presentation'
and language. This suggests gothic distortions – and gothic excess –
in the process of conversion. It also suggests that the emancipatory
power of this process might thus be less 'impaired'. Although, of
course, the conventionalised patterns of language remain, and remain
as a gendered problem, liberation and potential emancipation are
suggested by the intrusion of gothic excess in the autobiographic
writer's 'conversion' of her 'mental presentation' into the narrative of
the – gothic – text: a narrative that not only connects with the writer's
life but moreover with a whole web of 'excessive' writing. The narrative of the self multiplies.

When in *Lives* this process of conversion is thematised, it is often metaphorically linked to the strong photographic discourse of Del's story: the photographic process, like memory, is paradoxically both subjective and mechanical. Both recollection and mental presentation in Del's story are very visual. Papp-Carrington, discussing the retrospective narration as 'split point of view', sees the narrator as 'watcher' (1989, 6), and the function of 'translat[ing] the watching of the split point of view into a photographic or cinematic metaphor' as 'distancing or objectification' (8). However, it seems that the photographic process as metaphor for the complications and paradoxes of representation highlights the subjectivity of perception and the speaking subject's self-consciousness about the workings of language – and memory – as sets of codes and signs: distancing and *subjectification*, in the sense outlined by Blodgett: 'rather than photographing the object, [Munro] illumines the subject' (1988, 10). Thus, the photographic memory in Munro's self-conscious feminine life-writing gothicises not only female experience but also the subject processes of gender formation.

The linguistic, or rather, narratological aspects of 'conversion' are also thematised in *Lives* and work similarly. Godard discusses Del's self-conscious explorations of her mother's autobiography and of that form in general in these terms. As Del depicts the clashing of the uncle's and the mother's account of – once again – the house they grew up in, she realises how presentation relies on who's talking: 'Storytelling she instinctively understands exposes more of the subjective elements than the facts of the situation' (Godard 1984, 60) – a typically feminine gothic recognition that her own story, then, seems to reflect. As Del writes about the 'lives of girls and women' around her, her own subjectivity is constructed and inscribed in various ways. First, through her relationship with these female figures, she inscribes her simultaneous connectedness and separation, and (in some ways) the female desire underlying her (gothic) story of growing up. Second, her retrospective double-voice 'exposes more the subjective elements' of her perception: both then and now; both in isolation and in relation to others' views. Therefore, writing the 'lives of girls and women' around her, Del inscribes the multiplicity of female experience in her own subjectivity: a dynamic subjectivity that is thus recognisably in-process, but also in-relation. Here gothic excess intrudes.

The gothic auto-graph

Both the subject-in-relation and the multi-voiced subject are important concepts in the contemporary rethinking of auto-bio-graphy as
self-life-writing and specifically in the feminist/post-structuralist focus
on 'Autogynography' (Stanton 1984; Bree 1988) or 'Auto-Graph(e)'
(*Tessera*, 1990). In the latter the 'bio' is excised 'to bracket the traditional emphasis on the narration of "a life," and that notion's facile
presumption of referentiality' (Stanton 1984, vii) or to emphasise 'the
text as text ual mater ial', as a 'person's own handwriting' and to raise
'questions about what is written when the hand that writes is a woman's
hand' (*Tessera*, 12). Michel Foucault's documentation of 'technologies
of the self' in different cultures and historical contexts emphasises the
importance of active work and practice, in addition to discourse, in the
constitution of the self. Self-inscription or writing can be seen as such
a practice: 'there is a certain tendency to present the relationship
between writing and the narrative of the self as a phenomenon particular to European modernity. Now, I would not deny it is modern, but
it was also one of the first uses of writing' (Foucault 1984, 369).
Foucault's theory of sexuality relies on these presuppositions of the
technologies of the self, and so do Judith Butler's *Gender Trouble* (1990)
and Teresa de Lauretis's *Technologies of Gender* (1987). As we have
seen, these feminist readings take into account the 'differential solici-
tation of male and female subjects [and] think of gender as the product
and the process of a number of social technologies, of techno-social or
bio-medical apparati' (de Lauretis 1987a, 3). The construction of gender comes to be seen as 'both the product and the process of its
representation' (5); e.g., on its self-inscription through the technologies of cinematic as well as linguistic representation. In a critical extension of these post-structuralist ideas, Butler demands 'a return to the
notion of matter, not as site or surface, but as a process of effect of
boundary, fixture and surface we call matter' (1993, 9). These ideas
inform my reading of Munro's texts as gothic auto-graphs and thus
will be briefly outlined here.

No matter how the shift from writing a life to the frequently self-
conscious *graphing* the *auto* occurs, it implies – maybe fearful, maybe
desiring – emotional relations with the – literary or biological or symbolic – (m)other, as well as the multiplicity of the speaking subject.
Domna Stanton writes: 'The female "I" was thus not simply a texture
woven of various selves; its threads, its life-lines, came from and ex-

tended to others. By that token, this "I" represented a denial of a notion essential to the phallogocentric order: the totalized self-contained subject present-to-itself' (1984, 15).

Both aspects recall Julia Kristeva's subject-in-process and the particular dimension it assumes in her autobiographical essay 'My Memory's Hyperbole' (1984a). This text illuminates Munro's neo-gothic treatment of memory, with the related notions of hyperbole and excess and with the reflections between spoken story and speaking subject. The opening is remarkable as it invokes Simone de Beauvoir – whom Kristeva, in a personal interview (Becker: interview), has acknowledged not only as a central figure in twentieth-century feminism, but also as a 'literary foremother' when she links her own recent *roman-à-clef, Les Samourai* (1990), to de Beauvoir's *Les Mandarins de Paris* (1954). In 'My Memory's Hyperbole', she alludes to de Beauvoir as somebody who 'has not been properly evaluated as a *chronicler* who knew how to *construct* an entire cultural phenomenon' (1984, 219; emphasis added). This complex recognition underlies all that follows as Kristeva emphasises the personal impossibility of herself being (merely) 'a good witness', due to her 'own history' but also to 'the disturbing abyss that the psychoanalytic experience shapes between "what is said" and undecidable "truth"' (219); she, too, will both chronicle and construct a cultural, intellectual phenomenon. Her glimpse of the gap between experience and language, world and word she proceeds to address by writing 'an autobiography in the first person plural', where the narrating 'I' alternates with a 'we' that encompasses the *Tel Quel* group, itself composed of 'persons' with their own specific 'profile' (for a critique, see Bree 1988, 178). The speaking subject is introduced as 'hyperbolic' subject-in-process which is always in relation, never the same, and thus alive. What is important here is, once more, the role of memory: its mechanical aspects and 'adherence to the conventionalised patterns of language' (Hornung) are undermined as, unreliable as it is, memory becomes in its own turn the subject of hyperbole. This multiplying gesture complicates notions of origin and creates a sense of suspension, especially as the text ends with a (hopeful) glimpse of the future. Hyperbole recalls the excess that marks feminine gothic fictions and brings us back to Munro's neo-gothic writing (of) the self.

'I am not able to be the best of witnesses. I can only try to be well-disposed' muses the writer/narrator in Munro's 'Home' (150). This story shares the metafictional structure of *Lives of Girls and Women* – and, above all, the explorations of the gothic auto-graph. The quoted reflection echoes Kristeva's narrator between chronicling and constructing. It occurs in a self-reflexive section that situates the speaking subject in the process of writing, specifically in a gothic situation after a dream in which the narrator's dead mother returns to prevent changes in the house by the father's second wife, stepmother Irmla. Thus, it signals the daughter's emotional involvement with what she 'chronicles': the life in the changed house and around it. The scenes of house and country, and the characters, especially the ill father and the pragmatic stepmother, reflect back on her – writing and changing – self. The sense of abjection, the suspension between connectedness and separation, is then, as in Kristeva's auto-graph, linked to the powers of a specific, hyperbolic memory that undermines conventionalised patterns and here works to undercut closure of the text and stability of the subject. 'Home' ends, not with an idea of the ill father's fate or with the planned 'And so I went and wrote this story' (152), but with the uncanny evocation of 'the first scene I can establish as a true memory in my life' (152) and an apostrophe that highlights the *effects* of such a scene for the speaking subjects and for the reader (see also Heble 1994, 9). The emphasis is clearly on the tensions of separation from m/other: the reader is introduced as 'you' (recalling the Lacanian principle of absent presence in Alfred Hornung's reading of similar texts, but also the gothic need for an open listener) and as another multiplying relation in a self-inscription in process.

These dynamics also structure the other Munro story that self-consciously explores gothic (auto)graphing, 'The Ferguson Girls'. When the death of her older sister brings the family back together, Bonnie's memory evokes the sister as supportive of her own creativity and of her early stories. As in the earlier 'Home', the underlying structure is shaped by abjection (separation from the sister and the shared life of the past); the ending is in tension, as the future promises repetition of the sister's fate (which itself can partly be seen as repetition of the mother's). This accounts for the gothicism in the whole scenery of grotesque or extreme figures around various kitchen tables in various houses that reflect back on the perceiving – and unconsciously changing – Bonnie.

Similarly, albeit less overtly, self-inscription turns gothic in Del Jordan's story, even beyond the self-reflexive epilogue. As a novel of childhood and adolescence, the text is structured through the tensions of separation and connectedness, and especially through the dynamics of desire and abjection in relation with the mother. Addie Jordan, a progressive woman in the rural surroundings of the 1940s and a proto-type of Redekop's 'conspicuous mock-maternal figures', is an important figure for the young Del in many ways, but most notably in terms of her writing and even the choice of narrative form. Here is the matrilinear connection as mentioned by Stanton and others. However, as Barbara Godard has clearly shown, 'Munro chooses eclectically from both mothers and fathers, a combination which blurs boundaries' (1984, 45). Thus, Godard sees *Lives* as an 'encyclopaedia of narrative from the joke and gossip to history and epic ... It should not be difficult to guess which are the creations of the mothers and which of the fathers' (54). The encyclopaedia image comes from the mother's activities of selling encyclopaedias as a travelling saleswoman in the country but it is also related to Uncle Craig's activities of 'collecting facts' in the form of newspaper clippings and lists, as a history writer of Wawanash County. The notion of the encyclopaedic novel thus shows how Del is influenced by both of them as well as by the other mentioned oral forms of narration. Again, the gothic auto-graph, hyperbolically, excessively, multiplies.

In terms of gothic contextualisation, historiography – and the related collection of documents and facts – certainly becomes one of the realist modes against which the ensuing gothic distortions play off. Again, photographs offer a good example: Uncle Craig is, from the first, associated with them and, in this context, they function as documents that preserve the past and can be specified in time and place. However, Del distances them right away, relating them to 'another country, where everything was lower, muddier, darker than here' (24; see Carscallen on Munro's 'other countries', 1993, esp. 4). Her challenges make the uncle connect the pictures to the changes the future has brought (25); Del's perception thus prefigures the uncanny processes of her own later 'Photographer'. Although her actual act of 'writing things down' is linked to Craig's (210), her choice of subject matter only partly reflects his historiographic focus – as in her view of the religious history of the county in 'Age of Faith', but it is only important when it intersects with what interests her: the female every-day lives around her.

The other 'realist' discourse that serves as backdrop for Del's gothic distortions is, in a way, life-writing itself – but that form is structurally linked to the mother and, as we have seen, gothicised from the start. The image of the farmhouse, with the mother's mother inside – the grandmother who was a schoolteacher before marrying and becoming a 'religious fanatic' (63) – forms the mother's life-story. The house/story also gothically contains a violent brother; references to his 'tortures' betray – possibly sexual – abuse (65). The mother leaves the poor, repressive home – courageously exceeding what is expected of a young farm girl – for education at a boarding school. With the advent of love and romance, there enters 'a young man who remained a shadow – no clear-cut villain, certainly, like her brother' (66) – but the 'wrong man'. Del's father then has not married for love and passion, but because he is a gentleman (67). At this point, Del sums up the facts of her mother's life as she has just heard them, in this way:

> Was that all? I was troubled here by a lack of proportion, though it was hard to say what was missing, what was wrong. In the beginning of her story was dark captivity, suffering, then daring and defiance and escape. Struggle, disappointment, more struggle, godmothers and villains. (67)

An abusive and repressive female childhood and youth is thus 'magnified' and with characteristic hyperbole transformed into a gothic romance. This becomes one of the patterns operative in all Del's writing of the female lives around her. Hyperbole in this sense also marks her gothic auto-graph. The effect is interesting: the hyperbole of the daughter's story reveals the understatement of the mother's tale – and highlights the hidden truly gothic aspects of the mother's experience of becoming her/self.

Moreover, as has been indicated, Del's mother also becomes a writer: her letters to the newspaper offer a (non-canonical) form of writing that she uses both for feminist information (for example, on the new possibilities of contraception) and for romanticising (as in her 'long decorative descriptions of the countryside from which she had fled ... that made the roots of my teeth ache with shame' (68)). That the chapter on her is entitled 'Princess Ida', her pen name, emphasises her role as literary mother and relates her to other women writers (for example, the Brontë sisters) who function similarly in Del's story of becoming a writer. 'Within the pages of *Lives of Girls and Women* many literary progenitors are alluded to or pastiched' writes Godard (1984, 49); she enumerates the relationship of Uncle Craig and Alice Munro's father as historiographers (see also Redekop

1992, 234), the Tennysonian reverberations in 'Princess Ida's' letters, as well as her model in Canadian literature: Isabella Valency Crawford (1850–87). These connections add to the hyperbole of her literary memory (in Kristeva's sense) that interweaves and further multiplies her gothic auto-graph.

The gothic auto-graph in Del's story can thus also be shown by intertextualising her narration within gothic filliation. However, traditionally, the first-person retrospective voice emphasises subjective perception and implies that the speaking subject is in a safe position and has survived all horrors. By contrast, Del is, at the end of her story, still between the 'real thing' and her narration: the epilogue and the meeting with one of the Sherriffs on which her novel had been based paradoxically precede in narrated time her idea of going to the city to start 'real life'. Like the narrator's role in 'Home' – and like Kristeva's narrator's hyperbolic memory – Del's position as speaking subject is suspended in time and situated in-relation: through similarity with literary foremothers, as in Kristeva's 'Hyperbole', or by juxtaposition with completely different female figures, as in Munro's 'Home'. Moreover, as both show, the speaking subject is also – certainly gothically – connected with the reader, her 'you'. This suggests further multiplying – and a liberating feminist twist to the functions of memory. And as Del's story self-consciously explores its voice, her auto-graph assumes gothic texture as interrogative text and as dynamic form for gender construction.

Engendering the subject

Munro's neo-gothicism also rewrites gothic texture: as narrative of a female subject's growing up through childhood and adolescence. Fredericke van Leeuwen's humanist/feminist discussion of the 'Female Gothic' maintains that often 'the Gothic mode [is used] to reveal, in an indirect and grotesque way, the female condition' (1982, 43). She sees the form as 'discourse of the Other' in Simone de Beauvoir's sense and discusses the works of modern writers like Djuna Barnes, Sylvia Plath and Carson McCullers as 'instances of twentieth-century female Gothic used by women writers to articulate the situation of women in a society that denies them the status of subject' (39). The position as Other in this system accounts for the central gothic conflict faced by the adolescent heroines: the '[t]error of growing up and the

simultaneous realisation that it is not to be avoided' (39). Their stories
are marked by a 'reluctance to enter adulthood: to become adult women
is what they fear most' (39). Van Leeuwen's conclusion has been introduced above: 'they read like *The Second Sex* in novel form' (1982, 43).

Lives belongs to those feminine gothic texts that are, quite literally,
the story of becoming a woman, in conflict with the woman-as-Other
in the sense of de Beauvoir's emphasis on *becoming* a woman – that
structures, as we have seen, much of the contemporary debate of (gendered) subjectivity. In this sense, *Lives* does inscribe the 'discourse of
the Other' and is intertextually related not only to van Leeuwen's
examples but also to *Jane Eyre*, a good example of a gothic female
Bildungsroman – and, as indicated in the subtitle, a woman's 'autobiography'. Recalling and rewriting such feminine gothic texts, *Lives*
self-consciously uses the powers of gothicism to highlight the discourses of gender construction in general – and, similarly, the even
more complicated making of the female artist in particular, evoking
Elizabeth Barrett Browning's poetic gothic *Aurora Leigh* (1856). Munro
does this with her characteristic humour and a lightness of voice that
both continues and deconstructs the classics of feminine gothicism.

The discourses that 'engender' the subject in *Lives* are, in some
ways, those usually considered universal: rites of passage through
family life, sexuality, religion, education. But they are also firmly linked
to a whole set of conditions and values that constitute Del's specific
surroundings on the Flats Road and in Jubilee; values attached to the
land, to the community's religious history, to education during war-
time, and to living conditions after the mid-1930s. These discourses
situate her subject processes in the (Canadian) context that, as we
have seen, Heather Murray has called the 'pseudo-wilderness': a space
in between city and forest, marked by the possibilities of both and
emphasising the movement from one to the other. In *Lives* this suspended space comes to underline 'the process of female coming-of-age
… as a weaning from childhood's natural realm' (Murray 1986, 76), as
Del moves from the Flats Road – which 'was not part of town but it
was not part of the country either' (5) – to the small town, Jubilee,
and then considers going on to the city and university. As Murray has
shown, 'the question of how and where to live is also a choice of
literary style and voice, when … writer-heroines must decide between
an acquired diction or a local language, and between inherited or in-
digenous literary forms' (76). In Del's story, this process is very much

linked to this space as domesticated wilderness (Murray), marked by the influence of women who create a community there. The lives of girls and women in the pseudo-wilderness can both be more free and more stifled in surroundings that are removed from the centres of politics and culture but are small enough to construct local systems of social control. It is in this dynamic context that Del's story of becoming is situated.

Del's engendering processes are most obviously constructed through the girls and women around her: through their personalities but also through their discourses, rituals and 'connectedness'. In the exploration of these female figures, the neo-gothic tone of ironic humour dwells on imagery of the grotesque, a gothic move that aptly highlights the 'denial of their status as subjects' (van Leeuwen). As is often the case in narratives of artistic growth, and especially so in the pragmatic 1970s, one of the outstanding problems is that of female role models: to Del all women around her are problematic in various ways.

There is, for example, the advent of Madeleine in the first chapter, reverberating with Poesque overtones of domestic horror: a young mother full of violence – against her child. She is a terrifying female figure who disappears and is, paradoxically and ironically, remembered 'like a story' – with laughter and 'strange, belated, heartless applause' – as 'Madeleine! That madwoman!' (23). There is the mentally disabled cousin, Mary Agnes, similarly associated with abuse and introduced through cautionary tales (another important educating discourse here) as victim of male violence. It is she who provokes Del's own cruelty and physical attack, in a truly gothic scene with vampiristic overtones. Significantly, Del sees this as an act of self-liberation: 'When I bit Mary Agnes I thought I was biting myself off from everything' (46), recalling the physical aspects of what Ellen Moers has called 'the savageries of girlhood' in the female gothic. These scenes inaugurate a whole series of freakish female figures, typical gothic distortions, resulting not only from the girl's childish perception but also from the woman's gaze, the adult retrospective narrative voice. Related to this is a clash of discourses: of hyperbolic experience and understating memory, of defamiliarising presentation and the refamiliarising retrospective voice – a clash that accounts for the challenging potential of the neo-gothic text.

Munro's gothic glimpse of becoming a woman emphasises women – as opposed to 'Woman', or any other impression of something as general and unifying as 'the female condition' – most notably by the presentation of an entire array of female figures who represent both multiplicity, within the small Canadian rural world, and connectedness. Most striking are the older women: with their radically differing but equally vibrant sets of value-judgements regarding femininity but also with the presentation of their own lives, they set the notions of *le propre* and the 'monstrous-feminine' and their implications for gender construction.

There are the giggling, chatting, tale-telling and hard-working aunts Elspeth and Grace, devoted to taking care of their brother and judging their (female) neighbours not only severely, but also with a clear double standard. This is obvious to Del when, for example, Aunt Moira's ability to drive a car is considered brave, while Addie's is seen as 'reckless and unnecessary' (33). These aunts value acts of denial such as that of a cousin who turns down her college scholarship and decides to stay home because '[s]he preferred not' (32). Del finds the implied heroism rather strange:

> There it was, the mysterious and to me novel suggestion that choosing not to do things showed, in the end, more wisdom and self-respect than choosing to do them. They liked people turning down things that were offered, marriage, positions, opportunities, money ... Like certain subtle harmonies of music and colour, the beauties of the negatives were beyond me. (32)

These values come to construct a border for an ironic 'monstrous-feminine' – the irony clearly emphasising the socio-cultural construction of both *le propre* and the 'monstrous'. Most eccentric, according to these values, is Del's mother, with her 'clear and dangerous voice' (47) as well as her 'grave, hopeful, lecturing voice' (146). She is 'unpredictable, unreliable' according to her daughter (47), 'a wild-woman' in the aunts' eyes (54) – and 'monstrous' to all others: rejecting the Flats Road (where she is not well-liked) for the town (where she is an outsider as well); rejecting the expected ironing for the selling of encyclopaedias, and 'normal' family life for town life with her daughter and female boarders. Munro's neo-gothic narrative shows how the expectations of a proper femininity come into being, and how digression from these is coded as 'monstrous'. Moreover, Addie Jordan – an early feminist who refuses to assume a place that she experiences as limiting – in the spatio-temporal context of *Lives* is constructed into the 1940s' version of the 'monstrous-feminine'. The impact on Del is easily recognisable: 'exceeding' her female role with her artistic aspirations, she is closely related to this outsider–mother figure, which she realises with hesitation: 'I myself was not so different from my mother, but concealed it, knowing what dangers there were' (68). There is a clear recognition of a similarity (as in the 'classic' Jane–Bertha relationship) and of its implications vis-à-vis the male gaze – the pervasive presence and constraining constructions of which are both highlighted and mocked in the presentation of a women's culture in the domesticated wilderness. The aunts' artificial value scheme anticipates masculine control (and negation) where male figures actually seem weak, harmless or abusive.[7]

Like aunts and mother, another female figure similarly works as ambiguous model for living as a woman: Addie's middle-aged boarder, Fern Dogherty. With her work at the post-office, her past career as opera singer and present activities in the church choir, and through her sad relationship – or, in Del's terms, her 'tragic romance' – with Art Chamberlain, she is a typical spinster figure. Like the aunts and Addie, she is presented in relation to *le propre*, especially the feminine values of domesticity that she does not fulfil. Of course, all of these female figures are shown to 'exceed' *le propre*: the aunts with their jokes, the mother with her travelling, Fern with her career. Furthermore, they all come to influence Del's writing life – most notably the mother, but also the aunts, whose chatting and joking teach her a 'whole new language'. Fern's unmarried life as a singer makes Del wish to live 'differently': like an artist – and like a man (147). These female figures suggest alternative ways of living as a woman. And the gothicism in their depiction points to the complications of such deviation that are also realised by Del.

Lives of girls and women: multiplicity and deviation become key terms. The two other female figures who can be seen to be directly related to Del's subject-processes and who present two different extremes of female lives – and negative examples for Del – are her girlfriend Naomi and her teacher Miss Farris, aptly introduced in the Chapter 'Changes and Ceremonies'. Naomi shares the troubles, mockery and curiosities of Del's adolescence, but her story ends 'normally' – and sadly – with pregnancy and then marriage. By contrast, Miss Farris can be seen as female artist figure with her school operetta, her eccentricities (the clothes, the ice-skating), the yearly 'hypothetical romance, or scandal … between her and Mr Boyce' (102)

– and somehow also with her suicide. Her story is that of a tragic figure, an almost stereotypical romantic heroine torn between art and (unrequited) love. Both Naomi and Elinor Farris offer opposing versions of how to live as a woman, but both these lives appear tragic and unfulfilled to Del; in her story they seem like grotesque half-lives, each missing something important and obviously limited to only one of the multiple aspects of female life that she herself wants to live out.[8] What all of these female lives around Del confront in different ways and degrees, however, is a deep conflict with *le propre* of the 1940s – a conflict that anticipates postwar women's 'problem without a name' with the feminine mystique. This conflict behind that whole landscape full of strong but grotesque or 'monstrous' female figures is once again pointed to by gothic form.

As we have seen, *le propre* is produced in various, more or less institutionalised, discourses. Thus, in Munro's neo-gothic narrative, the presence of a whole series of normal-but-strange women is extended into the realm of other – literary – discourses that shape the process of becoming a woman. These are the '[l]ovely, wistful, shabby old friends' – the heroines of popular romances from the library, most notably Sigrid Undsed's 'Kristin Lavransdatter', a desirable heroine for Del mainly because of the hero, romantically outlined as 'a flawed and dark and lonely horseback rider' (100). The characters of such romances spark the girls' imagination, both in visions of their own lives as women and in looking at their surroundings, as fact and fiction blur. Del muses, once again mixing experience and gothicism and thus emphasising the everyday life 'realism' of the latter: 'They were like people you saw on the street day after day, year after year, but never knew more than their faces; this could happen even in Jubilee' (99). However, this recognition is instantly confronted with gothic excess: when Miss Farris becomes the subject of the girls' mockery and of Del's early 'gothicising' explorations, she and Naomi play out imagined dialogues of Miss Farris and the married Mr Boyce, thereby viciously dwelling on the inevitable, conventionalised fate of the first wife in the gothic romance formula since Radcliffe:

> 'What are we going to do about Mrs. Boyce? O my love?'
> '... I will make her swallow arsenic and saw her up in little tiny pieces and flush them down the toilet. No I will dissolve them with lye in the

bathtub. I will melt the goldfillings out of her teeth and make us a lovely wedding ring.'

'O you are so romantic, O my beloved.' (106)

Such exaggerated plots are familiar, part of the girls' growing up. However, as tempting as the dark romances displayed in them seem, their desirability is greatly (and gothically) undermined by the related notions of physical love for women – sex and pregnancy and birth. This more mysterious, more dangerous aspect is presented in different texts, texts that are related throughout to mothers: to Addie's letters on contraception, and most notably to Naomi's mother's book on inter-course, with its characteristic emphasis on positions and the male partner's pleasure (123). There are also stories related to her experi-ence as a nurse, stories that are again handed down from mother to daughter to girlfriend, stories in which the body comes to be seen as sensationalised and horrific:

> On [Naomi's mother's] authority – or what Naomi claimed was her authority – I had heard that babies born with cauls will turn out to be criminals, that men had copulated with sheep and produced little shrivelled woolly crea-tures with human faces and sheep's tails, which died and were preserved in bottles somewhere, and that crazy women had injured themselves in ob-scene ways with coat hangers. (100)

The grotesqueries of the body: a typical gothic view of sexuality and reproduction, and a typical liberation from romantic myths. The body's imagery in *Lives* comes to represent the central fear of the female subject here: the very realistic fear of pregnancy and of what is com-municated and perceived as the horrors inescapably related to it. Munro again uses the powers of gothicism to represent real female fears; she uses the gothic defamiliarising processes here to effectively avoid the glamours of maternity as natural vocation and to instead highlight the danger of it. Magdalene Redekop writes: 'Trying to understand this danger must also involve trying to understand what the danger means in the life of the writer as a young girl. In the epilogue, the impregnated womb is a dead metaphor contained in the dead body of Caroline, who is herself a character in Del's stillborn novel' (1992, 62). And the discourses and images that both construct and reflect that danger circle – as in Moers's Female Gothic – around the grotesqueries of the female body, darkly connecting physical and artistic creativity.

◆

Communicated among women, the idea of the body as grotesque also influences the complexities of love in *Lives*' gothic romance aspects. Del's growing interest in the other sex is marked by her perception of the darkly threatening horrors of the female body, pregnancy and maternity, extended into the explorations of sex and of the male body. Munro's self-conscious use of feminine gothic form in the representation of love and sex distinguishes *Lives* from the two strong female genres of the 1970s: the popular 'bodice-rippers' and the feminist 'confession'. Whereas the sensationalism of (soft-porn) sex-scenes in the former of course ignored the issue of potential pregnancies completely, the latter dwelt on it, and on the related issue of contraception, not only as an essential problem of the heterosexual relationship but also as interrupting whatever pleasures could be found in the erotics of the scene.

The introduction of sex in *Lives* defies romance and glamour as well as didacticism; it rather produces a critical image of becoming a woman typical of neo-gothicism. Del first physically encounters men through the 'dirty old man' Mr Chamberlain, with his groping hands on her breast (134) and his tapping fist in her crotch (142), and through a discovery scene of what amounts to an elaborate ironic mockery of the erect penis, as Mr Chamberlain proudly exposes himself and masturbates in front of her (141). That mockery is extended as the episode becomes transformed into another grotesque story, communicated to Naomi. In another scene, young Jerry Storey's curious eyes on her naked body are humiliating but comically anti-climactic in comparison, as Del thinks: 'Did he feel my body as inappropriate, as unrealisable, as I did his?' (169). Both episodes evoke a decisive scene of Esther Greenwood's engendering processes in Sylvia Plath's *The Bell Jar* (1962), an important feminine gothic intertext of *Lives*. As Buddy Willard undresses and shows himself to Esther, all she can think of is 'turtleneck'. The scene does not result in sex but in a conversation about it that leads to Esther's recognition of Buddy's – completely 'normal' – misogyny; and to her subsequent break with him. The parallel scene in *Lives* ends whatever relationship there had been between Del and Jerry.[9]

But what about the heroes? Obviously, in *Lives*, the relationships and desire between girls and women, and the related rites and narratives, are of consistent power and work to challenge those that only start out with boys and men. However, the male figures, too, appear surrounded with an aura of strangeness and represent not only the whole range of gothic heroes (from the villainous to the romantic) but also another set of discourses and texts that partake in Del's gender formation. Uncle Benny, for example – mockingly Byronic with his 'heavy black moustache, fierce eyes, [and] delicate predatory face ... the sort of man who becomes a steadfast eccentric almost before he is out of his teens. In all his statements, predictions, judgements there was a concentrated passion' (2) – is also the source of a tabloid that Del devours as soon as she can read: 'bloated and giddy with revelations of evil, of its versatility and grand invention and horrific playfulness' (4). Only a few pages into the text, this is the first trace of the conjunction of the gothic and the real. Her father's stories fit the same incongruous pattern – for example, that of the dead husband coming back to take revenge on his wife for marrying again (8) – only to be undercut by her mother's 'explaining how it was all coincidence, imagination, self-suggestion' (8). The figures of the father and Uncle Benny blend together at a later point in the story, when both are associated with killing – the usual hunting, but also the shooting of Major, the dog – and set off Del's most terrible dreams. In these nightmares, in complete contradiction to the amiability of his representation, her father is a killer – in one dream even of his own family, including Del, who feels paralysed with fear:

> It won't hurt, he told us, as if that was all we had to be afraid of, it'll all be over in a minute. He was kind and calm, reasonable, tiredly persuasive, explaining that it was all somehow for our own good. Thoughts of escape struggled in my mind like birds caught in oil, their wings out, helpless. I was paralysed by this reasonableness, the arrangements so simple and familiar and taken for granted, the reassuring face of insanity. (95)

Again, as in the mother's story, 'the simple and familiar' is evoked and shown in its gothic dimensions. The image of the 'x-rays' through idyllic relationships that Kristeva has analysed in romantic love comes to mind here, related to the nightmarish fears of familiar figures or to the domestic horrors in gothic houses in which anything might happen – especially to the (female) body. Del's emotions recall those of Emily in Udolpho at the mercy of Montoni, a 'bad father' figure. What happens is that through these stories and discourses and nightmares Del becomes (visually) aware of an existing other world 'alongside our world ... [I]n that world people could go down in quicksand, be vanquished by ghosts or terrible ordinary cities; luck and wickedness were gigantic and unpredictable; nothing was deserved, anything might happen; defeats were met with crazy satisfaction' (22). This other, darker (gothic) world, it seems, has much in common with the one that arises out of the aunts' stories, simultaneously true and unreal (28), just as their language is one that has many layers (31). There is a 'nimble malice that danced under their courtesies to the rest of the world' (33). This world also reverberates in other stories: those of Del's great-aunts (the fathers' aunts) about the Catholic church. They 'know' and joke about 'all there was beyond jokes, babies' skeletons, and strangled nuns under the convent floors … It was all true, they had books about it. All true' (79). Del's comment reveals her desire for what seems like sensational and mysterious plenitude and excess. At the same time, it reveals her scepticism, echoing her mother's dry irony in similar situations: 'the church building seemed inadequate; too bare and plain and straightforward-looking to be connected with such voluptuousness and scandal' (79). Such 'true stories' and discourses around Del expand the notions of the real world around her into that of gothic structures and relations.

There is yet another 'different' world that Del encounters through her brother Owen, who 'seemed to me to inhabit a world so far from my own (the real one), a world so irrelevant, heartbreakingly flimsy in its deceptions' (88). At this point, the world of the younger, male sibling is seen from the perspective of the older, female one; however, Owen later comes to be the major challenge to Del's religious phase when he produces 'the unavoidable collision … of religion and life' (96) and thus ends her temporary faith in that other, better world introduced through the various churches and denominations around her. In Del's quest – as in that of other gothic heroines or that of her own mother – it is the darker, gothic world that works to expand her space and possibilities, rather than that of hope encountered in her 'age of faith'. Significantly, this age of faith is also her age of love. In Del's story, the discourses of religion come to be closely intertwined with those of sexuality. This provocative connection is most strongly enforced through the figure of Garnet French, her first lover and (since a conversion during his stay in jail) an orthodox Baptist. Significantly, their relationship is marked by the meetings of the 'Baptist Young People's Society', where Del feels 'always amazed and lonely as somebody thrown up in a shipwreck' (179); it ends through Garnet's insistence on her conversion and his related, rather violent attempts at 'baptising' her himself in the river. This scene between the two is a struggle for appropriation of and power over the other; but it is also another example of 'x-rays through love' – the horror in an idyllic situation. Both love and faith here lose their power as 'master narratives' for a female life-story.

The baptising scene coincides with Del's recognition of pregnant Naomi's limited life, and her refusal to suffer the same fate; the discourses of faith and love are further extended into that of literature. First, Del's recognition parallels an earlier instance of differentiation between the two girls. In a scene that again recalls the related rites of passage in *The Bell Jar*,[10] Del (like Esther) escapes from the drinking and necking that Naomi (like Becky) enjoys as 'normal life', seriously concluding: 'I was not going to be able to do it. No. Better Charlotte Brontë' (161). This radical choice of art over love and a manifold life over a limited one – a choice that is disrupted by both Jerry Storey and Garnet French later on – occurs after she has read Elizabeth Gaskell's *The Life of Charlotte Brontë* (161). Later Del stores her own novel in her copy of *Wuthering Heights*: the Brontë sisters become Del's foremothers in her writing, even her life – after all, life on the Haworth moors does not seem altogether different from that in the Canadian pseudo-wilderness. At the same time, love and romantic relationships come to be treated like stories. Del and Jerry Storey romanticise their intellectual relationship as 'couple who dazzle all beholders with the unique and indescribable style of their dancing' (164). The humiliating experience of being locked naked into the Storeys' basement gets 'transformed … into a Great Comic Scene, something jerky and insane from a silent movie' (171). However, subsequently, Del's 'need for love [goes] underground, like a canny toothache' (173). And the affair with Garnet French becomes a fiction, transformed romantically at first: 'I talked to myself about myself, saying *she. She is in love. She has just come in from being with her lover. She has given herself to her lover. Seed runs down her legs*' (192). For the ending of the relationship, she stages herself, self-consciously, as tragic heroine, before she utters the decisive line:

> I combed my hair and waited, classically, behind the curtains in our front room … I was suffering. I said into the mirror a line from Tennyson, from my mother's *Complete Tennyson* that was a present from her old teacher,

Miss Rush. I said it with absolute sincerity, absolute irony. *He cometh not, she said.* (200)

The sincerity/irony paradox in this scene, like the similar paradox of rejection in the epilogue, enforces the gothicism of the scene. Del's own commentary – 'From "Marianna," one of the silliest poems I had ever read' (200) – extends this paradox and emphasises that the discourses of romantic poetry are appropriate for representing the ending of her love relationship. This ending marks the beginning of a new life: as 'real life' replaces 'Garnet French', Del sets out to be a writer.

This, then, is the 'happy ending' of a self-consciously neo-gothic story. To return to the earlier mentioned intertexts *Jane Eyre* and *Aurora Leigh* – with their own, subversive 'happy endings' – means to realise the possibilities of a modern, twentieth-century artist heroine.[11] However, this is not a clear choice of art over romance. Although Del's juxtaposition of her lover's name, 'Garnet French', with 'real life' (201) signifies that she renounces the romantic fantasies tied to him and the shared relationship, the ensuing vision of her future is clearly based on yet another fantasy:

> [T]he future could be furnished without love or scholarships. Now at last without fantasies or self-deception, cut off from the mistakes and confusion of the past, grave and simple, carrying a small suitcase, getting on a bus, like girls in movies leaving home, convents, lovers, I supposed I would get started on my real life. (201)

This movie-like fantasy of female life – 'made in Hollywood' – undermines the rejection of the romantic fantasy. It thus also functions similarly to the vigorous but only seeming rejection of gothicism: fantasies are important and they are emphasised as important aspects of a strong, dynamic, female subjectivity.

And Del's subjectivity is dynamic, beyond the sense of an ending of her narrative. Throughout her story, the totalising discourses that would work towards enforcing *le propre* have been dispersed by gothic excess – or, rather, by the self-conscious narrative explorations of its possibilities. In the intermediate landscape of the domesticated wilderness, the panorama of many different female figures suggests multiplicity: diverse, eccentric, and uncontrollable, they challenge the intense sense of social control within the small and isolated community. Similarly liberating are fantasies and imagination forming stories and lives that exceed control and containment. Del's creative processes as an artist, and her subject processes are composed from these contexts as well as from her own fantasies: her horrific dreams and nightmares (such as the one about her father as killer) but also romantic fantasies (as romantic heroine, as celebrity).

Del's story ends with a sense that she is still adolescent, growing up, 'in-the-making'. As Alfred Hornung has shown, such 'concentration on fragments of life only' is also an aspect of the contemporary autobiographic mode (1985, 71); furthermore, Del becomes a typical female subject-in-process in Kristeva's sense. This recognition is reinforced by comparison with 'classic' gothic intertexts: whereas these are told from a position *after* the encounter and survival of the unreal/supernatural/horrific, Del is speaking from an in-between state: between the constructions of experience, the 'real thing', and her own (gothic) story which we have just read. In Munro's neo-gothic narrative, the female subject processes even exceed the ending.

Connectedness: haunted houses – haunted texts

Del's gothic auto-graph further inscribes the shape of the house of fiction – a house haunted by the gothic traces from the web of women's writing. The neo-gothic text becomes a sign of filliation, and intertextuality offers another excess – of the containment of the house/text. In Munro's neo-gothic fictions, this process can best be shown by means of a metaphor that is also linked with the functions of memory: *connectedness*.

This term runs like a red thread through this chapter; Heather Murray has used it in formal terms, characterising the short-story novel, which is exactly the narrative structure of *Lives*, with its first-edition subtitle 'A Novel'. As mentioned above, Del tells episodic stories about her surroundings that, when pieced together, construct her own stories of growing up. Murray writes:

> The loosely linked short story collection or short story novel is a distinctively (although not uniquely) 'Canadian' structure … it seems especially suited to the telling of lives of girls and women, whether because of the flexibility of its format for publication, its fit to the busy (and often interrupted) schedules of authors and readers, or its structural suitability to the exploration of affiliation, interconnectivity and separation. (1990, 363)

All of these choices are explored in Munro's *Lives*, as well as in some of her other texts, both thematically within these stories and inter-textually between these and other stories in the web of women's (gothic) writing.

Neo-gothic 'connectedness' also further outlines how the notions of hyperbole and excess are extended within the realm of filliation; the haunted houses of feminine gothic fiction seem to multiply as 'relation-ship is the sustained subject ... between and among people, places, words, things, past, present' (Murray 1990, 363). These latter aspects also suggest connectedness through time: both within the text, con-structed by memory and the retrospective voice, and among texts of different times that haunt each other. Both levels will be explored here, as they highlight neo-gothic excess as liberating disruption of order and control within and beyond houses/texts.

In *Lives*, the time structure is not linear, as a story of growing up might lead one to expect. Rather, a new episode might go back in time, before the previous episode's time-frame. For example, the be-ginning of the chapter 'Age of Faith' goes back to life on the Flats Road, after 'Princess Ida' has just told about life in Jubilee. The effect of such non-linear time in the narrative is a further undermining of a fixed subjectivity; it adds yet another layer to the retrospective narra-tion that can shed new light on the preceding passage and thus puts the conclusions of that passage in relation. Most notably this is the effect of the particular placement of the epilogue, which, in fact, pre-cedes in time the ending of the chapter before. In that ending, and contrary to the epilogue, Del already knows that she has not won the scholarship that could 'carry [her] away from Jubilee' (207). The re-cognition of this (for her) devastating fact is also interesting itself in its 'timing': it is ironically interspersed with Garnet's marriage pro-posal, clearly explaining why she answers 'yes' to his question about whether she would like a baby – which means, for her, the real danger – and why she then comments with a characteristic paradox: 'Where would such a lie come from? It was not a lie' (196). The epilogue shows that her actual novel-writing – itself vaguely timed as 'A time came when' (203) – precedes the recognition that 'the future could be furnished without love or scholarships' and, romantic visions to the contrary, this underlines the possibility of her 'real life' as a writer.

Furthermore, such non-linear 'timing' emphasises the notion of change. 'Changing' is an important concept in the text, as might be

expected in a novel of adolescence; however, there are further connotations that take gothic turns. These are explored mostly in the
pointed mother–daughter talks. Take Addie's utopian vision of life
and death on the occasion of Uncle Craig's heart attack: she voices her
reflections while getting dressed and made up for the funeral. This
feminine activity of visual and physical transformation, watched by
the daughter, expands the notions of change that the mother's speech
evokes and desires:

> If we weren't thinking all the time in terms of persons, if we were thinking
> of Nature, all Nature going on and on, parts of it dying – well not dying,
> changing, *changing* is the word I want, changing into something else, all
> those elements that made the person and going back to Nature again and
> reappearing over and over in birds and animals and flowers – Uncle Craig
> doesn't have to be Uncle Craig! Uncle Craig is flowers! (40)

The metamorphosis of form from one shape to the other emphasises
the dynamics of subjectivity (extending the notion of 'person'), recalls
the cyclical powers of nature and – in a typically paradoxical gothic
move – defamiliarises the familiar notions of (natural) death. The call
for a changed perspective on living matter implied here then gives way
to the coming possibilities of science:

> They are already able to transplant eyes, not whole eyes but the cornea, I
> think it is. That's only the beginning. Someday they'll be able to transplant
> hearts and lungs and all the organs that the body needs. Even brains – I
> wonder, could they transplant *brains?* So all these parts won't die at all,
> they'll go on living as part of somebody else. Part of another combination.
> Then you won't be able properly to speak of death at all … We would all
> be heirs of one another's bodies, we would all be donors too. (41)

There are uncanny reverberations of Victor Frankenstein's creative
activities in this idea of parts of human beings or fragments of bodies
pieced together after death – and it is the grotesque, the morbid in the
image, not the hope that Addie sees in this kind of bodily connectedness, that sharpens Del's subsequent view of her parents' embracing
and her desire that they 'turn back into their separate, final, un-
supported selves' (41).

This idea of 'heirs of the living bodies' introduces the fantastic into
the story (see Godard 1984, 45). Importantly – as in the haunting
forms of *Udolpho*, *Jane Eyre* or *Wide Sargasso Sea* – it is the mother-
figure who introduces it: the sense of mystery; the sense of exceeding

what is controllable and conventionally assumed; the sense of a perspective beyond the containment of an ending. Moreover, and here we
encounter another dimension of the 'haunted house' idea, it is also
typical for these gothic texts that it is the body that plays a part in
such consciousness-extending ideas. In one sense – related to post-
structuralist thought – this questions once again the idea of the
'natural' and the 'given'. In a further sense – related to gothicism – it
further questions *le propre* and even the maternal. The effect, of course,
is often monstrous – especially to the narrating daughter – and thus,
in the gothic scheme, liberating.

This introduction of the fantastic and the – very physically –
monstrous through the mother-figure also recalls the gothic 'refamiliarising' of the strange or supernatural that makes *Frankenstein* so provocative. A good example from the Canadian postmodern is Gloria
Sawai's story 'The Day I Sat with Jesus on the Sun Deck and a Wind
Came Up and Blew My Kimono Open and He Saw My Breasts'
(1986). Decisively, the mother herself is the narrator. The story opens
with a sense of the gravity of domestic demands in a family with five
children; added to an eerie feeling that here, in the face of the endless
prairie (another version of the pseudo-wilderness), anything might
happen. And it does, as Jesus appears and has wine and tea with her
on the sundeck, while the laundry airs out in the living room, and as
her body – accidentally? – comes to manipulate the scene. This is told
very visually and virtually shows Jesus' most human dimension. Very
excessive, very 'normal': a gothic fantasy in a story of female, motherly,
everyday life.

In *Lives*, 'connectedness' suggests yet another context related to change
and the mother's vision:

> There is a change coming I think in the lives of girls and women. Yes. But
> it is up to us to make it come. All women have had up till now has been
> their connection with men. All we have had. No more lives of our own,
> really, than domestic animals. (146)

This statement addresses the underlying feminist emphasis on process
in *Lives* in various ways. First, there is the emphasis on 'us'; on women
as active and as assuming the position of subjects in a context that
places them in that of objects: Addie here implicitly addresses the
hierarchies of binary oppositions shown by Simone de Beauvoir and

challenged today by post-structuralist thought. Second, this major change means, for Addie, an expansion: *more* connections than only those with men – connections with women. This, of course, refers back to the text itself as *Lives* has shown throughout how female lives are connected, how they connect the past and the present and the options for the future, and how these connections account for the possibilities of a female subject.

Feminine connectedness also evokes the subject processes of separation and abjection. *Lives* draws attention to these processes, mostly by contrasting them to the different processes for mothers and sons. Del reflects on Jerry Storey: 'He could not do otherwise; he was what he seemed. I, whose natural boundaries were so much more ambiguous, who soaked up protective coloration wherever it might be found, began to see that it might be restful to be like Jerry' (166). Magdalene Redekop has shown how Del is positioned as borderline case in *Lives* (1992, 66–8) and concludes, in line with Kristeva's concept of abjection: 'Del discovers the other in mother and acknowledges the impossibility of constructing herself as subject without pointing to that figure' (1992, 86; see also Irvine 1983, 101–4).

An element that both underlines such processes of discovery and connects women is time – time as constructed through some kind of collective female memory. Julia Kristeva's 'Women's Time' links the second generation of feminism to notions of time that are contrary to the common (and male) notions of history and linearity:

> [B]y demanding recognition of an irreducible identity, without equal in the opposite sex and, as such, exploded, plural, fluid, in a certain way non-identical, this feminism situates itself outside the linear time of identities which communicate through projection and revindication. Such a feminism rejoins, on the one hand, the archaic (mythical) memory and, on the other, the cyclical or monumental temporality of marginal movements. (1986, 198)

There is no clear-cut sense of separation from the linear time-scheme. There is abundance in Addie Jordan's sense: to 'rejoin' means to form an additional bond with the female community in both its collective memory and its (possibly liberating) marginality. This sense of time structures many of the neo-gothic texts, especially their mirror-plot of female desire. It also shapes many of Munro's stories, most notably her second short-story novel *Who Do You Think You Are?* (1978). In the story 'Home', the grave encounter with both the father's present life and his dangerous illness are seen in the perspective of the earlier family, before the mother's death; there is a haunting presence of the past, and of the dead mother. This is emphasised by juxtaposition with a real-time notation: the narrated time is from Saturday to Monday, marked by journal-like headings. How irrelevant and artificial this kind of order is becomes clear when it becomes self-reflexive, both in terms of the speaking subject and her situation: 'I never stay longer than Friday night to Sunday night when I come here, and now because I have stayed longer it seems to me I might stay forever. The buses which run from place to place no longer seem so surely to connect with me' (151).

Chronology does not hold either, for once, because it is similarly disrupted by the self-reflexive episodes of writing in progress. Moreover, past scenes intrude unbidden, as in the final scene in the stable. This moment of the 'true memory in life' (152) is a scene of the father milking a cow, which again can be dated precisely as happening during the winter of 1935. Most importantly, it is a very visual scene, the beauty of which outshines both the reflections on the date and the note on 'the beginning of panic' (152); it is this image of togetherness with the father, whose loss is to be feared at the moment of memory, that stays. The writer/narrator is aware of this effect, as her apostrophe shows:

> You can see this scene, can't you, you can see it quietly made, that magic and prosaic safety briefly held for us, the camera moving out and out, that spot shrinking, darkness. Yes. That is effective.
> I don't want any more effects, I tell you, lying. (153)

This self-reflexive break marks yet another dimension of connectedness: that with the reader. And while in one sense it might disrupt the effect by pointing to the fact that it is 'made', written, constructed, it (effectively) enforces its appeal to a shared, maybe collective sense of time and memory that – less linear and more associative – corresponds to Kristeva's idea of 'women's time'.

So does another Munro episode in 'The Ferguson Girls Must Never Marry': the less self-reflexive, but just as visual and very gothic intrusion of the dead figure of the sister – and thus of the shared past – into the present-time family gathering before the funeral. Non-linear narration and multiple perspectives in this story open up gothic dimensions in the relationship of the three sisters. The death of Nola, herself isolated in life (43), re-affirms connectedness through memory: of a last meeting with her in Toronto that reveals her emotional and physical distance from her husband; of a scene in high school when Nola announced that the Ferguson girls must never marry, precisely because of the possibility of an early death. With these patterns of connecting and separating, the story produces a sense of repetition, of a cyclical return of the same, as the end suggests that Bonnie will repeat Nola's fate. There are parallel layers of life, this ending suggests, just as there are different layers of reality that exist simultaneously, as Del notices at one point in *Lives of Girls and Women*: 'My mother inhabited a different layer of reality from the one I had got into now' (140). Nevertheless, the expression of that recognition affirms the mother's presence and importance – similar to the absent presence of the dead sister in 'The Ferguson Girls' – rather than explaining her away.

This constitutes time in Kristeva's sense and thus as recognisable as an important connecting element among women (and constitutive of a female subjectivity). This collective female memory also works to connect, to 'affilliate' female texts; it is particularly powerful in feminine gothic texts, with their haunting presence of the past, of dead and absent figures and, self-reflexively, of other gothic texts. I will outline here a striking example of one neo-gothic text haunting the other.

'Time is not a line but a dimension' opens Margaret Atwood's novel *Cat's Eye* (1988). Its strong sense of connectedness with Munro's *Lives* is displayed in much more than the recognition of the layers of reality and memory. Like *Lives*, the later text explores the uses of gothicism and self-consciously gothicises women's experience. Like Munro, Atwood recalls, reconsiders and – in another rejection–affirmation play – rewrites feminine gothic form. And, in a further narrative twist, her connectedness with Munro's earlier experimental explorations offers excess of the containment of the earlier texts.

The visualisation of recollection, as well as the related paradoxes of spatial and temporal fragmentation, are traces of the gothic filliation going on here. Using a first-person 'retrospective' present-tense narration, fifty-year-old Elaine – like young Del – explores the processes of becoming a narrator, 'in flux' on a short (or endless?) return visit to

Toronto where her paintings are shown in a 'retrospective'. She too
has a sense of layers of time and layers of story; like Del she visualises
these recognitions:

> But I began then to think of time as having a shape, something you could
> see, like a series of liquid transparencies, one laid on top of one another.
> You don't look back along time but down through it, like water. Sometimes
> this comes to the surface, sometimes that, sometimes nothing. Nothing
> goes away. (3)

The theory of relativity structures the text's levels of time and perspective; it is tied to brother Stephen and 'male' science (which in
Lives is explained by Jerry Storey), but it also comes to characterise
'women's time'. Chronology, evoked by the opening of every chapter
with Elaine's present movement through Toronto and the following
flashback to her youth there, is an illusion: it is disrupted through
memory that connects associatively. The idea of 'nothingness' is another disturbing structuring category, almost personified in the figure
of girlhood friend Cordelia: characterised by paradoxes, provocative
and weak, ambitious and misunderstood, tragic and heroic, she recalls
Shakespeare's Cordelia. Moreover, as both cruel tormentor and tragic
victim, Cordelia is the absent presence in the story; her central position in the vicious power-plays of girls – when Elaine suffers a long,
terrifying period of victimisation – accounts for her haunting presence
throughout the text. From the beginning, Cordelia is one focus of
Elaine's directionless quest through downtown Toronto and, in many
ways, the female desire underlying and 'mirroring' the story is for her.

It is the uncanny connectedness of these two girlfriends in *Cat's
Eye* that shows well not only the gothicism with which the story is
told but also the dimensions of time that construct it, linking it back
to the neo-gothicism of *Lives*. Nine-year-old Elaine becomes Cordelia's
victim through a gothic event: a virtual live-burial that she claims not
to remember (113), but that she later indirectly associates with the
image of a grave: a 'square of darkness and of purple flowers' (272).
This is a truly gothic image in terms of the text's power relations, but
also in its treatment with regard to the layers of memory. Another
gothic scene ends the time of torment: the symbolic live-burial in a
ravine, in which Cordelia and the other girls have left Elaine, and from
which she is rescued first by an apparition that she recognises as the
Virgin Mary and then by her mother – a typical refamiliarising of the

fantastic in her story. This is not forgotten but represented, in a gothicised autobiographic mode, in one of Elaine's paintings called 'Unified Field Theory'. It shows the Virgin on the bridge with an oversized cat's-eye marble (430), just as does the cover of the book the reader holds. Elaine's paintings are both the self-reflexive dimension and the fourth dimension of time – like Del's novel in the epilogue to *Lives*. Here gothicism is not rejected but re-affirmed. It points to the relationship between life and art – and to the uses of gothicising the processes of female experience. In this sense, it teaches us how to read *Cat's Eye* the book, for example through 'Cat's Eye', the painting, in a narrative move that recalls the functions of the epilogue in *Lives*.

The 'Cat's Eye' painting is described as 'self-portrait, of sorts' (430), showing part of Elaine's face with 'the eyes looking outwards' and '[a] few grey hairs. This is cheating', the narrator comments, with characteristic (self-) irony, 'as in reality I pull them out' (430). In the artwork they are necessary time-markers (which the woman, in a social context that devalues signs of ageing for women, refuses). The further description of the painting shows, in gothic terms, the 'I' in it as split subject, fragmented between a present that is relative and a past that freezes the time of terror and torment:

> Behind my half-head, in the centre of the picture, in the empty sky, a pier glass is hanging, convex and encircled by an ornate frame. In it, a section of the back of my head is visible; but the hair is different, younger.
> At a distance, and condensed by the curved space of the mirror, there are three small figures, dressed in the winter clothing of the girls of forty years ago. They walk forward, their faces shadowed, against a field of snow. (430)

This painting, then, works similarly to Del's gothic novel of the epilogue to *Lives* as one centre of the text's 'anti-structure' (Redekop): it has the same title as the book we read, and we read it also through the other paintings, the names of which are all together the titles of the various sections of Elaine's story.

Moreover, female life-writing connects *Cat's Eye* and *Lives*. 'Why do you paint all those women then?' (98) asks a journalist. Elaine's reaction is defensive, as the female figures of her paintings represent much of her life, in which the connectedness of female figures 'mirrors' and subverts the romances, the marriages and the divorce. But they also reflect back on her self, and on her processes of becoming:

becoming a woman, an artist, a female speaking subject. In this sense, Elaine's story, like Del's, becomes a gothic auto-graph.

In this reading, *Lives of Girls and Women* and *Cat's Eye* show well the intertextual possibilities of connectedness, and of neo-gothic writings' filliation. They are 'haunted houses': they appear as gothic 'sister texts', both telling of a similar time, around and after World War II in Canada, with the war songs in school, the royal visit and other events seen through the eyes of girls and women. And both of them do so by gothicising experience, thereby drawing attention to the processes involved, both those of memory and representation and those of subjectivity of women writing. Reading them in relation to and through each other adds a further dimension to the explorations of connectedness and the powers of gothic: desire not only for the other woman but also for the other feminine (gothic) text.[12]

If women's time, as Kristeva suggests, is linked to their marginal position, feminine gothic texts of adolescence and becoming suggest a shift of the power relations, a recentring that puts female relations and women's connectedness into the foreground. Both adolescence and adulthood are reflected back on the female subject through the lives of girls and women. However, they avoid what Kristeva points out as 'the dangers that ensue when power changes hands without changing its nature' (Belsey 1989, 241) precisely through their 'gothicising' that here marks the affirmation of difference in the processes of representation as well as of subjectivity. One example of this is the idea of the natural and specifically of the body, as treated in these texts. Where female powers like procreation could easily be celebrated and mythologised into another Absolute, feminine gothic excess opens up further realms. Magdalene Redekop (1992) has shown how a whole parade of Munrovian 'mock mothers' resist idealisation, or else, rejection – even in 'Friend of My Youth' (1990), possibly Munro's most autobiographic approach to the experience of her own mother's death. In *Lives*, Addie Jordan's utopian image of every/body becoming heirs and donors of the living body presents a profound provocation to the patriarchal separation of the productive (male) and reproductive (female) spheres and the related power structures. This provocation also affects narrative form, as suggested in the chapter in question. Entitled 'Heirs of the Living Body', it shapes Craig as a haunting figure in Del's story, representing the dead body. The gothicism here is emphasised through the house metaphor: the gothic perception and experience of Craig's house:

> The house was like one of those puzzles, those mazes on paper, with a black dot in one of the squares, or rooms; you are supposed to find your way in to it, or out from it. The black dot in this case was Uncle Craig's body, and my whole concern was not to find my way to it but to avoid it. (42)

Just as he is 'the black dot' in the house as perceived by Del, the dead body is the dark spot in the house-like gothic text. And with the transformations of this dark spot – from the dead into the 'living body', from the fear of death into the (female) fear of birth (and of pregnancy) – gothic form transforms as well.

Alice Munro herself has likened a good story to a commodious house whose every room possesses an exterior door (Shields 1991, 22). She has also explored this idea in gendered terms, for example in her complex story 'Meneseteung': 'A man may keep his house decent, but he will never – if he is a proper man – do much to decorate it. Marriage forces him to live with more adornment as well as sentiment' (Munro 1990, 57). The implication of adornment, attributed to Almeda Roth's, the poet's house in 'Meneseteung', refers us back to the deep caves beneath the kitchen linoleum that end Del Jordan's story and that still present a most powerful image of feminine gothic writing. Alice Munro's commodious structure, then, the house-like neo-gothic texture, exceeds into a haunted internal labyrinth, or maze.

The gothic form of the text as maze that I have in mind here shapes a later neo-gothic text: Margaret Atwood's *Lady Oracle* (1976). In *Lady Oracle*, the processes of recalling, rejecting and (ironically) rewriting of feminine gothic form are self-reflexively repeated. The maze, with its multiplicity, choice and secret centre, seems to be an appropriate image for this further neo-gothic excess. During the process of writing *Lady Oracle*, Atwood has mused on her new interest in labyrinths: 'They were in fact a female religion. What you were supposed to find originally at the centre of the labyrinth was the Mother' (Varseveld 1975, 68). This view of the maze (as explored by gothicists like Kahane 1980, 343) connects back to *Lives of Girls and Women* where the mother's fantastic visions beyond the real and the natural order highlight not only the commodities and constraints of that order but also the intensely liberating effect of the gothic that celebrates excess. This emphasis is repeated in the maze-like texture of *Lady Oracle* with a complex twist, as fantasy can also take the shape of popular horror, 'escape literature'. The haunted house of feminine gothic fiction exceeds into a haunted maze – with multiple centres.

Notes

1 See Struthers's much-quoted interview 'The Real Material' (1983, esp. 26–9) and Munro's own important article 'What Is Real?' (1982b, esp. 5, 36). On the 'relationship between feeling and language' see Gold (1984, 1); on the Canadian context and her stories' 'probability and authenticity' see MacKendrick (1983, esp. 2); on the complexities of her realism, symbolism and presentation as sense and sensibility see Carscallen (1993, 5, 7); on her 'paradigmatic discourse' and her 'awareness of [the] textual dimension of the world' see Heble (1994, esp. 14); on the rejection of her (painterly) 'superrealism' see Cooke (1996, esp. 82). Convincingly, Garson shows synecdoche to be 'an important technical device by which Munro communicates the inscrutability of human experience' and 'the figure that constructs the Munrovian sublime' (1994, 424f).

2 For example: 'Somewhat ironically, it is the underpinning of autobiography in Munro's stories which lends them considerable validity as fiction' (Thacker 1988, 153–62; see also Hanly 1988, 163–74). Various book-length studies begin with a chapter on her life (Blodgett 1988, Rasporich 1990); others directly link her life and her art (Murphy 1993, 13); Papp-Carrington links Munro's description of herself as 'thin-skinned' to his recognition that 'the key words *shame* and *humiliation* recur with disquieting frequency in all six of Munro's books' (1989, 5). Illuminating, also because of personal interviews, is Ross (1992; on autobiographic traces in *Lives* see 69f).

3 Munro has characterised Southern Ontario in these terms: 'The part of the country I come from is absolutely Gothic' (Munro in Gibson 1973a, 248); critics who do discuss her gothicism mostly relate it to these spatial aspects; e.g., Atwood in her radio feature 'Southern Ontario Gothic' (1986).

4 York aligns Munro's 'fascination with paradox' with 'the very same paradoxes which surround photography' (York 1988, 33); Blodgett sees the 'photographic' as 'the dark core of her work' (1988, 6); Cooke explores the critical comparisons of Munro's texts to the photographs of Walker Evans and Diane Arbus (1996, 75f).

5 One critic writes: 'In a relatively brief novel, there are two drownings, four unattractively retarded people, one hermetic eccentric, one case of voodoo, one case of severe child abuse, one community associated with perpetual violence, two cases of neurotic religious zeal, one case of possible incest, rumors of bestiality, and one albino. With the exception of Marion Sherriff's drowning, this list extends only to page 124; things are

somewhat tamer after that' (Tautsky 1986, 68). Things might get tamer on the outside, but certainly not within Del, whose explorations then address emotions and physical experiences of gothic dimensions.

6 Hornung sees the autobiographic mode in this way as 'a new viable narrative medium' at a time when 'the steady decline of the concept of self is paralleled by the exhaustion of both autobiography and novel as narrative media' (1985, 71); he goes on to define it as characterising 'those contemporary texts which explore some aspects of the writer's self in a factual or fictional way and use narration as a form of recollection and presentation of earlier stages in life' (72). Godard has worked out the related traces of Munro's autobiographical and novelistic discourses in *Lives* (1984, esp. 57).

7 Munro here suggests what has become a contemporary feminist concern: women's collaboration with patriarchal power structures. Her irony in the aunts' appreciation of (female) negation anticipates women's collaboration with a totalitarian system in Atwood's *The Handmaid's Tale* (1985), where the 'Aunts' enact and enforce male control over women's lives, minds and bodies.

8 This half-conscious recognition on Del's part is a typical feature of contemporary feminine gothic. I think that Flannery O'Connor's story 'A Temple of the Holy Ghost' (1987 [1954], 236–48) aptly shows the implications: a twelve-year-old girl, growing up like Del in the country (a typical American Southern small town), comes to reject femininity as represented by her cousins' present and her mother's past lives at the convent, and by their views of the female body as spiritual 'temples of the holy ghost'. She dreams of a future as engineer or doctor, always emphasising head over body, a fantasy which is taken up in her Catholic-influenced dreams. The masculine principle, however, is no solution either, as male figures appear as either animal-like or stupid. Ironically, but with a typically gothic twist, the only positive image remains that of the hermaphrodite in a freak show, whom the girl herself never sees but who becomes a vision of the possibility of the incorporation of body and spirit as well as of the female and the male.

9 Furthermore, in both texts the boys' mothers play an important role as protectors of their sons against their girlfriends and as instances of perpetuation of a double standard for male and female lives that greatly inhibits the girls' sense of self. In this way the boys' mothers are juxtaposed to the complicated, albeit less conservative, narrators' mother-figures, who are themselves shown to be victims of this double standard. Mrs Willard's simile of 'the man as arrow and the woman as the place where the arrow shoots off from' is a good example, and so is Mrs Storey's 'matter-of-fact' disclaimer of a marriage that could hinder her son's career; both of these images are secretly rejected by Esther and Del, who have very different, if unspoken, plans for themselves. Both want to be writers, and their stories gothically represent the making of the female artist, respectively in the American 1950s of McCarthyism and the feminine

mystique and the Canadian 1940s of isolated rural life. Like Del, Esther experiences adolescence as horrific (although she is already at college and her story is essentially that of one summer, told in complicated flashbacks). Esther faces a whole series of female anti-examples, girlfriends who are too adapted to the restricting ideal or too 'liberated' from it to succeed in what they want from life, mothers in suburbs who have no life of their own, professional women in women's magazine publishing who seem superficial and cold, women of all ages who have been pronounced 'crazy', a famous writer (Philomena Guinea) who writes formula romances. Like Del, Esther has no community of women with desires similar to her own; for both of them, this is what the generic gothic isolation means, and what makes them feel incapable, insufficient, monstrous.

10 Both texts also relate the discovery of love and sexuality to another discourse: psychoanalysis. *Lives* shows the traces of the pop-Freudianism of the 1940s and 1950s that *The Bell Jar* partly reacts against (although Plath's text also attacks institutionalised psychiatry and its practices). Del's discovery of her body in front of the mirror is related to idealised love in her romantic fantasies, as she expresses in front of Fern's three-way mirror (127) or in ironic recognitions like 'Love is not for the undepilated' (150). Some of this irony is directed against 'a famous New York psychiatrist, a disciple of Freud' (150) and his reductive, sexist interpretations of women's ideas when looking at the moon or at art, which are discarded in Del's reflections. But her misery is clear too: 'I wanted men to love me, *and* I wanted to think of the universe when I looked at the moon. I felt trapped, stranded; it seemed there had to be a choice where there couldn't be a choice' (150).

11 I would like to refer here to the abundance of criticism on *Lives'* intertextualisation of James Joyce's *The Portait of the Artist as a Young Man* (see Martin 1979, 120–26; Struthers 1975, 32–46; Perrakis 1982, 61–7; Blodgett 1988, 37, 39; Rasporich 1990, 51; Carscallen 1993, 13f; Garson 1994, 416–18, 424). Godard convincingly shows that 'the opposition of "*Lives*" to "Portrait" as well as the sexual difference of "Girls and Women" to "Man" points to a *bildungsroman* written *against* Joyce' (1984, 65–8) and finds further revisionary links to *Ulysses* (69). Moss is virtually alone in seeing no literary allusions in Munro's work (1989, 8).

12 Atwood and Munro have both thematised the desire for filliation. Munro's latest example is the story 'Meneseteung' (1990 [1988]) in which the narrator/writer discovers and reconstructs the story of a – typically three-named – nineteenth-century writer. That story is told in the present tense; it starts from a photograph and other documents, as well as from the writer's found work. The moving story ends with a sense of its own gaps that only enforces the recognition of the overwhelming desire to write the other woman's life-story: 'I may have got it wrong. I don't know if she ever took laudanum. Many ladies did. I don't know if she ever made grape jelly' (73).

Chapter 5

Exceeding even gothic texture: Margaret Atwood and *Lady Oracle*

Re-experiencing gothicism: parody

'For years I'd been trying to get love and terror into the same title' says Joan Foster, the narrator/protagonist of *Lady Oracle* (1976, 32): a writer of popular gothic romances who is, at the moment of the quoted reflection, in pursuit of a working title for her latest work. Her expertise in the basic emotional trajectory of the gothic, thus early established, suggests a self-conscious treatment of the form's layers of love – and layers of plot. Moreover, the focus on an artist figure displays the strong interest in the creative processes that has marked Margaret Atwood's varied and wide-ranging work, especially her fiction, and that evokes – like Alice Munro's stories – the postmodern awareness of the paradoxical relations of creative process and artistic product. Linda Hutcheon has called Atwood the 'epitome of this postmodern contradiction' in *The Canadian Postmodern* (1988b, 138). In *Lady Oracle*, this contradiction is self-consciously played out in terms of a gothic paradigm: the formula of the popular gothics that Joan is in the process of writing but also the narrative conventions of the feminine gothic as they come to structure her own life- (and love-) story, making her a 'product' of the gothic plot. And it works, as we shall see, towards a certain 'repetition' of the experience of writing/reading the gothic, and by 'using and abusing' its conventions in a way that Hutcheon has called 'repetition with difference' or 'a reverential parody'.

'A Gothic Romance' was an early subtitle for *Lady Oracle* (Atwood Papers, Box 23: 'Early Drafts'). Indeed, a structural outline of the story can easily be rendered in gothic paraphrase: a young female figure comes to a lonely house in Italy, to escape from the complications of her life in Canada. In the isolation of this house now develops the generic paranoia of the gothic protagonist (Radway 1977, 158), as the new surroundings (her Italian landlord and the village Terremoto) as well as the past (somebody has followed her) seem to reach out for her. The paranoia induces romantic yearnings for her Canadian husband as knight-to-the-rescue. This outline characterises the narrative situation of the speaking subject in Parts I and V of the novel. In the embedded Parts II to IV, she tells – in the fashion of a *Bildungs-* and *Künstlerroman* – her life-story from childhood to married life. And she tells it by clearly enacting gothic narrative conventions, most notably that of the generic recollecting voice that periodically enforces the 'truthfulness' of the tale. For example, the occasional (but systematic) temporal prolepses into her present situation work this way; as Gérard Genette explains: 'Prolepses ... are testimonies to the intensity of the present memory, and to some extent authenticate the narrative of the past' (1980, 69). However, this narrative strategy also points to one major departure from the gothic convention, in which the tale is told from the secure position of the survivor of all horrors. By contrast, Joan speaks from a typically gothic situation in Italian exile – thus intensifying the generic effect of 'provoking unease' (Carter 1974, 133) and a sense of process rather than that of an ending.

This example of how a narrative convention is treated in *Lady Oracle* suggests what the structural outline misses – an implicit critical distance and an important aspect of Atwood's style in general and of this text in particular: her ironic voice. If Atwood rewrites the gothic in *Lady Oracle*, she does so with an ironic double-voice that allows for self-reflexivity and an implicit critique. That this voice has firstly a profound effect on the gothic's 'affective form' (Haggarty 1989, 8) and transforms it into a comedy, becomes clear from the novel's opening:

> I planned my death carefully; unlike my life, which meandered along from one thing to another, despite my feeble attempts to control it ... The trick was to disappear without a trace, leaving behind me the shadow of a corpse, a shadow everyone would mistake for solid reality. At first I thought I'd managed it. (3)

This opening initiates the ironic play with the gothic pattern. While instantly evoking one basic emotion structuring the typical gothic

romance, the fear of death (Rosowski 1981, 87), it works to undercut
that emotion as it installs it. The idea of death as self-constructed and
-controlled performance, does not evoke threat, but rather ridicule, an
effect enhanced by the concluding hint that the performance might
have failed. On the other hand, it suggests a takeover of destiny; Joan
seems to assume an uncanny authority over her life (and the 'end'
thereof), to construct it as she needs it (like a plot); her wish to change
the past (6) further reflects this desire for control. At the same time
the laconic narrating voice provides a disillusioning comment on such
desires as doomed and on the chosen destiny as failed; what should be
a new beginning, a rebirth, abounds in metaphors of murder, death
and destruction. The dark humour here continues the typical
neo-gothic tone already displayed by *Lives of Girls and Women*. But
Atwood's ironic double-voice effects more. It becomes the marker for
yet another aspect that positions *Lady Oracle* also at the intersection
of postmodernist and feminist discourses: the 'use and abuse' of narrative conventions, of 'similarity with a difference', that marks parody
and its self-reflexive explorations of traditional, canonical, dominant
literary forms (see Hutcheon 1987, 226). Parody has thus become
prominent in feminist ironic explorations of 'male' discourses and
genres. In *Lady Oracle* this strategy is extended: it does not take off
from a 'dominant discourse' but from a marginalised – feminine –
form, a form with a strong web of filliation. It thus draws attention to
this phenomenon in the same way as does Ellen Moers's chapter
'Female Gothic' in *Literary Women*, which appeared in the same year
as Atwood's novel: 1976.

Critics have been quick to read *Lady Oracle* as a parody (e.g.,
Sandler 1977, 157; McMillan 1988, 48), after its obvious gothic trivi-
alities had first provoked confused reviews announcing Atwood's
literary decline (e.g., Lehmann-Haupt 1976, Tyler 1976). These readings usually emphasise the comedy traditionally associated with the
term without considering the implicit ironic critique. For example,
Sybil Korff Vincent, speaking from a gothicist position, praises Atwood
for having created 'a new genre: the comic/gothic ... As women move
out into the crowded streets of contemporary life, the piercing scream
of the terrified gothic heroine seems to be giving way to the nervous
giggle of the uncertain comic/gothic heroine' (Vincent 1983, 163).
However, the gothic has early been self-reflexive and comic (see
Haggarty 1989, 82); and the 'nervous giggle' seems a phenomenon of

contemporary horror-comics that Atwood poetically parodies in *Murder in the Dark* (1983) and in *Power Politics* (1980). In the 1990s, more postmodern perspectives have influenced the many book-length studies, collections and essays on Atwood's work; here, *Lady Oracle* appears as: self-conscious 'Plot against the Gothic Romance Plot' (Bouson 1993, 63–85); textual 'funhouse' with a 'bitter parody' of gothic romance with 'tragi-comic' effect (Staels 1995, esp. 103); or 'instructive parody' with deadly serious humour (Worthington 1996, 287) – to give a brief overview.[1] Rather, it seems, *Lady Oracle*'s relationship to the gothic recalls and continues Jane Austen's parodic gothic *Northanger Abbey* (for a detailed comparison see Rao 1993, 28–32). Atwood herself has emphasised this affiliation (Becker: interview), and I think that, as in Catherine Morland's story, there is much more than a 'nervous giggle' to Joan Foster's twentieth-century terrors. And the 'uses and abuses' of gothic conventions and possibilities in *Lady Oracle* (as in *Northanger Abbey*) point to an effect that transcends the ridiculing as well as the instructing functions of parody.

The narrative technique of installing and subsequently ironically deconstructing gothic details and structure recalls a form that Linda Hutcheon has called a 'reverential parody' (1985, 32). In this sense, a parodic text is defined as 'a formal synthesis, an incorporation of a background text into itself. But the textual doubling of parody (unlike pastiche, allusion, quotation, and so on) functions to mark difference' (53). Ridicule is a possible effect of this difference, but only as 'one of a range of possible ethos or intended responses' (67). Rather, 'reverence' comes in 'as underlying the intention of parody … Like Pope's mock epics … many parodies today do not ridicule the background texts but use them as standards by which to place the contemporary under scrutiny' (57).

Read in this sense, *Lady Oracle* rewrites the conventions – and repeats the experience – of feminine gothicism to explore its possibilities in contemporary female literary culture, not just to ridicule it. However, that culture of the mid-1970s was precisely marked by both the women's movement and the 'gothic boom'. The popular 'gothics', as we have seen, demonstrate the transformation of an already highly conventionalised form into a formula – ultimately reaffirming 'love triumphant' despite the implicit disturbing emotional 'transformation from love into fear' (Modleski 1982, 60). Thus, they offer an ambiguous *escape* (Modleski 1982, 435) – but also a vicarious experience of

power that Atwood calls 'lion-taming' (Becker: interview). Both moves
are directed against patriarchal oppression, which was loudly attacked
by the feminism of the time. These terms perfectly characterise the
scope of *Lady Oracle*'s repetition, as it obviously places the gothic as
a popular cultural phenomenon and its effects under scrutiny. Its
protagonist successfully writes such 'gothics', aware that 'love was a
big seller' (32), but her own story also teases out gothic possibilities
and horrors, as Joan herself becomes a contemporary version of a
'beauty in distress'. This narrative exploration of (female) popular
culture shows Atwood's parody also as part of the contemporary attack
on the 'Great Divide' – the high modernist 'categorical distinction
between high art and mass culture' (Huyssen 1986, viii). And it
suggests the development of neo-gothic form, from Munro's ways of
gothicising female experience – into the text as house – towards
Atwood's further elaborations of self-reflexive gothicising repetitions
– into the text as maze.

Atwood's parodic 'repetition' of gothic texture involves a thorough
system of inscribing and undercutting its popular as well as its traditional conventions. This starts with the above-quoted opening. What
is successfully 'installed' here, in faithful repetition of the gothic
system, is the introduction of a mystery: a gothic feature since
Radcliffe's aptly named *The Mysteries of Udolpho*, and a decisive
element in popular gothics, as Phyllis Whitney's classic 'Writing the
Gothic Novel' shows: 'From the first, there must be a sense of mystery, urgency, of growing threat, of fear that amounts to terror ... the
building of suspense is all important. How well this element is handled
is the test of a good gothic novel' (1967, 13). The mystery of Joan
Foster's staged death is revealed at the end of Part IV as a fake drowning in Lake Ontario, which she has arranged to escape – from her
husband, whom she suspects of blackmailing her! This revelation is a
comic comment, enhancing the irony in Joan's romantic yearning for
that very husband to come to her rescue in Italy. But more importantly, this mystery solution also reveals a decisive gothic element in
the 'autobiographical' part of the narrative, which it ironically turns
on one level into a (self-reflexive) version of the popular 'suspicious
marriage plot' (Mussell 1984, 45). A mixture of narrative forms is
indicated in the opening, where Joan announces she will tell her story
as she sees it. This evokes that other important form of female writing

of the 1970s: the realist feminist confession as derived from feminist practices like consciousness-raising. Now her story paradoxically appears as a confession in tone but a gothic in form. Joan's expertise in popular gothic adds another layer, as her own embedded bestsellers become another part of that story. So, too, does her embedded gothic and ironic high-modernist poem 'Lady Oracle', which becomes yet another level of 'telling her story'. These various forms of narrative and of the (parodied) generic gothic layers and embeddings will raise questions as to 'confessional' versus 'gothic' representation and, again, as to the narrative construction of female subjectivity. And they already point us to the notion of 'hyperbole' in Carter's definition of gothic and thus to the 'excess' of Atwood's neo-gothicism.

Yet another level reinforces this recognition of formal excess: it is tempting to read the opening of *Lady Oracle* also as a parody of the reader's position when reading the romance: Joan, too, has staged a 'disappearing act', escaped from her chaotic life to Italy (!) to now look at it – and tell it – 'from the other side'. This recalls the opening of *Jane Eyre*: simultaneously being alienated from the family by her surrogate mother's interdiction and alienating herself by withdrawing beyond the drawing- and breakfast-rooms into the window-seat, the 'spoken subject' Jane (Silverman 1983, 47), as we have seen, is introduced in complicity with the reader (Spivak 1989, 180). Similarly, in Joan Foster's exile, the reader becomes her accomplice in recreating her life-story. Thus the gothic narrative move for inclusion of the reader is 'repeated'; and the intertextual complicity with a feminine gothic classic displays the reinforcing function of the reverential parody: it *continues* this tradition of women's writing. However, whereas the disillusioned Jane's gothic journey arrives in her famous apostrophe 'Reader, I married him', in *Lady Oracle* the disillusioned Joan's gothic journey circles around the recognition that '[l]ove was the pursuit of shadows' (315). The gothic romance's 'love triumphant' becomes the target of the feminist parody's critique and of neo-gothic *deconstruction*.

As 'repetition with a difference' *Lady Oracle* employs and exploits the gothic conventions (thus continuing them) to comment critically on their possibilities as well as on their problems (thus deconstructing them). It functions as authorised transgression in Linda Hutcheon's terms:

> parody's transgressions ultimately remain authorised – authorised by the
> very norm it seeks to subvert. Even in mocking, parody reinforces; in for-

mal terms, it inscribes the mocked conventions onto itself, thereby guaranteeing their continued existence. It is in this sense that parody is the custodian of the artistic legacy, defining not only where art is, but where it has come from. (75)

Lady Oracle's neo-gothicism in these terms reinforces feminine gothic form since Radcliffe as well as the popular 'gothics' of the time by incorporating their conventions – thus continuing a feminine form into the late twentieth century. Its critical distance – by ironically undercutting these conventions in the next step – addresses especially the containing ideologies of romance, love, and (media) images of an ideal femininity. This effects an aesthetic as well as a cultural critique, an emancipatory postmodern move beyond narcissistic playfulness.

Formally speaking, the development in gothic texture has been suggested as transformation from the haunted house of gothic fiction into the gothic text as maze. The concept of the maze or labyrinth is not only another gothic theme or 'stock device', repeated as *locus classicus* in *Lady Oracle* and consequently re-read in formal terms. It is also a particularly suggestive concept here when seen in its mythical dimensions and in gendered perspective: Ariadne's thread leads the way out of the labyrinth – that she, as Arachne, herself has created (see Nancy K. Miller 1986, 284). In terms of textuality, this thread can be seen as a line through the text: 'Ariadne's thread', J. Hillis Miller writes in his essay of that title, 'is both the labyrinth and a means of safely retracing the labyrinth' (1978, 156). However, following the line means encountering numerous complications that Miller conceptualises as 'repetition': the emphasis here is on the repetition of the maze through the thread. In the case of *Lady Oracle*, as we shall see, such creative repetition works to exceed the gothic excess that always already constitutes the dynamics of gothic texture. And the parodic repetition with critical – and excessive – difference takes off from what suggests itself as an unfixed, paradoxical 'centre' of the maze, from what has marked the feminine gothic as interrogative texture: the female subject.

The subject-in-excess

'There is never only one, of anyone' – this reflection is one of the premises for Elaine Risley's autobiographical recollections in *Cat's Eye* (1989 [1988], 6), and it recalls not only one of the deepest gothic

– as well as twentieth-century – scepticisms of a 'whole' individual, but also the numerous split heroines and doubles in the classic feminine gothic. *Cat's Eye*, often considered Atwood's most personal book, is also closest to *Lady Oracle*'s gothicism in this sense. Almost viciously parodic of such ongoing – postmodernist! feminist! – doubling and splitting is her later novel *The Robber Bride* (1993) with its four different but interrelated female types and their different but shared melodramatic desire for a femininity which they do not have. *Lady Oracle* reads like a self-conscious exploration of Elaine Risley's reflection – and of the related narrative convention – which perfectly characterises its complicated subjectivity. Joan Foster is not one but many women; she has several selves which, in best gothic fashion, are differently named: Joan Delacourt, the fat child and teenager; Joan Foster, the wife of Arthur Foster – and secret lover of the Royal Porcupine; Joan Foster the cult figure and successful author of 'Lady Oracle', Louisa K. Delacourt, clandestine author of 'Costume Gothics' – to name only some of the 'conscious ones'. Joan's creation, recognition and treatment of these 'selves' and the related multiplying processes becomes one of the trajectories of her story; and much of her activity is concerned with ordering these selves by means of separation: 'I always tried to keep my two names and identities as separate as possible' (33).[2]

Separation is, as we have seen, on various levels the key to the construction of subjectivity; the recognition of the 'I' as separate from the 'you' constitutes the recognition of 'self' as opposed to 'other' as shown by linguists (Benveniste) as well as by psychoanalysts (Lacan). This (visual, acoustic, linguistic) process is founded in the disruption of the dyadic unity with the mother and it is different for male and female subjectivity-formation (see Chodorow 1978; de Lauretis 1984; Silverman 1983); moreover, it produces the state of 'abjection' in Kristeva's sense of the term. As we have seen, separation/abjection structures feminine gothic texture, motivating the mirror-plot of female desire. It also qualifies those aspects of the horrific narrative events that are related to the female subject's pain (at the separation from the mother) and desire for a continuing self-in-relation represented in the romance plot. This desire is fulfilled in the popular gothics by the hero's 'nurturing love' (Flax 1990; Mussell 1984; Modleski 1982) replacing the lost mother love. By contrast, it is confronted and questioned in classic feminine gothic form, in which the split subject effectively challenges the dominance of the love plot.

As the multiple subject of *Lady Oracle* suggests, Atwood's parody takes off from such issues of separation and thus from the basic conflict structuring feminine gothic texture – and in these terms, Joan's complicated self reads like that form's split subject driven to an excess! Keeping in mind Belsey's distinction between the conscious and unconscious aspects of the split subject, the above-mentioned 'conscious' selves and personae are 'mirrored' by another set of selves that are linked with the unconscious and the repressed: the 'Fat Lady' and the 'Little Mermaid'. These latter aspects of Joan's subjectivity suggest the aspects of the 'monstrous-feminine' that highlight cultural border-construction as well as the female subject on the borderline, like the 'affiliated' feminine gothic 'monsters' from Frankenstein's creature to Jane Eyre's 'Am I a monster!' (267). *Lady Oracle* thus continues the gothic's feminist critique of the monstrous dimensions of feminine ideals; it 'repeats' them, not only effectively to highlight the hidden horrors of the heroine but also to emphasise the close correspondences of female lives and gothic stories. Like Mary Shelley, Charlotte Brontë and Jean Rhys, and moreover self-reflexively evoking these writers' works, Atwood thus uses the gothic to 'engender' her subject as female. Her ironic voice again works to mark critical difference as Joan's (and other Atwood heroines') confrontations with the 'monstrous' can produce liberating laughter, thus radically discarding it as yet another constructed, constraining aspect of Woman. And as we have seen, this 'monstrous-feminine' is deeply linked with (gothic) excess.

Excess in *Lady Oracle* is introduced by Joan's striking excess of body as a young girl – which comes metaphorically to structure her story: the (female) body but also the (feminine) body of the text. In thematic terms, the female body and its dimensions of excess come to be associated with the monstrous as typical gothic excess of *le propre* (Cixous) – a 'proper' femininity.[3] Furthermore, the monstrous is related to the mother's body: her (pro)creative powers – feared by men – and the related separation, abjection – feared by the daughter. The separation from m/other is important to Joan's specific subject processes as an adult; her gesture towards order and control of her 'chaotic' life (as characterised in the opening) – namely the separation of *herself* into her private, married self; her professional, writing self; her secret, fantasy self – is a gesture that repeats her mother's obsessions with order and control of herself (the clothes) and her family (the house). As a consequence, as I would like to show in the following section, not only different versions of monstrosity are compared, but the notion of physical excess is also repeated in terms of texture.

Excess of body thus also structures *Lady Oracle*'s neo-gothic form. Male writers have compared the female body to a 'labyrinthine reservoir' (Updike). And the labyrinth, as has been suggested, is a good term for Atwood's neo-gothic text with its own excess and multiple (ironic/comic/critical) repetitions. Joan's separating of her 'large' self occurs largely for the benefit of husband Arthur (who 'would not understand') and is thus, in formal terms, related to her love plot. That fragmentation of the other is one of the violent, destructive aspects of amorous discourse has been highlighted by Kristeva's 'x-ray through love' and has always structured gothic 'tales of love' with their substitution of terror for love (Fiedler 1982; Restuccia 1986); Joan's separate selves thus suggest the parodic repetition with critical difference in these terms. Her creation of various personae and the resulting multiple subjectivity constructs yet another neo-gothic excess: beyond the containments of a 'proper' (even gothic) heroine's plot – and beyond the related ideology.

Exceeding the proper feminine

The idea of Joan as subject-in-excess recalls the feminist/post-structuralist emphasis on the dynamics of the speaking subject. Kristeva has emphasised that the subject-in-process is especially important for the construction of female subjectivity: 'Because in social, sexual, and symbolic experiences, being a woman has always provided a means to another end, to becoming something else: a subject-in-the-making, a subject on trial' (1981, 167). This 'hyperbolic' subject-in-process is put on trial because it engages with its own otherness. This image accurately describes some of the processes that 'engender' Joan in *Lady Oracle*, who finds herself 'unable to stay together' (Hite 1989, 146) but also has the need to separate and 'categorise by absolutes' (Godard 1987a, 22). Atwood's parody here exploits the gothic narrative conventions of gender construction – not without thriving in their own 'gothic excesses' – and suggests that this subject-in-excess is a reaction to, or maybe a transgression of (Kristeva 1986, 29), the feminine ideal of the time: *Woman* as produced by totalising discourses of femininity.

The beginning of the text abounds with such totalising discourses in a very contemporary way: visions of various feminine ideals are presented in contrast to Joan's sense of self. In rapid succession she visualises herself, first as incarnation of the contemporary media image of the summer beauty: 'a Mediterranean splendour, golden-brown, striding with laughing teeth into an aqua sea' (3) – for which she lacks the suntan lotion ('without it I'd burn and freckle'). Second, she sees herself as graceful romantic heroine on a nightly balcony – undercut by the actual balcony's banality: 'It wasn't the kind of balcony a man would stand under playing a lute and yearning or clamber up bearing a rose in his teeth or a stiletto in his sleeve' (4). And the last vision is of being 'rescued' by Arthur – undercut by the image of what he would look like, 'lanky Arthur ... uncertain, stony-faced, rescue-minded, in his uncomfortable shoes and well-aged underwear' (5), fulfilling the part not as mysterious knight-in-shining-armour but as well-known husband. The tone is set. However ironically undermined, what appears is the triangular reference system that Joan has developed for herself, or rather, that has been developed for her and that will now structure her story: the beauty ideal of the time as produced by the media; the romantic heroine of the contemporary 'mass-produced fantasies for women', and a male suitor or saviour figure to match. Ironically subverted as they are, stripped of their fantasy glamour, Joan still longs for these images to materialise, as her story shows. Their failure to do so fills her with feelings of inadequacy – and it fills her story with self-deprecating irony.

Images of the ideal feminine as well as female fantasies have traditionally formed feminine gothic texts – especially in terms of gender construction. In the popular romance they function similarly and work most successfully, as Phyllis Whitney (1967) and other authors have shown, considering female readers' identification with a heroine who introduces herself as not quite adequate at first – only to show that, despite these inadequacies, she will have her happy ending; her fantasies will come true. However, in *Lady Oracle* such subtle insufficiencies are soon exaggerated into a grotesque – and ridiculous – self-image, even in a most sentimental moment:

> I never learned to cry with style, silently, the pearl-shaped tears rolling down my cheeks from wide luminous eyes, as on the covers of *True Love* comics, leaving no smears or streaks ... As it was I snorted, my eyes turned the colour and shape of cooked tomatoes, my nose ran, I clenched my fists, I moaned, I was embarrassing, finally I was amusing, a figure of fun. The grief was always real but it came out as a burlesque of grief. (6)

And the sentimentality comes out as a burlesque of sentimentality, one might add. The self-deprecation that is at work here – and at other decisive points in the plot – ruins the popular gothic effect, the possibility for instant identification with the suffering subject.[4] However, what is at work here is a double-voiced self-deprecation, an irony which 'allows one to suggest that what is being ironically presented as inferior has its own implied superiority' (Hutcheon 1991, 6). Joan's self-deprecations seem to function this way; they effect a defamiliarisation that reveals her as 'inadequate' only with regard to a gaze or controlling instance which positions her as 'other', inadequate to the implied standards – and the irony draws attention to the *construction* of the 'inadequacy'. What then are these standards Joan cannot live up to: female images on covers of *True Love* comics?

Those images of a proper femininity offered to Joan throughout the text are mostly drawn from the media and popular culture. They are, fittingly for the urban, postwar context in which she is shown to grow up (specific time references in the text allow one to figure out 1942 as the year of her birth), related to the rise of an affluent consumer society, fixed on media, advertising, Hollywood melodramas, women's magazines – and romances.[5] Significantly, these images, constructing *le propre*, are just as 'other' (in de Beauvoir's sense) in this culture as (real) women are, and they are shown as options for women *not* as a separate, fantasy world but as a possibility within reality. In *Lady Oracle*, all female figures are affected by this model, as is shown by their fantasies – which Joan, as successful writer of costume gothics, reflects. She becomes a sympathetic expert in her readers' fantasies: 'when it came to fantasy lives I was a professional, whereas they were merely amateurs' (241); this means that she relates women's fantasies most importantly to the 'inadequacies' she knows herself only too well: 'Now I could play fairy godmother to them, despite their obvious defects ... I could turn them from pumpkins to pure gold' (35). Joan herself will discover that there is a *propre* for various stages and aspects of female life as well as for her various selves (the private as well as the professional) in terms of beauty, social status and, growing into the 1960s' context, even in terms of politics and feminism.

That such a feminine ideal can be reached is early shown to Joan: in the figure of her mother. Frances Delacourt's 'costume' (the navy-blue suit, the gloves) and activities (the house decorations, the parties) make her the perfect 1950s Woman, the embodiment of the 'feminine mystique' to the world. And a 'monster' to her daughter. The theme of the mother–daughter relationship in *Lady Oracle* exploits the related generic horrors: Joan as the unwanted, unloved child, unsure of who her father is, both tormented by and tormenting the mother – her *real* mother, not a surrogate mother as in the nineteenth-century gothic. But it also foregrounds – in what I think is a typically neo-gothic move – the mother's paradoxical function almost as another 'totalising discourse' in those 'engendering processes' that construct the horrific, the monstrous and thus point to the gap between the 'ideal feminine' and 'women'.

The beautiful mother is shown throughout the story as a woman sadly trapped within the ideal she embodies (Joan only realises this after her mother's death). Read this way, the mother-figure in *Lady Oracle* recalls Atwood's 'Rapunzel Syndrome' – her (fairytale) image for a sad but typical female figure in Canadian Literature. Atwood's terms for defining this figure recall feminine gothic form – and its dimension that relates the woman and the house: 'In fact, in Canada *Rapunzel and the House are the same*. These heroines have internalised the values of their culture to such an extent that they have become their own prison' (1972, 209). The 'order' of Frances Delacourt's house – in which the daughter perceives a sterile containment just like the mother's suit/gloves and figure – and its disintegration after her death (202) reinforce this link of female body and house. Joan's reading of Tennyson's 'The Lady of Shalott' – the image of a woman enclosed in a tower returns in her own poem 'Lady Oracle' – is a typical 'repetition' of this link. And her own (to some provoking, to others endearing) chaotic house later signifies her own excess in these terms. This link of body and house that Atwood evokes in *Lady Oracle* not only finds another 'repetition' in its own gothic form, but also anticipates the formal development towards the 'shedding' of the house's shell that we shall find in *No Fixed Address*. In *Lady Oracle*, the body–house–text link self-reflexively highlights a very gothic view of femininity and writing. This brings us back to the mother-figure in the text.

It is a striking effect of Atwood's neo-gothicism that the mother is perceived as both victim and victimiser, as she ironically – and typically – educates the (obese) daughter in the same terms, thus perpetuating exactly those structures that have been victimising her. This seeming paradox is a typical effect of patriarchal containment, as Barbara Godard has shown: 'In … *Lady Oracle* we are shown how mothers raise their daughters in rejection and turn them towards men' (26). This works, as Godard goes on to show, by an 'education [that] consists of confining girls in the conventions of manners and in getting them "hooked on plots" ... appropriate for this life, namely those with "happy endings," fairy-tales of magic metamorphoses' (26). And it shows, that 'this is the only legacy mothers can leave their daughters in a patriarchy which has made motherhood thus monstrous' (29).

The parodic rewriting of this typical feminine gothic conflict in *Lady Oracle* also extends the (defamiliarising, disturbing) gothic effect of destroying feminine myths. The liberating destruction of the myth of the naturally good mother (which Ellen Moers has exposed in *Frankenstein*) recurs, but extended to include a further critique of an assumed automatic 'sisterhood' that was, at the time, strongly proclaimed by feminism. Atwood has been one of the first feminist writers to acknowledge the problematics of yet another idealisation of 'Woman/hood', self-made this time, as exerting pressure on women who in the present state of power relations are still on the side of the powerless. The horrific side of 'that certain thing called the girlfriend' (Atwood) that has deeply marked *Cat's Eye* – and, clearly, its more gothic aspects – is anticipated in *Lady Oracle*'s images of the cruel Brownies. In both novels, the test of girls' friendships culminates in a metaphorical live-burial in a typical Toronto ravine; both tests are resolved according to gothic conventions. In *Cat's Eye* the girl is saved by a supernatural appearance of the Virgin Mary; in *Lady Oracle* she is rescued by a male figure who could be both good and evil. Both girls are then found by their mothers who (for different reasons) are oblivious to their daughters' girlfriend problems. These scenes are also good examples of how Atwood's parody here uses the gothic and its effects to address such female myths. The result is a change in the classic feminine gothic's (interrogative) form: what has been a covert 'mirror-text' (Belsey) of female desire, in *Lady Oracle* becomes one of outspoken conflict, metonymically 'spread' over Joan's story. At the same time, 'mirroring' becomes an image for projections but also a narrative technique of this multi-layered text (Godard 1983). And the mirror itself becomes the site for the classic female gothic trajectory of the female (the mother's) body; monstrosity and creativity as well as separation/abjection.

◆

'My mother was a monster' – this recognition of little Joan occurs in the dreamt 'repetition' of the often-witnessed scene of 'Mother put[ting] on her face' (69) in front of her triple mirror. The mother's vanity-table is the place of the girl's desire to be like the mother, a beautiful woman with the matching accessories: 'I was fascinated by her collection of cosmetics and implements: lipsticks, rouges, perfume in dainty bottles which I longed to have' (68). But it is also – in typically gothic conjunction of opposing emotions – a place for her horror at the procedure: 'some of the things she did seemed to be painful; for instance, she would cover the space between her eyebrows with what looked like brown glue, which she heated in a little pot, then tear it off, leaving a red patch' (68). No magic metamorphosis into the ideal beauty here; rather a painful, and moreover dissatisfying, process: 'Instead of making her happier, these sessions appeared to make her sadder, as if she saw behind the mirror some fleeting image she was unable to capture or duplicate' (70). That the looking-glass shows a different image from that desired by the woman in front of it has become an important metaphor in feminist art for the discrepancy between Woman (as produced by the male gaze) and women. That this discrepancy is cast in terms of the monstrous is a typical move of the feminine gothic. The inadequacy that the mother might feel, and that the girl surely senses in her dream about this process of putting on the face of Woman, is gothically exaggerated in the daughter's image of the mother's face in her triple mirror: 'instead of three reflections she had three actual heads which rose from her towelled shoulders on three separate necks' (70). This is a projection on the daughter's part (see Godard 1983, 33) and it is in one way related to the male gaze that has produced that unreachable ideal image;[6] the mother's efforts to reach that image result in the recognition that she (her face) is always the same, in spite of her seeming (three-headed) multiplicity. Joan's later multiplying can be seen as taking off from this recognition and as exceeding this sameness of the mother's image. However, the 'monstrous mother' is also related to the realm of power structures – as the mother, always able to overpower her daughter, here is also shown to be on the side of the powerless. And this is exactly the complicated condition that signifies the 'semiotic', the Imaginary, mother–child relationship in Kristeva's terms.

It is thus tempting to read the scene in front of the triple mirror as the place of that boundary-subjectivity that Kristeva has described as locus for abjection. The boundary, the borderline she describes (in twentieth-century literature and especially in Céline's work) as

> setting up not a beyond but two terms, face to face, each judging the other, in turn, and both reducing in the end to the same abjection. On the one side, what is base; on the other, the speech that I hold forth and that has me in its hold. Nature, the body, the inside. Facing the spirit, others, appearances. Truth being on the base side, a barren side, without makeup, without seeming, rotten and dead, full of discomfort and sickening horror.' (1982, 143)

In this sense, mother and daughter are both on the borderline of abjection in front of the mirror, each of them desiring 'the speech ... that has [them] in its hold', 'the spirit, others, appearances' – the mother in the image behind the mirror she desires, the daughter in the image of the mother she desires – but each of them having to realise the 'Nature ... Truth ... on the base side', and the related horror in the recognition of separation. Thus, in this scene, Atwood's parodic gothic foregrounds those processes of subject-formation that in popular gothics have been implied but not spelt out, thus effecting the reconciling fantasy ending as female self-in-relation.

A later scene echoes this borderline situation: adult Joan in front of her own triple mirror, on the point of her 'automatic writing' experiment – 'facing the spirit, others, appearances', this time within the specific position of the female artist – or rather, at the point of creation (by separation) of this female artist-self. In this context again the mirror is an important site, as Gilbert and Gubar have shown, speaking from the same 'stage' of (1970s') feminism:

> Before the woman writer can journey through the looking glass toward literary autonomy, she must come to terms with the images on the surface of the glass, with, that is, those mythic masks male artists have fastened over her human face both to lessen their dread of their 'inconstancy' and – by identifying her with the eternal types they have themselves invented – to possess her more thoroughly ... women must 'kill' the aesthetic ideal through which they themselves have been 'killed' into art. (1979, 15–17)

What Atwood herself calls her 'parody of the creative process' (Atwood, in Sandler 1977, 17) relates this metaphor of feminist criticism to the crucial confrontation of desire and horror of mother and daughter; it thus rewrites the early 'female gothic' association of mothering a baby with mothering art, or of giving birth with artistic processes of creativity. By contrast, masculine images of the creative process are often related to sexual potency (see the Betsy episode in Ronald Sukenick's *The Death of the Novel* (1969)).

Joan's automatic writing experiment is inspired by the spiritualists' lessons that provide much of the 'supernatural' in Atwood's parody. As she 'goes into the mirror' (only one of a whole series of allusions to Lewis Carroll's *Alice*), she feels a presence that she later realises is her mother. Showalter has emphasised the guidance of another female figure for the female writer to write herself into existence in 'the wild zone' behind the mirror (1985, 263), and this female figure has long been associated with the mother; Virginia Woolf famously reflected 'We think back through our mothers if we are women.' *Lady Oracle*'s exploration of creativity also recalls such feminist positions; it even suggests a border-blur between fictional and critical feminisms of the 1970s.

If the creative process is parodied in this scene, its 'product' sets in motion the procedures of criticism – which are treated with even more parody, albeit much less 'reverence'. The accomplished transcendence of the looking-glass surface suggests the possibility of a language or form 'beyond' the constraints of poetic conventions – and beyond the categories of critical classification. The ensuing discussions of editors, critics and friends are presented with much mocking irony that depicts generally masculine reactions to feminine texts, ranging from rejection (too chaotic, too threatening) to celebration and an effective appropriation into the publishing establishment. These scenes amount to a critique of the persisting double standards within the literary establishment when confronted with female art that does not 'fit in'.[7] First, the embedded fragments of Joan's prose-poem 'Lady Oracle' mockingly evoke a kind of feminine writing that she traces out, and thus can be read as parodic allusion to the French concept of *écriture féminine* much discussed in American feminist circles at the time. But they also parody the forms of 'High Art' as manifested in modernist poetry. Atwood's vicious mockery of the 'great divide' here is displayed in Joan's 'special treatment' of the poem throughout its genesis: she hides it not with her underwear like the ('low art') gothics, but in a recipe book in the kitchen! Moreover, the parallels with modernist poetry are implicitly undercut by gothic intertexts. 'Lady Oracle' can be seen as a postmodern neo-gothic, with its ironically mocking reminiscences of Romantic poetry (like 'The Lady of Shalott') and

Victorian 'trashy' bestsellers (like Rider Haggard's *She*).[8] Their popular nineteenth-century heroines (both, of course, doomed) and their
gothic affinities are spiced by feminist visions like 'the embrace of the
Iron Maiden and the hero in the inflated rubber suit' – a likewise
ironic/comic spoof of gothic effects. In this context, the embedded
poem 'Lady Oracle' represents a *mise-en-abyme* of *Lady Oracle*'s parodic incorporation of the gothic.

However, it can also be seen to represent a *mise-en-abyme* of the
mother–daughter relationship (see also Godard 1983, 33): the female
figure 'Lady Oracle' is described as 'one and three' and as 'enormously
powerful, almost like a goddess, but it was an unhappy power'. These
terms clearly relate her to the figure of Joan's mother: Joan seems to
inscribe her ambivalent relationship with the mother, but this process
also evokes the notion that separation will be impossible. The desire
for and horror of the mother in a sense then might be called with
Kristeva the 'crying-out theme' of 'suffering-horror ... at the heart of
twentieth-century writing'. However, neo-gothic fictions also have that
critical ironic edge that inverts the suffering – and the 'monstrosities
of femininity' into liberating laughter. In *Lady Oracle*, the impossibility
of separation from m/other comes to structure Joan's life-story in just
such a double-edged way; there is much comic irony in dealing with
the horrific recognition that the mother will not let her daughter go,
but also of the 'return of the repressed' from the time within the
mother's power.

Even after Joan's escape, even after the mother's death, Joan is
haunted by her mother's presence. There are the images of the mother
like the one that Joan feels 'like an iron locket, she was sitting in front
of her vanity table, painting her fingernails a murderous red and
sighing' (71) or, later, the recognition that 'all this time I carried my
mother around my neck like a rotting albatross' (238). These grotesque, horrific images disrupt Joan's married life just as much as the
appearances of the mother's 'astral body' that keeps 'materialising' at
three points in the daughter's life: at the spiritualists' meeting where
Leda Sprott sees it first; in London, like a telepathic announcement of
her death; and in Italy, where Joan confronts the 'loose ends' of her
life. Here, in a final parodic twist of the gothic pattern, she accepts that
she cannot satisfy her mother's demands or, by extension, the related
totalising discourses. She thus 'accepts' the 'monstrous'. The 'supernatural' in her gothic story is tied to the mother and to disturbing

The Lady of Shalott   The woman who wants both love and art is doomed. Tennyson's and Waterhouse's Lady famously incorporates this favourite archetype of Romanticism – and prominently haunts postmodern gothica.

'appearances of a female body' (Hite 1989, 136), disrupting Joan's wish to 'order' her life by means of separation – in this case from her childhood. In formal terms, these appearances disrupt her story, which by that time, according to her education, has turned towards men. They also point to another aspect of the 'boundary'-position (of mother and daughter): the 'ambiguous opposition I/Other, Inside/Outside – an opposition that is vigorous but pervious, violent but uncertain' (Kristeva 1982, 7), which highlights the ambiguity of the whole issue of separation from m/other – and thus suggests the resulting desire for order and control that will structure Joan's life as an adult. This wish for separation in *Lady Oracle* parodically recalls the 'split heroines' and doubles from the gothic tradition, especially the opposition of the 'monstrous' (Bertha Mason) to the 'proper' (Jane Eyre), but 'repeats' the convention with a twist – or rather, with another labyrinthine effect. Joan's multiplicity exacerbates this split into (gothic) excess;

however, just as gothically, her splits are not final. Kristeva's 'vigorous but pervious' I/Thou opposition at the point of separation for Joan becomes an 'I–She extension' as her 'selves' spread across her plot/s.[9]

A good example of this radical gothic excess of the subject would be the 'monstrous' – and, at times, ironic/comic – images of herself that disrupt Joan's life like the 'return of the repressed' – again, in the shape of the female body. Joan has formed these 'monstrous selves' largely as a result of the gender construction related to popular culture, her mother, other girls, Aunt Lou[10] and the 'feminine plots' she has learned – but which she will not fit into. Joan's obesity as a child and teenager, her 'excess of body', becomes the metaphor for these 'monstrous selves' in terms of exceeding *le propre*: a proper femininity – and, as a result, of exceeding a 'proper' narrative. These 'monstrous selves' then come to function like the 'unconscious' aspects of the split subject (Belsey): as a second set of selves they challenge Joan's life-story and her love plot – or rather plots.

As a fat daughter, Joan does not fit the image of the Joan Crawford her mother named her after, at least not her glamorous roles – an image of the thin successful woman that still haunts Joan as a thin adult. As a fat child she cannot plan to become a dancer – one of her first dreams about becoming an artist. This makes her associate herself with the Little Mermaid from Hans Christian Andersen's fairytale, fittingly also a 'monstrous female' in physical terms as well as a female figure torn between the desire for love and her artistic talents for singing and dancing (see Gilbert and Gubar 1979, 386f; La Belle 1988, 143; Dinnerstein, 1976). Her story teaches, just like the Hollywood movie *The Red Shoes*, which is also part of Joan's gender education, that a woman cannot have both art and love: 'You could either dance or have the love of a good man.' Thus the image of the mermaid which could be a problem of puberty, of feeling only half-human, becomes another 'self' that haunts Joan still in Italy:

> The Little Mermaid rides again, I thought ... a female monster, larger than life, larger than most life around here anyway, striding down the hill, her hair standing on end with electrical force, volts of malevolent energy shooting from her fingers, her green eyes behind her dark tourist's glasses, her dark mafia glasses lit up and glowing like a cat's. (370)

This quotation is also a good example of the laughter produced by the gap between the image of a woman walking down the hill and the

Borrowed Items 08/03/2017 15:59
XXXX4854

Item Title	Due Date
* Gothic forms of feminine fictions	05/04/2017
Feminicidal fears : narratives of the female gothic experience	12/03/2017
Moving targets : women, murder and representation	26/03/2017
Femicide : the politics of woman killing	26/03/2017
Serial killers : death and life in America's wound culture	26/03/2017
Gothic histories : the taste for terror, 1764 to the present	29/03/2017
21st-century Gothic : great Gothic novels since 2000	29/03/2017

* Indicates items borrowed today
Thank you for using this unit
www.bibliotheca.com

monstrous dimension typically constructed by Joan with the eyes of the 'normal' Italian women to whom she is 'other': 'If I got a black dress and long black stockings, then would they like me?' (370). It highlights the ironic comment on the cultural processes of producing difference as monstrous.

A similar 'I–She extension' occurs with another 'self' related to the same origins. As a fat child Joan does not fit into the pink ballet outfit, spangles and tiara of the butterfly-role that she longs for in dancing school. This distinguishes and separates her from the other, 'normal' girls able to fulfil this part in one of the 'appropriate plots' designed for them by their mothers and teacher. This early experience causes her to create another 'self': the Fat Lady, another physically 'monstrous' large female figure. A good example of how this fantasy-self disrupts Joan's love plot/s is the scene when she wants to tell Arthur about one of her secret selves. In front of a television hockey game, male and female fantasies clash:

> The Fat Lady skated out onto the ice. I couldn't help myself. It was one of the most important moments of my life, I should have been able to keep her away, but out she came in a pink skating costume, her head ornamented with swan's down. With her was the thinnest man in the world. (304)

Reminding her at this moment that there is just too much yet untold – as her obese childhood and the related 'self' have become one gothic 'unspeakable' for Joan – this other 'she' keeps the 'I' mute, and the story untold. The Fat Lady is a grotesque figure, a combination of the desired ballet outfit and Joan's image of the fat lady at the freak show of the Ex which she has never seen. She functions as another haunting reminder of the dark views of femininity highlighted in gothic form, exploring how Woman makes women feel like freaks or monsters – and how 'women' will disrupt the processes of 'ordering', the 'order' of story-telling included.

With her image of a fat woman as gothic female monster Atwood has anticipated much of the 'Beauty Myth' that Naomi Wolf has claimed as the 1980s' backlash on feminism[11] and that can be read as another modern means for gender construction in terms of Cixous's 'appropriation'. Molly Hite puts it like this:

> This is a book in which fat is a feminist issue, and in which excess of body becomes symbolic of female resistance to a society that wishes to constrict

women to dimensions it deems appropriate, using devices that range from
exemplars to definitions to diets. (1989, 132)

Excess of body then also comes to enforce the 'gothic excesses' that
Atwood uses and abuses throughout Joan's story – to resist *le propre* in
terms of femininity and to disrupt the 'proper' plots for heroines, thus
exposing their constricting and appropriating ideology.

One aspect of this resistance is displayed in *Lady Oracle* through
the imagery of excess: of spreading, floating, shifting, dissolving –
defying any 'order', neat separations, borders of characters as well as
plot. Such imagery is evoked at the beginning of the novel: 'my life
had a tendency to spread, to get flabby, to scroll and festoon like the
frame of a baroque mirror' (3). What is here initially and then throughout the story presented in negative terms, as something that Joan
wishes to overcome in favour of a neatly ordered life/story, turns out
paradoxically as a *liberation* from that 'order' that had marked – and
destroyed – her mother's life, as symbolised by her synthetic, sterile
but exemplary houses and contrasted to Aunt Lou's comfortably messy
sitting-room. Joan's persistent efforts to order and control, most notably by separation of her various 'selves', seem related to that very
ideal she wants to depart from. However, the avoidance of affirming
her multiple personality comes from fears: 'If I brought the separate
parts of my life together (like uranium, like plutonium, harmless to
the naked eye, but charged with lethal energies) surely there would be
an explosion. Instead I floated, marking time' (242). Joan's 'floating'
between times of productivity and seeming inactivity, between the
worlds and selves she has created, marks the transcendence from the
mother's myth-fulfilment – and the possibility of transcending the
mirror that had contained it. Although Joan is not (yet) aware of this,
it signals a potentially liberating effect of such uncontrollable chaos,
and thus again points to the order/separation desired by Joan as a
form paradoxically complicit with (male) concepts of constriction.

Heroines of Atwood's earlier novels have confronted the same paradox in different ways, for example the unnamed narrator of *Surfacing*
(1972) who learns to accept the 'chaos' of nature, or Marian in *The
Edible Woman* (1969), who realises that the stability she desires can
threaten her very existence. For Joan, this paradox is related to her art
and the processes of creating formula fiction – which she perceives as
desirable order but also as dangerous, unsettling and tempting fantasies. As in *The Edible Woman*, in *Lady Oracle* art and love share this

paradox; and what the earlier novel's preoccupation with consuming constructs as the danger of being fixed as possession (Hutcheon 1988a, 142), *Lady Oracle*'s focus on escaping (as another connotation of excess) evokes the threat of being contained/constrained as *propre*. In both Joan's art and her own life, escape becomes an important move; one that she adopts as necessary strategy to avoid being fixed and doomed, like her mother. However, the early-learned feminine ideal and the related plots are seductive, as we have seen from Joan's fantasies, and so is the myth underlying these plots: love triumphant. Thus Atwood's parodic gothic 'repeats' and highlights not only the layers of mother–daughter love but also 'x-rays' the labyrinthine layers of what structures the conventional surface romance: romantic love.

Exceeding the proper plots

When Joan, late in the book, wandering through Toronto after a dramatic meeting with her first lover Paul, realises that 'Love was the pursuit of shadows' (315), she is in a state that resembles what Roland Barthes's solitary (male) lover calls *errance*/errantry. The lover helplessly discovers 'in himself a kind of diffusion of amorous desire; he then realises he is doomed to wander until he dies, from love to love' (1978, 101). This state gets worse with the question 'How does a love end?' and the recognition that 'no one – except for the others – ever knows anything about it.' Barthes writes:

> This phenomenon results from a constraint in the lover's discourse: I myself cannot (as an enamoured subject) construct my love story to the end: I am its poet (its bard) only for the beginning; the end, like my own death, belongs to others; it is up to them to write the fiction, the external, mythic narrative. (101)

Such recognitions are unbearable for Joan, who writes love stories for others that end 'happily' and who – in her deep desire for order and control – treats her own life like a plot that she arranges according to the situation (or according to the Other). This recognition is thus the first step towards escape – through her staged suicide – from her Canadian life and chaos. However, this 'death' gets another connotation when put into the context of the plots in which her various selves perform. Her private self, her fantasy self, even (as we shall see) her professional self, all play exactly those specific roles in their various appropriate plots, which are doomed and typically end in death. *Lady Oracle*'s parodic reversal, death as a (more or less) happy beginning, as well as other narrative take-offs throughout the text, then mark Joan as 'subject-in-excess': excess of the proper plots. And, accordingly, exceeding even the complexities of gothic texture, the neo-gothic plot is transformed from the haunted house of gothic fiction into the text as maze.

Joan, in the state of errantry, sadly reflects: 'I was a shadow for Paul, doomed to flee before him, evanescent as a cloud ... Once he had me, he wouldn't know at all what to do with me ... I was not the same as my phantom' (315). The female 'phantom' evoked here is a typically gothic one: the maiden-in-flight. No wonder Paul writes nursing novels, alias Mavis Quilp, and would like to adopt the heroic role of rescuer to save Joan from 'villain' Arthur. But although she refuses this plot/ting, Joan in a way has played the part of the 'maiden-in-flight' with a twist: she has throughout adopted the role of the moment but avoided being 'fixed' in it by multiplying, and thus extending into another plot – even into the plots of her own gothics. Although circling around love plots, it is not the amorous discourse that Kristeva described as 'fragmenting of the other' that is at work here, rather, it is Joan's self-fragmentation.

In Atwood's parodic gothic, Joan's 'romance' is important: while rigorously using and exploiting its conventions with much ridicule and melodrama, it also provides just as rigorous a critique of the ideological implications of the 'love triumphant' theme. As indicated by her recognitions quoted above, one of the narrative strategies involved is 'excess', as Joan does not have one love plot, she has plots in the plural: the fling with the Polish Count in London, with a demystifying, satiric seduction scene; the marriage with Arthur, with a hilarious, unromantic wedding; the affair with the Royal Porcupine, with displaced, melodramatic ballroom dancing and other romantic fantasies-come-true. Moreover, Atwood engages in mirroring, superimposing and multiplying Joan's various romances in her life, and her art: the popular romances. Related to this multiplying of love stories is Joan's own further multiplying, again, she is 'I' and 'she', a 'subject-in-excess' defying unifying notions of Woman just as much as those of a 'proper' romance. In *Lady Oracle* the desire for love is related to an education in feminine plots as taught by mothers as well as by cinema's

most effective encoding of 'love triumphant' in – at the time unignorable – Hollywood melodramas. But what in such romance plots
is the desired, and usually achieved, goal and sign of success – the
happy ending – in *Lady Oracle* becomes a focus for Atwood's mockery
and critique of the romance.

How Atwood's parodic challenges work might best be shown with the
example of *Lady Oracle*'s wedding scene. From Arthur's matter-of-
fact proposal in Queen's Park (220) to the 'white cotton dress with
nylon daisies on it [bought] at Eaton's Budget Floor' (222) to the
actual ceremony itself, performed in a 'standard Braeside living room'
transformed into a 'grotto' (227) by the former spiritualist Leda Sprott,
this wedding reads like a bizarre burlesque of every 'happy' ending.
But what might be mocking irony on the level of 'rewriting' this generic outcome of the 'heroine's plot' turns into a critique on a level that
is also part of parody's 'pragmatic range' – its ideological critique.

    The scene causes terror for Joan. This terror seems ridiculously
exaggerated at first. The wedding takes place too close to her childhood memories: her parents' house that she had left at sixteen to get
away from her mother; the spiritualist meetings that she attended with
her aunt when she was an extremely fat young girl – aspects of her life
which Arthur doesn't know of, for 'he wouldn't understand', and which
she fears will be uncovered now. The bride's terror is with comic
gothicism mirrored in the scene's decorum and in other details that
reflect death: Arthur, 'skinny as a funeral brass' (223), the bride 'bloat-
ing up like a drowned corpse' (222), the wedding picture, 'in which
our faces were a sickly blue and the sofa was brownish-red, like dried
blood' (229). Gothic tone is effectively displaced into what would conventionally be a romantic scene; it works to enhance the dark side of
the event and the fears of the heroine at what should be the 'happy
ending' of her love story. Ironically, as the gothic shows, it literally is.
'The time of love would be that of the present moment ... and marriage, as continuity, is its opposite' writes Kristeva (1987, 213). In
'formal synthesis' with the popular gothic romance formula, *Lady
Oracle* will show exactly this development, in gothic terms, of 'love
turning into fear' (Modleski 1982). Joan's terror, her fears (however
far-fetched they might seem at the time of her wedding), turn out to
be appropriate when read in conjunction with the account of her

'perfectly normal' marriage in Part IV and her struggles with being thus safely positioned within her culture's gender conventions.

The wedding scene is a good example of how Atwood's reverential parody displays complicity with the gothic conventions it repeats and incorporates, but is also a critique of their ideological problems (especially in the conservative popular formula gothics). Moreover, this scene shows well Atwood's technique of mirroring and superimposing gothic traces on one single scene, the sheer hyperbole and abundance of which effect that level of 'today's self-referential fiction [that] has the potential to be an "auto-critique" of discourse in its relation to reality' (Hutcheon 1985, 82). The maze of neo-gothic texture comes to attack radically the ideology of romantic love.

'Gothic writers substitute terror for love' writes Frances L. Restuccia (1986, 247), and Joan as a writer is well aware of that – as her quoted reflection that introduced this chapter shows. Atwood's reverential parody of this trajectory explores with much implicit ironic and comic distance gothic possibilities for contemporary feminist fiction. It is the *uses* of gothic form for Joan's story that most effectively highlight the 'other', darker side of the myth of 'love triumphant'. In a first step, this becomes obvious when – linked with the male gaze – heterosexual love also is presented as reinforcing (as we have seen in *Jane Eyre*) the 'engendering' processes that structure much of the gothic text. These totalising discourses and prescriptive processes function, like the mother's education (and example) exercised under that same gaze, to produce feelings of inadequacy and monstrosity. *Lady Oracle* self-consciously enacts and explores the gothic representation of such darker aspects of a female life-story, and Joan's relationships with men – in reality and in her fantasies and fictions – are all problematic in this sense.

A good example of this is one of Joan's earliest experiences with the 'male gaze'. Obesity as a child and adolescent had meant demonstrating an unignorable presence, but also resistance to her mother. Joan only reduces her weight upon the promise of financial independence and liberation from the mother (ironically, leaving her family at sixteen repeats her mother's life). This physical change also 'reduces' Joan into a female who is attractive to men – which in Western culture invariably means being (at least) whistled at in the street. As this is a situation fat Joan had not known and therefore not, like other girls, 'grown into', the effect is a defamiliarisation and critique of gender interactions that have come to be accepted as 'normal' in (street)life. Such defamiliarisation is a typically gothic as well as ironic critical effect.

This experience with the male views of women – or rather Woman – refers us back to the mirror-scene, the mother's efforts to 'put on her face' and the daughter's fear that an imagined man outside the door could come in and see her without that face of 'Woman'. The aspect of 'looks', of beauty, is important for this creation of Woman or 'woman as fantasy' (Lacan), as Jacqueline Rose has shown:

> we know that women are meant to *look* perfect, presenting a seamless image to the world so that the man, in that confrontation with difference, can avoid any apprehension of lack. The position of woman as fantasy therefore depends on a particular economy of vision. (1987, 232)

How this economy – which recalls Virginia Woolf's famous image of women as magnifying glasses to men – functions in terms of gender construction and 'appropriation' has always been explored in the feminine gothic's interrogative form. In *Lady Oracle*, Arthur's gaze and standards are a case in point, as throughout the first part Joan narrates her story in relation to him. A good example is her reflection that he 'had a strange relationship with my clothes' (20). Clothes, of course, 'make' the gothic heroine, as Joan-the-author knows well ('I thought if I could only get the clothes right, everything else would fall into place') and as her emphasis on costume gothic suggests. Her own clothes are eccentric, 'excessive', and unfashionable. Related to her fascination with the nineteenth century, with romantic style, they contribute to the imagery of flowing, spreading, distributing associated with her throughout the book: 'my red-and-gold sari, my embroidered caftan, my apricot velvet gown with the ripped hem' (20). Arthur's various objections are (ironically) well analysed by Joan:

> He ... thought we couldn't afford it, so at first he said they clashed with my hair or they made me look too fat. Later, when he took up Women's Liberation for flagellation purposes [!], he tried to tell me I shouldn't want to have clothes like that, I was playing into the hands of the exploiters. But it went beyond that; he found these clothes an affront of some kind, a personal insult. At the same time he was fascinated by them, as he was by all the things about me he disapproved of. I suspect he found them arousing and was irritated with himself because of it. (21)

Arthur's desire is for 'reduction' and control; it can easily be read in terms of *le propre* as the 'desire to reappropriate for himself that which seems able to escape him' (Cixous 1981, 80). Female sexuality is part of this 'uncontrollable', and Arthur in this aspect displays a twentieth-century version of Rochester's fears of female sexuality as shown towards Jane as well as Bertha – and thus positions Joan within the typical feminine gothic pattern of gender-construction.

Joan's reaction is illuminating because, despite her acute recognitions, she changes her habits: 'At last he made me so self-conscious that I found it hard to wear my long dresses in public' (21). She adapts, thus ironically displaying the problem of female complicity with their own 'reduction' that Atwood has been concerned with throughout her work. Joan's complicity characteristically remains on the surface, as she proceeds to live out her related fantasies separately, behind closed doors: first alone 'waltzing with an invisible partner' (21) and then with her secret lover, the 'Royal Porcupine'. A new 'self' is thus created, another 'she' that extends into and lives the female fantasies separated from 'real life'. This separation is clearly a response to the husband's gaze, to male 'order'. Ordering and separating then become increasingly related to masculine systems. The implicit duality of male order and female chaos, however, is ironically played out and not resolved in 'straight' terms.

Consequently, the separation remains synthetic for the extending Joan. The flamboyant lover in her own acted-out fantasy transforms himself back into Chuck and the flamboyant lovers in her gothic fantasies, her popular art, increasingly react like 'real' Arthur: ironically fulfilling the fantasy formula. 'Contain yourself' says Redmond to Felicia in Joan's latest gothic.

> He'd become tired of the extravagance of Felicia: of her figure that spread like crabgrass, her hair that spread like fire, her mind that spread like cancer or pubic lice … but she couldn't contain herself, she raged over him like a plague, leaving him withered. (351)

Felicia certainly figures as another one of Joan's selves; they are joined by their long, red hair and 'spreading' qualities – which will, as we shall see, put Joan into a fatal position within her own love plot. Again, the separations are ironically played off against each other; the borders are blurred between 'reality' and (popular) art as Joan extends into her fantasy world. As Hite writes about the missing separation here: 'Lady Oracle is not a novel in which the costume gothic stands in opposition to the naked truth' (1989, 134).

This becomes most obvious in Joan's various levels of love plots. At the same time, these love plots also display the most self-conscious system of parodic installation and provocation of the gothic romance form in Lady Oracle. 'Costume gothics' and 'real life' intersect in multiple romance plots and are superimposed upon each other like layers of love stories. Joan, 'hooked on plots', shifts between the process of constructing these romances and the various female figures she incorporates in them: always on the 'borderline' of separation (Kristeva), always extending into another 'she' in a new plot. She enacts a naive 'mistress' for the Polish Count, a kinky lover for the Royal Porcupine, and a true heroine of romance for Arthur. This last part is the most complex: it includes the development from the under-standing helpmeet of Arthur's varying political and academic pursuits, to the happy-housewife heroine with an illuminating twist of the domestic test. Ironically, it turns into a success because of Joan's failure in the kitchen: 'My failure was a performance and Arthur was the audience. His applause kept me going' (235). Joan thus also self-consciously plays the role of the endearing 'fool-heroine' (Thomas 1981), superior behind the clumsiness; and her self-deprecations pay lip-service to the male gaze only to undercut it secretly. This last recognition raises further questions about Joan's self-representation and her reliability as a narrator.

All of these roles that Joan plays in her love plots are ironically exposed to ridicule. They work to discard popular gothics' ideologies by their sheer abundance and the violence they most obviously do to Joan's manifold talents and possibilities, 'reducing' her to the one role that best suits her partner of the time. Most notably, her writing is done on the sly throughout – there seems to be no room for such creativity in her romance pattern. The effect is another neat separation on Joan's part between her 'private' and her 'professional' self – and the latter, as we shall see, will also be subjected to a masculine system inscribing le propre for a female writer! However, the Polish Count also writes – as Mavis Quilp – on the sly; and the Royal Porcupine's other dimensions only suggested by Chuck Brewer are not acceptable to Joan's scheme. 'Proper plots' are problematic for both sexes in Lady Oracle's abundance of stories. And of course, Joan is not only the object of others' plots for her. She is also the one who places others within her romance plots.

Joan's 'transforming eye' (McMillan 1988, 48) parodically links her to Emily St Aubert and other traditional gothic heroines and their abilities of perception. It perceives the nobly-named male figures around her as Byronic heroes and projects her own image for them, neatly separating them into the rescuer–villain categories within which her mother had first introduced her absent father: nice men did things *for* you; bad men did things *to* you. Arthur is a case in point – he is characterised as Canadian political activist and introduced as 'skinny, confused-looking young man' (184), acting 'stoically' and 'gloomily', but she perceives him as more and more 'dashing', until he transforms: 'a melancholy fighter for almost-lost causes, idealistic and doomed, sort of like Lord Byron, whose biography I had just been skimming' (184). The self-reflexivity here adds to the comic effect. But unlike the romance hero and the related expectations, his 'existential gloom' and 'inertia and the absence of a sense of purpose' (218) – an ironic twentieth-century kind of academic Byronic brooding – don't stop after the wedding; neither are they transformed into selfless fairytale love. The romantic perception is here parodically installed and undercut, and this turns out to be only one of the ironic twists that deconstruct the myth of romantic love for Joan. Her reaction, at first, is to 're-order' her view:

> There were two kinds of love, I told myself; Arthur was terrific for one kind, but why demand all things from one man? I'd given up expecting him to be a cloaked, sinuous and faintly menacing stranger. He couldn't be that: I lived with him, and cloaked strangers didn't leave their socks on the floor … I kept Arthur in our apartment and the strangers in their castles and mansions where they belonged. (241)

Joan typically shifts between the romance world and its stereotypical characters and 'real life' where men 'are both villains and rescuers and more and have to be recognised as such' as Godard puts it (1983, 22). Joan refuses this for a long time; instead she seeks to separate, to 'order'. And in the process she again creates what Sherrill Grace has called 'violent dualities' (1980): synthetic separations, their artificiality aptly displayed by the comic critique of Atwood's ironic voice.

What these constructions and separations show is how romantic love functions to appropriate, to deny female excesses, when cast in

the plots that Joan and her readers are 'hooked on': romance as presented in the Hollywood melodramas she goes to see with her aunt as
a teenager, or in her own trance-written costume gothics, or in the
Mavis Quilp novel she reads when reflecting on her own 'love-life':

> I longed for the simplicity of that world, where happiness was possible and
> wounds were only ritual ones. Why had I been closed out from that impos-
> sible white paradise where love was as final as death, and banished to this
> other place where everything changed and shifted? (316)

Again, there is Joan's apparent desire for 'finality'; for absolute categories, dualities, separation. Paradoxically – and just as revealingly – she
seeks this order in the world of fantasy, traditionally associated with
shifting shapes and chaos. This late stage in the novel plays with the
confusion between the real narrative space experienced as 'other place'
and shifting in the way dreams and fantasies do, and the world of
romantic fantasy, desired for what can only be an artificial, formulaic
or violent order. This confusion signals both Joan's error in how she
'orders' her life and this order's failure – or *monstrosity*.

Joan's desire for the 'order' of gothic romance plots, with its seductive link of love and death, is radically questioned when Joan really
finds herself in the centre of such a plot. The categories of reality and
art don't hold any more when gothic threats happen in Joan's life: the
threatening notes, the telephone calls, the dead porcupine on the doorstep, the blackmailing. Her life-story has turned gothic. It now parodies the 'suspicious-marriage plot' of the popular romance – and Joan
suspects Arthur to be the villain. What happens here is more than the
fearful projections of a romance-ridden mind: Atwood shows how
'reality becomes gothic' (Becker: interview) at this point in a female
life-story, thereby radically discarding the 'order' of the romance plot
as a masculine order, a patriarchal fiction extending gender constructions into the monstrous, and love into terror.

As her love plots unfold, Joan is presented as a beautiful and successful woman. In the best gothic fashion, the heroine's looks are first
introduced from the perspective of an outsider. And in best Atwoodian
parody this happens through press quotations from what are identified
as the two most important English-Canadian newspapers:

> Joan Foster, celebrated author of *Lady Oracle*, looking like a lush Rossetti
> portrait, radiating intensity, hypnotised the audience with her unearthly

... ' (*The Toronto Star*). Prose-poetess Joan Foster looked impressively Junoesque in her flowing red hair and green robe; unfortunately she was largely inaudible ... (*The Globe and Mail*). (11)

However, such qualities of beauty and success signify a tragic gothic position: they position Joan as 'the sexual woman' who is, as we have seen, 'beautiful and damned' (Mussell 1975, 84–9). The prototype for the sexual woman in the popular gothic, Rebecca, is basically a dead wife, killed by her husband, and owes much to Bertha Mason – the mad wife, imprisoned by her husband. As expert in the gothic fantasy system, Joan 'repeats' this: 'In my books all wives were eventually either mad or dead, or both' (352).

Seen in this context, her seemingly ridiculous staged drowning enacts the formula in a vicious parody: as in Hutcheon's 'authorised transgression' the formulaic ending is incorporated but simultaneously rigorously questioned. Joan's 'death', while displaying form(ula)-fulfilment, radically questions the ideological implications of this 'ending' for the 'other woman' in the gothic fantasy. Moreover, now the blurring border between her life and her gothics shifts back to influencing her fiction-in-progress. As her Italian exile starts to resemble the situation of the 'mad wife' (again a hyperbolic effect in Atwood's parody), she identifies with her own doomed-wife figure Felicia and 'saves' her from her formulaic death. At this point, becoming the product of her own gothic plots, she realises their limitations – and explodes them.

The explosion of plot and the dissolution of separations happen at the occasion of a dramatic clash – the 'meeting' of Joan's gothic romances and her own gothic life-story. This clash occurs in a highly overdetermined space: the centre of the maze in Joan's last gothic. In a first step, her construction of the fictional maze extends to a metonymic dimension of her own quest, as Felicia faces Redmond – and the male figures of Joan's life:

'Don't touch me,' she said, taking a step backward. She refused to be doomed. As long as she was on *her side of the door* she would be safe. Cunningly, he began his transformations, trying to lure her into his reach. His face grew a white gauze mask, then a pair of mauve-tinted spectacles, then a red beard and moustache, which faded, giving place to burning eyes and icicle teeth. Then he stood looking at her sadly; he was wearing a turtle-neck sweater ... 'Let me take you away,' he whispered. 'Let me rescue you. We will dance together forever, always.' ... Once she had wanted these words, she had waited all her life for someone to say them ... 'No,' she said. 'I know who you are.' (377, emphasis added)

The horrifically transforming male figure at the centre of the maze is Bluebeard from Perrault's as well as the Grimm brothers' fairy-tales. Bluebeard replaces the Byronic heroes whose magic transformations from brute to lover had made the endings of the heroine plot 'happy'. By contrast, Bluebeard's transformation is from seducer to killer – into the murderer of all his wives, punishing them for their desire to know (about) him. This figure has been much explored by feminist gothic writing: for example, in Atwood's own story 'Bluebeard's Egg' (1983) and in Angela Carter's 'The Bloody Chamber' (1979). In *Lady Oracle*'s maze, men are discarded as Bluebeards: 'every man has more than one wife' (376). At the same time, Joan/Felicia encounters various of her other 'selves' who incarnate dead-wife figures in the maze. This image emphasises the multiple subject-in-process; moreover, containment, reduction and violence of romantic love and the related plots undergo a dramatic exposition in this playfully understated and spectacular mock-cathartic scene. The incessant repetition and rewriting of gothic texture into the text as maze is self-reflexively underlined in phrases like '[s]uddenly she found herself in the central plot' (375). It both connects and further extends the threads of subjectivity and plot/s. This is particularly illuminating in terms of the feminist exploration of subject processes against the ideology of traditional plots – and of traditional endings.

Joan Foster discards 'her men' as threatening Bluebeards in a fantasy related to her new gothic plot. Consequently (and anti-climactically), she hits the next man who crosses her doorstep over the head with a Cinzano bottle. However, isn't it the destiny of the Rochesters to be punished and maimed by the time of the happy ending? Indeed, 'there is something about a man in a bandage' Joan admits, playing the nurse like a Mavis Quilp character, planning her way home to Canada. Moreover, she has transformed from the beautiful-wife figure into a new self: 'the birth of my new personality (a sensible girl, discreet, warm, honest and confident, with soft green eyes, regular habits and glowing chestnut hair)' (206). The transformation scene is noteworthy, as it must be one of the most sentimental and ludicrous in contemporary women's literature. Joan cuts her long red hair with her nail scissors and subsequently burns it on the gas burners in the kitchen: a grotesque, displaced, ritualistic sacrifice, underlined by melodramatic memories of Arthur who 'liked brushing my hair for me' (12).[12] What happens is the ironic reversal of a central romance convention linked to the plots of femininity she knows so well: the transformation of the plain girl into the beautiful woman or, to use the adequate terminology, the transformation of poor Cinderella into the glamorous princess (for a different reading see Davey 1984, 121). Joan, by contrast, reduces her optical effect as a nineteenth-century-style beauty into that of a 'secretary on vacation' (11) – for once ignoring the powers of the male gaze that had so influenced her before – and thus, ironically, saving herself. This newly created self then reads like a stereotypical gothic heroine: like Radcliffe's Emily or like Joan Foster's own Charlotte. In the repertoire of gothic female figures, the transformation from the beauty into 'plain Jane' can be seen as transformation from the beautiful wife into another version of the maiden-in-flight. The narrative seems to have come full circle as Joan is ready for the next romance.

However, there are – despite Joan's introductory strategies to the contrary (3) – 'loose ends', which, in best gothic fashion, are not to be subsumed under some 'supernatural-explained' or 'evil-punished' or 'virtue-rewarded' pattern: the blackmailing that had made Joan's married life truly gothic is not explained away – the problematics of the 'happy ending' for a female subject are not resolved. The generic destiny of the beautiful-wife figure is one of the most important questions that Atwood has asked of the gothic romance: 'Of course the thing about the mad wife in *Jane Eyre* is that you kill off the mad wife and then you become the wife. Does that mean that you'll also go mad?' (Becker: interview). That this question is addressed but not resolved in Joan's story is another parodic treatment of feminine gothic texture with its generic happy ending questioned by a mirror-plot of female desire. Joan's multiple identities, her position/s as subject-in-excess, shape her plots still as interrogative in that sense. Her own abundance, and mobility, in a gothic scenario that highlights the terrors of love without explaining all threats away, thus works like Kristeva's 'x-ray' that shows the violence in romantic love in her reading of 'the most beautiful love dream of the Western world' – Shakespeare's tragedy *Romeo and Juliet* (1597) – and in her illuminating paraphrase of Juliet's desire: 'Lose your symbolic entity to enable me, on the basis of your loved, fragmented body, to become entire, whole, one: out of myself and myself alone there becomes a couple!' (Kristeva 1987, 212). Kristeva also displays the violence (and horror) in Juliet's

'blind love', her 'unconscious desire to break up Romeo's body' in the
famous image of him 'cut out in little stars, and he will make the face
of heaven so fine, that all the world will be in love with night' (III.ii.9–
25). In this view, Juliet is 'killed' into her seeming death, into 'this
body, erroneously dead and beautiful, … the image of a contained,
padlocked, one could say frigid passion because it was not able to give
its violence free rein' (Kristeva 1987, 216). The awareness of this violence points to 'death's immanent presence with love', which Kristeva
finds in Shakespeare but founds on Freud's theses on Eros and
Thanatos. This is exactly the awareness which the gothic romance
evokes (in the heroine's horror of the hero) but denies (in his magic
transformation). The ideological implications of this denial become
clear in a feminist gothic like *Lady Oracle*. Joan's terror at her wedding
was justified: her 'better than average' marriage functions like an institutionalised reduction of her 'excesses', in vain, which is why the
violence of the process is exposed. Molly Hite calls this 'the most
fundamental source of violence in the genre: in a society that defines
all possible male–female relations in terms of masculine control and
constraint, heterosexual love *is* terror for women' (1979, 154).

In *Lady Oracle*, and in its characteristic labyrinthine excess, this violence
is explored on yet another level of gothic texture. Not only Joan's
private, but also her professional self is exposed to the 'masculine
control and constraint': as a writer Joan encounters another 'male
system'. By her parodic (and partly self-parodic) exploration of Joan's
interaction with the 'male gaze' exercising 'reduction' in this other
context, Atwood extends the feminine gothic's conventions of highlighting engendering discourses for the female subject; at the same
time she uses the gothic's possibilities of presenting the complicated
situation of the female artist that Mary Shelley had introduced in
Frankenstein. As in her later novel *Cat's Eye* (1988), Atwood examines
notions of artistic fame in general, and a female artist's fame in particular. Joan's position offers firstly a critical view of the 'double critical
standard' that Anglo-American feminist criticism has uncovered and
that Atwood has elsewhere called 'Sexual Compliment/Put down'
(1982a, 199). Joan experiences this in the form of compliments on her
hair and put-downs of her writing: 'hair in the female was regarded as
more important than either talent or the lack of it' (11). Mostly these

turn out to be 'the unexpected personal attack on her by a jealous male writer' (185) – like the Polish Count (180, 309) or Fraser Buchanan, who expects that she 'got the book published by using ... feminine wiles' (321); or a jealous male artist like the 'Royal Porcupine':

> 'I guess you're a publishing success,' he said. 'What's it like to be a successful bad writer?' I was beginning to feel angry. 'Why don't you publish and find out?' 'Hey,' he said, grinning, 'temper. You've got fantastic hair, anyway. Don't ever cut it off.' (266)

The irony here highlights the ambiguities of value judgements, subjectivity, criticism.[13] But also another, more gothic image of the female writer is presented to Joan, which Atwood has elsewhere called 'Ophelia: ... a female version of Doomed Dylan usually with more than a little hope on the part of the interviewer that you'll turn into Suicidal Sylvia and *really* give them something to write about' (1982a, 184). Ironically, it is exactly this role that Joan fulfils with her staged (and not, as Atwood had planned at first, actual) suicide. In this context, *Lady Oracle* can be read as cruel parody of a 'feminine ideal' founded in the tragedy of the life and death of Sylvia Plath, a writer of gothic poetry but also of a very gothic autobiography, *The Bell Jar* (1963). Joan's gothic story thus both underlines the uses of the gothic for contemporary women writing in the autobiographic mode, and gothically enacts Atwood's ironic recognition:

> Female writers in the twentieth century are seen not just as eccentric and unfeminine, but as doomed. The temptation to act out the role of the isolated or doomed female artist, either in one's life or through one's characters, is quite strong. (1982a, 226)

Again, it is a romanticised role, and again the tension between form-fulfilment and subversion is played out ironically instead of being resolved. Moreover, it is another part which carries a death sentence.

Joan's position as a writer accounts for what must be Atwood's most hilarious and most vicious depictions of the publishing scene. They culminate in Joan's Canadian editor's idea to model her as a kind of female Leonard Cohen – unfortunately, Joan does not play the guitar. But Joan's position as a writer also leads us back to another formal aspect of *Lady Oracle*'s labyrinthine texture. It is, as we have seen, a highly metafictional novel, with its multiple layers of plots that recall fairy-tales, Victorian romance, Romantic poetry, and (of course) popular as well as classic gothics. What all these intertexts share is the mockery of mimetic realism, and what their superimpositions in *Lady Oracle* effect is the refusal of any 'master'-plot, of any hierarchy of discourses and especially of the traditional critical evaluation of high and low art and realist versus fantastic narrative. However, gothic texture as maze defies the playful eclecticism that might be suspected in this context. As a feminine form it rather confronts questions that were central to feminism in the mid-1970s – and still are today. One of these anticipates the 1990s' discussion of the relationship of high or popular art, female culture, and an acceptable idea of 'truth'. *Lady Oracle*'s address of this body of issues might best be discussed within the larger context of Atwood's gothicism as well as of gothic filliation.

Terrific escapes: the text as maze

'Reality becomes gothic', Margaret Atwood once said (Becker: interview), referring to her novel *The Handmaid's Tale* (1985). Although it has been critically treated as dystopia, 'there is nothing in this book', Atwood insists, 'that has not actually happened, that could not happen or that we wouldn't have the technologies for' (Becker: interview). The collection of clippings from international newspapers and transcripts of news in her extensive research folder for that book (preserved in the Atwood Papers) effectively confirm this statement. Although this dark, private story of a totalitarian system might seem a far cry from the neo-gothic comedy *Lady Oracle*, 'reality becomes gothic' for Joan as well. As we have seen, her 'autobiography' turns into a gothic plot with layers of dark insights, of femininity perceived as monstrous and love discarded as threat – features not that different from Atwood's vision of Gilead's order in the near future of *The Handmaid's Tale*. The relationship of gothicism and realism, of fiction and truth, is addressed here. And it is explicitly put into the context of the 'escapes' that Joan produces with her writing of popular horror. *Lady Oracle*'s neo-gothicism makes a case for escape from the constraints of a misogynist order while at the same time – through its own excessive maze-like texture – vigorously addressing the violence of these constraints. And its feminist politics uses texts and types of everyday escape.

The dark insights of Joan's story about women's lives and love virtually read like the basic ingredients of one of her costume gothics, like the products of her touch-typing sessions. These creative sessions themselves are an escape of sorts. They parodically recall the cliché of the gothic writer: Horace Walpole claimed to do inspired writing, Charlotte Brontë described herself as trance writer, Mary Shelley referred to the origins of *Frankenstein* as waking dream. These claims suggest an escape from – or a conscious refusal of – responsibility for the gothic excesses. Moreover, Joan's excessive subjectivity sheds more light on these formulaic fantasies than the mere critique of their functions as escape from, and reconciliation with, the 'real' everyday torments suffered by the female reader. Joan accepts escape as necessity, not only in sympathy with her readers but from her own experience. The fantasy effect here is not an object of critique but of celebration.

This can best be shown by Joan's imagined defence of her work before Arthur. He, the theoretically Marxist and actually anti-establishment intellectual, represents the (male) sceptic vis-à-vis such (female) 'trash', as well as a similarly disposed implied reader of *Lady Oracle*. It is interesting to note that the first draft of *Lady Oracle* (Atwood Papers, Boxes 23–25) was written in epistolary form to Arthur (then named, equally royally, George) – in letters which were extremely melodramatic in tone. In the published novel, Joan's explanations to her husband are mute; like the figures of Barthes's solitary lover they are only told in her mind. Joan keeps the information that she is a bestselling novelist from Arthur beyond the ending. However, her *imagined* explanations predispose the reading of her story and of her gothics from the very beginning in Italy.

'Why did I never tell him? It was fear, mostly. When I first met him he talked a lot about wanting a woman whose mind he could respect, and I knew that if he found out I'd written *The Secret of Morgrave Manor* he wouldn't respect mine' (33). In the light of Joan's sense of inadequacy around Arthur's university colleagues and their theoretical endeavours, her desire is for a new, intellectual version of old-time heroines' 'respectability'. Arthur's permanently shifting – but always Marxist – ideas demand academic discourse, just as much as experience within the workers' world, just as much as a cooking wife. The constant in all this is that within his circles, Joan's work – her gothics – would be considered 'trash of the lowest order. Worse than trash, for didn't they exploit the masses, corrupt by distracting, and perpetuate degrading stereotypes of women as helpless and persecuted?' (34). Joan's awareness of the leftist critique of her fantasies is disarming, and so is her personal defence of escape. For her readers – and for herself, as according to the teachings of Mavis Quilp the romance has to provide escape for the writer as well – '[e]scape wasn't a luxury ..., it was a necessity' (34). And her own marriage puts her emotionally into the lonely position of the typical romance readers that she so pointedly outlines throughout the story. Revealingly, she stops writing her romances as soon as she starts the affair with the Royal Porcupine. Moreover, she also realises the necessity of 'male escapes'. For example: 'War, politics and explorations up the Amazon, those other great escapes were by and large denied them [the romance readers], and they weren't much interested in hockey or football, games they couldn't play' (35) – games that are a persistent part of Arthur's life. Arthur in front of the television, lost to the world, watching hockey: that is his 'disappearing act'. His changing theories and ideologies of a better world: they are his fantasies. One of Joan's various imagined justifica-tions (tried out in different discourses like the 'materialist–determinist angle' or the emancipated woman's perspective) attacks exactly this point:

> who the hell was Arthur to talk about social relevance? ... The truth was that I dealt in hope, I offered a vision of a better world, however preposter-ous. Was that so terrible? I couldn't see that it was much different from the visions Arthur and his friends offered, and it was just as realistic. So you're interested in the people, the workers, I would say to him during my solitary midnight justifications. Well, that's what the people and the workers read, the female ones anyway, when they have time to read at all and they can't face the social realism of *True Confessions*. They read my books. Figure that out. (35)

In one way, it is *Lady Oracle*'s form which then works to figure out the seeming paradox proposed here. Its 'repetition with a difference' of the popular gothic formula unfolds not only the implied ideological critique but also an analysis of the workings of the assumed escape-effect. Atwood's parody, at the time of Germaine Greer's (1977) and other prominent feminists' public rejection of the romance, thus an-ticipates much of the 1980s' feminist critical interest in female popular culture and the 'gothic boom' in general.

Lady Oracle has been called an 'anti-gothic' by Atwood herself. It was written in the context of her explorations of women's culture in the mid-1970s, as her extensive research for the book collected in the

Atwood Papers testifies. Looking back, she realises that what was most important to her was the recognition of the prevailing fascination of gothic writing for women:

> [The gothic] is a specific women's form and I think one of the questions that were interesting me at the time was why so many women read those kinds of book. What was it in the gothic form specifically that was interesting and appealing to them? Now we could talk about that ... I would say the *Jane Eyre* pattern is more or less how the gothic has evolved, the Female Gothic – and some people who have written about it have mentioned the masochism, you know, the heroine gets put through all these terrible things, and then there's the sell-out in the end because she marries the man. But I don't think it's that at all. I think it's lion-taming. (Becker: interview)

'Lion-Taming' – exercising female power in the 'heroine's plot' – is most dangerous for the heroine in the gothic romance with its cruel-but-tender Byronic heroes. This recognition has early been the subject of gothic filliation. *Lady Oracle* parodically explores this theme, in classic as well as popular gothics, but it also 'repeats' and anticipates the related feminist intertexts. It 'repeats' most notably Jane Austen's own reverential parody *Northanger Abbey*'s exposition of misogynist power structures through Catherine's hyperbolic gothic sensibility. And it anticipates a novel that explores – with a similarly ironic double-voice – the vicarious experience of female power in popular gothics.

Fay Weldon's *The Life and Loves of a She-Devil* (1983) is important in terms of filliation, as it also inscribes a dark, satiric view of the notions of popular horror and its relevance to women's lives. As throughout Weldon's work, the passions of love in *She-Devil* are inextricably intertwined with those of hatred and revenge. Moreover, here it is related from the first to the most profitable tales of love: romantic fiction. Initially read for consolation by heroine Ruth, a betrayed wife, sad mother and overweight suburban housewife, and written by her pretty and rich rival Mary Fisher, these romances come to structure Ruth's story – with a neo-gothic difference. The reverential parody of the gothic romance pattern here works by literally inscribing the vicarious reading experiences of hatred and revenge. In formal terms, it thus effects another labyrinthine repetition: Ruth proceeds to turn her husband's new romance into a nightmare by turning it into a normal family life. And she destroys him socially and psychologically by female cunning and illegal intrigues tied to her role as 'she-devil'.

At the same time, large Ruth transforms herself *physically* into her 'shapely' rival Mary. The plastic surgery involved carries uncanny overtones of Frankenstein's dreary processes of creation. And the perfect feminine beauty achieved in the end is truly monstrous: a vicious gothic twist that Susan Seidelman's film adaptation *She-Devil* typically leaves out for a more feminist-heroic ending (1989). Once again, the notions of a female monster and of love as terror evolve as a gothic fantasy comes true. Ruth's ironic happy ending relies on the complete reversal of the initial emotional, domestic, financial power relations. Throughout the book, misogynist power structures are shown as 'normal' and pervasive, as Ruth's own manifold personae spread across middle-class households and their domestic discontent. Weldon's gothicism defamiliarises this accepted order, and the shift between such discontent and the related fantasies recalls Atwood's subject-in-excess. Gothic lion-taming.[14]

The gendered focus on power-relations implied in a novel like *She-Devil* (and, albeit less self-consciously, in all of Weldon's novels) modifies the arguments of masochism and escape that still influence even the latest gothic criticism. This understanding of the gothic system of fears and fantasies as related to power politics has structured, I would argue, Atwood's work throughout. Most notably, as in *The Handmaid's Tale*, in her novel *Bodily Harm* (1981) – which she calls her 'Edgar-Allan-Poe-type gothic' (Becker: interview) – gothicism points to the violence of the body politic and to women's bodies. *Bodily Harm* also touches the colonial power relations that Atwood has been concerned with throughout, and that she again gothically explores in *The Robber Bride* (1993) with its striking female figures and their plots and 'post-imperialist heroine' Zenia (see Hengen 1995). Gothic traces in Atwood's poetry, since her first collection *Double Persephone* (1961), point to the complications of – gendered, national, cultural – identity and use gothicism, besides the typical Atwoodian ironic humour and sharp satire, to attack 'master narratives' and the legitimation of power structures. Her recent collection of poetry, *Morning in the Burned House* (1995), carries gothic overtones in its title. The poem of that title evokes the uncanny, domestic situation of a virtual ghost speaking from the burnt breakfast table:

> In the burned house I am eating breakfast.
> You understand: there is no house, there is no breakfast,

yet here I am

...

(I can almost see)
in my burning clothes, the thin green shorts
and grubby yellow T-shirt
holding my cindery, non-existent,
radiant flesh. Incandescent.

(1995a, 126f)

This invocation of existential transience concludes a collection that variously depicts states between life and death – as in 'Half-hanged Mary', where the uncanny voice narrates Atwood's ancestor Mary Webster's survival of a whole night while being hanged from a tree in 1680, and her related transformation into the witch she was pronounced to be before her execution (58–69). More and more, gothic signs incorporate oppositions, both life and death, both love and revenge, as the horrific 'hairball' in the story of that title in Atwood's 1991 collection of short fiction, *Wilderness Tips*. This book also recalls her historicising of Canadian ghosts; as in *Surfacing* (1972) and in *The Journals of Susanna Moodie* (1970), the forest is seen as place of possibility beyond the constrictions of classic power structures, a place of supernatural mystery. When young, dreamy Lucy simply vanishes from a cliff in summer camp, to haunt her friend Lois for ever with the puzzling sensation of a shout ('Death by Landscape', 1991, 124f), Atwood displays once again that 'there is more to Kanada than meets the eye' (Atwood 1982a, 252) – or, as she put it in a letter: 'Canada is very gothic' (March 1988).[15]

Within her wide-ranging work, maybe Atwood's poetic prose pieces collected in *Murder in the Dark* (1983) and *Good Bones* (1992) play out most self-consciously her academic familiarity with the gothic tradition in both its popular and its canonical dimensions. The fragments of her Harvard dissertation on the late-Victorian 'Metaphysical Romance' in the Atwood Papers display her early analysis of the female figures as mostly 'split heroines' produced by the gothic structures of these texts; her recognitions here anticipate Anglo-American images-of-women criticism of the 1970s. Her concept of the gothic is self-consciously connected to Victorian traditions but also to the patterns of popular art: ' "Popular art" is a collection of rigid patterns, "sophisticated" art varies the patterns. But popular art is material for serious art in the way dreams are' (Sandler 1977, 10). Atwood's selection of her intertexts

from myths and popular culture points to her interest in fairy-tales
and gothic forms that she contextualises with a specifically *female*
popular culture. And the seductions of these forms are seductively
played out in her satire 'What is a Woman's Novel?':

> *She had the startled eyes of a wild bird.* This is the kind of sentence I go mad
> for. I would like to be able to write such sentences, without embarrassment.
> I would like to be able to read them without embarrassment. If I could only
> do these two simple things, I feel, I would be able to pass my allotted time
> on this earth like a pearl wrapped in velvet.
>   *She had the startled eyes of a wild bird.* A, but which one? A screech owl,
> perhaps, or a cuckoo? It does make a difference. We do not need more
> literalists of the imagination. (1983b, 35f)

A similar play with feminine literary 'trash' and its seduction, a play
that pointedly incorporates postmodern and feminist scepticism about
big concepts like truth and identity, occurs in the opening of *Wilderness Tips* (1991). The first story, 'True Trash', is structured by a group
of teenage girls' communal reading of *True Romance* magazines, the
embedded story parts intercut with the girls' differing comments and
the actual happenings at the typical late-1950s' summer camp at which
they spend the summer. The originally collectively mocked 'Moan-o-
dramas' (11) – only Ronette seems to take them seriously (15) – get a
completely different connotation in retrospect, when one of the girls,
Joanne, eleven years later comes to figure out Ronette's mysterious
pregnancy of that summer. Joanne, characterised as being 'addicted to
endings', suddenly sees 'the end of the story ... or at least a missing
piece' (36): Ronette's seduction of the then fourteen-year-old Donny.

Joanne considers the revelation of her recognition to grown-up Don.
'Should she tell him? The melodrama tempts her, the idea of revelation, a sensation, a neat ending.' But the story ends with her decision
against the act because 'it would not be an ending, it would only be
the beginning of something else. In any case, the story itself seems to
her outmoded. It's an archaic story, a folk-tale, a mosaic artefact. It's
a story that would never happen now' (37). What clashes here are first
of all the categories of popular art and life, of 'trash' and 'truth', *the*
postmodern clash. As in *Lady Oracle*, this clash is related to the clash
of present and past in the perception of the subject. While Joanne
realises the truth in the trash they read as teenagers, she perceives a
line between now and then that becomes clear when related to the
romances and the way they treated sex at a time when it was 'sin'.

Sick with desire. Three dots had expressed it perfectly, because there had been no ordinary words for it.

On the other hand there had been marriage, which meant wifely checked aprons, play-pens, a sugary safety.

But nothing has turned out that way. Sex has been domesticated, stripped of the promised mystery, added to the category of the merely expected. It's just what is done, mundane as hockey. It's celibacy these days that would raise eyebrows. (37)

The early 1990s' reader could supplement these last reflections with the consideration of sex and celibacy in the age of AIDS – and realise that, while there has been another 'line to separate the past', 'true trash' stories *do happen*.

Both 'True Trash' and *Lady Oracle* bring about such recognitions by a retrospective perception of life-stories. The story unfolds an abundance of differing feminine plots with 'happy' or tragic endings on which Joanne reflects – while her own career defies such patterns altogether. The novel, while recalling the gothic romance's 'trashy' pattern, incorporates a whole range of possibilities to be told differently. First, there is a whole set of 'ghost stories': Joan's untold stories and her lies, or rather fictions, about her life to Arthur. There is the benevolent (and dead) mother she invents 'for his benefit' (41). There is the Montreal sailing instructor who replaces the Polish Count as more modern romantic first-lover figure (167). There are the university courses that she claims to take and never finish to hide her successful romance-writing – an economic basis for her as well as Arthur (33). These fictions work to reinforce myths of the feminine: the good mother, the romantic lover, the inadequate intellectual. And they highlight once again, enforced by Atwood's ironic double-voice, the gothic's radically defamiliarising critical potential with regard to these myths. Moreover, these fictions, by being less gothic, ironically turn out to be also less real!

Of course, the last sentence is rendered problematic by the book and its gothic maze again. For – in a second alternative to the story as read so far – in the end we have to realise that we might have read another such fiction, this time fabricated for the Canadian reporter in Italy and maybe even transcribed by him. While this narrative move again suggests the use of a gothic convention, most notably in the style of Henry James's governess story of *The Turn of the Screw* – which is, as we have seen, mediated by its male audience as introduced in the opening as well as by the (probably) male narrator's transcription – *Lady Oracle* self-consciously foregrounds this mediation as well as the fabrication: 'I guess it will make a pretty weird story, once he's written it; and the odd thing is I didn't tell any lies. Well, not very many' (378). It is not only a central subjectivity that is further relativised here: so is gender. Throughout the story Joan has presented herself as a liar, and the incongruity of the narrated events and her mode of narration (her above-discussed 'inadequacy') underline her unreliability as a narrator. This is another gothic narrative convention, a Poesque turn, which reappears in *Lady Oracle* in postmodern self-reflexivity. In typical parodic hyperbole, Joan's unreliability is exaggerated by the opening suggestion of the death of the (speaking) subject, and of the ensuing narrative voice as being that of a ghost. This effects a further undercutting of a central subjectivity, similar to Joan's position as subject-in-excess as outlined throughout this chapter. Thus, holistic notions of identity and truth become unreliable concepts – and gothic excesses become probable alternatives.

All these layers of stories and probable narrative voices reinforce the formal qualities of feminist gothic texture as maze. What its various creative repetitions of both gothic traditions and contemporary feminine gothic rewriting highlight is the vain quest for the true story. After all, 'true confessions' are also excessively deconstructed – feminist confessions included. At the time of writing, as we have seen, confessional life-writing presented an important, and almost a 'dominant', form of feminist 'self-expression' – and the parodic gothicism challenges this tendency for new versions of dominant stories and discursive hierarchies. The scepticism also addresses the related creation of female role-models: the position of a 'proper feminist' can be just as constraining as that of the ideal 'feminine' when subjected to totalising discourses, and can thus again be used against women: Arthur takes up women's lib for 'flagellation purposes'.

At this point, I would like to evoke another feminist classic, although it is usually critically placed far from gothicism: Doris Lessing's *The Golden Notebook* (1962). However, I think there are strong intertextual ties between Lessing's novel, often seen as one of the rationalist feminist manifestos of 1960s' radical realism, and the highly emotional *Lady Oracle*. The protagonist/narrator Anna Wulf tells her story – around her emotional as well as creative block – in four carefully separated notebooks as well as in a traditional novel. What connects her with Joan is not only the particular situation of the woman writer but also the desire for separation, control, order – which her own life, characterised as 'experimental', refuses. The same desire structures her writing, as her notebooks separate her into the successful author, the active Communist, the fictitious figure in another novel and the private person in psychotherapy. However, the desire prompting that separation is to write *truthfully*. And the form of the text – a highly experimental form that refuses the genre categories it alludes to – demonstrates complex concepts: that fiction can be truthful without being true, that writing and other sign-systems are lies, that truth can be approached (through experimentation) but not reached, etc. All this contextualises the cultural/political crisis and the ongoing 'sex war' of late-1950s' Britain (and Africa, and America, and the Soviet Union). Like Joan, Anna has to realise that separation is not the solution and that chaos can be accepted productively. And like Anna, maybe even in playful response to the serious Anna, Joan confronts and accepts the lies of her writing and story-telling imposed by narrative form and language. The labyrinthine gothicism of *Lady Oracle* in this sense intertextually responds to the rational questions for truth mapped out in *The Golden Notebook*.

What has been called Atwood's 'lack of closure' in *Lady Oracle* – or, in formal terms, her refusal to lead the way out of the labyrinth by accepting instead its multiple choices and possibilities – effectively challenges constraints, also for feminist plots and for feminist heroines. The gothic then, in this Atwoodian version as self-conscious, maze-like, parodic form, tells female life-stories with a liberating difference. It reveals the persistence of feminine myths and plots, that of romantic love included – and points to the powers of fictionalised challenge in a two-centuries-old form. Its parodic form at the same time deconstructs the gothic's fantasy reconciliation with existing power-relations, through 'loose ends' that remind us of the truth in romantic trash (the monstrousness of Woman, the terrors of Love) and that suggest escape into new fictions of yet unexplored 'selves' and aspects of femininity. Atwood's neo-gothicism is interwoven with women's gothic writing but already exceeds the space created here – anticipating a 'wilderness' that itself escapes the constructions and enclosures of houses – and even mazes. This is the space for the gothic forms of feminine fictions of the 1980s.

Notes

1 This can only suggest the scope of the abundance of Atwood criticism; for a detailed overview of readings of *Lady Oracle* see Fee (1993, 20–29). Fee's own position on its gothicism starts from the presupposition that Atwood 'wrote the novel to combat ... Gothic thinking' (77) and insists that 'Atwood's main point in the novel is that Joan's concept of what women should aspire to is limited by those stereotypes that form the currency of the popular media' (35). She continues: 'The media generally thrive on the extremist thinking that Atwood describes as Gothic, and require that complicated human beings fit into their simplistic hero/villain pattern' (35). By contrast, I would like to show how gothic excess points to such sensationalism and offers perspectives beyond – throughout Atwood's work, and most clearly in *Lady Oracle* and *Alias Grace* (1996).

2 For critical readings of Joan's fragmented identity as unable to accept her 'whole self' see Ross (1980), Thomas (1981), Hill Rigney (1987); as 'multiple personality disorder' (Rosenberg 1984, 116), as forming a new self and thereby challenging 'the pathology represented most obviously in this text by the figure of Joan's husband, Arthur' (Hengen 1993, 73); they see a danger to the 'self' in fantasies and ignore that Joan's story itself is told in gothic terms. By contrast and from a more postmodern perspective, Rao emphasises the 'liberating aspects of a multiple, plural subjectivity' and concludes: 'Deconstructing the homogenous ego, *Lady Oracle* yields a gendered vision wherein the figure of woman assumes a multiplicity of roles and positions' (1976, 133).

3 Similarly, Hite (1989, 141ff) and Godard (1983, 13ff) discuss *Lady Oracle* in terms of Irigaray's critique of the Selfsame and containment as masculine, hierarchical systems of control.

4 Critics have seen her as 'inadequate', as 'victim' and impossible (feminist) role-model (e.g. Hill Rigney 1987, 74). However: remember Austen's introduction of Catherine Morland as unfit for romance in *Northanger Abbey*!

5 Significantly, it was by researching women's magazines that Friedan discarded the 'feminine mystique' of the 1950s; and it was by analysing fashion and advertising that Wolf uncovered the 'beauty myth' of the 1980s. For an exploration of 'the masculine myth in popular culture' see Easthope's *What a Man's Gotta Do* (1990 [1986]).

6 This vision causes fear in the daughter – although it is 'the confirmation of something I'd always known' (70) – when put in relation to a mysterious man imagined outside. Joan fears the male gaze to which the mother would appear 'monstrous' before 'made up' into the ideal feminine image; later she wants reality to be recognised as truth (see also Godard 1983, 33 and Hengen 1993, 71ff on this scene).

7 Atwood's own research on such double standards of the early 1970s is reflected in her satiric 'Paradoxes and Dilemmas' (1971; in 1982a); *Lady Oracle* parodies her own public image of the time.

 8 See Atwood's unfinished doctoral dissertation on Haggard (and other
   metaphysical romances) in the Atwood Papers and her essay 'Superwoman
   Drawn and Quartered: The Early Forms of *She*' (1965) in *Second Words*
   (1982a).
 9 The concept of the I–she extension is complicated when put in relation to
   Benveniste's work on the function of pronouns; in this sense, the 'I' would
   represent the author/narrator and the 'she' the figure/character in the
   text. This recognition underlines the artificiality of these 'shes'. However,
   in my view, such a split or separation is not possible in the gothic; thus
   Joan's personae and fantasy figures remain connected, however widely
   their uncanny influence across the plot might spread.
10 Aunt Lou, a 'large woman' and also a woman of various identities, represents a godmother for Joan's art; and her name, Louisa K. Delacourt,
   becomes Joan's pen-name.
11 Wolf's study, especially her chapter on hunger, seems to owe a lot to
   Atwood's *The Edible Woman* as well as to *Lady Oracle*'s imagery of the
   Iron Maiden (Wolf 1991, 186) and the daughter's view of the mother's
   achievements in terms of beauty (compare the above quoted mirror-scene
   to Wolf's autobiographical account, 204). Both Wolf and Atwood offer
   biting ironic comments on the paradoxes of being 'immersed in flesh ...
   [but being seen as] beyond its desires' (192).
12 This scene is praised by Thomas as 'one of the funniest vignettes in
   Canadian Literature' (1981, 164). In a similar ritualistic scene, Joan buries
   her Canadian clothes. These clothes gothically signify a former self: 'I
   still felt as though I was getting rid of a body, the corpse of someone I'd
   killed' (18). Again, the gothic death-motif is displaced and extended into
   a rebirth, when the clothes are returned, of course, freshly washed.
13 Consequently, her photograph as fat woman – or Louisa Delacourt – is
   never printed on the back of her costume gothics, as it does not fulfill the
   image of the 'fairy godmother': 'The women who wrote my kind of book
   were supposed to look trim and healthy, with tastefully grayed hair. Unlike the reader, they had brisk shoulders and were successful' (176).
14 For a closer analysis of *She-Devil* in this sense see my 'The Haunted
   Voices of Fay Weldon' (1992a).
15 'Atwood Gothic': Eli Mandel first discussed Atwood's poetry with this
   focus in the *Malahat Review* dedicated to Atwood's work (1977) when her
   art as well as her politics had made her into a controversial Canadian
   cultural icon. This situation accounts for much of the self-parody in *Lady
   Oracle*. For Atwood's own view of that time see the introduction to *Second
   Words* (1982a). She emphasises that her politics have never been 'separate
   from my writing' (1982a, 14) – and her writing has, as I can only suggest
   here, never been separate from the gothic.

Chapter 6

Stripping the gothic: Aritha van Herk and *No Fixed Address*

Border experience: naked North

With Aritha van Herk's *No Fixed Address* (1986), my discussion of neo-gothicism reaches the context of the 1980s. This decade, in cultural terms, might best be characterised by the emancipatory turn of post-modernism (Hornung) from playful self-reflexivity to more pronounced politics, a turn that has been influenced by ex-centric voices (Hutcheon) from the postcolonial, the multicultural and the feminist (and larger gender-oriented) movements. It is also the decade of a conservative 'backlash' (Faludi) that produces, among other anti-feminist conse-quences, the most traditional feminine ideal since the 1950s. Just like the 'feminine mystique', this new femininity is constructed through the media, which on the one hand bedevil 'career women' as monsters (see Michael Crichton's influential bestseller and subsequent Holly-wood success *Disclosure* [1993]), and which on the other celebrate a pop star like Madonna precisely for her ability to 'sell' – albeit less her music than a typically 1980s' image of 'clean sex'.

Of course, the 1980s were also the decade of Charles and Diana, and Alison Light has shown how, in the aftermath of the Royal Wedding (1981), the public and media-empowered awareness for love plots exploded into an abundance of romance literature – and romance criticism (1986, 140). The *gothicism* of the decade is related: popular horror forms are always successful at conservative times that focus on the home and reinforce the ideology of the happy family. Philip Brophy, speaking mainly of popular cinema, observes a trend he calls 'horrality':

the audience's pleasure is derived from the destruction of the family –
'it being the object of the horror and us being the subject of their
demise' (Brophy 1986, 7) – and from the destruction of the body, as
these plots tend to 'play not so much on the fear of Death, but more
precisely on the fear of one's own body, of how one controls and
relates to it' (8). In formal terms, Brophy emphasises 'the act of showing over the act of telling; the photographic image versus the realistic
scene ... and a perverse sense of humour' (2) – aspects that highlight
the rising intertextual influence of comics (12). These are key aspects
contextualising neo-gothicism in the 1980s. *No Fixed Address*, as we
shall see, parodically 'repeats' some of these cultural and aesthetic
developments, using the ironic/comic voice that marks postmodern
gothicism and specifically its feminist critique. It is at its most powerful through the wide range of intertextual repercussions that evoke a
sense of the paradoxical dynamic 'stability' of neo-gothicism in a
typically 1980s' way.

My focus on form suggests, to start with, the haunted house of
gothic fiction. This early 1970s' form that gothicised female experience at the time of 'feminist confessions' had extended into more
labyrinthine constructions – with attentive parodies of both real and
fantasy, both literary and popular horrors and desires. In the context
of 1980s' literary culture, gothicism continues this process, which
might be characterised – as suggested in van Herk's title – as further
'unfixing' from master narratives; the generic excess addresses the
ideological constructions of Western culture and of our lives. The
development since Munro's gothicising of everyday life becomes even
clearer when comparing the setting: Munro's space within a domesticated wilderness, narrow, almost crowded with familiar faces – house-
like, after all – opens up into another truly Canadian setting: the
'frontier' in the wide open West and towards the North, a space of
bare nature and few people; of shifting forms and new visions. Moreover, the 'unfixing' from everyday reality (and its own texts) means
more and broader intertextuality, as anticipated by *Lady Oracle*. But
whereas here the labyrinthine repetition had a strong self-reflexive
(albeit not exclusive) focus on various forms of gothicism, *No Fixed
Address* in addition extensively parodies a whole range of texts, from
popular culture – and specifically visual (and multimedia) forms like
Hollywood movies or MTV – to canonical twentieth-century feminist
'classics'. Here again space is important, as the Canadian prairies

appear as a border space to this Western culture at large. In this border space, van Herk's novel thus continues the unfixing processes of gothic form. This means a shedding of shells and enclosing constructions, and the uncovering of the mirror-plot that constructs, as we have seen, the feminine gothic's interrogative texture: processes that I have come to read as 'stripping the gothic'.

This image is in some ways linked to the metaphor of texture that I have used throughout this study, but also to the metaphor of weaving that structures *No Fixed Address* – as instantly indicated by the heroine's name, Arachne Manteia, which evokes the web of the myth just as much as the narrative thread through the labyrinth. These emphasised connotations of spinning and weaving address form and 'texture' itself and deconstruct it back into its qualities as woven fabric. This is a transformation particularly illuminating in gendered terms as the weaving of threads into fabrics is traditionally women's work, and the weaving of narrative text/ure thus suggests a feminine textual form. A second thread that leads to the image of 'stripping the gothic' comes – like the house and the maze – from the idea of enclosure and containment of the heroine. All that is left in Arachne's story are the clothes she wears on her body. The heroine's dress has been important throughout feminine gothicism, as *Lady Oracle*'s 'costume gothics' self-consciously highlight; and it is important to note that they signify not only the containment of corsets and other fashionable shapers, but also representations of desire and of the powers of seduction. Again, as with the haunted house and the maze, I would like to explore the formal and cultural dimensions of this gothic theme. And the title 'No Fixed Ad/Dress' suggests, I think, the formal unfixing – and excess – that we shall find in this neo-gothic story of the 1980s.

'No Fixed Address' also suggests the other dynamics that has always characterised the gothic: the desire for travel, mobility, escape. Birgitta Berglund's study of Radcliffe, Wollstonecraft and Austen in terms of the image of the house stresses the illuminating ambivalence of eighteenth-century women writers concerning terrible feelings of containment within the houses' official security (1993, esp. 16ff). Similarly, Gilbert and Gubar's reading of nineteenth-century women's texts in these terms offers a good background for the discussion of a contemporary feminine text through the formal metaphor of 'dress':

> Dramatizations of imprisonment and escape are so all-pervasive in nineteenth-century literature by women that we believe they represent a uniquely female tradition in this period. Interestingly, though works in this tradition generally begin by using houses as primary symbols of female imprisonment, they also use much of the other paraphernalia of 'woman's place' to enact their central symbolic drama of enclosure and escape. Lady-like veils and costumes, mirrors, paintings, statues, locked cabinets. (1979, 85)

Such domestic furnishing not only contains but also, as we shall see, *engenders* everyday lives, like the very textures that contain and en-gender female bodies. A neo-gothic text like van Herk's self-consciously evokes and continues these metaphors from filliation – highlighting that 'engendering' function. Moreover, it also evokes the related twen-tieth-century feminist discourses on the 'look'. This concept is based on the one hand on feminist film criticism (e.g., Mulvey 1975; Kuhn 1985; Doane 1991) and especially on its controversially discussed as-sumption of the male gaze (Berger 1972; Kaplan 1983b; Humm 1997). On the other, taking off from Roland Barthes's explorations of the communicative possibilities of vestimonary codes (1969) it includes recent theories of fashion and fabrication (e.g. Gaines and Herzog 1990; Garber 1992) as well as revaluations of women's textile art and work (e.g. Hedges 1993).

Much of this twentieth-century discussion of fashion is still influ-enced by Simone de Beauvoir's views on dress and costume. In one sense, she takes up the idea of dress as enclosure – as thematically discussed by Gilbert and Gubar, and with the formal potential that I am interested in – when she speaks of fashion as enslavement for women:

> A man's clothes, like his body, should indicate his transcendence and not attract attention ... he does not normally consider his appearance as a reflection of his ego. Woman, on the contrary, is even required by society to make herself an erotic object. The purpose of the fashions to which she is enslaved is not to reveal her as an independent individual, but rather to cut her off from her transcendence in order to offer her as prey to male desires; thus society is not seeking to further her projects but to thwart them. (1989, 529)

In this sense, 'excess in dress' would open up the chance to act in the world – and it would be essential to the transition from (sexual) object to subject in the same way as excess of a house would – insofar as the house is not only 'woman's place' but also the product of (her) work and creativity, of both upkeeping and adorning. De Beauvoir is again illuminating on the relationship of body and dress when she writes: 'the costume may disguise the body, deform it, or follow its curves; in any case it puts it on display' (529). The presence of the gaze is assumed here, which de Beauvoir also suggests when she speaks of dress as intended 'to indicate the social standing of the woman', but also to put 'feminine narcissism in concrete form' (528). The subject's gaze and its relationship to the (dressed?) object is essential to the effects of dress – and other 'shells' around the body – as representation of the (gendered) 'self', in the sense that John Berger's *Ways of Seeing* (1972) has suggested and that feminist film criticism has expanded. The question whether the gaze is male assumes that men look at women and this is the organising principle in visual arts, from high-art oil paintings to popular forms like movies, videos, advertisements (see Gaines 1990, 3). It is in response to and even anticipation of this gaze that the female body is 'put on display', and that a certain image of femininity is created – and such images are reproduced and distributed extensively and effectively, as Laura Mulvey has shown in her influential essay 'Visual Pleasure and Narrative Cinema' (1975). Annette Kuhn's reading of glamour photography further highlights the relationship of nature and artifice (to remain within de Beauvoir's classification):

> A good deal of the groomed beauty of the woman of the glamour portraits comes from the fact that they are 'made up', in the immediate sense that cosmetics have been applied to their bodies in order to enhance their existing qualities. But they are also 'made up' in the sense that the images, rather than the women, are put together, constructed, even falsified in the sense that we might say a story is made up if it is a fiction. (1985, 13)

In one sense, this promotes, as Kuhn writes, 'the ideal woman as being put together, composed of surfaces and defined by appearances' (14). But this recognition also reflects back on the construction – or, to use Jane Gaines's fitting term: the 'fabrication' (1990) – of the body itself through the textures around it. 'Not biology but signs are the stuff that bodies are made of' writes Barbara Vinken (1993, 15; my translation). The German term *Stoff* here connotes not only 'stuff' but, more precisely, material or fabric; it thus reinforces the recognition that nature and artifice, body and dress, are interwoven textures, and that dress is one of the signs that 'make' the texture of the body.

I would like to use these new approaches to dress as 'texturing' sign in two dimensions. First, as the brief summary of positions suggests, shapes of dress are mainly seen as reinforcing the confinement into the male gaze and power structures. However, I think they also work, like romance plots, on different levels of feminine fantasies, desires, and maybe provoke a paradoxical escape, another 'disappearing act'. At the same time, the enclosures – and escapes – of dress suggest, in formal terms, the possibilities of the text/ure of feminine plots. Arachne Manteia's story is shaped, as we shall see, like the layers of her dress: with paradoxical suggestions of its enclosures but also of its possibilities of escape (and disappearance from sight) – and, of course, of excess.

First of all, the idea of dress as 'texturing' sign becomes crucial to the discussion of subjectivity and gender construction, where another typical aspect of 1980s' feminine writing in general and of stripping the gothic in particular is suggested: a version of subjectivity-in-process where 'subject' is transformed into 'verb'. Then the notion of clothing as enclosure, confronted with gothic excess and 'stripping' tendencies, offers a good starting-point in discussion of neo-gothic contextualisation of ex-centric border experience in van Herk's novel.

As has been suggested, clothing is the only enclosure left around Arachne: her story is set, not in a family home or small town or other small circle of familiar people, but in the wild prairies of Canada. Through the wide open space of the Canadian West and North, the fabric of her neo-gothic story spreads. It continues and thus reinforces the web of women's gothic writing, with all its various excesses of enclosures: in thematic terms as houses/costumes; in the related formal terms of the textures of dress; or in the cultural terms of *le propre*. At the same time, as we have seen, neo-gothicism also means deconstructing its own enclosures, promising liberation – and this is the 'stripping' dimension of *No Fixed Address*. In this section, I would like to discuss how 'stripping the gothic' works in terms of form – dress – and space – the 'naked North' of Canada.

'How do you make love in a new country?' asks Robert Kroetsch, 'Mr. Canadian Postmodern' (Hutcheon 1988b, 160), in his article on women and prairie fiction. His answer begins by connecting love-making to story-making to the functions of containment of both:

> In a paradoxical way, stories – more literally, books – contain the answer. How do you establish any sort of *close* relationship in a landscape – in a

physical situation – whose primary characteristic is *distance*? The telling of story – more literally, the literal closedness of a book – might be made to (paradoxically again) contain space. (Kroetsch 1989, 73)

Kroetsch's textual examples are modernist; despite the fact that he once pronounced the absence of modernism in Canadian literary history and declared a 'Canadian bravura leap' (Bessner 1992, 16) from Victorianism straight into postmodernism (Kroetsch 1989, 1). I would like to use his idea of love- and story-making in a space marked by distance to look at feminine writing and prairie fiction in a postmodern context; a context which celebrates process and defies notions of containment. Aritha van Herk's heroines, Judith, Jael and Arachne, are all 'prairie women' of the Canadian West, and their stories address the question of close relationships and open space in different ways and varying narrative and formal strategies. What these – strong and in different ways complicated – heroines share is their appreciation of or love for the open space of Western Canada. That Canadian women's prairie fiction has long 'ungarrisoned' Canadian literature and criticism (Buss 1993, 125) has been shown, for example, by the collection *A Mazing Space: Writing Canadian Women Writing* (Kamboureli and Neuman 1986); by Carol Fairbanks's proposition that '[f]rom the early nineteenth century Red River settlement to contemporary life in works by writers like Byrna Barclay, Sharon Butala, and Aritha van Herk, the prairies are predominantly described as a positive force in women's lives' (1986, 35); and by Helen M. Buss's demand for new metaphors 'of a more erotic and maternal nature' (1993, 133). Van Herk herself has mused on 'love of the prairie landscape [as] a dominant structure in stories about prairie women' (1990, 2) and I think that her fiction as well as essays explore such new metaphors in gothic terms.

In Kroetsch's view, this landscape and its scope of distance complicates the notion of love and physical proximity and develops the books that paradoxically could contain that scope/space in a way that is crucial to a gothicist reading:

It seems to me that we've developed a literature, on the Great Plains, in which marriage is no longer functional as a primary metaphor for the world as it should or might be. The model as it survived even in Chaucer (for all his knowledge of the fear of women), through the plays of Shakespeare, through the novels of Jane Austen and D. H. Lawrence, has been replaced by models of another kind. What that kind is, I've only begun here to guess. (Kroetsch 1989, 83)

Gothic horror is family horror, and overcoming the marriage metaphor might suggest overcoming the related type of horror as well.
Seen in this context, the figure of the prairie woman indeed faces new
and, again, 'open' possibilities for her love story, without the constraints and control of a crowded, and, in the twentieth century, mass
society, without the conventions that society constructs for love – and
for love plots.

Although this 'new country' is not characterised by the enclosed
space traditionally so essential to the construction of horror, gothic
traces mark it nonetheless: 'The geography of love and the geography
of fear: on the prairies it's hard to tell them apart' (Kroetsch 1989,
77). This evokes the gothic's conjunction of love and terror, which in
No Fixed Address appears in a postmodern 'disguise', as we shall see.
But this geography is also that of the sublime – of the grand open
space that terrifies (and, in Radcliffe's terms, 'heightens the senses')
by its sheer extension, by its vastness, by its 'looks' – and that, by the
same means, attracts and seduces. Margaret Atwood summarises this
image of seduction and terror with characteristic irony as 'the idea of
the North as a mean female – a sort of icy and savage *femme fatale*
who will drive you crazy and claim you for her own' (1995b, 88).
Feminine plots, especially contemporary ones, she writes, have played
with the fascinations of that imagery. In the context of the 1980s, it
seems that this geography of the great wide open becomes the site of
postmodern plots, and, as in *No Fixed Address*, a site of neo-gothicism
– and of the prairie woman's 'love' plot.

Notions of space are constitutive of the *Canadian* postmodern. Neil
Bessner notes that 'Canada's evolving ideas about its history and its
geography, about its past and its natural setting, have always been
charged with Canada's awareness of its colonial ties across the Atlantic
and of our apprehension – and "apprehension" is probably an apt
term – of our North American space' (1992, 18). This Canadian sense
of space and of perspective, it seems, is a movement that does not
consume itself – like the American dream – from East to West, but
towards the (frozen) North – a space which connotes the impossibility
of any permanent settlement, the deferral of arrival, and the necessity
of motion for survival.[1] These postmodern concepts are reinforced by
titles of Canadian criticism like 'North of Intention' (McCaffery 1986)
with the emphasis on the process rather than the reached product.
Linda Hutcheon has shown this liminal space to be that of possibility

(1988, 3), and it seems that this idea provides the background to Aritha van Herk's uses of it for staging an escape on the Arctic Sea:

> And yes, I always want to go farther, push back another boundary, cross another invisible line. Yes, reader, what I am about to confess is heresy, but I long, finally, to escape the page, to escape ink and my own implacable literacy, altogether. (1991, 4)

This 'confession' comes five years after *No Fixed Address*'s exploration of such escape with postmodern, feminist and gothic strategies. The central female figure of that novel does go further and pushes back boundaries, crosses lines – though not as writer or artist, but as heroine of the prairie, on the road. The lines she crosses are, therefore, in a primary sense geographical/spatial and thus suggestive of the view of the Canadian postmodern sketched out above. But there will be other, related 'line-crossings': of the moral – into the erotic; of the rational – into the chaotic; of the natural – into the gothic; of the conventional – into excess. In terms of texture, 'line-crossings' or 'unfixings' explore gothic possibilities both for constructing a female subject and for telling her story. And, in the same sense in which these terms indicate that they still acknowledge and reject that which they thus 'address', *No Fixed Address* also shows that boundaries of form, of genre itself, are 'unstable' – and that they can be neo-gothically exceeded, and 'stripped'.

Arachne's physical mobility is important in this sense. In her black 1959 Mercedes she drives through the small towns of Alberta and Saskatchewan. It is the pleasure of driving, of 'explor[ing] all the weird little towns in the West' (14), of desiring roads and maps, that in one way links her to the writer. 'Mapping with words' is what van Herk has suggested as one, however problematic, possibility of 'map[ping] this country' and 'ourselves'. In the introduction to a collection of short fiction from Alberta she writes:

> How do we live here, how can we understand the hugely magnificent country? All of our puny attempts, our mappings, our drawings, in no way capture its mystery, its presence ... Perhaps only fiction allows us to do that, map ourselves with words. Although words, of course, are dangerous, can be misleading, can deceive. (1990b, 5)

Her *Places far from Ellesmere* (1990) presents such a verbal map; it poetically explores not only the Canadian frontier landscape between her hometown Edberg and the frozen Ellesmere Island but also, in yet another postmodern border blur, the intersections of geography and fiction. It is illuminating to realise how this is part of van Herk's own journey around recognitions about Canada and fiction: far from home, as a guest professor in Germany, she writes the introduction to another collection, *Boundless Alberta* (1993), in these terms:

> Albertans are from Japan, Italy, New Delhi, Toronto, Trinidad, China, Holland, and heaven. Their literary travels take them not just back to earlier homes, but on first-time journeys to Prague, India, Germany, Zaire, Iceland, New York, and the moon. And what experience these travels offer is not always comforting, not merely indolently exotic. Characters discover the shifting nature of what we call home. Canada as a desirable address is called into question, any assumption of Alberta as a provincial safety zone, predictable and well-fed, is challenged. We are now part of the global community, and our literature reflects that connection. (van Herk 1993, ix–x)

I think that van Herk uses the gothic to explore such globalising developments, and that Canadian neo-gothicism in the 1980s anticipates such recognitions of a new sense of space. So much for mapping the grounds for exploring its textures.

In van Herk's *No Fixed Address*, the desire for maps is inextricably linked to the love plot. Arachne's 'apocryphal lover', and the man she lives with between her travels, is the cartographer Thomas Telfer. 'He maps the roads; she drives them. His is the product; hers is the process', as Linda Hutcheon puts it (1988b, 130), emphasising once again this aspect of the Canadian postmodern. Perhaps not surprisingly, the obsession with mobility, with process – or rather: the avoidance of the product/stasis – will here take over and motivate the plot. For her desire for exploration and motion also takes Arachne away from Thomas. Driving is her job: she is a travelling salesperson, selling women's underwear – and representing Calgary's – aptly named – 'Ladies Comfort Limited' company.

The underwear is the first trace of dress in the text; not surprisingly, it is not only important as a theme. The novel opens with an ironic reflection on underwear's age-old function – 'to aid physical attractiveness, a standard inevitably decided by men' (9) – and on its effect: imprisonment of the female body and the general discomfort of women until recent, more androgynous fashions. In this sense, underwear becomes a sign for the larger fashion system, which is in some ways suggested not only as another form of containment, but also as totalising discourse in gender construction. This 'containment' works similarly to that in *Lady Oracle*, and it provokes similarly gothic reactions: the activities of expanding and exceeding, in terms of the body and in terms of the text. Where Joan eats and thus resists, Arachne resists as she 'wears nothing at all' (12) underneath her dress or jeans. This also draws attention to her body – a body that does not at all fit the 1980s' ideal of slimness (in contrast to the sketch on the cover, Arachne is 'chunky') but which she thoroughly enjoys. And it draws attention to the function of surface clothes, which turn out to be 'disguises' – or even masquerades – while, paradoxically, putting the body on display (de Beauvoir). Appropriately, it is Arachne's official job to get rid of the underwear by selling it to men: small-town shopkeepers. Her own treatment of these complex garments is a first trace of Arachne's treatment of related aspects of *le propre* – and of her own story's treatment of the proper plots.

Underwear suggests layers of clothes, which suggest layers of narrative voices. *No Fixed Address*, with its lightness of voice in typically neo-gothic fashion, is marked by that 'double-layered phenomenon' so characteristic of the Canadian postmodern in Hutcheon's definition: irony. The opening elaborations on the 'proper' underwear conclude with an ironic reversal of the very connotations of *le propre* itself: 'All that has changed, and now, if we wear satin and lace, we do so desirous of the proper consequences' (10). The irony ridicules convention; again, as in *Lady Oracle*, it turns into liberating laughter that overturns constrictions – and thus other 'standards, inevitably decided by men'. However, 'feminist ironic challenges' also imply a critique of such constrictions, most notably because 'double-talking irony' allows for, and even celebrates, the sense of contradiction that totalising discourses have produced in women. 'Contradiction, division, doubleness – these are the contesting elements that irony lets in by the front door' (Hutcheon 1991, 97) – to challenge forms of containment in a text like *No Fixed Address*.

Moreover, layers of clothes, layers of voices also suggest layers of text and of subjectivity. The notion of the hidden (underwear) shaping the surface refers us to the possibility of a subtext forming the plot as well as to the possible subversion of the surface story of *No Fixed Address*. 'They [the women] will buy panties patterned with spiders or eggplants or pigs or skulls ... They dress conservatively enough on top, but underneath there's more to be found than flowers and polka dots' (11). This playful mockery of the commonplace cliché of feminine mystery also recalls the feminist challenges to textual surface: feminine gothic structure as 'interrogative' texture with its challenging mirror-text of female desire. The idea of a different love plot on the prairies suggests a new development of neo-gothic texture; however, as we shall see, the powers of ideology and of totalising discourses remain a force to be contested – or, gothically, exceeded.

Criticism on *No Fixed Address* has so far only related the novel to genres that are not at all gothic: the Western, a very masculine American genre, and the women's travel tale, with a solid Canadian tradition and well-known literary foremothers like Nelly McClung or Sara Jeanette Duncan, women's prairie fiction. Moreover, the heroine on the road, as well as the opening's suggestion – 'No art, no novel, no catalogue of infamy has considered the effect of underwear on the lives of petty rogues' (10) – self-consciously suggest the picaresque. Van Herk comments:

> It's the first modern picaresque novel written from a female point of view – with one exception, Erica Jong's *Fear of Flying* ... it's also the first picaresque novel about a woman which is not written in the first person, although I've maintained many of the other conventions, including the episodic chapter headings. (in Lacey 1986, C11)

That *No Fixed Address* actually feminises this masculine genre with much ironic inversion, and that this means a change in 'literary, social and ideological reverberations', is shown by Linda Hutcheon's discussion of the novel as feminist postmodern parody of the picaresque (1988, 126). However, the picaresque is closely connected to the gothic. In fact, a diagram of the gothic in Todorov's style might place the gothic at the structural intersection of the picaresque and the sentimental, just as Todorov's fantastic is placed at the intersection of the uncanny and the marvellous (1975, 45). Ellen Moers has convincingly characterised Radcliffe's Emily not only as 'Pamela's sensible sister' but also as 'Moll Flanders' indestructible cousin': 'in Mrs. Radcliffe's hands, the Gothic novel became a feminine substitute for the picaresque, where heroines could enjoy all the adventures and alarms that masculine heroes had long experienced, far from home, in fiction' (1976, 126). Ironically, as we have seen, it is the villain whose power and violence offer the possibility of travelling and of exceeding the containment of the heroine's 'proper sphere' (Moers 1978, 126). This recognition of the maiden-in-flight's liberation also highlights how the gothic magnifies that sphere itself:

> For indoors, in the long, dark, twisting, haunted passageways of the Gothic castle, there is travel with danger, travel with exertion – a challenge to the heroine's enterprise, resolution, ingenuity, and physical strength ... It was only *indoors*, in Mrs. Radcliffe's day, that the heroine of a novel could travel brave and free, and stay respectable. (Moers 1978, 129)

'Respectability' still resonates in neo-gothicism. While the gothic heroine of the late twentieth century exchanges the gothic castle for the roads of the *picara*, she continues radically to expose the stifling stability of *le propre*, rapidly changing cultural standards notwithstanding. Esther Greenwood's struggles with, and step-by-step rejection of, 'respectability' in the shape of the 'feminine mystique' in Plath's *The Bell Jar* (1963) – also a 'road novel' in its own time (see Tucker 1994, 35) – are a striking example. As has been suggested, the monstrous-feminine in the 1980s is the successful, economically and sexually independent career woman. At the same time, the sexual woman becomes an icon of popular culture, for example in the shape of pop goddess Madonna, with her first video *Like a Virgin* (1985). Madonna's success, I think, has less to do with the development of sexual liberation in the aftermath of the 1960s than with adapting to the (male) gaze: her 1980s' videos make female sexuality a commodity, a (repeatedly) consumable, neatly packaged product. As such, it loses its threat: it can be controlled and enjoyed at a distance. Rosalind Coward has suggested that perhaps such 'sex-at-a-distance is the only complete secure relation which men can have with women' (1985, 76). She argues: 'The aesthetic appeal of women disguises a preference for *looking* at women's bodies, for keeping women separate, at a distance, and the ability to do this' (1985, 76). In the video age, such representations of female sexuality become, paradoxically, 'proper'. It seems that the neo-gothicism of *No Fixed Address* reacts precisely against this version of domesticating female sexuality and women's bodies in 1980s' media culture. And it does so in two ways: by undercutting the distancing look through Arachne's aggressive sexuality, and by enforcing the traditional gothic challenge to the constraints of gender conventions: excessive mobility.

Late-twentieth-century gothic heroines no longer need villains to travel; however, the old perception of 'man's world – woman's place' persists. Witness Kroetsch:

> We conceive of external space as male, internal space as female. More precisely, the penis: external, expandable, expendable; the vagina: internal, eternal. The maleness verges on mere absence. The femaleness verges on mystery: it is a space that is not a space. External space is the silence that needs to speak, or that needs to be spoken. It is male. The having spoken is the book. It is female. It is closed. (1989, 73)

Linda Hutcheon has shown how his dialectic 'Erotics of Space' is transformed into feminised alternatives in *No Fixed Address* (1988, 123). These alternatives not only play with gender reversals but also draw attention to the boundaries that are exceeded. Arachne's life-story before the 'professional' travelling is marked by such excess and by motion: climbing out of the crib as a baby (39); climbing the fence and running away as a child (42); avoiding home by working double-shifts as a bus-driver and thus again as always moving (75); leaving Vancouver in a carefully plotted trip East with Thomas (94). Her travels actively, persistently, exceed enclosures, including *le propre*, into the great open space, a parodically hyperbolic space for postmodern process and gothic provocation.

The Great Plains offer the possibility of border experience; in *No Fixed Address* they become the space for gender exploration, for reversals and parodic allusions to the gothic love plot. Arachne's and Thomas's gender roles are reversed, as she goes on business trips and he tends to the home, but this is only the start. Throughout the story, Thomas is credited with having 'saved' Arachne in leaving Vancouver with her, 'with preventing her from becoming an escapee' (62). The irony here is obvious: not only is this just the function of the villain in the traditional gothic novel, but it is also 'heroine' Arachne who has plotted the trip in the first place. This complex situation reflects back on the traditional gothic novel's *covert* liberating processes – and presents another trace of the neo-gothic 'stripping' process. Enhancing the ironic reverberations here, Thomas as 'saviour' figure carries almost religious overtones. However, his character is quickly recognised as that of a hero 'too good to be true' (van Herk 1986b) – a hyperbolic romantic figure devoid of the traditional Byronic hero's threats and thus uncanny in his own way. This self-consciously fantastic male figure further works to deconstruct the romantic myth of the patriarchal male's mysterious transformations through love: his positioning as 'saviour' does evoke the generic rescuing motif of the gothic romance with ironic mockery and reversal as it is initiated by Arachne. Consequently, *No Fixed Address* avoids the subsequent idealised image of stability – of the couple in the home – and thus the restoration of the liberated, travelling female figure into a patriarchal structure. Rather, the indoors and its related domesticity – traditionally the heroine's 'happy ending' and relief from bravely endured horrors – here are ironically reversed into the very site of the gothic condition to be escaped: 'the horror of what [Arachne] calls house arrest' (38), the feminist dimension of 'horrality' (Brophy 1986).

With such gender explorations, Arachne's story evokes and 'strips' the covert desires of traditional gothic heroines: Emily St Aubert could have eloped with and secretly married Valencourt, but she goes to Italy with Montoni under the pretext of obedience; Jane Eyre – with a passionate desire to travel – accepts Rochester's first proposal with the promise of travel through Europe after the wedding. In *No Fixed Address*, this desire for mobility is no longer concealed in a subplot. Here neo-gothic texture is structured by a range of plots that 'strip' and uncover the dynamics of emotional challenges. Arachne's plot also 'strips' with ironic mockery the compromise of happy endings. In the border space of the North, the possibility of a new, different gothic love plot is thus suggested: the vastness of the 'new country' demands and offers new, flowing dynamics of texture.

The subject-in-process – and in disguise

The texture of the neo-gothic love plot as flowing dress will be discussed in this section, with a focus on the processes of the female subject. I think that in this text of 1980s' neo-gothicism, the idea of subjectivity itself is further transformed, in a way that is linked to the emancipatory turn of postmodernism under its feminist influence, and that further highlights the development of gothicism towards new dynamics of form and of gender construction.

Arachne's jobs as bus-driver and travelling saleswoman are a case in point. These travels, in their particular contextualisation, construct her, literally, 'physically', as 'subject-in-process' in the sense outlined by Kristeva. Formally speaking, the dimensions of both spatial and gender 'unfixing' are constituted through the dynamic qualities of texture as dress. If such texture also constitutes gendered subjectivity, the texture of dress participates in 'making' the female body and the female subject in this neo-gothic text in a specific way: I think what happens in *No Fixed Address* is a narrative move towards Alice Jardine's concept of 'women-as-verbs'. Jardine defines this concept as the 'putting into discourse of woman as that process ... intrinsic to the condition of modernity' (1985, 24). In her argument, this is a feminist answer to the crisis in legitimation of the master narratives as diagnosed by Lyotard. It offers a possibility to encounter what she sees as 'violent refusal of the maternal ... [in] ... the contemporary male American text' (1985, 237), in the face of an interrogative return to the sources of our knowledge in the West that is tied to the return to the mother's body. Thus contextualised, it seems that 'women-as-verbs' constitute new feminine narrative forms: neo-gothic fabrications that use different forms of excess to dynamise notions of gender and writing.

Both the travel motif and the related more flexible form of dress suggest a self-conscious treatment of this kind of dynamic subjectivity, which will be discussed here with regard to the love plot and to female desire. It intertextually relates Arachne to other heroines of contemporary gothic texts, and to their own processes of 'unfixing'. For example, Joan Foster in *Lady Oracle* represents an ironic escapee from 'love'; or, to introduce a new figure from Canadian neo-gothicism, 'Lola Montez', alias Shirley Kaszenbowski (Weinzweig 1980), represents, as we shall see an ironic pursuer of her absent/present 'lover'. The title of her story – *Basic Black with Pearls* – alludes to a classic of feminine fashion in the late twentieth century and thus already indicates the specific fabrication of her plot. What 'Lola', Joan and Arachne (and similar female figures) share is the mobility, constructed through this multi-layered feminine gothic texture, that exceeds – and at the same time ironically highlights – the persistent traditional notions of a domesticated and 'respectable' female subjectivity. For all of them (and this is the focus of this chapter) this physical mobility also, in different ways, means 'unfixing' the female body from the related moral constraints and expectations – physical, sexual, erotic liberation is an important aspect of their travels. This is a theme that not only contextualises the consequences of the various 1960s' liberation movements but that also contributes to an ongoing (ironic) dialogue with

those feminine gothic classics that have early inscribed these constraints as horrors. Elsewhere, van Herk has emphasised that 'the
body's true inheritance is its imagination ... transcending both corpo-
rate and corporeal' (1996a, 'Introduction'). Accordingly, these travels
turn into 'amorous journeys' in different ways. And the female subjects of – or verbs through – these travel stories 'cross the line' that
had, in the gothic classics, separated and characterised 'the dark lady
and the fair maiden': the doomed sexual woman and the proper 'angel
in the house'.

The femme fatale: an amorous journey

Arachne's travels in her black 1959 Mercedes Benz are, as the subtitle
aptly indicates, 'An Amorous Journey'. As such, they radically contest
le propre: Arachne, with her need to 'keep ... herself amused' (14),
enjoys innumerable sexual encounters, with 'road jockeys' (34), as her
friend and 'confidante' Thena disapprovingly calls them. But for
Arachne, these lovers are 'just bodies, you could put a paper bag over
their heads':

> Arachne is not unselective: she has an instinct for men who are clean,
> residually polite, who are decent lovers without being nasty or dangerous.
> Some of them she even sees again on return trips. They are easy and
> cordial; she may or may not take them back to her room, it's no matter.
> They follow her no further. If they even recognise her again, it's because of
> the Mercedes. Arachne jokes that the car is better than any aphrodisiac.
> (33)

The casual voice that rejects any moralising regulating instance, the
tales told to a female friend, the hyperbole in these sexual excesses: all
these produce irony's 'splitting images' (Hutcheon) here and construct
a new image of the *femme fatale*. The irony undercuts the didacticism
attached to that figure in the tradition of Mary Wollstonecraft's
eighteenth-century feminist gothic; however: Arachne's sex life is just
as provoking, as it explicitly undercuts the male gaze and the related
control-through-distance that makes *femme fatale* figures attractive and
consumable – especially in the world of 1980s' commercial audiovisual
media. Arachne's aggressive sexuality mocks that 'sex-at-a-distance'
in a parodic gender reversal that 'strips' the figure of the modern
macho. It also alludes to the recent feminised versions of that figure:
the type of the cruel woman depicted in popular punk texts or

provocative feminist fiction, such as that of American writers Kathy Acker or Lynne Tillman. However, what is more important than the sex scenes themselves is their communication among women: when cast into stories for Thena, these adventures, these lovers, are reduced to objects of narrative. Consequently, Arachne's sexual excesses as well as their – equally excessive – discursive repetition also mock the myth of romantic love that has shaped feminine gothic form, at least on the surface, into the 'heroine's plot'. This is effected by another ironic twist of the gothic convention.

Arachne incarnates both the heroine and the 'sexual woman in gothic fiction' (as defined by Mussell 1975): two female figures that have, throughout the gothic romance tradition, been narratively separated and functioned as foils. That the figure of Arachne presents a conjunction of both suggests a reversal – and a trace of parodic hyperbole. Arachne incorporates the effect of instant attraction for men that characterises Blanche Ingram (one of the first 'sexual women' types in Mussell's reading), and Bertha Mason's sexuality in *Jane Eyre*. In the feminine gothic, these figures function traditionally as the heroine's rivals for the hero's love (Blanche), and as monstrous female figures highlighting the heroine's (surface) respectability while doubling her own (secret) desires (Bertha). The perceived monstrosity of the sexual-woman figure is most memorably rendered in Jane Eyre's only encounter with Bertha Mason:

> In the deep shade, at the farther end of the room, a figure ran backwards and forwards: what it was, whether beast or human being, one could not, at first sight, tell: it grovelled, seemingly, on all fours: it snatched and growled like some strange wild animal: but it was covered with clothing, and a quantity of dark, grizzled hair, wild as a mane, hid its head and face. (321)

The 'madwoman in the attic' is seen as 'clothed hyena', crazy, imprisoned and *voiceless*. Her presentation in *Jane Eyre*'s attic scene as Other to the 'proper' Jane reveals a remarkable narrative construction: it occurs within the powers of the hero's gaze. Rochester's view of his wife, which controls this passage casts Bertha as monster. As various critics have shown, this view – like Bertha's imprisonment – is related to the male fear of women and, more precisely, of the sexual woman and her 'passions', of adult sexuality, affirmation of physical pleasure, articulation of desire, a fear of the powers of the female body.[2] The figure of Bertha Mason has thus become a prototype of the sexual

Medusa She who tempts and kills: the attractions of archetypal *femme fatale* figures assume new powers at the centre of neo-gothic plots and designs.

woman in the feminine gothic: the beautiful wife turned monstrous, her presentation as half human, half animal effectively foregrounded by her status as voiceless (textual) object, controlled by the hero's gaze. However, while on the one hand the male gaze produces a contrast between the two female figures, Bertha and Jane, on the other this gaze is what they have in common, and it points to the recognition that Bertha is also a double of the 'wild', passionate, and – to herself – 'monstrous' Jane (see Gilbert and Gubar 1979, 348).

This power of the male gaze is put on trial when the silenced 'madwoman' starts to speak, as Jean Rhys's *Wide Sargasso Sea* (1966) has shown. This modernist gothic is Bertha's, the sexual woman's, story, and thus overtly tells what Atwood has suggested are contemporary women's secret plots (Oates 1978). The sexual woman's dark gothic story does more or less overtly motivate much feminist writing today, and *No Fixed Address*, with its narrative unfixing processes, participates in this provocative intertextualisation.

Arachne Manteia. Her name alone points us to a reading in these terms. It signals a first formal quotation of the myth of the mortal woman whose wonderful weaving provoked the goddess Athena to turn her into a spider. This myth then, repeated with much post-modern parody, becomes another intertext of Arachne's multilayered story – and yet another dimension of her story as (spider's) web (see Hutcheon 1988a, 123). But 'Arachne' also evokes a type of *femme fatale* – the spider woman:

> The dark lady, the spider woman, the evil seductress who tempts man and brings about his destruction is among the oldest themes of art, literature, mythology and religion in Western culture. She is as old as Eve, and as current as today's movies, comic books and dime novels. She and her sister (or *alter ego*), the virgin, the mother, the innocent, the redeemer, form the two poles of female archetypes. (Place 1980, 35)

This definition opens Janey Place's essay on 'Women in Film Noir', and thus brings us back to cineastic discourse and the idea that texture engenders – and unfixes – the subject. Place argues that the spider woman is constructed only in relation to men: 'Film noir is a male fantasy, as is most of our art. Thus woman here as elsewhere is defined by her sexuality: the dark lady has access to it and the virgin does not' (35). The spider woman – like the *femme fatale* of late romanticism (see Hilmes 1990) – is tempting and threatening in her own domain, the erotic: she promises death, not only for her lover but for herself. However, her eroticism is combined with an extraordinary activity and ambition which uses the erotic (and the lover) for intrusion into male domains, thus subverting male control and power. Place emphasises the provocation of a special 'mode of control that must be exerted to dominate her' (1980, 54) – by those (men), for whom she represents a threat and in whom she produces fear: thus, the *femme fatale* myth comes full circle. Her discussion of the 'spider woman' in film noir emphasises forms of visual signification that subvert this circle and its 'regressive ideological function' – for example, film noir's 'uniquely sensual visual style which often overwhelms (or at least acts upon) the narrative so compellingly that it stands as the only period in American film in which women are deadly but sexy, exciting and strong' (54). She also emphasises the related subversion of generic closure:

> Even more significant is the form in which the 'spider woman's' strength and power is expressed: the visual style gives her such freedom of move-ment and dominance that it is her strength and sensual visual texture that is inevitably printed in our memory, not her ultimate destruction. (1980, 54)[3]

The figure of Arachne can be read as a narrative version of such a 'spider woman' with an ironic difference. She is characterised as 'amoral, selfish, dishonest' (103) but in her story, freedom of move-ment is the key term, not dominance or ambition for a specific goal. Her aggression and her mobility are aimed at avoiding enclosure, con-striction, that of her body included. Still, her sexuality, devoid of these more 'dangerous' attributes and explicitly lived out because 'I like men' (33), presents a threat to men. In one sense, what they (have to) fear is (only) ridicule – the ridicule of two women chatting. How-ever, as Naomi Wolf has put it, to be ridiculed is the male fear (of women) that parallels the female fear of being killed (by men).[4] This recognition adds yet another level to one of the basic emotions – fear of death – in gothicism. And Arachne's matter-of-fact affairs and their virtual dependence on being told to the *confidante* (154) viciously mock those fantasies that define women only in sexual terms and only in relation to men.

However, despite the lightness of voice and the mocking irony shaping *No Fixed Address*, Arachne's erotic 'amusement' is quickly overshadowed by gothic traces that typically thicken throughout her story and become grotesque, criminal, violent, un-real – and deadly. The gothic in this context recalls once again Kristeva's 'x-rays through love' (Becker: interview): love without the idyllic aspect; rather with the recognition of the violence in its passion, as the form plays through the interrelatedness of romance, sex, horror. Arachne's 'amorous journey' – which is, to emphasise it once again, a story fabricated through wit, liberating laughter and much mocking irony – becomes darkest in its last part. What can be traced throughout the plot is a gender reversal also in sexual terms of the traditional romance constellation. Female masochism and passivity[5] is here transferred to the male characters: their hands (palms up) signal submission; they mostly react to Arachne's initiative; they are objects in her 'brutally honest' reports to Thena. They are victimised by her sexuality, and later by her violence: she robs one and kills another man in self-defence.

This murder occurs in the typically gothic situation in which the immobility of the subject triggers violence. A classic example is Lockwood's encounter with Catherine's ghost in *Wuthering Heights*, as Eve Kosofsky Sedgwick has shown (1986, 99). 'Terror made me cruel': thus Lockwood, aptly described as 'buried-alive' and so immobilised, explains his famous maltreatment of the ghostly arm. In *No Fixed Address*, Arachne is 'immobilised' by a male figure's advances in a nocturnal scene on a boat that has overtones of rape and vampirism (286); the gothic combination of immobility and violence is thus extended to representing female self-defence against male physical abuse. Again, in terms of violence, as in terms of sexuality, there is, in typical postmodern fashion, no moral judgement on the horizon; Arachne has just escaped again, crossed another line. But this part of her story has turned into a poetic prose-piece of gothic border-blurs between shades of fear and the terrors of the imagination. Arachne thinks she is dead and all action means the recognition of her living body. Another good example is the treatment of 'making love' in this part, in her completely fantastic sexual encounter with what turns out to be a literal ghost of an airman who had drowned in 1944. This uncanny – and in a sense supernatual – scene in this most dark and death-ridden episode (294) can be read as another hyperbolic postmodern rewriting or parodic repetition of a truly gothic excess, namely Poesque necrophilia. That it is here evoked *without* the thrilling single-effect suggests a further excess: exceeding the classic gothicism that would have relied on this effect.

How to make love in a 'new country'? Arachne's story treats this question in narrative layers. Another such layer is in her relationship with Joseph – a relationship which is death-ridden, but also comic; which has redeeming qualities, but also excessive ones. Joseph is Arachne's ninety-year-old lover who is romantically – and ironically – described as a man 'who has been alive for a long time'. He not only appears as hyperbolic distortion of the always older and more experienced and traditionally somehow physically maimed Byronic hero, but also provides the possibility of an ironic reversal of a gothic elopement, when Arachne kidnaps him from an old people's home – one of the truly nightmarish spaces in the text, with its 'endless white corridor that seems like an entrance to a dream where walls are terrifying and forever' (225). Their affair is also a good example of the functions of (excessive) irony in this love-story: when Joseph and Arachne see their reflection in a window, what that mirror shows is the socially constructed surface: a very old man and a young woman – an impossible couple. What the text has constructed, however, is a deep parallel between the two. They meet early in the plot, in an introductory grotesque scene in a graveyard, in which they find, guard, and finally bury a skull together in wordless understanding. They share the fascination with motion: Joseph's desire for movement is demonstrated for example in the copper plates decorated with dancers that he creates (104), and they both fear stasis and death. They are outsiders, marginalised in terms of the 'improper' use of language: Joseph as Hungarian immigrant and Arachne as working-class girl. This parallel ironically and grotesquely works to present them as the only matching couple in the text – and thus to exceed another line, that of society's gaze, formulating a *proper* 'look' and a proper couple.

Gothic heroines typically clash with society's ways of seeing – and, consequently, with the related ways of constructing subjectivity. The function of social control and the gap in perception involved is often, as has been suggested, metaphorically represented through the hero's gaze. In the feminine gothic – as in much feminine writing – this gaze has traditionally been represented by the powerful image of the female figure in front of the mirror. Arachne, as female rogue and 'spider woman', exceeds the frame of the mirror and the boundaries of this construction of femininity – especially, as we have seen, when it comes to constricting the female body. But, as the term 'excess' indicates, she must still be seen in relation to it, and she still has to acknowledge it somehow. Her story self-consciously acknowledges this recognition:

> There is nothing slender and light about Arachne; when she walks she thumps, the floorboards shudder. She knows she contradicts every ideal. Women are cherished for being soft and pliable, for their grace. Instead, Arachne displaces mass. (113)

In an ironic reversal, her very contradiction of that ideal makes her, in turn, a 'saviour figure' for Thomas. This idea reinforces, like their mutual love, once again, the equal terms of their relationship. But it also constructs a gothic provocation to the feminine ideal of the conservative and once-again domestic 1980s: 'she has saved him from life with a blue-eyed and bouncy-assed fembot who would spend hours making casseroles and buying laundry soap, who would hang pink drapes.' Moreover, this recognition unfolds the themes of house and other enclosures: 'Arachne has not changed his house one jot. He likes that, the way she took on his surroundings without rearranging one chair or cupboard. He knows it's a camouflage she has pulled around herself, but she is still Arachne underneath, a stormy-faced orphan whose speech is a little coarse, who responds' (113).

The house has a changed function in this neo-gothic text: no longer the space of exclusively female activities – and moreover, by contrast, ignored by the woman within – it has lost both its containing and its engendering functions. Instead, it works as an unlikely hiding-space from Arachne's 'real life' on the roads. Moreover, this section evokes the idea of the 'camouflage', suggesting the layers of Arachne's dynamic subjectivity – who is 'underneath' this camouflage that Thomas recognises? Where does this orphan come from? And moreover: where does the camouflage come from?

In feminist criticism, the idea of camouflage is related to the idea of masquerade.[6] Judith Butler's double reading of the term suggests the possibility that 'masquerade suggests that there is a "being" or ontological specification of femininity *prior to* the masquerade, a feminine desire or demand that is masked and capable of disclosure, that, indeed, might promise an eventual disruption and displacement of the phallogocentric signifying economy' (1990, 47). *No Fixed Address* seems to defy notions of any prediscursive femininity, with its endless layers of camouflage, disguises, constructions of subjectivity and desire for motion and escape. However, it self-consciously explores its possibilities.

Arachne uses creative constructions of camouflage that replace the pre-fabricated shells of femininity she sheds. Such notions of disguise, cover and camouflage present self-conscious traces of one of the questions interwoven throughout the web of women's gothic writing: how is femininity produced socially and culturally? Or, with de Beauvoir: how does one become a woman? Van Herk's neo-gothic text tackles the question in terms of fabric: introduced by the exploration of underwear, and the related text/ures of the hidden and the surface, questions of engendering processes also structure Arachne's story in a play that is finally named on the last page: 'You began to understand the connection between the inner and the outer appearance, began to comprehend the philosophy of the accoutrements of women' (318). Accoutrements – created textures themselves – create appearances; create gendered subjects: a sketch of the dynamics of the text/ures of dress. That gothic form should be 'stripped' in this way precisely in the 1980s is suggestive: in a context perceived as post-feminist, gender borders have become debatable; cross-dressing and other forms of transvestism start to develop into the liberating and popular functions they adopt in the early 1990s. That 'clothes make the man' – or the woman – has become an accepted aspect of the border-crossings of gender (see Garber 1992). Neo-gothic texts like *No Fixed Address* link this context to the intertexts from the web of feminine gothicism and to their gender-related excess.

Thus, clothes as theme connect Arachne to the classic gothic heroines and their struggle with the respectability–monstrosity conflict – in terms not only of gender, but also of class. The challenge of class assumptions is first introduced in conjunction with assumptions of race, as Arachne is confronted by the world of art and fame of a black concert pianist. *No Fixed Address* on many levels unfolds a postmodern play of recognition concerning aspects of difference and marginality. Thomas's bourgeois world 'displaces' Arachne, who has a working-class background and above all a relative lack of education (school to her was yet another 'prison'). The result is a feeling of inadequacy and even, in typically gothic dimensions, monstrosity: 'I'm a freak. I can't dress right, I can't talk right' (135). What follows is a typically postmodern parodic repetition of the related romance motif: the classic hero's attempt to make the heroine a product of his wealth and status by buying her new clothes. This is the *stuff* of fairy-tales: in romances it works to effect the magic transformation from Cinderella into princess; even more popular, made in Hollywood for a much larger audience, it still transforms the 'Pretty Woman' on the street into the millionaire's wife. In feminine gothic writing, with its interrogative texture, this motif has early on been refused: Jane Eyre's monologues on equality spoken to Rochester as well as her estrangement from herself in her wedding dress before the (first) wedding are good examples (281). In *No Fixed Address* Arachne's neo-gothic story recalls these situations – and inverts the procedure with irony and excess. In the aptly entitled episode 'Disguise',[7] 'Arachne agrees to let Thomas turn her into a respectable woman, or at least the appearance of one' (137).

The ensuing scenes in the (again aptly named) dress shop, 'Woman's Move', self-consciously play out the dressing theme in these formal terms.

> When Arachne steps out [of the dressing-room] to present herself to Thomas, she does not need to ask how she looks. She turns in front of a bank of mirrors and confronts this quiet transformation. Oh, she hasn't been turned into any princess, but she looks respectable. (137–8)

Respectability is discarded as appearance in neo-gothicism; it becomes a desired appearance, a chance to transform and thus another type of mobility. Arachne's permanent desire for appearances and disguises suggests with Mary Russo that '[t]o put femininity on with a vengeance suggests the power of taking it off' (1987, 224).[8] The dress shop scenes suggest this view, but simultaneously undermine it – especially given the outfit chosen in the end.

> And when Arachne emerges from the dressing room, they are all silent. This is not a disguise, this is Arachne, disturbingly so. It is silk, a fine, watered silk, two pieces, a tunic and narrow pants slit at the ankle, the green of Arachne's eyes. It catches green lights in her hair, makes her sloe-eyed, remote. She is more than beautiful, she has stepped from a carved wall, her mutinous face, the glaring question of her eyes, her wide bones. The costume makes her almost frightening; certainly Arachne is frightened. The clothes are supposed to cover her nature, not blare it out. (139)

Disguise, costume, cover, appearance – clothes do not necessarily work this way: ' ... [C]lothing is a necessary condition of subjectivity – ...

in articulating the body, it simultaneously articulates the psyche' writes Kaja Silverman (1986, 147), quoting Eugénie Lemoine-Luccioni and reflecting on the functions of clothes that 'draw the body so that it can be culturally seen, and articulate [it] as meaningful form ... Clothing and other kinds of ornamentation make the human body culturally visible' (Silverman 1986, 145).[9] In the example of Arachne's trans-formation through the green outfit – a scene which emphasises once again the layers of dress, cover and artifice, and of body, exposure and nature – the effect is 'disturbing' and 'frightening', to the spectators just as much as to Arachne herself: she seems to recognise her reflec-tion in the mirror as the spectacle that others perceive.

'Are women again so identified with style itself that they are es-tranged from transgressive effects? In what sense can women really produce or make spectacles of themselves?' Mary Russo has asked (1987, 217). Arachne in her green outfit could present a fictionalised 'spectacle' in the sense that it has 'to do with a kind of inadvertancy and loss of boundaries' (Russo 1987, 213) – but not as a role model in any way. As we have seen, postmodern feminist gothic stories refuse to present new idols and icons, and *No Fixed Address* is no exception, even in this scene. In Arachne's story, once more it is Thomas who works to undercut the idealisation of the heroine. Thomas's role in the choice of costumes is important and it is he who chooses the green outfit that 'blares out' her nature. Again he shows himself to be 'too good to be true', as this choice means exceeding the male gaze that had led to different forms of imprisonment – through dress – of sexual woman figures in traditional romances. Moreover, instead of making her look 'respectable', he helps to bring out her 'self'[10] – a reversal that effectively and ironically highlights the Rochesters', de Winters' and other Byronic heroes', fears of female sexuality.

Of course, if clothes articulate the body, the notion of 'camouflage' that Arachne attributes to and desires from them does not hold. This is further problematised in another situation: 'There are moments, standing in a plain dress with black pumps, her hair combed, her nails clean, jotting down an order, when she does not believe that the body she inhabits is hers' (191). This reflection triggers a flashback to Arachne as fifteen-year-old leader of the 'Black Widows' gang, thus disrupting the outside integrity and suggesting yet another 'real self ... underneath' (193). However, this idea is undermined again, as the gang is 'a cover, an excuse' (192) – and thus only a further construction of that 'real self'. *No Fixed Address* radically undermines conventional assumptions of identity, self, even the body with its neo-gothicism. What Arachne wants to camouflage is more than her body: 'she sometimes steps back, expecting disaster, her real self to emerge, bow, recapture her' (193). Such reflections suggest a deep gap between how she feels about herself and how she acts according to the expectations of *le propre* – precisely the gap that has produced many of the fears, horrors and monstrosities in the feminine gothic and that neo-gothicism 'strips' from the narrative covers that had made it a 'covert story'. Arachne's strategy is to create a new, more 'adequate' figure of her/self; in a process that intertextualises Joan Foster's various life-stories, created with similar motivation, Arachne's dresses become the textures of her different fantasy plots.

Not surprisingly, Arachne's self-presentation as an orphan to Thomas turns out as yet another fabrication of her/self. It is a construction she has created, as she rejects seeing herself as her parents' daughter. And this fabrication again highlights the layers of subjectivity with which this novel is concerned, rather than one unified centre of consciousness. It also further draws attention to the processes of subjectivity-construction. Arachne's story, the texture of *No Fixed Address*, shows neo-gothic possibilities in a feminist text critically concerned with 'engendering processes'. It continues the formal excess of neo-gothic writing towards the further 'stripping' of textual 'covers'. Thus, in this formal dimension, the idea of dress as texture also 'strips' subjectivity construction in the tensions of the surface romance plot and the covert mirror-plot of female desire.

Female desires

Feminine gothic texture has, as we have seen, the structure of an interrogative text where the surface romance is challenged by a mirror-plot of female desire – desire for the mother or for another woman. In the postmodern reverential parody, this formal challenge is increasingly brought to the fore, thus stressing its function as feminist critique of homocentrism – with a narrative emphasis on female relations in Munro's *Bildungsroman* or with an intricate web of inner-textual repetitions of romance and mirror-plot in *Lady Oracle*. *No Fixed Address*, with its 1980s' neo-gothic 'stripping' processes, continues this development by an extensive play with covert and 'stripped' narrative sequences. Female desire here is brought to the fore by different narrative techniques, most notably by breaks in subjectivity and focalisation and by a related, additional plot that emphasises a female subject's desire for another woman.

I would like to start the exploration of female desire in *No Fixed Address* with a discussion of the mother–daughter relationship in its thematic and formal dimensions. Arachne's refusal to recognise her family as a basic 'given' amounts to another one of her line-crossings: the 'unfixing' of origins. Her self-presentation as orphan connects her intertextually to the generic gothic orphan; her doubts as to who her father is (Toto? Gabriel?) repeat the drama of *Lady Oracle* where Joan Foster wonders about the 'other man' and his role in her mother's photo-album; moreover, Arachne's ambivalence about her mother Lanie associates her with such nineteenth-century motherless heroines as Jane Eyre and Aurora Leigh. These are first traces of the female desire that has marked feminine gothic texture and its deconstruction of the 'happy ending'. Formally speaking, in Arachne's story, the question of female desire and her relationship with Lanie suggest a second set of narrative layers: the mirror-plots to the already multilayered and parodied romance. However, these mirror-plots of female desire are 'stripped' into a plot of their own; a plot that introduces a shift in subjectivity as the mother, Lanie, becomes another dynamic subject. With this neo-gothic narrative move, female subjectivity-in-process is multiplied and extended, as has been suggested, into the idea of 'women-as-verbs' through the neo-gothic text.

Lanie first appears in the episode entitled 'Progenitors' (37), which sketches, in an ironic dry tone, the mother–daughter dilemma: 'Arachne acknowledges Lanie, but she doesn't endorse her. She isn't convinced that she has a mother; Lanie's connection to her feels tenuous and unproved. But once or twice a year Arachne will submit to biology' (38) – and meet with her mother. This constellation recalls again Kristeva's 'ambiguous opposition I/Other, Inside/Outside – an opposition that is vigorous but pervious, violent but uncertain' (1982, 7). The spatial separation from as well as the cynical rejection of the mother suggest Arachne's own 'unfixing' of the related 'borderline' – her own constructed separation. This process is incomplete and results in Arachne's rejection of her life in Vancouver: she never speaks about her past either with Thomas or with Thena. 'Like Thomas, Thena can only imagine the chisels that worked Arachne before she came to Calgary' (141). This negation of one part of her 'self', and its exclusion from her own, self-fabricated life-story, is once again a typical motif in gothic gender construction. However, as we shall see, in *No Fixed Address* it is not the 'return of the repressed' that haunts the female subject (as for example the 'Fat Lady' in *Lady Oracle*), but, in a parodic reversal of the convention, her return *to* the repressed that enacts the 'powers of horror' at the borderline of time – the past – and space – the West. I think that this narrative move is one aspect of 'stripping' the gothic of covert plots and repressed emotions, both fears and desires.

As we have seen in the reading of *Lady Oracle*, the mother–daughter drama is played out with ironic hyperbole; other well-known hyperbolic mother-figures from contemporary feminine gothic fictions are Leah in Oates's *Bellefleur* (1980), Mrs Greenwood in Plath's *The Bell Jar* (1963) and all three mothers in Tillman's *Haunted Houses* (1987). By contrast, in *No Fixed Address* the whole Lanie–Arachne relationship is presented in a dry tone that understates their 'gothic condition'. However, despite their sketchy aspects, the difficult positions of the two female figures are also explored and exposed. Lanie's story circles around characteristic situations in a very concise and self-reflexive (and self-assured) way: 'Lanie never played. Once she discovered there was no romance in being Arachne's mother, she simply backed away' (39). Again, as in the earlier neo-gothic texts, the dilemma can be traced back to the temptations and frustrations produced by the expectations of fairytale transformations and romance. 'Technically an orphan' (54–6) in 1945; escaping her foster parents as an English war-bride at seventeen; escaping poverty in Vancouver as a teacup-reader; escaping pregnancy (or, as she puts it, 'I ain't getting stuck at home with any brat'); escaping the two-room apartment into a little house with Toto – Lanie's mobility works to highlight the desire for the romance plots that nourished the popular culture with which she has grown up. However, van Herk's mother-figure – like Atwood's and Munro's – displays pragmatism when dealing with the gap between the necessities of postwar life in Western Canada and the promises of fairy-tales and Hollywood. Lanie is characterised as a 'pragmatist, without sentiment, although she likes movies where the right people kiss in the end' (40). Her pragmatism – and, more importantly, her mobility – is then (like Frances Delacourt's in *Lady Oracle*) disturbed and disrupted by her unwanted pregnancy. Her story-in-the-story becomes a *mise-en-abyme* for a feminine gothic *locus classicus*: it exposes – neo-gothically repeating and continuing feminine gothic classics – the threats of 'happy endings'.

One of Lanie's post-happy-ending scenes is illuminating. In an ironic narrative move, the pregnant Lanie finds herself in an archetypal fairytale situation. Like the queen in the Grimm brothers' *Schneewittchen*, she sits at a winter window, 'strangely content, caught in a web of quiet' (81) – with the undermining difference that the queen desperately wishes for a baby, while Lanie, waiting for the birth, 'ignored the child inside her'. Like the queen, she will name her child after what she sees at that time within the window-frame: in the fairytale it is the combination of blood, snow and ebony; in *No Fixed Address* it is a spider. The parody is extended when the actual naming, with all its highly unromantic implications, occurs with Gabriel's reflections: 'Arachnid … spiders are rogues' (83). Undermining the original fairytale sentimentalism even further, the mother-to-be identifies with the spider:

> It was a large spider with a belly as rotund as Lanie's. Her legs were swift and hairy, seemed almost to dance, drawing the silvery filament out from her anus, weaving with her hind legs. Lanie saw that the spider had been injured; it had only seven legs. But that did not hinder her design or ambition. (82)

The provocative association of injury and pregnancy ironically evokes the confrontation of the myths around motherhood that have constituted the female gothic since *Frankenstein* (Moers) and that here contextualise a society that has yet to accommodate families' (and especially mothers') needs into its Western work ethic. The construction in a displaced or 'trans-contextualised' (Hutcheon 1985, 37) fairytale scene aptly highlights the connectedness of gothic romance and fairy-tale, not only in terms of form but also of ideology. The form of reverential parody is used once again to continue a convention – in this case that crucial generic connection – and to expose that convention to a feminist critique 'from within' (Hutcheon, 1987, 226).

Moreover, the spider links Lanie with Arachne[11] – a parallel that is reinforced throughout the text and that circles around the fear of losing self-determination. 'Only in movies did characters long for adventure, follow it, seize it' (82), Lanie fantasises. Mother and daughter 'wanted the same thing', as Arachne realises, looking back on how her mother followed her own 'design and ambition' (for mobility) despite the baby (41). Yet, once again this is a typically neo-gothic text which presents us with the complex and paradoxical consequences of a demystified motherhood. Like Atwood and Hébèrt, van Herk uses the gothic to explore, in Barbara Godard's terms, 'how mothers raise their daughters in rejection and turn them towards men' (Godard 1983, 26). However, Arachne's perpetual 'unfixings' prevent her from the related danger of getting 'hooked on plots' of romance, and thus might be suggestive to the development of engendering processes in the 1980s: the time when feminism has provoked a new consciousness of female plots.

Consequently, Arachne fears and abhors the conventions of traditional marriage and especially motherhood (and thus the conventional trajectory for a female subject): 'She is without a scrap of motherly feeling herself ... Motherhood rouses no idealised sentiment in her. That is something socialised, something incubated in a girl child with dolls and sibling babies. Arachne had neither' (38). Besides drawing attention to the processes that construct this motherly aspect of femininity, thus refusing notions of essentialism with its related myth of the 'natural' female desire for motherhood, this reflection also provokes a reaction on the mother's part that must seem sadly ironic when read in the context of her own story: 'Why don't you marry [Thomas]? Sew him up?' (60). *No Fixed Address* here repeats the feminine gothic conventions of highlighting this typical paradox in the mother–daughter relationship: the mother, ironically, cannot imagine a pattern for the daughter's life different to that of her own, and thus proceeds to perpetuate the enclosures of private life and love that have been so convenient for traditional power structures and frustrating for her. The feminist gothic critique of this paradoxical process – patriarchy perpetuated by mothers who are shown as suffering from it – is here effectively highlighted in two ways. First, through structure: Lanie's suggestions of marriage are positioned in the same chapter as her own problematic story. And second, through repetition: another mother (or 'progenitor', as the chapter title has it), namely Thena, divorced and cynical about men, nevertheless recommends marriage to her friend Arachne. And it seems important to note, that the mother's advice uses the metaphor of sewing for what seems to her to be Thomas's inclusion in Arachne's power.

Arachne's position on marriage is clear enough: 'I don't want no ring in exchange for screwing' (69). Like Joan Foster, she breaks away from her mother geographically but is subject to undesired visitations. Her mobility defies the expected 'reproduction of mothering' (see Chodorow 1978, esp. 169). She travels to travel: to get away from her past, which she invariably associates with imprisonment and the mother's power; and to get away from her future, which appears as the inevitable 'happy ending' with Thomas. What explicitly occurs in *No Fixed Address* is the association of such a 'happy ending' – which has, as we have seen, been implicitly questioned early by feminine gothic texture – with 'the horror of what [Arachne] calls house arrest' and with the role-reversal in Arachne's and Thomas's household. The ultimate horror, the 'unspeakable' in this neo-gothic text, is stasis: the immobility as a child in the power of the mother – and, as Lanie's example shows, vice-versa – just as much as the immobility as a wife in a house. In a complete inversion of the gothic romance pattern in which 'love triumphant' consumed in domestic bliss marks the (surface) end of all horrors, here this (overtly) becomes the trap – and, ironically, the real terror – to be feared most. Formally speaking, again, it is the narrative exploration of the mother–daughter relationship and of female desire that gothically questions the conventional love plot – albeit in its neo-gothic, 'stripped' version.

Throughout the web of feminine gothicism, gothic texture has exposed a clash of the very different sets of values that constitute the surface romance and those that shape the mirror-plot of female desire. In *No Fixed Address*, the interrogative texture of feminine gothicism is 'stripped' in such a way that the layers of these different emotional motivations are laid open and interwoven into a – nevertheless multi-layered – plot that mocks romantic constructions of love and sexuality (through Arachne's excessive and emotionless sex life) and reinforces a plot of female desire that exceeds the relationships with mother and female friend. These relationships, as we have seen, connect Arachne's story to that of Joan Foster or Emily St Aubert. In *No Fixed Address*, these connections are repeated, but moreover extended by yet another plot: a plot that frames and interrupts Arachne's story.

No Fixed Address opens with a mysterious voice that tells the elusive Arachne's story. This disembodied voice constructs a 'You' that becomes, as Linda Hutcheon has shown, 'the most inclusive pronoun possible: it includes the narrator, the reader, and the protagonist' (1988b, 132) and that is early on engendered as female: 'The first-person plural "we" furthers that inclusion [of readers] and en-genders it female: "we" women have come to be what we are' (Hutcheon 1988b, 131). This You disrupts Arachne's story with her 'Notebook on a Missing Person', which both suggests the reality of the missing Arachne – who is reported dead in a newspaper report – and self-reflexively draws attention to her as fiction, as her life is told again and again – by Lanie, Thena and 'eye-witnesses', people she has met on the road. But this repetition of life-stories that constitutes a search of its own also forms another, both inter- and intra-textual repetition: it forms the plot of female desire not for the mother but for the other woman, as the female 'You' goes on a search for the ever-escaping female protagonist Arachne. And the 'Notebook' begins as well as ends this plot-in-motion, exploding the conventions of narrative closure, of genre and of subjectivity. The female-desire plot exceeds the boundaries of these traditional constructions.

However, female desire, desire that liberates from the homocentrism of the romance and constitutes the emotional motivation of plot around female figures, does not produce another dominant discourse: neo-gothicism of the 1980s, with all its 'stripping' processes, maintains the dynamics of the interrogative text. And it does so in a narrative move that has been anticipated by 1970s' feminist gothicism: the deconstruction of any feminine or feminist ideals or role models. *No Fixed Address* does not only question the conventional notions of consciousness and identification, and the ideology of a clear moral ending. Like Atwood and Munro, van Herk uses gothicism to disrupt and contradict notions of femininity, and to highlight the monstrous aspects of Woman for women. The gender-reversals, the unfeminine or even anti-feminine layers of the female subject, work further to contradict all notions of even 'female role models'. Moreover, *No Fixed Address* is, as has been suggested, in many ways a post-feminist book (it also contextualises culture after the women's movement of the 1970s) and accordingly the gothic mirror-plot deconstructs the idealisation of women's lib. The critique is here thus extended – and this is what I mean by a typically 1980s' critical reaction to 1970s' idealising feminism – even to new images of women created by the women's movement itself. Explicitly problematic appear to be the idea of 'the liberated woman', when this means just another norm, and the 'ideal feminist', as yet another unreachable, even if self-made, goddess. Such ideas have early been used against women, as the sociological studies of Edith Schlaffer and Cheryl Benard have convincingly shown (e.g. 1985), and as a neo-gothic text like *Lady Oracle* (with Arthur taking up women's lib for 'flagellation purposes') anticipates with feminist irony. They can also mean yet another homogenising effect that perpetuates de Beauvoir's categories of subject/other *within* female groups (that is, in terms of race and class) and thus defies the dynamics of difference so important to the feminist project of changing the status quo. Authors like Atwood, Carter and Weldon have exposed and refused such traps in their feminine gothic works with much provocative, and to some (feminists) even offensive, irony. Incidentally, all of them combine ironic tone and neo-gothic form. And I think that the irony is even stronger in texts – which are usually not considered gothic but do share some of the feminist critique in neo-gothic texture – by lesbian writers like Daphne Marlatt (for example in her *Ana Historic*, 1988) or by women of colour like Maxine Hong Kingston and Toni Morrison.

In *No Fixed Address*, the ironic representation of the post-feminist dilemma is effectively (dis)placed into a mock-gothic setting: 'the castle-like hotel on top of the hill' in Banff (251). The very closed scenario of a hotel contrasts with the open space associated with Arachne and enhances a striking scene. At first, the all-female drama is signified through dress. 'Five hundred women dressed in blue jeans and sweaters' (Women First, a feminist gathering) and 'five hundred women in polyester dresses' (Women's Ministry, a religious gathering) clash in coinciding meetings:

> The women in dresses are standing in demure knots, nodding their permed heads and keeping their eyes fixed on each other's faces. The women in blue jeans are swinging from the banisters and luggage racks. One is doing leg raises off the horns of the buffalo head over the door. Women are balancing luggage on their heads, pinching the bums of bellhops; they are sprawled over the gothic chairs, the courting chairs, the stately Queen Anne wing chairs, the demure Princess Mary chairs, they are whistling at their friends on the mezzanine, dropping their suitcases and flinging coats and waving keys. They are booking messages and whipping out their business cards and demanding suites with jacuzzis and the location of the swimming pool. (242)

This scene is a great example of neo-gothic voice: both of the liberating laughter and of the biting satire with which the feminist gothic depicts the grotesqueries and the 'monstrosities' of Womanhood and of some effects of women's liberation. This image works to criticise possible polarisation and militant intolerance within a movement – feminism – that is, in fact, liberating when realised as plural – feminisms. The presentation of women in the shrillest terms, with weird individuals characterised in careful caricature and monstrous impressions of female masses crowded in 'their' indoor space carica- tured without hesitation, aptly culminates in the enclosure of a sauna from which Arachne escapes.

But this whole episode does more in terms of neo-gothic decon- struction. From the first, the two groups of women are identified and characterised by their clothes; Arachne, in jeans and sweater (and naked in the sauna), is throughout associated with the feminists. She even changes into a (stolen) silk blouse to match them at the banquet in which the two groups hilariously clash in terms of fabrics. Van Herk here enforces the play with the cultural functions of dress, and in this context clothes make visible not only the contrasts between these two groups but also their insurmountable, aggressive antagonisms – as the feminists win the war for the elevators on account of their 'briefcases, wielded as weapons [and] ... stampede the other group, crushing cor- sages and trampling on open toes, tearing a lacy sleeve, unbuttoning a high collar' (249). But if Women First members are implicitly blamed for martial behaviour, Women's Ministry members are revealed in all their 'righteousness' thinking 'Women's libbers, all the trouble in the world comes from women's libbers' (249). This exemplifies a stubborn split between two different groups (in which each positions the other as Other) as well as the scepticism about maybe one of the most dif- ficult and most important ideas of feminism, namely solidarity among women.

A further sceptical view on feminism is presented through the scene with the 'guest speaker' (250–52). One of the initiators and stars of the women's movement, she has become 'an icon, a figurehead, a priestess ... a golden Amazon ... the titan'; her listeners 'love her, Oh they love her' and her words 'are tensible, they lift worlds, she has shaped these thousand bodies into one concerted effort'. The military connotations – 'The women are half on their feet, they are hot, they can storm battlements' – address, with pointed irony, contemporary dominant anti-feminist positions, especially in North America and Germany. At the same time, she seems to be the object of the group's desire to consume her. She is first mentioned along with the promise of the dessert, but she 'looks tired, as if she's been breathing life into banquets for months, years. She helped to start everything, she is supposed to be brilliant. She has no choice.' Ironically, her talk focuses on 'choice'. Further ironic twists abound. For example, there are two men in the audience: 'They are diffident and assertive; they belong here as much as anyone, they have paid their fee and come to hear the women's libber, to hear if she is really as great as their wives say she is. Their wives are at home taking care of the children, making sure no one breaks into the house. They'll want an objective report' (251). For some, clearly, these times are not that post-feminist after all. The comic gothic scenery in the hotel thus turns out to be a set for a parody of feminism itself – and it is thus an excellent example of the wide range of effects of feminine gothic and of emancipatory post-modernism.

Because of the politics of postmodernism and feminism, Arachne will not become a triumphant heroine, feminist icon or otherwise ideal female figure. Accordingly, she defies the plots of the 'proper' heroine of romance or of the spider woman with their alternative endings of marriage or death. Her incessant mobility, with 'no fixed address', instead introduces other textures and layers that unfix the subject. Just as Arachne moves through the narrative, so she changes subject positions. In keeping with Benveniste's relational subjectivity (1971, 224), Arachne's subjectivity is related to both her mother's subjectivity that interrupts her story and to the enunciating voice that introduces her as a discursive subject, then turns her into an object of desire and knowledge. Lastly, this voice loses her – maybe to become her: the mysterious 'You' meets the helicopter pilot, supposedly the last person to have seen Arachne – thus suggesting another repetition of the elusive Arachne's story (317).

In *No Fixed Address*, these complex subject-processes exceed the conventions of narrative form. If this form functions as dress, it not only engenders the subject, but it also accompanies the body (at least in the sense of the androgynous fashions suggested in the opening and throughout the descriptions of Arachne's clothing habits). Neo-gothic form itself adopts the mobile qualities of female subjectivity or women-as-verbs, motivated no longer by the emotions that 'make' the romance but by the conflicting emotions of female desire. Consequently, the very idea of female desire is redefined: taking over the plot, it escapes self-definition *against* (and thus inclusion within) the romance. Moreover, as we have seen, a female subject's aggressive sexuality exceeds the control of the male gaze (see Coward 1985, 76). New dimensions of these central metaphors of gothicism are thus suggested, when neo-gothic form adopts the flexibility of dress as the only enclosure left.

The formal possibilities of vestimonary codes include the trajectory of the look: a perceiving subject, an audience or narratee, or an address. Having discussed the possibilities of dress as form in a border space like Canada's geographical margins, and of dress as engendering and disguising the subject-in-process, I will focus in the next section on the look and its effects for neo-gothic texture, especially in terms of an ending.

Escaping (en)closure: the textures of dress

One way of neo-gothic escape is exceeding narrative closure. In *No Fixed Address*, the subject-in-process can no longer 'arrive' in the safe h(e)aven of a 'happy ending' – not even in the ironic one of feminine gothic classics. Arachne escapes the (en)closure of her story in incessant process: she 'arrives' in motion, in a helicopter, beyond the spiderweb of roads – and the web of the text – that have contained her movements: 'She watches the roadless world below her, knowing she has arrived' (310). This sentence is not only the last in her story but also the last of a series of traces that signify a desire to move into 'a world different from the one she was stuck in' (176) when looking at the stars in the night sky or when rising into the sky in a balloon with Thomas on her birthday, 'above that map of road and land and slough and fence' (223). Arachne's look in these sections suggest her own distancing from systems of containment and control. At the same time it connects her to the reader surveying the web/map/world of her story.

Here the question of the look intersects with the question of address. As we have seen, in its postmodern and feminist dimensions, *No Fixed Address* does address, with its inclusive 'You' narrator, a specified female audience. In its gothic dimensions – which often connect with (female) readers' situations through parodic repetition of everyday life – the title, with its emphasis on *no* fixed address becomes suggestive: compared to *Lives of Girls and Women* and Munro's gothicising of everyday life, *No Fixed Address* shows the development towards excessive intertextuality. Van Herk's filliation emphasises connectedness by self-consciously interweaving textures and by nevertheless demonstrating a typically gothic openness where anything might happen. This is, indeed, the case in the last section of the book, which Arachne's travels lead her into: a section that is most obviously and most intertextually gothic.[12] Taking off from the Banff hotel episode, it also engages in a further exploration of dressing and disguising, and of addressing escape from (en)closing textures.

Before this gothic section, Arachne's travels could have been read as quest, through the various flashbacks even as formal exploration of an extended *Bildungsroman* around 'the conflict between the ideal of *self-determination* and the equally imperious demands of *socialisation*' (Moretti 1987, 15). However, Arachne's travels do not end in the 'harmonious solution' expected of that genre (Moretti 1987, 15), namely the 'conclusive synthesis of maturity' (Moretti 1987, 19) or, in other words, the positioning of the subject with a 'stable' and balanced identity as part of a 'social pact' that lets the plot come full circle; a 'ring' relying on happiness (see Moretti 1987, 22–4). Nor do they end in marriage or death, as the traditional heroine's plot would have it: rather, this last section engages in what we could call 'gothic flirtation', which explores both of these possible endings over and over again.

First of all, this gothic section intertextually recalls numerous endings of well-known 'feminist classics' of the twentieth century. There is Edna Pontellier's liberating suicide by drowning in Kate Chopin's provocative and sensuous novel *The Awakening* (1899) – a New Woman who escapes husband, lover, motherhood by escaping the shore. In *No Fixed Address* Arachne is throughout seduced by water, on the ferry she dreamily 'could plunge into that darkness' (286). There is Marian, 'consuming herself' in the shape of a cake in Margaret Atwood's *The Edible Woman* (1969). Arachne in a sushi restaurant reverentially eats an artistic, beautiful sushi-spider by 'circling the web inward to the body of the spider in the centre of the plate' (283). There are the heroines from Doris Lessing's *The Golden Notebook* (1963): both Molly and Anna return from their lives as 'Free Women' to security and roots; Anna chooses social work, Molly a loveless marriage. Arachne is throughout tempted to return; in a coffee shop she muses about going back, '[p]erhaps she will be able to find a place to settle in, colonize'

(302). Such allusions recall a whole landscape of strong twentieth-century heroines and their alternative endings; however, Arachne's go on and on.

This intertextual 'gothic flirtation' self-consciously explores possibilities for a 1980s' 'heroine's text' and leads to an ending in motion by flying. Arachne's story is not linear, but proceeds like a spiral, moving virtually into space. It thus recalls Nancy K. Miller's idea of the absence of an aim, of 'a maxim' as marker for a feminine plot:

> To build a narrative around a heroine without a maxim is … to fly in the face of a certain ideology (of the text and its context), to violate a grammar of motives that describes while prescribing, in this instance, what … women should or should not do. (1986, 339)

Rather, Miller continues, such a text is 'about the plot of literature itself, about the constraints the maxim places on rendering a female life in fiction' (1986, 356). *No Fixed Address*'s 'stripping' processes disclose the constraints of 'a maxim' throughout; the last section self-consciously addresses it again. Instead of resolving the various strands and sets of narrative levels, this last part thus 'x-rays' their darkest layers, into the gothic's trajectories of love and death, sex and violence, sublime and terror. Arachne escapes from jail and drives West, 'her inevitable direction' (288), returning to her past, 'back to her own escaped history' (278). This movement signals the folding over of escape episodes – another formal excess that structures van Herk's neo-gothic texture. Throughout Arachne's story, her 'line-crossings' have not only been spatial; they also involve the 'unfixing' of conventional notions of temporal structure, especially when wholly disjunct events are presented in sequence in the present tense (13). This disorienting narrative move also structures the last part, in which present and past become associated[13] and Arachne loses all sense of time: 'somewhere she has lost three months' (288). Her incessant motion does not stop: 'on the edge … the border, the brink, the selvage of the world' (291), she drives North – 'farther, not toward, away' (270). This escape thus postmodernly defers her 'arrival' beyond the Canadian North. Even this ending is marked by gothic traces: it occurs on the border between the horror of imprisonment (279) and the fear of 'going nowhere, into a lost and limitless world she might not emerge from' (391). What provokes her last gothic escape North is a Mountie, who enters the plot just as Arachne fantasises about the possibility of returning (302). To her he signifies not only threats of jail but also the order and strictures of a patriarchal culture that she has escaped from all her life.

Throughout *No Fixed Address* there have been traces of dread. The landscape Arachne travels is haunted from the first – not only by her own visions but also by intertextual traces. It begins with comical optical illusions – 'a disembodied head floating' (35) in a virtual ghost town of dubious existence (36), or 'wild' paranoid visions of forgotten lovers' ghosts (29); these events 'repeat' Joan Foster's early – and less threatening – visions in *Lady Oracle*. Coming from the panorama of British Columbia, Arachne is filled with 'cautious horror' at the first sight of the prairie (102) – repeating with playful irony Emily St Aubert's first encounter with the Alpine sublime in *The Mysteries of Udolpho* – before she is magically drawn to explore this 'mournfully gothic world' (164). Driving West through the Rockies, and then North towards the frozen Arctic, means an encounter with the Burkean sublime, characterised by the attributes of what he has called 'terrible privations: Vacuity, Darkness, Solitude and Silence' (Burke 1987, 71): the West Coast mountains, the cliffs of the Pacific coast, the shipwreck disaster (294). The emphasis on sensory perception is Burkean as well; for example Arachne's 'pupils dilating' in utter darkness (262), in a situation that generically results in pain and fear: the 'terrors of dark- ness' (Burke 1987, 145). Van Herk's gothic flirtations here amount to emotional encounters with the terrors of a late-twentieth-century story that thus acknowledges its connectedness to the gothic web and uses the gothicism to emotional excess.

The epitome of the encounter with the sublime is the blue (another typical sublime colour) Bear Glacier, which Arachne finds with a group of geologists:

> blue shaft flaking thunder to float bluer in the melt, pale blue, electric, icing everything, even the trees crawling up the mountain beside it, even the black rock of the scree … she stumbles to where they stand in a silent row facing that terrifying blue. Arachne sinks to her knees. It is the last thing she sees, blue. (307)

This scene then also ends the obsession with death that structures this last part of the novel in various ways. Arachne's flirtation with suicide is balanced by her thoughts of Thomas (293), suggestive of a return to love. However, as in Kristeva's 'x-ray', only love's darkest layers are explored here, and sex is linked to violence: vampirism, murder and death. It is not only the figure of the spider woman that becomes associated with death, but also the male figures she encounters: the drowned man (294), the 'ferry man' (285), the sushi chef (284f). However, all of them also recall her own sense of being alive, of recognising her body and her needs for sex and food. Another gothic *locus classicus* is repeated in a doubly grotesque parody: Arachne's 'live-burial' between two sleeping drunks in a pitch-black coalminer's shack. Its terrors – darkness and immobility – are balanced by its sexual connotations: '[she] feels herself wedged between two sodden bodies, covered by them, held by their arms and legs in a grotesque parody of post-coital tenderness' (262). Typically, this place has irresistibly drawn her towards its darkness (261) and is associated with Arachne's border-crossings and unfixing motions since childhood, for example when she peers into 'the receding tunnel' of a coal mine: 'If only she could get in there. But it is impossible … Arachne peers into the unseeable. Her body pressed against the gate is a body caught in the act of escaping, struggling to get over a last fence' (267).

The desire for fence-crossings, transgression, excess – here it points to a dive into darkness erotically associated with death. However, it is also associated with the North: 'It grows dark, the dark of the North that each day lengthens itself until it takes over, wraps all' (305). This increasing darkness can also be seen as further liberation of incessant mobility. And the metaphors in these reflections evoke the chance implied for the female subject: the possibility of getting into what van Herk has elsewhere called an 'indifferent landscape': the 'male West … garrisoned by the art that represents it', aestheticised into a surface without entrance:

> In the real West, men are men, and life a stern test of man's real attributes. The fabric of this living breathing landscape has been masculinised in art, descriptive passages of a land instinctively female perceived by a jaundiced male eye. Description, description, and more description, an over-looking. Prudence, caution. They are afraid to enter the landscape. They describe it instead. To get inside a landscape, one needs to give up vantage, give up the advantage of scene or vision and enter it. To know prairie, one has to stop looking at prairie and dive. (van Herk 1984b, 16f)

Arachne's very physical, very erotic, very gothic dive into the darkness towards the Canadian North thus means both another 'unfixing' of gender roles and another excess of the distancing, cautious, self-protective male gaze. This move presents another escape from the en/closure of the text, through intertextual connectedness: it allies her (flirtatiously) with other female heroes, created by women writers, whom van Herk sees as 'spies' in that indifferent landscape (1984b, 24). Most notably, this ironic reversal of the gendered connotations of 'entering' or 'penetrating' (while underlining notions of manifesting male desire in the gaze versus female desire in touching) evokes yet again the notion of feminist undermining from within: 'We have found our own geography of love and fear, and live now within it, burrowed like insistent gophers, no masculine gun can dislodge us all. And we have new passwords' (1984b, 20). One of the passwords van Herk offers here is 'stay in the house', which aptly characterises Alice Munro's radical domestication and gothicising of the everyday lives of girls and women, 'caught in the house but using the structure of house to enter fiction, the still-indifferent landscape beyond the house a reverberation of the fiction within' (van Herk 1984b, 20). 'One final password' in van Herk's system is, accordingly, 'explode': the female subject 'leaves the house and sinks into the landscape' (1984b, 23) – a move, it must be noted, that cannot occur without violence – which comes to be seen as part of exploding the being 'defined by other eyes' and of the 'earth-quaking' and 'infiltrating' of the male West (van Herk 1984b, 24).[14]

If the 'passwords' throughout Arachne's story have been 'unfixing', 'stripping', 'escaping', they certainly adequately describe her ending, with its aura of death, however, in van Herk's (and Robert Kroetsch's) sense of 'death [as] a happy ending ... the one ending we know but cannot know, the loveliest of endings because it is utterly imaginary and mysterious' (van Herk 1991, 194). Arachne has, in best gothic tradition, given up her body for dead: 'I died, she thinks. I'm dead' (285); 'She had been back to Vancouver and died there, one of her lives certainly over' (301); 'Perhaps they would let her stay here ... sleep her last life away' (309).

The implication of lives – and deaths – in the plural reinforces once again the construction of a multiple subject that had been introduced into her story by the early metaphor of underwear and clothes in general. It is further and self-consciously emphasised by a typically gothic convention that here in its playfully ironic flirtation almost functions as comic relief: Arachne encounters her *Doppelgänger* – a woman with a bear whom she picks up on the road with a strange sense of *déjà vu*. In the gothic tradition, the uncanny closeness of the same often indicates disintegration (Trautwein, 1980, 46; see also Gilbert and Gubar 1979). Here, however, it seems that the *Doppelgänger* enhances the intertextual flirtation with gothic possibilities. This woman is a grotesque female figure, herself pointing out that they are *Doppelgänger* – as they share a shower – and otherwise calling herself 'a poet manqué' (275). Arachne, associating her more with the bear, calls her a 'bearwoman'. Allusion is made to numerous 'affairs with bears' in Canadian folk tales as well as Canadian women's writing (see Atwood 1977, 108): most notably van Herk's own *The Tent Peg* (1981), in which Jael encounters a female bear in a sublime, ceremonial scene; and, of course, Marian Engel's *Bear* (1976), in which the bear parodies the Byronic romance hero. A similar parody occurs in Joyce Carol Oates's (very American) *Bellefleur* (1980) in the episode 'Fateful Mismatches', in which a typically stubborn female Bellefleur, Hepatica, marries a Canadian streetworker who subsequently changes into a black bear – and is killed by the male members of the family (276–82). These parodic allusions to the animalistic and sexual ingredients in gothicism are part of the humour that remains, although in darker shades, until the ending.

However, in the feminine gothic context, the 'bearwoman' also re-calls drastic images of incomplete – or monstrous – femininity. It is tempting (from a European point-of-view) to read it as parodic Canadian version of the Danish 'fishwoman', the mermaid, who figures, as we have seen, in *Lady Oracle* and other feminist gothic texts. The figure of the bearwoman thus also highlights the non-feminine layers of Arachne as female subject. Moreover, she also, once again, draws attention to the aspect of 'cover' and disguise, not only because she, too, deals with 'concealed products' (274) but also because Arachne has just put on another 'disguise' by getting her hair cut and dyed 'an awful blond' (279). Otherwise, as Arachne realises, staring 'in the steamy mirror, … she would look exactly like the woman. No, the woman would look exactly like her' (277). The success of 'covers' is questioned once more – just as, in *Lady Oracle*, the success of dramatic transformations is called into question.

Consequently, Arachne's travels amount to an excessive play with end-ings that escape (en)closure in both formal and ideological dimensions. It leaves the reader with such an ambiguous image – the 'You' on a trail of traces (that are, fittingly, panties) venturing North – that the ending becomes a provocative sign of neo-gothic excess, and of female desire. Another Canadian novel – mentioned above because of its heroine, who is, like Arachne, a travelling woman and a female subject-in-disguise – suggests a similar escape from (en)closure: Helen Weinzweig's *Basic Black with Pearls* (1980). I would like to briefly outline its connectedness to *No Fixed Address*. This novel ends in a self-conscious deferral of arrival with the sentence: 'but for once I didn't have far to walk' (135). This first-person narrator, Shirley, has a lot in common with both Joan Foster and Arachne Manteia. There are the 'disguises': the (fake) name – Lola Montez – of a famous royal mistress, Eliza Gilbert (1820–61), who is thus almost an archetypal sexual woman; another disguise is the most conservative costume of the Western 1950s' female middle class: the basic black dress with a single strand of pearls.[15] The heroine is constantly in motion, travelling by reading the complicated and constructed signs that her lover – an unspecified, mysterious male figure – seems to leave for her. Simultaneously, through memory, she works out her relationship with her mother, and this is where the typical interrogative texture of the feminine gothic sets in: all her travels throughout the world for romance (travels that thus echo the amorous travels of the real Lola Montez through nineteenth-century Europe) are challenged by her strong and emotional encounters and connections with other women.

The 'amorous journey' for the ever-absent Coenraad – whose absent presence functions as a (respectable) pretext to keep the narrator (virtually) going – is ambiguous: the plot itself is set completely in the streets of Polish-Canadian Shirley Katzenbowsky's home town Toronto; and all references to more exotic parts of the world are related to a pack of postcards that are the only entertainment on the many loverless evenings. Just as the mysterious and ever-changing Coenraad appears more and more as a fantasy-figure – maybe for a conservative woman who thus 'controls' her adventurous love-life or, more likely, for a conservative wife who thus escapes into an adventurous amorous fantasy life – the ambiguous journeys around the world appear more and more as a fantasy, and maybe as the armchair-travelling of a 'proper' woman in the 'proper' dress – in the process of escaping the textures of a 'proper' plot.

Read in this way, Shirley's – or, her alter ego Lola Montez' – story can be seen as another reverential parody on the position of romance readers since Radcliffe's times. Its own gothic form is noteworthy, as the interrogative texture also challenges the romance with Coenraad: the numerous meetings with other women on the way multiply the female subject's own plot as these female figures invariably come to tell their own, similar stories that thus work to replace the (constructed) lover's function as other. The lack of such an other is clear early in her story – 'My voyage has meant nothing to anyone' (12) – and early in her life – 'More insistent than the memory of such moments of happiness was the picture of myself at the age of ten on these sidewalks in a cruel November rain such as this, searching for my mother' (52). Such traces of abjection are complemented by suggestions of ghosts and visions (37, 83), and by the fears and paranoia of a woman travelling alone, whose terrors are – of course – linked with love (79).

Love, although the romantic motor of the plot, structures it in a typically 'x-rayed' version. The figure of Coenraad is cruel and ever-absent; a parody of both a romantic Byronic hero and the uninterested husband evoked in the numerous other women's stories and in Shirley/Lola's own marriage to Zbigniew. The love story itself is illicit and hidden – however, ironically, Coenraad's interdiction of writing it out as a fiction is productively subverted by the text we read. The borders of life and art are fluid and easily exceeded: one of the other women comes straight out of a painting (57), a typically gothic/surreal incident. Moreover, like Arachne, Shirley/Lola encounters her own death before the ending (121); here it is told as story by her husband to his mistress – another 'other woman' – before she leaves him. This act is perhaps her only 'real' action in the text, combined with throwing out the postcards, and, most importantly, with exchanging the obvious 'disguise', the basic black dress and its related 'respectability', for a colourful spring dress at the close. This new dynamic thus defies the enclosure of the marriage and the narrative closure of a solution by arrival. It links the figure of Shirley/Lola (and of the other women) to the ever-moving Arachne, and suggests the escape from the enclosure of this ideologically charged 'basic' stiff and narrow texture into a new beginning and towards new forms of femininity and subjectivity.

This suggestive, emancipatory dimension of postmodern writing is related to the ex-centric voices – in terms of gender, culture, nationality, geography, class, age – of heroines like Polish-Canadian Shirley/ Lola and Western-Canadian Arachne Manteia. I emphasise their 'hyphenated' situation here because I would like to suggest that their plots are related to a larger context of postmodern feminine writing that uses gothicism to emancipatory dimensions in a cultural context in the 1980s that is increasingly perceived as international, multi-cultural and global. For example, *Granta* as early as 1980 lamented 'The End of the English Novel' only to celebrate 'the beginning of the British one' and the recognition that 'the fiction of today is using a language much larger than the culture' (Buford 1980, 16). Indeed, the 1980s have shown how 'the empire writes back', as Pico Iyer has demonstrated by his analysis of Booker prizewinners since Salman Rushdie's *Midnight's Children* won it in 1981 (Iyer 1993, 50–55); the decade has seen a flourishing of postcolonial and multi-ethnic writing, especially in the English-speaking world. Among the most powerful voices that narrate contemporary and historical America are those of a mixed cultural background; with regard to my focus on the possibilities of gothicism I am thinking specifically of women writers like Chinese-American Maxine Hong Kingston and African-American Toni Morrison. Their explorations of the American experience rely on interweaving a wide range of narrative traditions and genres from different cultures. Hong Kingston's novels often rely on the autobiographical mode (as defined by Hornung 1985), and Morrison's on historiographic fiction as 'stabilising' and politicising devices. The gothicism that permeates their stories works on various levels; importantly, it connects a whole range of different cultural forms with the literary tradition.

Toni Morrison's *Beloved* (1987) shifts a historical child-murder of the nineteenth century 'to the sphere of culture and cultural memory' (Hornung 1996, 216). Contextualising American 'Reconstruction' – which for the African-American protagonists is more a time of disintegration – the novel opens with the description of a haunted house: '124 was spiteful. Full of a baby's venom. The women in the house knew it and so did the children.' This house adopts a life of its own as Morrison combines 'references to the family history with American history' (Weissberg 1996, 110); and it occupies the very centre of a ghost story (intermingled with other narrative forms) that is also a mother–daughter drama, with multiple layers and emotional disasters, a violent death at the mother's hands and the revenge of a seductive but cruel ghost. As this ghost woman, Beloved, comes out of the river,

she also comes out of Black folklore. However, as Liliane Weissberg
has shown, Morrison's familiarity with the gothic tradition is exhibited
for example in her treatment of American plantation homes 'as Gothic
settings that feature slaves as invisible Blacks', and her related political
reframing 'has consequences not only for the contemporary Black
novel, but for a new evaluation of the British literature of the past'
(1996, 116). The gothic, it seems, attracts a Black as well as a white
readership, and thus empowers Morrison's politics. Similarly, Maxine
Hong Kingston in *The Woman Warrior* (1976) narrates 'Memoirs of a
Childhood among Ghosts' – and these ghosts possess, even if Hong
Kingston outspokenly situates them in the Chinese tradition, gothic
dimensions. For example, when the mother's story revolves around a
nocturnal encounter with a 'Sitting Ghost' in 'the horror [of] the
ghost room' (69), it connects with heroines from the Chinese as well
as from the Anglophone gothic traditions, and again the gothic connection communicates the politics implied. Lothar Bredella has recently shown the novel's ambiguities in a postmodern context: 'whereas
postmodern critics read *The Woman Warrior* as self-referential text,
others read it as a sociological report' (1997, 426); and, I think, the
gothicism enhances this complex and highly experimental novel's anticipation of postmodernism's emancipatory turn. Both Morrison and
Hong Kingston use internal, feminised gothic spaces to show women
to be the bearers of children as well as the bearers of history, mainly
through memory (see Weissberg 1996, 115). And both show the cultural constructions of women also as physical constructions of gender
and power – as in *The Woman Warrior*, where culture is literally inscribed on the body in a painful ritual between parents and daughter.
The critical ambiguities of how to read these writers (see, e.g., Bredella
1997, 421–33 on Hong Kingston; Tucker 1994, esp. 102f on Morrison's
'ghost story') signify radical 'unfixings' that nevertheless point to something new.

Arachne Manteia and these other unfixed, multiple, female subjects-
in-process are good examples of the emancipatory turn of postmodernism through feminism[16] – and of their uses and abuses of gothic
form. Formally speaking, like Del Jordan and Joan Foster, they recall,
and moreover virtually enact, Alice Jardine's concept of 'women-as-
verbs'.[17] Read with regard to such contexts, a (Canadian) feminine
gothic text like *No Fixed Address* shows once more the possibilities of

the postmodern rewriting of gothic form: in Jardine's matrix, such a text can be seen as 'internalising' and 'practising' *gynesis*: the female body, and also a more general 'feminine', are here explored in its discursive contradictions and constructed (not just 'naturally' narrated) as 'verbs'. This way, they productively challenge the subject of the enunciation, but they also challenge narrative form itself. 'Women-as-verbs' in one way resist the production of yet another 'master narrative', of another such 'subject' or heroine or Woman or role model, thus avoiding readers' identification (and even a *fixed* reader-*address*) just as much as any one-dimensional prescription for contemporary 'heroism'. In a further step, they provoke questions as to the balance and conventional workings of traditional narrative structure. In a text like *No Fixed Address*, with a flexible, unfixed female subject like Arachne, the problematising processes of 'gynesis' and the concept of 'women-as-verbs' have the effect that Jardine ascribes to modernity: a return to the mother's body, 'an erotic merging with maternal boundaries' that disturbs the subject of the enunciation (237), and that unfixes the narrative.

Moreover, this last image can be extended into a further version of merging: the connectedness with sister texts. This connectedness in the sense of gothic filliation both includes intertextual relations into the (open) question of address and thus maybe responds in a typically feminine way to the need for a certain stability that Alfred Hornung (1985) has diagnosed for the culture of the 1980s: in feminine writing of that time it seems that filliation replaces the earlier focus on 'experience' and that the ongoing web of women's textures offers an alternative space for the liberating dynamics of 'excessive' forms like the gothic. Neo-gothicism has come to expose, through the process of stripping layers of textures and of unfixing subjectivity into 'women-as-verbs', the connectedness of the gothic forms of feminist fictions, in the feminine shape of the text as flexible dress and in a feminine way of connecting that anticipates the new decentralised forms of communication of the coming century.

Notes

1 This necessity is aptly demonstrated by van Herk's essay *In Visible Ink* (1991, 1–11). Wiebe's 'On Being Motionless' (1989) links language and

space, the grammar of Inuktitut and the 'vast expanses of the arctic land-scape, either tundra or ice ... In order to live a human being must move; to live in the Arctic a human being must, generally speaking, move quite a lot to acquire enough food' (49).

2　Kristeva, situating horror with regard to the mother, convincingly writes on such male fears in 'Those Females Who Can Wreck the Infinite' (1982, 158): 'To what end is castration embodied in the mother? Is it the representation of an abiding blame, the appeasement of a precocious narcissistic wound? Or, a way of expressing a love that only the weak can receive without those who utter it being threatened? – The theme of the two-faced mother is perhaps the representation of the baleful power of women to bestow mortal life.'

3　There are strong similarities between some narrative/cinematographic strategies of film noir and feminine gothic: in both a mirror can represent self-absorbed narcissism as well as 'women's duplicitous nature' (Place 1980, 47); or the framed portrait of a woman can function as 'a "safe" incarnation' of a 'nagging, ambitious, destructive bitch highlighting the contrast to the living woman' (50).

4　Wolf credits Atwood with the recognition of this phenomenon and concludes: 'When men control women's sexuality, they are safe from sexual evaluation' (1991, 153).

5　It is important to note that gothic classics have always suggested the *perception* of female characters as masochistic and passive. For example, the Lady Rowena in Poe's 'Ligeia' or Georgina in Hawthorne's 'The Birth-mark' die poetically enough at their husbands' hands – but with a terrible vengeance.

6　'Woman as masquerade' – woman 'appearing as being the Phallus' – has been explored by feminist critics like Irigaray (1981) and Modleski (1986), and by post-structuralist film critics like Heath, Armatage, Silverman; see also Joan Riviere's much-quoted essay 'Womanliness as Masquerade' (1929, in Burgin 1986). However, as has been indicated, my reading focuses more on the cultural than the psychoanalytical context for the gendered subject here.

7　Titles throughout signal double meanings. For example, 'Routes of passage', a chapter about Arachne's 'rites of passage' on her routes as bus-driver; or 'Swath', meaning 'the movement of a blade' as well as 'a great stir', in the chapter when Arachne and Joseph first make love in a field; or 'Ferryman', the chapter in which Arachne first thinks she is dead and then murders a man on a ferry. Titles also frequently point to gothic references, for example, 'The Disinterred', in which Arachne flees with Joseph from the old people's home; and 'Live-Burial' indicating the gothic *locus classicus* to be discussed on the following pages. Titles, then, form another focusing frame for our reading of this neo-gothic text.

8　Russo sees 'masquerade as the most potent form of "acting out" the dilemmas of femininity' (1986, 225). This is questioned by Armatage: 'I would have thought that the "pleasure of transgression" (Hebdige) would be less closely tied to dressing the way women are supposed to dress, even if to an excessive degree' (1989, 211).

9 Silverman concludes, emphasising at once the dynamics of subjectivity construction and the dynamic functions of the fashion system: 'If ... clothing not only draws the body so that it can be seen, but also maps out the shape of the ego, then every transformation within a society's vestimentary code implies some kind of shift within its ways of articulating subjectivity' (1986, 149).

10 One chapter later, Arachne (who can 'pass now' in terms of looks and manners) reflects upon Thomas's decisive support in these matters: 'She wonders, though, if she should let Thomas manage her, even, by God, dress her up and fix her manners. She is disgusted by women who need men to rescue them' (141). However, the self-reflexive treatment of the rescue-motif has established their mutual saving of each other.

11 This overdetermined scene suggests yet another reading. If the spider's web becomes a metaphor for the female text, its production by an injured spider becomes a metaphor for the female writer who still has to be a 'rogue' in the present state of the arts.

12 It is also the most controversial. Reviewers have ignored or rejected it. In terms of filliation, it exceeds the interrogative returns of feminine gothic classics, e.g., to a pastoral La Vallée (*Udolpho*) or a fairytale Ferndean (*Jane Eyre*).

13 For example in Vancouver, when 'she is back where she started', and thinks of herself at fifteen, about to lose her virginity (279). It is important to note that in van Herk's spider-text the introduction of sex occurs at the same age as that of violence: as 'a crude fifteen-year-old, the one girl in the gang, the leader' (191) she takes physical revenge on a tough guy (193); this is also a formal foreshadowing of her later treatment of McKay.

14 This position recalls van Herk's situating of the woman writer with regard to her art but also with regard to death:

> Writers must remember to remember that their inevitable position is beneath, below. We stand beneath the stars, the sun, beneath our own pasts and implacable futures. Underground, buried even ... The writer writes underground, a mole or more appropriately a gopher, tunnelling quietly through the earth of being and language, although the writer might know shamefully little philosophy, just as she is eternally aware of her poverty of expression, that she has not the tongue to celebrate properly the incandescence of this beneathedness. It is *beneath* that points writerly chins toward the stars or the beclouded sky – looking toward heaven, light, the possibility of angels ... And the absolute certainty of death. (1991, 191–2)

15 This telling garment is also evoked in the opening of *Lady Oracle* as ironic image of the 'neat and simple' ideal that her chaotic, meandering life is contrasted with (3).

16 Michael (1996, esp. 217) names these two novels among a whole range of
    women's writing in the same context, focused on the politicising powers
    of feminism for postmodernism (albeit without the gothic dimension).
17 Jardine situates this idea in her illuminating analysis of 'Gynesis – the
    putting into discourse of "woman" or the "feminine" as problematic'
    (Jardine 1985, 236) in between French and American writing of moder-
    nity. Her argument presupposes that '[t]he interrogative return to the
    sources of our knowledge in the West has involved an obligatory return to
    the mother's body – a female body, no matter how unrecognizable; no
    matter how hysterical, textual, inanimate or actual' (237), to conclude: 'It
    could be argued that there is in the contemporary male American texts a
    refusal, even a violent refusal, of the maternal ... that female body re-
    mains traditionally *in representation* no matter how unrepresentable it
    might at first seem to be; it remains an image in representation un-
    questioned by the feminine and maternal as process, as internal to the
    workings of signification' (236–7). Seen in this context, the enlightening
    possibilities of the contemporary feminine gothic become once more
    obvious.

PART III

Gothic times again: two hundred years after Radcliffe

Chapter 7

The neo-gothic experience

Two hundred years after Radcliffe: the pull of the millennium, the sense of economic and ideological crisis, the advent of huge cultural shifts on a global basis. Gothic times again? Yes: I think that in the 1990s we do live within a neo-gothic culture that not only recalls a comparable political and philosophical situation from the 1790s but also begins to suggest a major shift in postmodern culture on the threshold of a new century. In this part, I will outline 1990s' culture in this sense: after a brief review of the developments of neo-gothicism over the previous two decades, I will turn to recent literary developments. It is my proposition that neo-gothicism might exceed postmodernism in its present self-reflexive state: my argument is based on a discussion of A. S. Byatt's *Possession* (1990) and Margaret Atwood's *Alias Grace* (1996), and of the cultural issues these novels contextualise. In the last section, I will extend my discussion to the larger audio-visual popular art forms that characterise the present international entertainment culture.

Angela Carter's postulate that 'we live in gothic times' reverberates with unbroken force at this moment of change. Indeed, as she suggested in the early 1970s, and as for example Linda Hutcheon's theories have since demonstrated, *ex-centric* voices and genres have come to unfold their powers: postmodernity recognises the potential of difference and connectedness. Ex-centric *voices* from women, from the postcolonial world and those marginalised due to race or ethnic or class politics; ex-centric *genres* from related oral cultures or Western popular and entertainment culture: the 1990s' cultural appropriation of these voices and genres is linked to the increasing globalisation of thought and communication. Neo-gothic fictions, as I have outlined, are deeply related to this experience of our 'gothic times'; I would like to show their role not only as shaping but also as enlightening force in the culture before the new millennium.

Outlining this culture more closely in terms of its literature, it seems important to consider the advent of new technologies and new forms of communication that rely on digitalisation and create new forms of texts. I think this recognition suggests a link between our own and Radcliffe's gothic times that goes beyond comparing the influence of the French Revolution then, and the breakdown of the Iron Curtain since 1989. It can be argued that while the Industrial Revolution marked culture and texts in the 1790s, a similarly profound transformation marks the last decade of this century: the Media Revolution. The expanding connectedness of computer, telephone and television is in the process of changing not only communication, but also our lives – and texts. The developing new textures, I think, come from an intersection of the powers of ex-centric texts with the ways of both production and communication of texts via computers. And neo-gothicism, as a popular, gendered and thus doubly ex-centric genre, offers a form that is both archaic and dynamically interrogative; a form that thus virtually exceeds into the new, computerised textures of the media-dominated 1990s.

I opened this study by emphasising the prevailing powers of gothicism at the end of the twentieth century, and I would like to review here their developments towards the 1990s before turning to anticipations. I have tried to show that gothic form is marked by specific feminine and feminist dynamics that have ensured its strong persistence, and even revival, throughout two hundred years of modernity and the recent postmodern decades. One of these dynamics I have come to call *excess*. It structures, first, the gothic heroine: a female subject, multiple and mobile, who comes to assume the provocative textual position that Alice Jardine calls *women-as-verbs*. Second, it is productive of gothic texture: a multilayered texture, motivated by the erotics of romance, which is mirrored and challenged by a subplot of female desire. Third, it effects the gothic liberation from the enclosures of feminine myths between *le propre* and the 'monstrous-feminine'. Moreover, such excess connects the web of feminine stories from different ages, nationalities, ethnic traditions and both high and popu-

Where the Wild Roses Grow   Rock-poet Nick Cave as murderous
Byronic hero and pop-idol Kylie Minogue as his doomed love: their
neo-Romantic video *Where the Wild Roses Grow* hits the nostalgic nerve of
the 1990s.

lar cultures. This intertextualisation – or, in Barbara Godard's term,
filliation – of the gothic has been continued and, at times, deconstructed by the neo-gothicism that I have outlined here. Still, as I have
tried to show, the attractions of gothic form for women writers and
readers seem connected to gothic excess, as it contextualises the
experience of everyday life and of culture at large in hyperbolic, emotional, or parodic dimensions. Moreover, it also shapes the typically
gothic attacks on and sense of liberation from the containment and
limitations of existing power structures.

    In this sense, as we have seen, neo-gothic texts from the early 1970s
to the late 1980s demonstrate these narrative dynamics through the
growing flexibility of gothic form that I have called a 'stripping'
process. Alice Munro's early 1970s' fictions gothicise everyday life,
thus highlighting both gender construction, and related horrors for
the heroine, a creative young woman, within her culturally assigned

place: the house. Such enclosures then are exceeded in Margaret Atwood's – and other late-1970s neo-gothicists' – parodic incorporations of the popular gothic formula: they celebrate the fruits of feminism, for example, with their independently travelling heroines; but they also explore the seeming paradox of women's persistent fascination with the seductions of popular romance. Formally speaking, the earlier postmodern fictions use gothic excess to critically ultra-domesticate their textures as *haunted houses* (Munro). Later gothicists, I have argued, create more self-conscious spacey textual and intertextual *mazes* (Atwood). And the 1980s' further formal flexibility I have compared to the *texture of dress*: a dynamic and erotic form that suggests the gothic escape from enclosures – from the house as woman's place, but also (formally) from the house of the text, and (culturally) from the related traditional power structures, as Aritha van Herk's *No Fixed Address* demonstrates. In this sense, neo-gothic fiction continues gothic form with its provocative, challenging, liberating excess. And the formal 'stripping' processes signify a typical effect of this excess: it reveals and attacks a gender culture that, once again, is turning conservative. Gothic times again!

Extending my discussion of the gothic forms of feminine fictions into that larger 1990s' culture and its popular audiovisual media developments means realising how gothicism persists and once again unfolds its enlightening powers and provocative excess at the moment when postmodernism is folding back upon itself. It seems that after 1989 – with its attendant social and ideological turmoils and the recognition that we live increasingly within powers that operate globally – the postmodern practices of infinite deferral and self-referentiality give way to new desires for answers, even for knowledge, for identity, for origin – and for other taboos of postmodernity. These desires and the related turn to self-awareness of postmodernism become more and more outspoken as well as emotionalised as the decade proceeds. As I have suggested throughout, the gothic always contextualises what is most virulent and active in its time and culture. The recognition that critical interest in it is today more lively than ever (see Tinkler-Villani and Davidson 1995, 3, 5) prompts a scrutiny of recent literary developments.

One of the most discussed novels of 1997 was Arundhati Roy's Booker prizewinning *The God of Small Things* – a family story set in India in the last half of the twentieth century, told in a combination of Indian narrative forms and English novel conventions. An early image which opens the sense of mystery and drama that permeates the text is the seeming live-burial of an English girl, Sophie Mol, as perceived by her seven-year-old Indian cousin Rahel. This image signifies the deceiving end of the plot's unfolding mysteries; it thus points to the urgent desire to *know* as a (neo-)gothic experience: in the postmodern world there are no easy answers, but there are gothic ones. Put differently: the postmodern deferral of answers and of any sense of knowledge or truth gives way to the sense of an answer – but from the gothic, unreal, excessive world. Similarly, another writer from the younger generation, Norwegian-American Siri Hustvedt, opens her (neo-) realistic novel *The Enchantment of Lily Dahl* (1996) with Lily's recognition that 'old man Bodler had buried his wife alive back in 1932' (15). Her immediate desire for and dread of Helen Bodler – she steals, and later wears, the dead woman's shoes – become a mirror-plot against her simultaneous erotic romance with the attractive, Byronic, macho artist Ed Shapiro. Here again, gothic form shapes the story of a female life. The plot unfolds with the menstrual cycle between two periods, and the story of contemporary American life: a small town, a scenario of normal, strange and eccentric people, an older woman friend with a lost daughter, a prostitute with a dramatic transformation, an old friend and his cave with uncanny 'twins', a sense of violence and a suicide, a heroine enchanted by the shadow of Marilyn Monroe and haunted by a sense of dread about her past. Throughout, Lily tries to figure out what is 'real'. And again, the desire to *know* – about origin and identity – finds a neo-gothic response.

Furthermore, these live-burials also signal another desire closely related to the postmodern theorising of difference: the question of corpo-reality that has sparked such important studies as Elisabeth Bronfen's *Over Her Dead Body* (1992) and Judith Butler's *Bodies that Matter* (1993). Katherine Binhammer opens a whole issue of *Tessera* (1995) on 'Bodies, Vesture, Ornament' with the recognition that it is an 'assumed female body that permeates feminist history' (1995, 7) and that suggests the present urgency of critical interest in clearing these assumptions in the larger cultural context. As Bronfen's history of Western aesthetics shows, patriarchal art – and not only in the work of Edgar Allan Poe, who famously called it the world's most poetic subject – figuratively begins and ends in the death of a beautiful woman. Whether as punishment for a sexual woman or as sacrifice of a pure maiden, it confirms and re-establishes traditional order. It also points to the two extremes that invariably construct femininity and that contemporary women writers explode by parodic – or, in Bronfen's related terms, hysteric – strategies. I have shown the similar possibilities of neo-gothicism to exceed such constructions and I think that the recurring image of a live-burial draws attention to the positioning of femininity and the female body as well as to the desire for its retrieval and renewal with typical neo-gothic excess.

It also draws attention to the postmodern doubts concerning truth and representation. All of the writers I discussed in Part II are turning or returning to these questions in their more recent works, showing how they are linked to the emotionalised climate of the 1990s with its nostalgia, its sentimentalism and its sensationalism. For example, one of Alice Munro's recent long stories, 'The Love of a Good Woman' (1996), delineates the issues it raises in its subtitle – 'A Murder, a Mystery, a Romance' – by way of an elaborate exploration of the possibilities of reticence, lies, revelation and truth. There is the body of the optometrist in his car in the lake: should the boys who find it tell or not? There is the agonising presence of lies – for example, for Enid, who nurses the young, dying Mrs Quinn and who realises that her patient is also sick with hatred and bitterness. There is a tease of truth about the optometrist's violence towards Mrs Quinn and about his murderer – a truth that seems so hard to believe that Enid wants proof in an even more unlikely construction: her vision of a romantic blackmailing scenario that concludes the story. This plot also unsettles the order that, as Bronfen has shown, is traditionally re-established with a female corpse in the house: Mrs Quinn's death is ironised by the title of the story as well as by Munro's neo-gothic excess. As always with Munro, the horror is only thinly covered by everyday life and needs; but this story all the more ironically also dramatises what draws attention to it on the cover of *The New Yorker*: 'Sex! Adultery! Murder!' Similarly, Margaret Atwood's recent novel *Alias Grace* (1996), as we shall see in the following chapter, addresses the desires to know and to feel that within (high) postmodernism's intellectual pleasures were taboo and that now can be tackled with neo-gothic recklessness.

The 1990s seem set to become a time where neo-gothic experience responds to postmodernism's most critical questions. In this sense, Aritha van Herk problematises 'home' as 'still a concept that we inhabit, and a place that we begin from' to emphasise the 'challenge of xperience extra to grounded reality' (1993, xi). This neo-gothic experience happens, it has to be repeated, in the context of globalising processes and a related turn of the private and intimate into the public and collective. These epistemological and emotional developments, I think, have been anticipated by an important novel of the beginning of the decade: A. S. Byatt's *Possession* (1990); and reinforced by Atwood's *Alias Grace*. These novels use the gothic combination of romance and horror to explore the fears and desires of the 1990s, which are, as Byatt and Atwood also show, inextricably related to the mass media as a site for public horror and revelation. Just as the gothic played an important part in the origins of mass culture two hundred years ago, neo-gothicism now participates in its international and multimedia extension.

Chapter 8

Exceeding postmodernism

1990: *Possession*. A. S. Byatt's novel instantly became a literary event in the Anglophone world, an international bestseller of Booker Prize fame. It is a book that – in form, themes and its famously multi-layered parallel plots – bridges various contrasting worlds: the twentieth and nineteenth centuries; high poetry and pulp fiction; art and love – to name but the most notable ones. But, more importantly, it also bridges the different intellectual climates of the last two decades of our century, as I have tried to outline them here: the emancipatory, seriously academic and theory-conscious 1980s and the emotionalised, nostalgic, millennium-ridden 1990s. *Possession* uses parody but directs it at (1980s') postmodernism itself. And it uses neo-gothicism to encounter the (1990s') promise of knowledge and emotion that arises from this parody.[1]

A. S. Byatt has long shaped the more English form of post-modernism that she herself has called 'self-conscious realism' (1991a, 4). Recent critics have retained social realism as predominant frame of reference for her work and emphasise the self-reflexive and the fantastic as intrusions in her work (Todd 1997, 17, 77; Kelly 1996, ix; Buxton 1996, 217). *Possession* can be seen as a development, as Byatt's 'earlier interest in discussing theoretical ideas within the realm of realism emerges here with her more recent interest in forms of fabulation, namely in romance, ghost story and fairy tale' (Neumeier 1997, 18). Indeed, Byatt endows her fifth novel with a series of signals concerning its form of representation. The subtitle – *A Romance* – suggests that we read her voluminous novel beyond realism; and the first epitaph is taken from Nathaniel Hawthorne's famous celebration of the romance's 'latitude' and liberating powers over the novel's painstaking fidelity to man's experience in the preface to *The House of the Seven Gables*. Alfred Hornung has recently shown Hawthorne's immense influence on 'the witchcraft of fiction' in postmodern times, from Stephen King's popular gothics to Anne Rice's just as popular vampire chronicles (and the related film adaptations) (1997b, esp. 313ff). Hornung emphasises the powerful feelings aroused by these plots (1997b, 315); Byatt uses Hawthorne's 'romance' to gothic dimensions, with a similar emotional effect. The gothic has always thrived on the connectedness of extremes and feminine gothic excess has shown its emancipatory potential for postmodern culture. A. S. Byatt, I think, goes yet a step further; provocatively speaking, she uses gothicism to exceed postmodernism itself before the millennium.

> The man and the woman sat opposite each other in the railway carriage. They had an appearance of quiet decorum; both had books open on their knees, to which they turned when the motion of the carriage permitted. He was indeed leaning lazily back into his corner ... She had her eyes for the most part cast demurely down at her book, though she would occasionally raise a pointed chin ... An observer might have speculated for some time as to whether they were travelling together or separately. (*Possession*, 273)

This could be taken as a perfect opening of a nineteenth-century romance, or of a gothic romance, or even of a Mills & Boon paperback. However, it does not open *Possession* but marks the very centre of its plot. The travellers are Randolph Henry Ash and Christabel LaMotte, two fictitious Victorian poets, and the quoted scene reveals their illicit romance, despite his marriage and her assumed lesbianism. This romance has, from the start, been the subject of fanatic research by two 1980s' academics: Roland Michell, a despairing Ash scholar, and Maud Bailey, an expert in LaMotte. As these two – and with them *Possession*'s readers – voraciously consume documents as varied as diaries, letters, biographies, LaMotte's gothic *Melusina*, her fairy-tales, Ash's poems and other official and private, literary and historical writings, their own story gradually turns into a romance – or rather, into a reverential parody of one.

As if this was not intertextual enough, moreover, this contemporary romance plot develops amidst another collection of contemporary

genres – from television interviews to faxes and other electronic communication – and an abundance of related narratives of other academics: the patriarchal Ash specialist Blackadder, the frustrated 'woman
scholar' Beatrice Nest, the flamboyant Americans Mortimer Cropper
(a self-confessed Ash fetishist) and Leonora Stern (whose post-
structuralist-feminist criticism celebrates LaMotte) – to name only
the most striking figures in Byatt's scenario of academic eccentrics.
Her abundance of narrative forms and figures, it seems, is the perfectly
excessive form for an excessive plot which covers two centuries, large
estates and sublime landscapes, buried letters and hiding veils, family
horror of differing sorts, adultery, a tragic suicide, an invalid with an
important key, an illegitimate child that – alive or murdered? – haunts
the last part of the novel, and an apocalyptic graveyard scene. All this
– and that is the peak of her parody – for *possession*: the possession of
a secret that really happened: the possession of knowledge.

Read this way, *Possession* perfectly exemplifies gothic form. Byatt's
excessive genre (and media) mix draws attention to the multitude of
possibilities between gothic, historic, fantastic and realistic representation. However, it is important to realise that the gothic is positioned at
the centre of that narrative abundance. Thus if one of the driving
forces of the narrative is to uncover what *really* happened between
Ash and LaMotte, the solution is the plot of a gothic romance!

In some ways, this narrative play with the expectations of realism
and gothicism is a parodic and postmodern move. However, here the
parody is directed at the postmodern itself. Byatt uses parody in *Possession* to recall and repeat questions that postmodernism had rejected
as classic realist – questions of history, knowledge and even origin –
and then to defer the answers by shifting them into the ambiguous
realm of gothicism. However, as Hutcheon's theory of parody implies,
this parodic process does draw attention to that which is trans-
textualised, and *Possession*'s parody does repeat the basic questions for
the 'master narratives' that postmodernism has so proudly resisted.
And it does that with the narcissistic pleasure of pointing to the temptations of form and to the impact of emotion: 'Coherence and closure
are deep human desires that are presently unfashionable. But they are
always both frightening and enchantingly desirable' (422). They are,
in short, a gothic experience.

♦

'I want to – to – follow the – path. I feel taken over by this. I want to *know* what happened, and I want it to be me that finds out' (238) says Maud to Roland at a moment when they notice that their pursuit of the Ash–LaMotte affair 'isn't professional greed. It's something more primitive' (238). As has been suggested, possession of knowledge is one of the driving forces in the novel, and its most important object is Christabel LaMotte – who is searched for, as Byatt gothically puts it, like a 'hypothetical ghost' (251) and, I would like to add, like one of the many 'lost mothers' and 'other women' from the gothic tradition. Her life-story is gradually pieced together through her poetry, her letters to Ash, his letters to her, Ash's wife's diary, her reading of LaMotte's gothic *Fairy Melusina*, her French cousin Sabine's writing exercises, the contemporary feminist criticism of her work – and, most parodically, the omniscient narrator's occasional intrusions that mock all of these academic and reading discoveries with a gothic voice. Thus, LaMotte's narrative comes to assume the very centre of the novel. *Possession*'s mystery plot opens with a generic gothic transgression, as Roland steals Ash's fragmentary letters to Christabel from the library. They suggest his fascination with her own poetic designs (5) and start a lovers' discourse that elegantly parodies the Victorian gothic classics – for example, the famous dialogues between Rochester and Jane Eyre, where (as we have seen) *he* rails about her ethereal elusiveness while *she* emphasises her physical presence and, by extension, her sexuality.

In a further intertextualising move, Christabel describes herself continuously in metaphors of weaving, for example in her first letter to Ash:

> I live circumscribed and self-communing – 'tis best so – not like a Princess in a thicket, by no means, but more like a very fat and self-satisfied Spider in the centre of her shining Web ... Arachne is a lady I am greatly sympathetic to, an honest craftswoman, who makes perfect patterns, but is a little inclined to take unorthodox snaps at visiting and trespassing strangers ... The Spider in the poem however, is not my Silken Self, but an altogether more Savage and businesslike sister. (87)

Not surprisingly in this novel of abundance and excess, the spider imagery characterises Christabel in manifold dimensions: she uses it to present herself as the fabricator of a poetic web – her art – but also as a woman who works very hard to fabricate her own, independent home – her life. Her last letter to Ash displays her despair at the question whether by destroying the protection of that web for the affair with him, she ruined her chance of becoming – like him – a great poet (502).The parodic allusions to Tennyson's 'The Lady of Shalott' and Romanticism's feminine demise between art and love (181, 187), a persistent feminine gothic conflict, are here, once again, extended into the gothic figure of the spider woman. In feminine gothic fiction, as we have seen, the fate of the tragic temptress has always been illuminated with sympathy rather than idealisation. And thus, the life-story of Christabel LaMotte is further interwoven with the web of feminine gothic writing. As we have seen, feminine gothic textures, with their surface romance plot of love and sex and their mirror-plot of female desire, creativity and art, avoid the closure as well as morality of classic realism; rather, they poignantly narrate the pleasures and horrors of women's lives. In this sense, the multi-voiced, dynamic, web-like fabrication of Christabel's life narrative exceeds the postmodern parody into a gothic story about women's lives in the nineteenth century.

'I have been Melusina [her own gothic heroine] these thirty years' (501) writes Christabel as an old woman, after the love, the anger, the horror. The story of how she gives birth to her and Ash's daughter in Brittany in emotionally disastrous circumstances is the most gothic episode of her life's plot, reverberating with overtones of Moers's female gothic 'trauma of the afterbirth' (1978, 119). Significantly, this almost mythic, pan-European gothic narrative becomes entirely believable. It is embedded in a scenario of nineteenth-century family arrangements that parodically 'repeats' but subverts the well-known clichés. There is the famous poet, Ash, pampered by an 'Angel in the House', his wife Ellen, who, ironically, not only knows about his affairs but preserves the evidence for future generations; the jealous younger writer Sabine de Kerosz in Brittany; the tragic 'lesbian blue-stocking' Blanche Glover, Christabel's partner in the project of living as self-sufficient artists – and maybe lovers – in a hostile society. All these female figures represent marginalised women typical in Byatt's character scheme (see Todd 1997, 56); however, I would like to emphasise that although they seem to gravitate around Ash, their place in the plot is at the centre. The narrative thus effectively attacks those power structures that marginalise them. At the same time, Blanche's Wollstonecraftian suicide, as well as Christabel's own eventual compromise in a life she never wanted, are radical comments on the fates of women artists and writers not only in Victorian culture that have long been narrated best in the feminine gothic fiction that Byatt here recalls. Her own comment on the position as woman writer is striking: 'Literature has always been my way out, my escape from the limits of being female' (Dusinberre 1983, 186).

The solution to *Possession's* mystery responds to the mirror-plot – or rather, one of the mirror-plots – of female desire and thus offers another typical gothic connection: Maud discovers LaMotte to be her great-great-great-grandmother. 'How strangely appropriate to have been exploring all along the myth – no the truth – of your own origins' (503), one of her formerly competing and now sympathising colleagues comments. Of course, 'truth' and 'origins' are, like 'knowledge', virtual contradictions to postmodern thinking. However, it is the appropriate response to Maud's explicitly 'primitive' – and not only scholarly – desire to *know*. Thus, there *is* an answer to her quest, and it comes by way of uncovering her matrilineal tradition. However, here the parody gives way to an illuminating perspective on contemporary culture, and its pronounced need for answers. Byatt's contemporary romance plot in *Possession* is structured throughout by this desire to know, and contemporary readers are complicit in that desire as the book's success clearly shows. Following Maud's and Roland's plot thus brings us back to my proposition that *Possession* exceeds postmodernism.

A striking *fantasy* connects these two enlightened modern scholars of literature and theory:

> 'Sometimes I feel,' said Roland carefully, 'that the best state is to be without desire. When I really look at myself–'
> 'If you have a self–'
> 'At my life, at the way it is – what I *really* want is to – to have nothing. An empty clean bed. I have this image of a clean empty bed in an empty room, where nothing is asked or to be asked ...'
> 'I know what you mean ... That's what I think about when I'm alone. How good it would be to have nothing. How good it would be to desire nothing. And the same image. An empty bed in an empty room. White.'
> (267)

Fountain has shown that Byatt's imagery here exhibits nostalgia in the sense of 'a desire for an absence of desire' (1994, 203). He attributes this nostalgia to the majority of subject positions in the novel in the

sense that 'the disillusioned subject longs for non-existence or complete "satisfaction" ... the result is a static nostalgia' (1994, 203).
Static nostalgia as favourite fantasy: Byatt's parodic image for the
emotional state of late-twentieth-century academics?

Formally speaking, here the 'stripping' processes of neo-gothicism
continue, as mirror-plots are uncovered and (at least) two romance
plots comment on each other with provocative and enlightening effects.
Whereas Ash's and LaMotte's unconditional love is driven by powerful desires and, especially in LaMotte's case, by very legitimate fears
of loss, their contemporary counterparts deprive their lives of such
emotional drama. Roland, always on the shadow side of academic
hierarchies, in the beginning moves from one live-burial (in the mau-
soleum of the library) to another (his windowless basement apartment), and the illegitimate possession of Ash's letters seems his only
chance to break that cycle of doom. Maud is a successful scholar but
painfully stalked by her playboy colleague Fergus Wolff and her American sister in LaMotte criticism Leonora Stern. Their research on the
two nineteenth-century poets leads them into their quest for the past,
for history – and, ultimately, for love. Byatt narrates this contemporary quest, I think, also with a sharp eye on nostalgia as she herself
has defined it, as an emotion that we turn to at the end of the century:
'Where we fear the chaos of the contemporary, with its bombs at
airports and other uncontrollable threats, we turn to a nostalgia for a
past that suggests order and familiarity' (Byatt 1995). Significantly,
hers is not the well-kept Jane Austen garden of self-control that has
become a Hollywood favourite before the millennium,[2] but the wilderness of gothicism. Nostalgia in this sense points to more than fatigue
with postmodernism's infinite deferrals.

The nostalgia-fantasy is first openly shared in Yorkshire, to which
Roland and Maud have – led by intuition rather than logic – followed
their subjects of research. Here, in that literary and gothically most
overdetermined English landscape, the paradoxes of their quest become
obvious. For are these two nostalgics not, despite their fatigue, driven
by their desire to know? Accordingly, right after expressing that sterile,
intellectual, bodiless fantasy that they share, Roland suggests that they
'go and look at something for ourselves ... I just want to look at
something, with interest, and without layers of meaning. Something
new' (268). This 'new' place is described by 'abundance, ... growth,
... banks of gleaming scented life' (268), and it brings them closer to

the Ash–LaMotte romance than they could ever research. The scene is a parodic 'repetition' of the other couple's erotic experience there: responding to Roland's insistence to 'let it out' (271), Maud opens her usually fixed and covered braids and lets her long hair flow freely. A gothic moment: Roland 'saw the light rush towards it and glitter on it, the whirling mass … Maud inside it saw a moving sea of gold lines, waving, and closed her eyes and saw scarlet blood' (272). A gothic moment of intimacy, suspended between their nostalgia for the past and the promise of the future.

'What's love got to do with it?' asks Jackie Buxton in her reading of *Possession* as 'postmodern seduction' and appropriately answers: 'everything, it seems' (1996, 200). Indeed, Roland and Maud are able to theorise love, desire, the body, the drives, etc. (e.g. 423) but the theories they have internalised – post-structuralism, psychoanalysis, deconstruction, feminism, and so on – have alienated them so much from emotion that they 'have to make a real effort of imagination to know what it felt like to be them [Ash and LaMotte]' (267). Structurally, this realisation links their shared fantasy of nostalgia to the Ash–LaMotte romance that follows it in the next chapter: a self-reflexive idea that runs like one of Christabel's 'silk threads' through the novel's texture. Accordingly, late in the book, Roland finds himself caught in the web of romance:

> Maud was a beautiful woman such as he had no claim to possess. She had a secure job and an international reputation. Moreover, in some dark and outdated English social system of class … Maud was County, and he was urban lower-middle-class … All that was the plot of a Romance. He was in a Romance, a vulgar and a high Romance simultaneously, a Romance was one of the systems that controlled him, as the expectations of Romance control almost everyone in the Western world, for better or worse, at some point or another. (425)

However, while he recalls the considerations of class and propriety that in the gothic classics defer the happy ending, in his own plot, love and sex are deferred because he and Maud know too much. Thus, Byatt's late-twentieth-century romance plot works through an important paradox: knowledge defers the emotional happy ending, while the desire for knowledge that motivates the plot nevertheless works to liberate these emotions. I think Byatt's complex narrative in this sense not only illuminates a particular emotional vacuum – related to the nostalgia fantasy – in postmodern culture, but, by insisting on wanting to possess, anticipates the new desires of a new decade at the end of the century.

The pleasures of reading *Possession*, it seems, are related to a reading-effect that suggests that we actually possess something at the end of the novel. This effect comes about first, and most obviously, in the final sex scene that perfectly parodies both the struggles and the bliss-ful defeat of postmodern strategies:

> very slowly and with infinite gentle delays and delicate diversions and vari-ations of indirect assault Roland finally, to use an outdated phrase, entered and took possession of all her white coolness that grew warm against him, so that there seemed no boundaries, and he heard, towards dawn, from a long way off, her clear voice crying out, uninhibited, unashamed, in pleas-ure and triumph. (507)

However, this moment of *jouissance*, as one critic has called it (Foun-tain 1994, 205), could not have been reached without the most dra-matic gothic excess in the novel: Mortimer Cropper's robbing of Ash's grave on a dark and stormy night.

Cropper's own desire to know is decisively that of a necrophiliac. He pursues the black box that Ellen Ash had reportedly placed on top of her husband's coffin, and the traces of this compulsive desire thicken throughout the novel. When he finally starts digging – with the help of the just as adequately named Hildebrand Ash – the scene poign-antly reverberates with metaphors of potency and transgression. Ap-propriately, an apocalyptic storm ends it and closes the grave for ever – but not before Cropper actually secures the box. He then has to be rescued by his British competitors for scholarly achievement who, al-though explicitly shocked, have let him do the dirty work.

> Waiting for him was a dark figure with a flashlight, whose beam was swung in his direction.
> 'Professor Cropper?' said this being, in a clear, authoritative male voice. 'Are you all right?'
> 'I seem to be trapped by trees.'
> 'We can get you out, I expect. Have you got the box?'
> 'What box?' said Cropper.
> 'Yes, he has,' said Hildebrand, 'Oh, get us out of here, this is ghastly ...'
> Cropper spun round, and the beam of the other's flashlight revealed, peering through the branches, like bizarre flowers or fruit, wet and white, Roland Michell, Maud Bailey, Leonora Stern, James Blackadder, and with

streaming white woolly hair descended, like some witch or prophetess, a transfigured Beatrice Nest. (496)

This gothic scenario, then, transports us into another plot that has, throughout the novel, explored the underside of the academics' tension between nostalgia and the 'primitive' desire to know: their craving for excitement, their clandestine voyeurism and sensationalism. After all, their quest for the secret love of two people is also a quest for illicit sex, for child murder, and for other, related excesses.[3]

And that, I think, suggests much, not only about the contemporary academic scene in which the novel is predominantly set, but also about the larger cultural climate in the decade of reality-TV, confession shows, a booming tabloid industry and the related heroes and dramas. *Possession* in this sense contextualises an acute image of the late post-modernism anticipating the media-hyped 1990s. Another, more recent important novel continues that poignant power of neo-gothicism as appropriate form before the millennium.

At first glance, Margaret Atwood's *Alias Grace*, published in 1996, seems like her first historical novel, set in the nineteenth century. It tells the life-story of Grace Marks, a historical Canadian figure of dubious fame because she was suspected of murder and sentenced to life in a spectacular trial in Toronto in 1843. As Atwood points out in her 'Afterword', the book is 'a work of fiction, although it is based on reality' (461); she lays open her sources, declares her liberty 'to invent' and concludes: 'The true character of the historical Grace Marks remains an enigma' (463). Thus, we read a historiographic metafiction in Hutcheon's sense, which approaches its evasive subject in different ways and forms: there are historical documents like the confessions of Grace Marks and of her accomplice James McDermott; the newspaper reports about their spectacular crimes and trial; Susanna Moodie's account of meeting Grace Marks in the Kingston Penitentiary, as well as in the Provincial Lunatic Asylum in Toronto (*Life in the Clearings*, 1853); documents like the letters of Dr Joseph Workman, who was Medical Superintendent of the Asylum; and so on. Moreover, there are also the fictitious letters of the fictitious American nerve-specialist, Dr Simon Jordan, who investigates Grace's subconscious (she claims to have no memory of the murders); more letters between him, his mother and other men of professional (and sometimes private) interest in Grace's person and case; his personal story, with much emphasis on his dreams and fantasies. And, of course, there is Grace's own first-person narration, as she tells it to Dr Jordan, and as it appears in her reflections and dreams. Thus, like *Possession*, the novel is composed of an abundance of voices and narratives that circle around a mystery. Moreover, this plot of scientific pursuit of knowledge, as personified by Dr Jordan and followed closely by the reader, also is revealed, in the end, as having been largely a 'craving for the hot spots' of a mysterious woman's life-story.

Significantly, Grace Marks was a servant girl of fifteen when she became a 'famous murderess', and her youth and beauty as well as the erotic potential of her story – or rather the combination of sex, murder and rebellion – contributed greatly to her ambiguous career as a media celebrity in nineteenth-century Canada. Was she, for example, sexually involved with James McDermott, who allegedly was her partner in crime and who was hanged following their trial in Toronto on 21 November 1843? Was she, rather, involved with her master, Thomas Kinnear, Esq? Was her master involved with the housekeeper Nancy Montgomery? Master and housekeeper were murdered at the Kinnear estate on 23 July 1843. Did the two servants kill them? If so: because of Grace's wild jealousy, as Susanna Moodie has indicated, or rather out of rebellion? This is, indeed, good stuff for a gothic tale, and many have been told about Grace Marks, Moodie's own included. By contrast, Atwood uses the gothic combination of romance and horror once again to tell the story of a woman's life and, moreover, to expose the workings of celebrity, sensationalism and mass media. Set in the nineteenth century, her story reflects back on the same phenomena today.[4]

Formally speaking, gothic excess in *Alias Grace* works to focus the postmodern genre *historiographic metafiction* on the presently recurring questions of knowledge, history and identity. The novel, adequately, has more than one beginning: the well-known quote from Susanna Moodie before actually meeting Grace for the first time; a horrible fantasy of Nancy in the rose-garden that haunts the novel; the *Toronto Mirror* report of the spectacular McDermott execution, with its telling description of the 'immense concourse of men, women and children anxiously waiting to witness the last struggle of a sinful fellow-being' (9); a ballad that outlines the whole criminal story in popular rhymes.

Moodie's actual description of Grace, concluding: 'She looks like a person rather above her humble station' (*Alias Grace*, 19) sets the tone for the opening of Grace's own (fictitious) narrative. By now, we have circled around the celebrated murderess in both personal and official discourses, and (Atwood's) Grace Marks quickly and adequately puts an end to that approach in these terms:

> Sometimes when I am dusting the mirror with the grapes I look at myself in it, although I know it is vanity. In the afternoon light of the parlor my skin is a pale mauve, like a faded bruise, and my teeth are greenish. I think of all the things that have been written about me – that I am an inhuman female demon, that I am an innocent victim of a blackguard forced against my will and in danger of my own life, that I was too ignorant to know how to act and that to hang me would be judicial murder, that I am fond of animals, that I am very handsome with a brilliant complexion ... that I am a good girl with a pliable nature and no harm is told of me, that I am cunning and devious, that I am soft in the head and little better than an idiot. And I wonder, how can I be all of these different things at once? (23)

What better discarding could there be of the constructions of celebrity? Grace, facing a gothic ghost in the mirror, introduces herself like a romantic heroine through the eyes of the world; her sharp recognition of the firm enclosure within society's gaze and constructions addresses the abundance of contradictions that defy realising her as a fixed personality – an early recognition of her as both 'empty' and over-determined that will stay with us throughout her story.

That story, the life of a servant-girl in the nineteenth century, sur-prisingly turns out to be one of abundance as well. She tells it to Dr Jordan in so much detail – as one reviewer put it, she is 'gloriously commonsensical' (Prose 1996, 6) – that he suspects hidden informa-tion behind her accounts of female everyday work (185), whereas, ironi-cally, he never doubts the most cruel, violent and otherwise dramatic parts of her tale. Grace's childhood reads like a colonial version of Jane Eyre's. Her childhood is full of (domestic) violence; she re-members her father as a brutal man, a criminal and maybe a murderer, and her life-story is haunted by death. The emigration from Belfast to Toronto becomes a horrible passage during which her mother dies. Working as a maid, a strong friendship connects her to the slightly older, native maid Mary Whitney, who – much like Brontë's Helen Burns – gives her love and solidarity and, more dramatically, dies the cruel death of a young, poor girl in Victorian times. Throughout,

Atwood foregrounds class and gender issues, as in Mary's provocative verbal reversals of the master–servant relationship and Grace's own sharp observations that put her masters to shame, reveal her recognitions of recurring abuse and sexual entanglements, and make her fictitious account entirely sympathetic and convincing (see, e.g., Prose 1996, 6; Gussow 1996, B1).

The central relationship in the narrative, between Grace and Dr Jordan, brings these issues together, in an ironic and illuminating play of difference and similarity. Simon Jordan continuously reflects on the various housekeepers and maids around him – usually he feels badly treated and has fantasies of sexual overpowering. Listening to Grace's story of such a servant, he realises the similarity to his own 'happier days and the memories of them, and they too contain pictures of clean sheets and joyful holidays, and cheerful young maidservants' (185). This is only one signal that doctor and patient – or, put in different terms, the American, middle-class, educated gentleman and the Irish-Canadian, working-class, criminal woman – have more in common than first meets the eye. Both are about thirty; both are strangers to Kingston and the Governor's circles; both clearly look through the social conventions that surround them – for example the ruses and workings of the marriage market. What connects them, despite their carefully guarded distance, is the solidarity of outsiders, in a society that courts them with the fascinations of desire (Dr Jordan) and of horror (Grace). Thus Simon is careful when this society turns, as Grace clearly notes, the suspected and much romanticised murderess into a monster:

> My hair is coming out from under my cap. Red hair of an ogre. A wild beast, the newspaper said. A monster. When they come with my dinner I will put the slop bucket over my head and hide behind the door, and that will give them a fright. If they want a monster so badly they ought to be provided with one.
>   I never do such things, however. I only consider them. If I did them, they would be sure I had gone mad again. (33)

(Atwood's) Grace unfolds the drama of the monstrous-feminine from the perspective of the speaking subject, a heroine between clairvoyance, unreliability and deception. When she, with her matter-of-fact voice, tells of the everyday life in houses and dresses, of housework and of sewing, of loneliness and starvation in the prison, and of death in the attic and murder beneath the kitchen linoleum, readers have to negotiate a growing sympathy and the recognition of an equally grow-ing insecurity about her tale. Moreover, the complex composition of the novel as a whole works both to reinforce and to question the truthfulness of her narrative throughout: for example, Grace's reflec-tions on Dr Jordan's notes during their meetings unfold her clear recognition of how he not only perceives but also constructs her sen-sitive imagination, and a seeming honesty that privileges the reader:

> While he writes, I feel as if he is drawing me; or not drawing me, drawing on me – drawing on my skin – not with the pencil he is using, but with an old-fashioned goose pen, and not with the quill end but with the feather end ...
>
> But underneath that is another feeling, a feeling of being wide-eyed awake and watchful. It's like being wakened suddenly in the middle of the night, by a hand over your face, and you sit up with your heart going fast, and no one is there. And underneath that is another feeling still, a feeling like being torn open; not like a body of flesh, it is not painful as such, but like a peach; and not even torn open, but too ripe and splitting open of its own accord.
>
> And inside the peach there's a stone. (69)

However, if we think that she has been speaking 'openly' here, on the next page, in a (fictional) letter from the medical superintendent of the Toronto lunatic asylum, we read that Grace Marks is 'an accomplished and a most practised liar' (71). Similarly, her own reflections frequently relativise her account, for example, when she muses that 'little by little I found I could talk to [Dr Jordan] more easily, and *think up* things to say' (68, emphasis added).

At the same time, Dr Jordan increasingly and involuntarily suc-cumbs to the feminine wiles encircling him. His own, gothically acci-dental, affair with his married landlady within the orbit of the sullen housekeeper Dora is a disarming parodic repetition of the earlier erotic constellation at the Kinnear estate and might be the most excessive turn in a gothic plot full of nightmares and fantasies, dark mirrors, the grotesqueries of bodies, and horror tales.

The most sensational horror tale that haunts *Alias Grace* is Susanna Moodie's gothic history *Life in the Clearings versus the Bush* (1853), a history of Canadian life she was asked to write by her English publisher as a follow-up to her very popular *Roughing it in the Bush* (1852). Carol Shields, discussing Moodie's place in Canadian culture and literature, emphasises her *authentic* voice and the emotional power of her accounts (1989, esp. 338–40). Interestingly, her comment on the form of Moodie's writings – which assemble elements of travel writing, literary sketches, narrative fictions, meditations, poetry, and so on – concludes:

> *Life in the Clearings* is the kind of patchwork, unofficial document that allows us to 'read' a slice of our national history, and a rather large slice at that.
>   Trying to place such a text in a governing tradition is to miss the book itself. The form is Susanna Moodie's invention; it fits like a comfortable hand-knitted sweater. (Shields 1989, 339)

Atwood, I think, intertextualises that notion of a feminine form but she also, in a first step, uses the nineteenth-century scenario of her novel to probe the reactions an unconventional, and gothic, text like Moodie's has to provoke. As I have mentioned above, she has poetically intertextualised Moodie's ground-breaking journals for the Canadian-conscious 1970s (Atwood 1970, 1977); and her 1974 television drama about Grace Marks relies on Susanna Moodie's historical, but expressedly third-hand account of Grace's guilt (Moodie 1989 [1853], 197–209). In *Alias Grace*, she takes up these connections with Canadian filliation as well as historiography with a neo-gothic twist. She carefully revises Moodie's excessive rendering of the crimes as well as of the 'mad murderess' by poignantly disclosing the contemporaries' clandestine fascination with Moodie's gothic sensibilities. Of course, this happens with disarming sympathy for Moodie and for the temptations and attractions of melodrama – and with supreme Atwoodian irony. Everybody in *Alias Grace* seems to have read Moodie's book: most of the ladies shudder and most of the gentlemen sneer at the thought of it. And then, in a poignant, hilarious and ultimately revealing scene, the scientist (Jordan) and the priest (Verringer) discuss Moodie's history. Their reservations develop into confession: analysing Moodie's fabrications by repeating the salacious details one by one, they realise that

> 'she has the culprits cutting Nancy Montgomery's body up into quarters before hiding it under the washtub, which surely was not done. The newspapers would hardly have failed to mention a detail so sensational. I am afraid the good woman did not realize how difficult it is to cut up a body, never having done so herself ...' [says the doctor to conclude:] 'the public will always prefer a salacious melodrama to a bald tale of mere thievery ...'
>   [at which the well-read reverend responds, alluding to a literary Nancy-murder:] 'Mrs. Moodie ... has stated publicly that she is very fond of

Charles Dickens and especially of *Oliver Twist* ... Mrs. Moodie is subject to
influences ...'
    [he proceeds to recite her most gothic poem *The Maniac*, which makes
him confess a special memory ...][f]or verse of a certain type, unfortunately ...; it comes from too much hymn-singing.' (190–91)

This scene is noteworthy, as its disarming attack parodies the range of
both popular and more elitist reactions to Moodie and other gothic
history writing. Moreover, it also opens a large literary web: the two
learned men also admit to their own fascination with Nathaniel
Hawthorne, although he is 'accused of sensualism, and – especially
after *The Scarlet Letter* – of a laxity in morals' (192). Hawthorne's own
romances of guilt and redemption haunt, as we have seen, much neo-
gothic fiction and they (as well as to Robert Browning's poetry) a-
filliate *Alias Grace* and *Possession*. Of course, in the quoted dialogue,
Hawthorne remains appreciated, while Moodie's gothicism is mocked
– much like the 'scribbling women' in Hawthorne's own raging re-
proach – in gendered terms:

'Mrs. Moodie is a literary lady, and like all such, and indeed like the sex in
general, she is inclined to–'
    'Embroider,' says Simon. (191)

Embroidering history, gothicising experience: this is familiar territory
by now and brings us back to the interwoven metaphors of feminine
textures and fabrications. Shield's appropriate image of Moodie's
'patchwork' prefigures Atwood's own, self-reflexively feminine form.
Alias Grace thematises the metaphors of women's needlework in a
variety of ways: sewing is a household chore, it helps Grace to look
'proper' in a new, self-made dress (176) and it keeps her busy in the
Governor's household; but most importantly, sewing is Grace's (like
Hawthorne's own Hester's) talent and her art. While she tells her
story, she ornaments different quilts; thus the activities of narrating
and sewing are related right away. Moreover, as she explains the quilts'
patterns' names to her interested listener, Simon Jordan, another layer
of narrative is opened up that leads us from the 'Log Cabin' quilt she
makes for the Governor's daughter (98) via the 'Pandora's Box' that –
of course – greatly interests Dr Jordan (146) and the 'Snake Fence'
she tells him she would like to make (98), to the 'Tree of Paradise'
that is her secret dream since she first encountered the pattern with

Mary Whitney (98) and that she ends up making for herself before her own 'happy ending' (469). These quilt names come to be headings of the fifteen sections of *Alias Grace*. Atwood's novel is pieced together like a quilt, from the different genres outlined above: differing fabrics and fabrications shape her feminine gothic texture beyond conventional enclosures.

Recent feminist criticism has rediscovered quilting as both feminine work and art (see, e.g., Howe 1991), and, as for example the studies of Elaine Hedges show, quilts have become a 'major feminist icon' (Hedges 1993, 11). Some find that quilting represents feminine collective efforts from different contexts of race and class unified in a harmonious whole, whereas from a more postmodern perspective, the quilts' artful patterns that depend on very differing materials become the focus and force of the feminist argument. In *Alias Grace*, quilts are tied to female lives (they mark for example weddings, class status, death and mourning), and their formal function in the fictitious life-story of Grace Marks is important. To Grace, they represent both cover and ornament; they make for example 'the bed the most notice-able thing in the room' (161) in one of the scenes that thematise perception and 'ways of seeing' and that defamiliarise the everyday objects she is concerned with. The bed right away becomes a site of birth and death, of sex and despair, of peaceful sleep and of bad dreams (161). This double-edged view is emphasised when she speaks about how to perceive a quilt: 'you can see them two different ways, by looking at the dark pieces or else the light' (162). These are, of course, also the ways we can read the texture of her life, and the question of her guilt. One of the concluding images is, accordingly, her idea that 'The Fruit of Life and the Fruit of Good and Evil were the same' (459). However, the quilt pattern she likes, the 'Tree of Paradise', works in triangles, and her plan for her own quilt closes her narrative in these terms:

> Three of the triangles in my Tree will be different. One will be white, from the petticoat I still have that was Mary Whitney's; one will be faded yellow-ish, from the prison nightdress I begged as a keepsake when I left there. And the third will be a pale cotton, a pink and white floral, cut from the dress of Nancy's that she had on the first day I was at Mr. Kinnear's, and that I wore on the ferry to Lewiston, when I was running away.
>
> I will embroider around each one of them with red feather-stitching, to blend them in as a part of the pattern.
>
> And so we will all be together. (460)

An image of union of the three women, then, ends the novel with a suggested closure that is, of course, deceiving.

Formally speaking, Grace's vision of reunion with the two most important women in her life undercuts her 'happy ending' – her (fictitious) wedding to Jamie Walsh after her (historical) release in 1872 – and thus continues feminine gothic texture. It does so by also continuing the 'stripping' processes that uncover the layers of mirror-plots. Again, the quilt-like texture becomes important, where this final romance element is only a patch that seems completely disjunct with the previous texture of narrative. Accordingly, Grace's marriage to her former traitor, Jamie Walsh, is presented in ironic terms, like a pragmatic (452) as well as a literary (446) necessity. Jamie, first seen as a boy on the fence of the Kinnear estate in the chapter 'Snake Fence' (209), is remembered mainly because of his behaviour at her trial that turns the judges against her and cements his own career (451). He represents one of the traitors or 'snakes' in her story, the presence of which she has long accepted in the texture of her life and included into her final quilt, 'as without a snake or two, the main part of the story would be missing' (460). Significantly, the snakes border the quilt, while the central pattern, the 'Tree of Paradise', brings together the separate fabrics preserved from her own and from the two other women's lives. The quilt theme and form of *Alias Grace* thus works to foreground the threads of female desire, of creativity and emotional liberation, while the – treacherous – romance plot appears as mere function and frame. Fittingly, that last chapter itself is self-reflexively called 'Tree of Paradise', suggesting that actually, finally, 'ends meet'.

However, this sense of an ending could not have been achieved without Grace – who keeps deferring the subject in her meetings with Dr Jordan – actually speaking about the murder. Significantly, this 'moment of truth' happens in an utterly gothic scene of hypnosis. This scenario is so excessively overdetermined that it presents both the epitome of Atwood's own narrative deferrals and a perfectly neo-gothic experience. Intertextually, *Lady Oracle*'s, as well as Susanna Moodie's, spiritualists reverberate throughout the scene in the Governor's parlour; at the same time, the popular but derogated practices of nineteenth-century mesmerism are evoked (394–8) that constitute a similarly mysterious, decisive but much less comic scene in *Possession*. Grace is hypnotised by a doctor whom she has earlier met as Jeremiah the peddler; the scene is focalised through Simon Jordan – these and other narrative twists unfold an abundance of possible interpretations of Grace's performance, which suggests that at the time of the murders she was possessed by the ghost of Mary Whitney. That ghost seems to have entered the scene of hypnosis as well, and to be narrating the deed – as well as commenting on the scene itself – in Grace's place (395–404). Of course, the chapter is aptly called 'Pandora's Box' – and of course, it does not contain the answer to the increasingly pressing questions as to what *really* happened.

However, this neo-gothic scene draws attention to the audience's – as well as the readers' – increasing desire to *know* – and especially to Simon Jordan's eagerness (395) to know primarily the sexual situation around the murder (399). Grace – or rather Mary? – mockingly confronts him with more (or different) erotica than he is prepared for, and thoroughly attacks her audience's urge – not for knowledge, but, it seems, rather for horror and catharsis (400). The workings of sensationalism are fully exhibited.

As Grace, for the last time put on public display like an animal in a zoo (see also Moodie 1989 [1853], 209; and Atwood's 'Afterword', 462), nevertheless dominates the scene, the prevailing power relations are reversed, a process that is taken up again in Grace's last letter to Simon Jordan. Importantly, at this point, he has become not only a Civil War invalid, but he has also *lost his memory* (if we believe his mother's letter reporting this to his former lover): forgetting about Kingston and Grace, whom he had so desired, also means forgetting about his lover's (and landlady's) plot to kill her husband. This final parodic twofold repetition of Grace's demise stresses the haunting recognition that her fate could happen to anybody. For Grace, Simon has painfully disappeared; however, her final letter offers a conclusion of her tale. Not addressed to Jordan, this letter also implicitly addresses the readers, whose questions and emotional involvement, it seems, Jordan has been representing throughout. Maybe, Grace's final recognitions about their relationship thus also point to our own relationship to her. Her husband, she tells him (or us), finds the most cruel and the most horrific parts of her life-story in the Penitentiary, the Lunatic Asylum and the Kinnear estate arousing:

> [B]ut his favourite part of the story is when poor James McDermott was hauling me all around the house at Mr. Kinnear's, looking for a bed fit for his wicked purposes, with Nancy and Mr. Kinnear lying dead in the cellar,

and me almost out of my wits with terror; and he blames himself that he wasn't there to rescue me. (457)

Simon Jordan, she suggests, reacted similarly:

[Y]ou were as eager as Mr. Walsh is to hear about my sufferings and my hardships in life; and not only that, but you would write them down as well. I could tell when your interest was slacking ... but it gave me joy every time I managed to come up with something that would interest you. (457)

If Jordan represents the reader in the text, this leaves us with yet another recognition: about ourselves, rather than about Grace Marks. No sense of truth, certainly: as in *Lady Oracle*'s ending, there is the suggestion of lies put in for the entertainment of the audience (458). Atwood's life-story of Grace Marks does not answer our questions. It leaves us with as many as there are in the beginning, only different ones.

This complex novel's ending reminds us, in its final image of a quilt, that for strong patterns fabrics are not blended but kept within their own texture. Different Atwoodian themes are intertwined in this ending: the inextricable connectedness of apparently very different women, last played out in *The Robber Bride* with a similar, if darker, image of togetherness in the end. Or the unsettling open-endedness of *The Handmaid's Tale* – is she rescued or imprisoned? Similarly, Grace could be pregnant or growing a cancer. This very physical, very feminine and typically gothic twist also recalls once again Atwood's controversial story 'Hairball' (1991), where the heroine's operated embryo/tumour ends up in a revenge package to the betrayer/lover. These double-edged neo-gothic endings exceed closure. However, as *Possession* reminds us, there returns the desire for a sense of closure – and indeed, *Alias Grace* provides that: while the historical enigma of Grace Mark's guilt remains, we encounter a recognition of the present. For today, the aura of sex, violence and rebellion is again an attraction for public constructions of celebrity.

'What we really like to do is watch' writes Henry Louis Gates about America in the 1990s:

Today, we know more about what people do in bed – not to mention trains, planes, and automobiles – than ever before. Lawrence may have been right in saying that peeping, prying and imagining are activities that go back to Adam and Eve, but, like so many pursuits, they have since been professionalized. The culture of tabloidism is a social covenant between exhibitionism and voyeurism, which means that *Schaulust* is now a sustainable career choice. Secrets, it sometimes seems, are going the way of the spotted owl. (Gates 1997, 118)

This voyeurism, as a both startled and gratified worldwide audience realises, especially revels in the sex life of the American president, as the official public investigation of President Clinton betrays. The 'tabloid nation' that Gates has outlined is much larger than America: a media culture of soap operas, of public confession shows like Oprah Winfrey's, of reality-TV and of hyped and 'hip' courtroom dramas like O. J. Simpson's. The football and Hollywood idol was pronounced not guilty, after a spectacular trial, on 3 October 1995, then guilty on 4 February 1997 of murdering his ex-wife and her friend on 13 June 1994 in Los Angeles; he has remained a much-courted guest on television talk-shows. It is also the visual culture that has made Princess Diana an icon of female suffering and survival, a star of the media age who bridged the gap between her own 'royal' dysfunctional marriage and eating disorders and those of many modern women. Just as both confessional interviews and the incessant publication of indiscreet images obliterate privacy, the borders between the media narrative of a life as soap opera and that life itself are obliterated: the princess's life and death *become* a soap opera. The whole trajectory of celebrity, tragedy and media imagery makes Diana's a very 1990s' story.[5] It exemplifies a global culture the visual power and emotional excesses of which have been poignantly uncovered, I think, especially by the gothicism in Byatt's and Atwood's exploration of desiring, deferring and nevertheless possessing.

In the 1990s, postmodern strategies and ideas like that of infinite deferral have been increasingly controversially discussed. Feminist critics in the 1980s, preoccupied with construction and performance of gender, started to ask questions that Judith Butler sums up in these terms: 'If everything is discourse, what happens to the body? If everything is a text, what about violence and bodily injury? Does anything *matter* in or for poststructuralism?' (1993, 28). The related argument for the materialisation of sex (1993, 10) points to recent developments in both the critical and larger cultural discourse that novels like *Possession* and *Alias Grace* so poignantly address. Similarly, poststructuralist thinking, it seems, turns towards more 'materialising' angles. The concept of identity as displayed in a recent issue of *Grand*

Street (62: Fall 1997) might be a good example. That issue, entitled 'Identity', displays a collection of very contemporary and very inter-national textual and visual self-presentations that read like postcolonial, pragmatic answers to the theoretical deferrals of subjectivity and that fill the problematic concept of 'identity' with new, timely possibilities. At the same time, while critics of postmodernism pursue their 're-discovery of values' more strongly than ever (for example Cutler 1997, esp. 12), postmodern theorists come to explore – theoretically as well as emphatically – the representational effects, epistemological urges and other emotional dimensions re-emerging in the 1990s. The essays in *Emotion in Postmodernism*, edited by Hoffmann and Hornung (1997), display the range of discussion on the forces of feeling in postmodern thinking. I agree with the view of postmodernism as primarily an intellectual movement: its basic strategies of deferring, defamiliarising, de-doxifying, to name only a few, seem to provoke more intellectual pleasures than the emotional ones that in the face of the millennium are presently becoming more pronounced within public culture.

In this chapter, I suggest that neo-gothicism exceeds post-modernism. In this sense, *Possession* presents the reassessment of the desire to actually possess something (something material! something emotional!) beyond the intellectual pleasures of playful deferral. Byatt's own parodic voice in the novel, as we have already seen, suggests this: 'Coherence and closure are deep human desires that are presently unfashionable. But they are always both frightening and enchantingly desirable' (422). They are, in short, a gothic experience. Byatt ends *Possession* with a scene of gothic sublime that, just like the most intense moments of her novel, is suspended between nostalgia and desire. It starts like this:

> There are things which happen and leave no discernible trace, are not spoken or written of, though it would be very wrong to say that subsequent events go on indifferently, all the same, as though such things had never been.
> Two people met, on a hot May day, and never later mentioned their meeting. This is how it was. (508)

She then narrates the fairytale-like encounter of Ash and his daughter. It is an enchanted scene that the writer (Byatt) shares with us (the readers) in a complicity that excludes the other figures in the novel. Its fantastic dimension recalls the most powerful feminine gothic happy endings. Like them, it both undercuts classic realist closure and reinforces the pleasurable reading-effect of *possessing* ... a secret. It seems that the moment when postmodern deferrals fold back upon postmodernism itself is when it becomes the moment of neo-gothic excess.

Notes

1 For an extended version of my reading of *Possession* see my 'Postmodernism's Happy Ending: Possession!' (1998).

2 The revival of Jane Austen in British television series, the recording of her sheet music and most importantly the movie-adaptations of most of her novels reached its peak with the international box-office and Oscar success of Ang Lee's *Sense and Sensibility* (1996). Emma Thompson, who wrote the Oscar-winning screenplay, reflects on the phenomenon in these terms: 'I think of Jane Austen's stories as absolutely contemporary, because her limited settings are full of emotions and connections that still pertain today' (Becker: interview).

3 Byatt suggests this throughout the novel, for example, as Maud realises that they *know* so much and *feel* so little, she also muses about her 'generation that has learned to see sex everywhere' (266). Moreover: 'They were children of a time and culture which mistrusted love, "in love", romantic love, romance *in toto*, and which nevertheless in revenge proliferated sexual language, linguistic sexuality, analysis, dissection, deconstruction, exposure' (*Possession*, 423).

4 This recognition is all the more pertinent at the time when the execution of Karla Faye Tucker for murder in Huntsville, Texas (on 3 February 1998), not only raised a new international controversy about capital punishment – a debate that involved the UN as well as the Pope – but also about another, contemporary, contradictory media mystification of a 'famous murderess'. Tucker's Christian turn in prison, but also her gender, played an important role in the public and media-hyped discussions of her death-sentence. Atwood's *Alias Grace* mirrors such present-day vital issues in the nineteenth century.

5 Significantly, Diana's death (on 31 August 1997 in Paris) was both related *to* the media (in pursuit of yet another indiscreet and therefore all the more pleasurable and profitable picture) and related *by* the media, with the globally televised funeral as cathartic event for millions; at the same time, after her fatal accident, public emotion was a celebrated necessity. Both Salman Rushdie's reflection 'Crash' (*The New Yorker*, 15 September 1997: 68–9) and Carol Gilligan's *New York Times* essay 'For many women, gazing at Diana was gazing within' (9 September 1997, C4) situate Diana's story within this contemporary trajectory.

Chapter 9

Global escapes:
nineties' gothica

Looking back on the twentieth century, Linda Nicholson has high-lighted the 'therapeutic turn' in American culture that allowed for the thought *I feel*, and that in a further step helped to articulate the differences in class, race and gender that politicised the radical 1960s and 1970s (1997, 18). These democratic movements also set post-modernism in motion, albeit, I think, via an era of both confession and kitsch that did not make it into postmodern discourse but formed its – popular, tabloid, romance, pulp – underside. At the moment when postmodernism, originally a provoking force against the Establishment, threatens to become (part of) the Establishment, these subversive forces come to the fore. I have said in the introduction to this study that gothicism in some ways works like pulp – and this, I think, is part of its force to exceed postmodernism. Just as it emerged as a sign of mass culture at the underside of the Enlightenment and the Age of Reason, just as a virtual gothic romance boom paralleled the radical women's movement of the late 1960s and 1970s, so the gothic now shapes a media culture that feeds the need for emotional directness and instant gratification simmering beneath postmodern intellectualism.

Clive Bloom's study of *Cult Fiction* (1996) – a modern, alternative literary history about pulp texts that unfortunately excludes the romance – addresses the situation in these terms: 'We can trace four parallel and interrelated incarnations of fiction concerned with the erotic, the sensational and the horrific' he writes, and enumerates those of the Stephen Kings, the Thomas Harrises and the Bret Easton

Ellises, to then concede: 'The fourth incarnation is not in fiction at all but in current cultural criticism' (1996, 237–8). This concludes a linguistic analysis mainly of feminist criticism and amounts to Bloom's 'contention ... that contemporary post-structuralist criticism is the new "pulp"' (236):

> A language inherently metaphoric in pulp (gothic) fiction has been taken as literal (a description of actuality) in post-structuralism. Such analysis is drenched in the language of nostalgia – virally disturbed by its own rhetoric of violence, irrationality and death. (Bloom 1996, 240)

Although something rings true in that view of the state of the arts, pulps and academia in the 1990s, as always, fiction is just as much tuned to the times and beyond such critical cynicism. Byatt's gothic graveyard scene and Atwood's revealing hypnosis session read like parodies of Bloom's image of the convergence of criticism and pulp gothic before the millennium. The gothic, I think, does not lose its sting or the provocative powers of pulp; rather, it exhibits again its excessive form that not only challenges culture but also challenges culture criticism before the millennium.

Gothic times again – at the moment of ongoing globalisation this opens a range of possibilities. Theo D'haen – who sees the gothic as part of the postmodern/fantastic that complements aesthetic post-modernism from the margins – places gothicism with magic realism 'in the third world and with minorities and marginalized groups in the first world' and concludes:

> From a wider perspective, this distribution is itself a telling illustration of the globalization of the Western economic system. For non-Western society and for the marginalized in Western society – roughly speaking: Western 'non-society' – the postmodern fantastic signals resistance to the hegemonic discourse of Western society. (D'haen 1995, 292)

However, these ex-centric forces of resistance have worked throughout the history of modernity (summed up by D'haen as the 'supernatural explained'), and I think that they will also work beyond the post-modern scene. Neo-gothicism does resist, it does express fears and pressures of those marginalised (D'haen 1995, 292); but it also points to and profoundly challenges the grounds for the marginalisation (like the constructions of the monstrous-feminine) and suggests their excess. In this sense, neo-gothicism also points to the various workings of globalisation we presently encounter.

The sense of apocalypse that characterises the end-of-the-century atmosphere in general more specifically points to the dawning challenges of the – definitely multicultural, definitely electronic – twenty-first century. By these challenges I mean the changing treatment of difference in today's culture; the increasing lack of orientation or utopia (with its related rise of violence in everyday life as well as in popular art forms); and the surprising effects of the media age.

As has been suggested, the awareness of difference – in the sense of gender, race, class, and so on – that had been a radical cultural, intellectual and theoretical force throughout the last twenty years has now become 'institutionalised', and thus domesticated, into 'political correctness'. Chris Weedon has shown that it has also become commodified by communication through the media that suggests 'shopping for difference' (1997, 49) and the consumption of difference for pleasure (49) – for example in local (but globally controlled) 'lonely hearts' columns. She concludes:

> Postmodernity with its commodified celebration of difference does not in itself necessitate any fundamental shift in the racialised and gendered power relations of contemporary Western societies. To allow for the articulation of difference is not necessarily to revalue it. (Weedon 1997, 52)

Similarly, Kwame Anthony Appiah and Henry Louis Gates outline their vision of the 1990s in these terms:

> A literary historian might very well characterize the eighties as the period when race, class, and gender became the holy trinity of literary criticism … In the nineties, however, 'race,' 'class,' and 'gender' threaten to become the regnant clichés of our critical discourse. (1992, 625)

I think that the neo-gothicism of writers like Munro, Atwood and van Herk, with its interrogative texture and generic excess, has effectively disrupted such cliché-ridden discourse. Feminine fictions stretch into the climate of political correctness and the consumption of difference with gothic forms that maintain their critical edge and gender-conscious potential and refuse domestication. Two recent Canadian texts are apt examples: Susan Swan's novel *The Wives of Bath* (1993) and Barbara Gowdy's stories *We So Seldom Look on Love* (1993) gothically 'exceed' clichés of the (female) body and of female sexuality. Their heroines are female gothic subjects not only because they are motivated by the tension of abjection and desire, but also because their bodies radically challenge the notions both of a feminine ideal and of the monstrous-feminine. Mary Bradford in *The Wives of Bath* is a hunchback – and her story is structured by the contesting plots of a 'grotesque's' (31) fight for acknowledgement among 'normal' girls at college, and of a female *Bildungsroman*. In a similar exploration of 'normal' femininity and female sexuality, Gowdy's story collection revolves around figures like Sylvie with her double set of legs and sex organs, or Ali with her exhibitionist combination of art and auto-eroticism in front of the open window. These texts extend feminine gothic filliation and its challenges to the cultural notions of gender construction as well as to the politically correct notions of femininity. Swan and Gowdy have also created alternative forms of *performing* the excess of gothic fiction; their shared 'reading' tour through North America in the winter of 1993, dubbed 'sexual gothic', presented the adequate audiovisual dimension not only of gothic fictions but also – with clever *costumes*, and masquerade? – of gothic writers.

Beyond those related to fiction, 1990s' gothica have come to encompass a variety of phenomena. There are the popular audiovisual art forms: *gothic videos* like *Black Hole Sun* (by the Seattle-based grunge band Soundgarden, 1994), which playfully uses digital morphing technologies to distort human faces and thus to suggest the horrors of a peaceful family garden scene. Classically edited as well as performed and thus all the more powerful are Nick Cave's *Murder Ballads* (1996), especially the cult video *Where the Wild Roses Grow*, with its ironic and neo-romantic idealisation of the Poesque death – or rather murder – of a beautiful woman, sung and acted by Kylie Minogue. Similarly, the changed Madonna's *Frozen* video (1998) shows the sex-goddess's transformation into a High Romantic death goddess: tuned to wild nature, able to morph into ravens and dogs, to ascend heavenwards and to finally multiply into a female trinity. There is the dark *gothic rock* sound of bands like The Cure or Sisters of Mercy, and the related *gothic style* – a young fashion trend with provocative, sado-masochistic, or straightforwardly gloomy effects. These are good examples of commercial gothic pop culture that do betray darker visions shaping and challenging their polished popular surfaces but that still seem more fashionable than critical. Madonna's 1980s' version of the postmodern *femme fatale* is a good example: what some have seen as an ambivalent or ironic personification of male fantasies seems to have been rather a one-dimensional cliché of the sexual woman.

Chris Weedon observes a similar effect with Tina Turner, who 'takes on her stereotypical "embodiment" as sexualised Black woman and earns her living by it' (1997, 51). It seems that the neo-gothic disruptions of feminine myths – *proper* or *fatale* – contextualise a culture in which such myths have still not lost their power of seduction – or their power of defining gender culture. Filmmaker David Lynch, who made it his credo not to tell a story but to create an atmosphere or a sense of complexity in his films, has the fragmented plot, and the fragmented hero, of his movie *Lost Highway* (1996) circle around a *femme fatale* figure. Played by Patricia Arquette, Alice – or also Renee – presents a self-reflexive incorporation of both the dark and the blonde woman with parodic evocations of a whole range of sexualised media stars. In a blatantly self-reflexive scene, the 'magic moment' of the film as emphasised by Lou Reed's song of that title, the whole postmodern trajectory of the woman, the car and the money – or the *femme fatale* in the rich villain's Cadillac – rolls by in extreme slow motion. The parody is extreme as well, as it not only plays with the allusions to temptresses like Barbara Stanwyck (in *Double Indemnity*) or Jane Greer (in *Out of the Past*) and to other incarnations of male fantasies, but turns out to be a complete fantasy itself. Of course, as always with Lynch, the parody remains self-reflexive – exposing a whole set of male fears and desires, of masculine power games, pornography and violence – and leaving it at that: an exposition. Does Fred kill Renee – does Alice use Pete – does Pete replace Fred – a series of mysteries that are not solved. *Lost Highway* also means 'lost story'. Its complexities are deceptively held together by the familiar, attractive, ultimately empty image of the *femme fatale*: a perfect celluloid construction of the monstrous-feminine.

Elaine Showalter has spoken of the 1990s in terms of a 'Gothic revival', representing 'alternative strategies for depicting an ever more terrifying reality' (1991, 144). She stresses the 'enormous … gender gap in American Gothic', and defines it by comparing representations of the growing violence in American culture:

> The concerns of the Female Gothic are now consistent with a larger change in American fiction towards 'violence-centered plots' … If *American Psycho* is the masculine Gothic of the 1990s, Female Gothic looks more and more like a realist mode. (1989, 144)

It seems that Bret Easton Ellis's *American Psycho* (1991) and other serial killer plots, like Thomas Harris's *The Silence of the Lambs* (1988), gothically contextualise today's violence, and particularly violence against women, with a specifically voyeuristic effect and a commercial interest signalled by Hollywood's interest in these plots. Hans Ulrich Mohr analyses the box-office success of Jonathan Demme's movie *The Silence of the Lambs* (1990): '[It] now seems to intend to strike a subtle balance between a male audience that feels threatened by female independence and attractiveness and a female audience that feels threatened by male aggressiveness' (1991, 10). This balance is politically correct enough to win four Oscars (1992): after the initially misogynist allusions, the plot turns into a story of female emancipation. Leading actress Jodie Foster emphasises the political chances of such a film when talking about her role as feminist heroine of the 1990s: 'The story has a politically correct subplot ... This film has done more for women than feminist activism of the eighties' (von Dadelsen 1992). However, there is an obvious difference in politics and effect between a popular movie plot and the neo-gothic forms that refuse such subtle balances (and, maybe, the related international popularity) and that maintain the excess-effect of challenge and critique – especially with regard to (any form of) violence against women.

Besides the Jane Austen boom that does, I think, point to the prevailing nostalgia for visible complexities in the face of increasingly global and uncanny power structures, a range of gothic classics have been filmed, most recently Franco Zeffirelli's *Jane Eyre* (1996) – a tamed version of a rebellious plot. Kenneth Branagh's *Mary Shelley's Frankenstein* (1994) has little to do with Mary Shelley and is most revealing in its sensationalist mise-en-scène of the violence and the blatantly sexual horror. Neil Jordan's *Interview with the Vampire* (1994) – based on Ann Rice's bestseller of that name (1976) – exhibits, with similar sensationalism, a violent and sexual bloodbath that mocks the age of AIDS and political correctness at the same time. And Francis Ford Coppola's *Bram Stoker's Dracula* (1992) has even been called 'the end of Gothic' by Fred Botting, who shows how its romanticism 'presents its figures of humanity in attenuated and resigned anticipation of an already pervasive absence, undead, perhaps, but not returning' (1996, 180).

Fay Weldon, whose own intertextual connectedness to Shelley as well as to the vampire myth has always played out the (neo-)gothic as

Lara Croft Bit-girl with romantic legend, this action heroine of a three-dimensional computer game is a shapely construct from pixels and bytes; a pop star of the cyber-age.

an everyday phenomenon, comments on the new gothic wave from Hollywood with a strong statement for the role and success of gothicism in the 1990s:

> I think it's there because it's easy, because it has worked in the past, because it's morbid and mythic and a bit gloomy, really – people have an appetite for it at the moment, or an appetite for excess. It just works on an archetypal level. (von Dadelsen 1994)

The 1990s' 'appetite for excess' might meet, on the screen, a return to historical sets and a 'costume horror' that exploits gothicism for all its sensationalism. This is the escape-effect that feminine neo-gothic forms exceed. However, in Weldon's sense, the gothic turn in Hollywood also signals the repetition of the early entertainment culture and the fascinations of the 'Age of Frankenstein'. Gothic times again.

♦

In the time of Radcliffe and Shelley, with its radical cultural revolution related to industrialisation, 'the Gothic Novel [was] ... the first literary genre that helped to unfold the mass communication system', as Hans Ulrich Mohr has put it (1991, 12). His own comparison of the gothic times at the beginning of modernity and those of contemporary, postmodern culture concludes in these terms: 'At least one can say that television, this multiple genre and media mixture, may be for Postmodernism what the Gothic Novel was for Modernism' (15). This is convincing in terms of the entertainment value of popular culture's gothica, as well as in the formal terms that Mohr emphasises. However, in terms of cultural effect, television and the mass media system seem to present an affirmation that neo-gothicism, as I have defined it here, continues to undercut – especially with regard to gender and the gendered order of culture. This is especially interesting with regard to the ongoing, accelerating cultural revolution of the media age, at present signified by MTV which 'surrounds the globe like an electronic shell' (Mohr 1991, 15), but even more by the World Wide Web.

The media revolution, as has been suggested, is changing mass and private communication, and it has begun to create new thought about gender and genre. I think that this shift and the new texts of the electronic age – with their own *hyper*-textuality[1] and *world-wide* connectedness[2] – share some of the provocative and pleasurable excesses of neo-gothicism that I have outlined here. Extending the star system of Hollywood movies and of MTV pop culture, the Internet already has its own stars. In a perfect response to the postmodern recognitions of the constructedness of gender and celebrity, the digital age has its own, digital pop star, named Kyoko Date: a 'feminine' creature made not of flesh and blood but of pixels and bytes to be found at http://dhw.co.jp/horipro/talent/dk96/index_e.html. 'Born' in Tokyo on 26 October 1996, in the computers of the software company HoriPro, she has been topping the Japanese charts with her song 'Love Communication', before 'coming to Europe' to give autographs and interviews.

Similarly, another shapely cyber-babe is invading computer terminals, talk-shows, and some men's imaginations: Lara Croft, the digital action heroine of the internationally successful CD-ROM adventure game *Tomb Raider* (Eidos Interactive). This three-dimensional pixel girl comes with her own romantic legend: the fallen daughter of an English aristocrat, she becomes a fighter in Tibet; she is always unattainable, her only romance is with the player whose joystick steers her through her virtual adventure world. This would make the perfect Hollywood plot; however, her creator Ian Livingston points out the paradox of the virtual woman: 'She is what you want her to be: Lara is everything to everybody. Which actress could play her – which woman is good enough to be Lara Croft?'[3] William Gibson had just parodied, in *Idoru* (1997), the constructions of celebrity – and reality is already enacting it. A new monstrous-feminine for the electronic age?

The gothic forms of feminist fictions: they 'repeat', with provocative reassurance, the contemporary cultural and personal instability at the loss of gendered 'order' and 'master narratives', and they develop 'stripping' strategies – from the ultra-domesticity of the house of fiction to the flowing textures of dress as form – that resist incorporation into new gender ideologies of the 1990s. Rather, the powers of gothicism create new dynamics for gender and culture, and for the textures of a new age of communication.

Notes

1 The term was first used by Ted Nelson in 1965 for 'non-sequential writing' and elaborately explained in his *Literary Machines* (1980). Ever since, there have been versions of printed hypertexts, like the recent *Imagologies: Media Philosophy* (Taylor and Saarinen 1994); however, the form is inextricably linked to the computer and only exists in digital signs, and the famous non-linear plot structure.

2 Via the Internet, which is not only the space for new ways of communication and textuality, but also for electronic gothica like 'Romantic Ghosts and Gothics: Love in another World' (http://www.autopen.com/ghost .gothic.ahtml) or 'Romance Reader's Corner: The Well Dressed Heroine: Fashion Challenges for the Romantic Time Traveler' (http://www .autopen.com/romance.well.dressed.shtml), of 2 March 1998.

3 Susanne Becker, interview in television documentary, ZDF, 31 March 1998.

Bibliography

Achilles, Jochen (1991) *Sheridan LeFanu und die schauerromantische Tradition: Zur psychologischen Funktion der Motivik von Sensationsroman und Geistesgeschichte*, Tübingen: Narr.

Ahrends, Günter and Hans Jürgen Diller, eds (1990) *English Romantic Prose*, Essen: Die Blaue Eule.

Alcoff, Linda (1991/92) 'The Problem of Speaking for Others', *Cultural Critique* x:x, Winter, 5–32.

Altick, Richard (1957) *The English Common Reader: A Social History of the Mass Reading Public 1800–1900*, Chicago: Chicago University Press.

Appiah, Kwame Anthony and Henry Louis Gates, Jr (1992) 'Editors' Introduction: Multiplying Identities', *Critical Inquiry* 18, 625–9.

Armatage, Kay (1989) 'Fashions in Feminist Film Theory', in Douglas Fetherling, ed., *Best Canadian Essays 1989*, Saskatoon: Fifth House Publishers, 195–214.

Assiter, Alison (1998) 'Romance Fiction: Porn for Women?', in Day and Bloom, 101–9.

Atwood, Margaret (1969) *The Edible Woman*, Toronto: McClelland & Stewart.

Atwood, Margaret (1970) *The Journals of Susanna Moodie: Poems by Margaret Atwood*, Toronto: Oxford University Press.

Atwood, Margaret (1971) *Power Politics*, Toronto: Anansi.

Atwood, Margaret (1972) *Survival: A Thematic Guide to Canadian Literature*, Toronto: Anansi.

Atwood, Margaret (1976) 'On being a "Woman Writer": Paradoxes and Dilemmas', in *Second Words*, 190–204.

Atwood, Margaret (1977) 'Canadian Monsters', in *Second Words*, 225–31.

Atwood, Margaret (1978) *Lady Oracle* [1976], New York: Avon Books.

Atwood, Margaret (1981) *Bodily Harm*, Toronto: McClelland & Stewart.

Atwood, Margaret (1982a) *Second Words: Selected Critical Prose*, Toronto: Anansi.

Atwood, Margaret (1982b) *Surfacing*, Toronto: McClelland & Stewart.

Atwood, Margaret (1983a) *Bluebeard's Egg*, Toronto: McClelland & Stewart.

Atwood, Margaret (1983b) *Murder in the Dark: Short Fictions and Prose Poems*, Toronto: Coach House Press.

Atwood, Margaret (1985) *The Handmaid's Tale*, Toronto: McClelland & Stewart.

Atwood, Margaret (1986) 'Southern Ontario Gothic', CBC Radio, January; script in the Atwood Papers.

Atwood, Margaret (1988) 'Great Unexpectations: An Autobiographical Foreword', in Van Spanckeren and Castro, xiii–xvi.

Atwood, Margaret (1989) *Cat's Eye* [1988], New York: Bantam Books.

Atwood, Margaret (1990) *Conversations*, ed. Earl. G. Ingersoll, Princeton: Ontario Review Press.

Atwood, Margaret (1991) *Wilderness Tips*, Toronto: McClelland & Stewart.

Atwood, Margaret (1992) *Good Bones*, Toronto: Coach House Press.

Atwood, Margaret (1993) *The Robber Bride*, Toronto: McClelland & Stewart.

Atwood, Margaret (1994) 'Silencing the Scream', *Profession*, New York, 44–7.

Atwood, Margaret (1995a) *Morning in the Burned House*, New York: Houghton Mifflin.

Atwood, Margaret (1995b) *Strange Things: The Malevolent North in Canadian Literature*, Oxford: Clarendon Press.

Atwood, Margaret (1996) *Alias Grace*, New York: Doubleday.

Atwood, Margaret and Charles Pachter (1997) *The Journals of Susanna Moodie* [1980], with a memoir by Charles Pachter and foreword by David Staines, Toronto: Macfarlane Walter & Ross.

Atwood, Margaret and Robert Weaver, eds (1986) *The Oxford Book of Canadian Short Stories in English*, Toronto: Oxford University Press.

Atwood Papers, Thomas Fisher Rare Books Library, Toronto.

Austen, Jane (1989) *Northanger Abbey* [1818], London: Virago.

Baldick, Chris, ed. (1992) *The Oxford Book of Gothic Tales*, Oxford and New York: Oxford University Press.

Ballaster, Ros (1996) 'Wild Nights and Buried Letters: The Gothic Unconscious of Feminist Criticism', in Sage and Smith, 58–70.

Barclay, Glen St John (1978) *Anatomy of Horror: The Masters of Occult Fiction*, London: Weidenfeld & Nicolson.

Barfoot, Joan (1978) *Abra: A Novel*, Toronto: McGraw-Hill Ryerson.

Barthes, Roland (1969) *Système de la Mode*, Paris: Éditions du Seuil.

Barthes, Roland (1975) *The Pleasure of the Text* [1973], trans. Richard Miller, New York: Farrar, Straus, & Giroux.

Barthes, Roland (1978) *A Lover's Discourse: Fragments* [1977], trans. Richard Howard, New York: Farrar, Straus, & Giroux.

Barthes, Roland (1991) *Camera Lucida: Reflections on Photography* [1980], trans. Richard Howard, New York: The Noonday Press.

Bayer-Berenbaum, Linda (1982) *The Gothic Imagination: Expansion in Gothic Literature and Art*, London: Associated University Press.

Beauvoir, Simone de (1989) *The Second Sex* [1949], trans. and ed. H. M.

Pashley, New York: Vintage.

Becker, Susanne, Interviews with Margaret Atwood, Frankfurt: October 1987; Toronto: January 1989, October 1989 and February 1991; unpublished transcriptions.

Becker, Susanne, Interview with Julia Kristeva, Paris: 15 March 1991, unpublished transcription.

Becker, Susanne (1992a) 'The Haunted Voices of Fay Weldon', in Riedel and Stein, 99–113.

Becker, Susanne (1992b) 'Ironic Transformations: The Feminine Gothic in Aritha van Herk's *No Fixed Address*', in Hutcheon, 115–33.

Becker, Susanne (1996) 'Postmodern Feminine Horror Fictions', in Sage and Smith, 71–80.

Becker, Susanne (1998) Interview with Ian Livingston, 'Virtual Friends and Real Desires', ZDF Television, 31 March.

Becker, Susanne (forthcoming) 'Postmodernism's Happy Ending? Possession!', in Neumeier.

Belsey, Catherine (1980) *Critical Practice*, London and New York: Routledge.

Belsey, Catherine and Jane Moore, eds (1989) *The Feminist Reader: Essays in Gender and the Politics of Literary Criticism*, New York: Basil Blackwell.

Bendixen, Alfred, ed. (1985) *Haunted Women: The Best Supernatural Tales by American Women Writers*, New York: Ungar.

Benhabib, Seyla, Judith Butler, Drucilla Cornell and Nancy Fraser, eds (1993) *Der Streit um Differenz: Feminismus und Postmoderne in der Gegenwart*, Frankfurt: S. Fischer.

Benveniste, Émile (1971) *Problems in General Linguistics*, Coral Gables: University of Miami Press.

Berger, John (1972) *Ways of Seeing*, London and Harmondsworth: British Broadcasting Corporation/Penguin.

Berger, Renate, ed. (1985) 'Frauen Weiblichkeit Schrift', *Argument* 134.

Berger, Renate and Inge Stephan, eds (1987) *Weiblichkeit und Tod in der Literatur*, Cologne and Vienna: Böhlau.

Berglund, Birgitta (1993) *Woman's Whole Existence: The House as an Image in the Novels of Ann Radcliffe, Mary Wollstonecraft and Jane Austen*, Lund: Lund University Press.

Bernstein, Stephen (1991) 'Form and Ideology in the Gothic Novel', *Essays in Literature* 18, 151–65.

Bertens, Hans (1996) 'Out of Left Field: The Politics of Postmodernism', in Hoffmann and Hornung, 97–114.

Bessner, Neil Kalman (1990) *Introducing Alice Munro's 'Lives of Girls and Women': A Reader's Guide*, Toronto: ECW Press.

Bessner, Neil (1992) 'Beyond Two Solitudes, After Survival: Postmodern Fiction in Canada', in D'haen and Bertens, 9–25.

Bettelheim, Bruno (1976) *The Uses of Enchantment: The Meaning and Importance of Fairy Tales*, New York: Knopf.

Binhammer, Katherine (1995) 'Introduction', *Tessera* 19: *Bodies, Vesture, Ornament*, Winter, 6–12.

Birkhead, Edith (1921) *The Tale of Terror: A Study of the Gothic Romance*, London: Constable.

Birkhead, Edith (1925) 'Sentiment and Sensibility in the Eighteenth-Century Novel', *Essays and Studies by Members of the English Association*, Coll. Oliver Elton, Oxford: Clarendon Press, 92–116.

Birkle, Carmen (1996) *Women's Stories of the Looking Glass: Autobiographical Reflections and Self-Representations in the Poetry of Sylvia Plath, Adrienne Rich, and Audre Lorde*, Munich: Fink.

Birney, Earle (1975) *The Collected Poems of Earle Birney*, Toronto: McClelland & Stewart.

Blais, Marie Claire (1971) *Mad Shadows* [1959], trans. Merloyd Lawrence, Toronto: McClelland & Stewart.

Blau du Plessis, Rachel (1985) *Writing Beyond the Ending: Narrative Strategies of Twentieth-Century Women Writers*, Bloomington: Indiana University Press.

Bloch, Ruth (1987) 'American Feminine Ideals in Transition: The Rise of the Moral Mother 1785–1815', *Feminist Studies* 4:7 (June), 101–26.

Blodgett, E. D. (1982) *Configurations: Essays in the Canadian Literatures*, Downsview: ECW Press.

Blodgett, E. D. (1988) *Alice Munro*, Boston: Twayne.

Bloom, Clive (1996) *Cult Fiction: Popular Reading and Pulp Theory*, New York: St. Martin's Press.

Botting, Fred (1991) *Making Monstrous: 'Frankenstein', Criticism, Theory*, Manchester: Manchester University Press.

Botting, Fred (1994) 'Signs of Evil: Bataille, Baudrillard and Postmodern Gothic', *Southern Review* 27:4 (December), 493–510.

Botting, Fred (1996) *Gothic*, London: Routledge.

Bouson, J. Brooks (1993) *Brutal Choreographies: Oppositional Strategies and Narrative Design in the Novels of Margaret Atwood*, Amherst: University of Massachusetts Press.

Bovenschen, Silvia (1979) 'Gibt es eine weibliche Ästhetik?', in Dietze, 82–115.

Bowering, George (1981) 'Margaret Atwood's Hands', *Studies in Canadian Literature* 6:1, 119–36.

Brautigan, Richard (1984) *The Hawkline Monster*, New York: Simon & Schuster.

Bredella, Lothar (1997) 'Involvement and Detachment: How to Read and Teach Maxine Hong Kingston's *The Woman Warrior*', in Hoffmann and Hornung, 421–39.

Bree, Germaine (1988) 'Autogynography', in Olney, 171–9.

Brodski, Bella and Celeste Schenck, eds (1988) *Life/Lines: Theorizing Women's Autobiography*, Ithaca, NY and London: Cornell University Press.

Bromberg, Pamela S. (1988) 'The Two Faces in the Mirror in *The Edible Woman* and *Lady Oracle*', in Van Spanckeren and Castro, 12–23.

Bronfen, Elisabeth (1985) 'Die schöne Leiche: Weiblicher Tod als motivische Konstante von der Mitte des 18. Jahrhunderts bis in die Moderne', in Berger, 87–115.

Bronfen, Elisabeth (1994) *Over Her Dead Body: Death, Femininity and the*

Aesthetic, Manchester: Manchester University Press.

Brontë, Charlotte (1981) *Shirley* [1849], Oxford and New York: Oxford University Press.

Brontë, Charlotte (1982) *Jane Eyre: An Autobiography* [1847], New York: New American Library.

Brontë, Charlotte (1983) *Villette* [1853], London: Everyman's Library.

Brontë, Emily (1965) *Wuthering Heights* [1847], Harmondsworth: Penguin.

Brooke-Rose, Christine (1980) 'Where Do We Go from Here?' *Granta* 3, 161–88.

Brooke-Rose, Christine (1981) *A Rhetoric of the Unreal: Studies in Narrative and Structure, Especially of the Fantastic*, Cambridge: Cambridge University Press.

Brophy, Philip (1986) 'Horrality – The Textuality of Contemporary Horror Films', *Screen* 27:1 (January/February), 2–13.

Brown, Charles Brockden (1973) *Wieland, or, The Transformation: An American Tale* [1798], New York: Doubleday.

Brownstein, Rachel (1982) *Becoming a Heroine: Reading about Women in Novels*, New York: Viking.

Budd, Elaine (1986) 'Rebecca Redux: Phyllis A. Whitney', in *Thirteen Mistresses of Murder*, New York: Ungar, 137–50.

Buford, Bill (1980) 'Introduction', *Granta* 3: *The End of the English Novel*, London: Penguin, 1980.

Burgin, Victor (1986) *Between*, Oxford and New York: Basil Blackwell.

Burke, Edmund (1987) *A Philosophical Inquiry into the Origins of Our Ideas of the Sublime and the Beautiful* [1757], Oxford: Basil Blackwell.

Buss, Helen M. (1993) *Mapping Our/selves: Canadian Women's Autobiographies in English*, Montreal, McGill University Press.

Butler, Judith (1990) *Gender Trouble: Feminism and the Subversion of Identity*, New York and London: Routledge.

Butler, Judith (1993) *Bodies that Matter: On the Discursive Limits of 'Sex'*, New York and London: Routledge.

Butler, Judith (1997) *The Psychic Life of Power: Theories in Subjection*, Stanford, CA: Stanford University Press.

Butler, Marilyn (1980) 'The Woman at the Window: Ann Radcliffe in the Novels of Mary Wollstonecraft and Jane Austen', in Todd, 128–48.

Buxton, Jackie (1996) '"What's Love Got To Do with It?" Postmodernism and Possession', *English Studies in Canada* 22:2 (June), 199–219.

Byatt, A. S. (1975) 'American Gothic', *New Statesman* (6 June), 760.

Byatt, A. S. (1991a) *Passions of the Mind: Selected Writings*, London: Chatto & Windus.

Byatt, A. S. (1991b) *Possession: A Romance* [1990], London: Vintage.

Byatt, A. S. (1993) 'Reading, Writing, Studying', *Critical Quarterly* 35:4 (Winter), 3–7.

Byatt, A. S. (1995) *Imagining Characters: Six Conversations about Women Writers, A. S. Byatt and Igaes Sodrae*, ed. Rebecca Swift, London: Chatto & Windus.

Byatt, A. S. (1995) 'Interview', *METROPOLIS*, *ante* television (20 April).

Calinescu, Matei and Douwe Fokkema, eds (1987) *Exploring Postmodernism*, Amsterdam: Benjamin.

Cameron, Deborah, ed. (1990) *The Feminist Critique of Language: A Reader*, London and New York: Routledge.

Carroll, Noel (1990) *The Philosophy of Horror: or Paradoxes of the Heart*, New York and London: Routledge.

Carscallen, James (1993) *The Other Country: Patterns in the Writing of Alice Munro*, Downsview: ECW Press.

Carter, Angela (1974) 'Afterword', *Fireworks: Nine Stories in Various Disguises*, Cambridge: Harper & Row, 132–3.

Carter, Angela (1978) *The Sadeian Woman and the Ideology of Pornography*, New York: Pantheon Books.

Carter, Angela (1979) *The Bloody Chamber*, New York: Pantheon Books.

Cawelti, John George (1976) *Adventure, Mystery, and Romance: Formula Studies as Art and Popular Culture*, Chicago: University of Chicago Press.

Chafe, William (1972) *The American Woman: Her Changing Social, Economic, and Political Roles, 1920–1970*, New York: Oxford University Press.

Chernin, Kim (1986) *The Hungry Self: Women, Eating and Identity*, London: Virago.

Chessler, Phyllis (1972) *Women and Madness*, New York: Avon.

Chodorow, Nancy (1978) *The Reproduction of Mothering: Psychoanalysis and the Sociology of Gender*, Berkeley: University of California Press.

Chopin, Kate (1981) *The Awakening and Selected Short Stories* [1899], New York: Bantam.

Cixous, Hélène and Catherine Clément (1986) *The Newly Born Woman* [1975], trans. Betsy Wing, Minneapolis: University of Minnesota Press.

Cixous, Hélène (1981) 'The Laugh of the Medusa' [1975], in Marks and de Courtivron, 245–64.

Cohen, Matt (1981) *Flowers of Darkness*, Toronto: McClelland & Stewart.

Cohn, Jan (1988) *Romance and the Erotics of Property: Mass-Market Fiction for Women*, Durham, NC: Duke University Press.

Connor, Steven (1989) *Postmodernist Culture: An Introduction to Theories of the Contemporary*, Cambridge, MA: Basil Blackwell.

Cooke, John (1996) *The Influence of Painting on Five Canadian Writers: Alice Munro, Hugh Hood, Timothy Findley, Margaret Atwood, and Michael Ondaatje*, Lewiston: The Edwin Mellen Press.

Cornwell, Neil (1990) *The Literary Fantastic: From Gothic to Postmodernism*, Hemel Hempstead: Harvester Wheatsheaf.

Cott, Nancy (1978) 'Passionlessness: An Interpretation of Victorian Sexual Ideology 1790–1850', *Signs* 4:2 (Winter).

Coward, Rosalind (1985) *Female Desires: How They Are Sought, Bought and Packaged*, New York: Grove Press.

Coward, Rosalind (1986) 'Female Desire: Women's Sexuality Today', in Eagleton, 145–8.

Creed, Barbara (1986) 'The Monstrous-Feminine', *Screen* 27:1 (January/

February), 14–26.

Cutler, Hugh Mercer (1997) *Rediscovering Values: Coming to Terms with Post-modernism*, London: M. E. Sharpe.

Dahlie, Hallvard (1984) *Alice Munro and Her Works*, Downsview: ECW Press.

Dahlie, Hallvard (1985) 'Alice Munro and Her Works', in Lecker et al., 215–56.

Daleski, Hillel Mathew (1984) *The Divided Heroine*, London: Holmes & Meier.

Davey, Frank (1978) 'Lady Oracle's Secret: Atwood's Comic Novels', *Studies in Canadian Literature* 3:2.

Davey, Frank (1984) *Margaret Atwood: A Feminist Poetics*, Vancouver: Talon Books.

Davey, Frank (1986) *Surviving the Paraphrase*, Winnipeg: Turnstone Press.

Davidson, Arnold E. (1978) 'Margaret Atwood's *Lady Oracle*: The Artist as Escapist and Seer', *Studies in Canadian Literature* 3:2.

Davidson, Arnold E. and Cathy N. Davidson, eds (1981) *The Art of Margaret Atwood: Essays in Criticism*, Toronto: Anansi.

Davidson, Cathy and E. M. Broner, eds (1980) *The Lost Tradition: Mothers and Daughters in Literature*, New York: Ungar.

Day, Gary and Clive Bloom, eds (1988) *Perspectives on Pornography: Sexuality in Film and Literature*, New York: St. Martin's Press.

Day, William Patrick (1985) *In the Circles of Fear and Desire: A Study of Gothic Fantasy*, Chicago and London: University of Chicago Press.

De Lauretis, Teresa (1984) *Alice Doesn't: Feminism, Semiotics, Cinema*, Bloomington: Indiana University Press.

De Lauretis, Teresa (1987a) *Technologies of Gender: Essays on Theory, Film, and Fiction*, Bloomington: Indiana University Press.

De Lauretis, Teresa, ed. (1987b) *Feminist Studies/Critical Studies*, Bloomington: University of Indiana Press.

Degler, Carl (1980) *At Odds: Women and the Family in America from the Revolution to the Present*, New York: Ungar.

DeLamotte, Eugenia C. (1990) *Perils of the Night: A Feminist Study of Nineteenth-Century Gothic*, New York: Oxford University Press.

Delbaerre, Jeanne (1992) 'Magic Realism: the Energy of the Margins', in D'haen and Bertens, 75–104.

Derrida, Jacques (1980) 'The Law of Genre', trans. Avital Ronell, *Critical Inquiry* 7, 55–81.

D'haen, Theo (1995) 'Postmodern Gothic', in Tinkler-Villani, 283–94.

D'haen, Theo and Hans Bertens, eds (1992) *Postmodern Fiction in Canada*, Amsterdam: Rodopi.

Dietze, Gabriele, ed. (1979) *Die Überwindung der Sprachlosigkeit: Texte aus der neuen Frauenbewegung*, Darmstadt: Luchterhand.

Dinnerstein, Dorothy (1976) *The Mermaid and the Minotaur: Sexual Arrangements and the Human Malaise*, New York: Harper & Row.

Djwa, Sandra (1981) 'Deep Caves and Kitchen Linoleum: Psychological Violence in the Fiction of Alice Munro', in Virginia Harger-Grinling and Terry Goldie, eds, *Violence in the Canadian Novel Since 1960/Violence dans le roman Canadien depuis 1960*, St John's: Memorial University of Newfoundland, 177–90.

Doane, Mary Anne (1991) *Femmes Fatales: Feminism, Film Theory, Psychoanalysis*, New York: Routledge.

Docherty, Thomas (1990) *After Theory: Postmodernism/Postmarxism*, London and New York: Routledge.

Donovan, Josephine (1985) *Feminist Theory: The Intellectual Traditions of American Feminism*, New York: Ungar.

Douglas, Ann (1971) 'The "Scribbling Women" and Fanny Fern: Why Women Wrote', *American Quarterly* 23, 3–24.

Douglas, Ann (1976) 'Introduction: Rites of Passage for American Women', *Women's Studies* 4, 1–2.

Douglas, Ann (1980) 'Soft-Porn Culture', *New Republic* 30, 25–9.

Du Maurier, Daphne (1938) *Rebecca*, New York: Literary Guild of America.

Du Maurier, Daphne (1982) *The Rebecca Notebook and Other Memories*, London: Pan Books.

Duffy, Martha (1971) 'On the Road to Manderley', *Time* (12 April), 95–6.

Dusinberre, Juliet A. (1983) 'A. S. Byatt', in Todd, 181–95.

Eagleton, Mary, ed. (1986) *Feminist Literary Theory: A Reader*, Oxford: Basil Blackwell.

Easthope, Anthony (1990) *What a Man's Gotta Do: The Masculine Myth in Popular Culture* [1986], Boston: Unwin Hyman.

Ecker, Gisela (1985) 'Poststrukturalismus und feministische Wissenschaft: Eine heimliche oder unheimliche Allianz?', in Berger, 1–16.

Edgeworth, Maria (1895) *Castle Rackrent and The Absentee*, London: Macmillan.

Edmundson, Mark (1997) *Nightmare on Main Street: Angels, Sadomasochism, and the Culture of Gothic*, Cambrige, MA: Harvard University Press.

Eldredge, L. M. (1984) 'A Sense of Ending in *Lives of Girls and Women*', *Studies in Canadian Literature* 9, 110–15.

Ellis, Kate Ferguson (1989) *The Contested Castle: Gothic Novels and the Subversion of Domestic Ideology*, Urbana and Chicago: University of Illinois Press.

Ellis, S. M. (1923) 'Ann Radcliffe and Her Literary Influence', *Contemporary Review* 123, 188–97.

Engel, Marian (1976) *Bear: A Novel*, Toronto: McClelland & Stewart.

Eppstein, Grace (1993) '*Bodily Harm*: Female Containment and Abuse in the Romance Narrative', *Genders* 16 (Spring), 80–93.

Fairbanks, Carol (1986) *Prairie Women: Images in American and Canadian Fiction*, New Haven, CT: Yale University Press.

Faludi, Susan (1991) *Backlash: The Undeclared War against American Women*, New York: Crown.

Federman, Raymond, ed. (1975) *Surfiction: Fiction Now and Tomorrow*, Chicago: Swallow Press.

Fee, Margery (1993) *The Fat Lady Dances: Margaret Atwood's 'Lady Oracle'*, Toronto: ECW Press.

Felski, Rita (1989) *Beyond Feminist Aesthetics: Feminist Literature and Social Change*, Cambridge, MA: Harvard University Press.

Fiedler, Leslie (1982) *Love and Death in the American Novel* [1960], Harmondsworth: Penguin.

Fink, Thomas (1976) 'Atwood's Tricks with Mirrors', *The Explicator* 43, 60.

Fischer-Seidel, Theresa, ed. (1991) *Frauen und Frauen-darstellung in der englischen und amerikanischen Literatur*, Tübingen: Narr.

Flax, Jane (1978) 'The Conflict between Nurturance and Autonomy in Mother–Daughter Relationships and within Feminism', *Feminist Studies* 4:2 (June), 17–191.

Flax, Jane (1983) 'Political Philosophy and the Patriarchal Unconscious: A Psychoanalytic Perspective on Epistemology and Metaphysics', in Harding and Hintikka, 245–82.

Flax, Jane (1990) *Thinking Fragments: Psychoanalysis, Feminism, and Postmodernism in the Contemporary West*, Berkeley: University of California Press.

Flax, Jane (1993) *Disputed Subjects: Essays on Psychoanalysis, Politics and Philosophy*, New York: Routledge.

Fleenor, Juliann, ed. (1983) *The Female Gothic*, Montreal: Eden Press.

Flint, Kate (1996) 'Romance, Postmodernism and the Gothic: Fictional Challenges to Theories of Women and Reading 1790–1830', in Schöwerling and Steinecke, 269–79.

Foster, Hal, ed. (1983) *The Anti-Aesthetic: Essays on Postmodern Culture*, Seattle: Bay Press.

Foucault, Michel (1984) *The Foucault Reader*, ed. Paul Rabinow, New York: Pantheon.

Fountain, J. Stephen (1994) 'Ashes to Ashes: Kristeva's *Jouissance*, Altizer's *Apocalypse*, Byatt's *Possession* and "The Dream of the Rood"', *Literature and Theology* 8:2 (June), 193–208.

Fowler, Rowena (1984) 'The Art of Alice Munro: *The Beggar Maid* and *Lives of Girls and Women*', *Critique: Studies in Modern Fiction* 25:4, 189–98.

Frank, Frederick S. (1973) 'The Gothic Novel: A Checklist of Modern Criticism', *Bulletin of Bibliography* 30, 1–14.

Frank, Frederick S. (1984) *Guide to the Gothic: An Annotated Bibliography of Criticism*, Metuchen, NJ and London: Scarecrow.

Frank, Frederick S. (1988) *Gothic Fiction: A Master List of Twentieth Century Criticism and Research*, Westport, CT: Meckler.

Frank, Manfred (1988) *Was ist Neostrukturalismus?*, Frankfurt: Suhrkamp.

Fraser, Nancy and Linda Nicholson (1990) 'Social Criticism without Philosophy: An Encounter between Feminism and Postmodernism', in Nicholson, 19–38.

Freibert, Lucy M. (1982) 'The Artist as Picaro: The Revelation of Margaret Atwood's *Lady Oracle*', *Canadian Literature* 92, 23–34.

French, Marilyn (1977) *The Women's Room*, New York: Summit Books.

Freud, Sigmund (1955) 'Das Unheimliche', *Gesammelte Werke 12: Werke aus den Jahren 1917–1920*, London: Imago, 229–68.

Friday, Nancy (1977) *My Mother/My Self: The Daughter's Search for Identity*, New York: Dell.

Friedan, Betty (1963) *The Feminine Mystique*, New York: Norton.

Frye, Northrop (1957) *An Anatomy of Criticism: Four Essays*, Princeton, NJ: Princeton University Press.

Frye, Northrop (1971) *The Bush Garden: Essays on the Canadian Imagination* [1965], Toronto: Anansi.

Frye, Northrop (1977) 'Haunted by a Lack of Ghosts', in Staines, 16–32.

Fuss, Diana (1992) 'Fashion and the Homospectatorial Look', *Critical Inquiry* 18:4 (Summer), 713–37.

Gaines, Jane (1990) 'Introduction: Fabricating the Female Body', in Gaines and Herzog, 1–27.

Gaines, Jane and Charlotte Herzog, eds (1990) *Fabrications: Costume and the Female Body*, New York: Routledge.

Gallop, Jane (1982) *Feminism and Psychoanalysis: The Daughter's Seduction*, London: Macmillan.

Gallop, Jane (1988) *Thinking through the Body*, New York: Columbia University Press.

Garber, Marjorie (1992) *Vested Interests: Cross-Dressing and Cultural Anxiety*, New York: Routledge.

Garson, Marjorie (1994) 'Synecdoche and the Munrovian Sublime: Parts and Wholes in *Lives of Girls and Women*', *English Studies in Canada* 20:4 (December), 413–29.

Gates, Henry Louis (1997) 'The Naked Republic', *The New Yorker* (25 August and 1 September), 114–23.

Gay, Peter (1984) *The Bourgeois Experience: Victoria to Freud, Education of the Senses*, Vol. I, New York: Oxford University Press.

Genette, Gérard (1980) *Narrative Discourse: An Essay in Method* [1972], Ithaca, NY: Cornell University Press.

Gibson, Graeme (1973a) 'Interview with Alice Munro', *Eleven Canadian Novelists*, Toronto: Anansi, 237–64.

Gibson, Graeme (1973b) 'Interview with Margaret Atwood', *Eleven Canadian Novelists*, Toronto: Anansi, 1–31.

Gibson, Graeme (1983) 'Gothic Shocks from History: The Birth of a New Novel', *The Globe and Mail* (4 June), E1.

Gibson, Jennifer Ann (1991) 'Artificial Perplexities: The Paradigm of Gothic Fiction and its Postmodern Survival in the Work of Nabokov, Pynchon and Beckett', Dissertation, University of Wisconsin.

Gilbert, Sandra (1976) 'Plain Jane's Progress', *Signs* 2:4, 779–804.

Gilbert, Sandra (1978) 'Horror's Twin: Mary Shelley's Monstrous Eve', *Feminist Studies* 4:3, 48–75.

Gilbert, Sandra and Susan Gubar (1979) *The Madwoman in the Attic: The Woman Writer and the Nineteenth-Century Literary Imagination*, New Haven, CT and London: Yale University Press.

Gilbert, Sandra and Susan Gubar, eds (1985) *The Norton Anthology of Literature by Women: The Tradition in English*, New York: Norton.

Gilman, Charlotte Perkins (1985) 'The Yellow Wallpaper' [1892], in Gilbert and Gubar, 1148–61.

Giobbi, Giuliana (1994) 'Know the Past: Know Thyself. Literary Pursuits and Quest for Identity in A. S. Byatt's *Possession* and in F. Duranti's *Effeti Personali*', *Journal of European Studies*, 24:1 (March), 41–54.

Gitzen, Julian (1995) 'A. S. Byatt's Self-Mirroring Act', *Critique: Studies in Contemporary Fiction* 36:2 (Winter), 83–95.

Gnüg, Hiltrud and Renate Möhrmann, eds (1985) *Frauen Literatur Geschichte: Schreibende Frauen vom Mittelalter bis zur Gegenwart*, Stuttgart: Metzler.

Godard, Barbara (1983) 'My (M)other, My Self: Strategies for Subversion in Atwood and Hébèrt', *Essays on Canadian Writing* 26 (Spring), 13–44.

Godard, Barbara (1984) '"Heirs of the Living Body": Alice Munro and the Question of a Female Aesthetic', in Miller, 43–71.

Godard, Barbara (1987a) 'Telling It Over Again: Atwood's Art of Parody', *Canadian Poetry* 21, 1–30.

Godard, Barbara, ed. (1987b) *Gynocritics/Gynocritiques: Feminist Approaches to Canadian and Québec Women's Writing*, Downsview: ECW Press.

Godard, Barbara, ed. (1994) *Collaboration in the Feminine: Writings on Women and Culture from 'Tessera'*, Toronto: Second Story Press.

Goddard, John (1985) 'Profile: *Lady Oracle*', *Books in Canada* 14, 6–10.

Gold, Joseph (1984) 'Our Feeling Exactly: The Writing of Alice Munro', in Miller, 1–13.

Gowdy, Barbara (1992) *We so Seldom Look on Love*, Toronto: Somerville House Publishing.

Grace, Sherrill E. (1980) *Violent Duality: A Study of Margaret Atwood*, Montreal: Vehicule Press.

Grace, Sherrill E. (1984) 'Courting Bluebeard with Bartok, Atwood and Fowles', *Journal of Modern Literature* 2, 245–62.

Grace, Sherrill E. and Lorraine Weir, eds (1983) *Margaret Atwood: Language, Text and System*, Vancouver: University of British Columbia Press.

Graham, Kenneth W., ed. (1989) *Gothic Fictions: Prohibition/Transgression*, New York: AMS Press.

Grand Street (1997) 'Identity', 16:2 (Fall).

Greer, Germaine (1977) *The Female Eunuch* [1970], New York: McGraw Hill.

Griffith, Margaret (1980) 'Verbal Terrain in the Novels of Margaret Atwood', *Critique: Studies in Modern Fiction* 2, 85–93.

Griffiths, Naomi (1976). *Penelope's Web: Some Perceptions of Women in European and Canadian Society*, Toronto: Oxford University Press.

Griggers, Cathy (1990) 'A Certain Tension in the Visual/Cultural Field: Helmut Newton, Deborah Turbeville, and the *Vogue* Fashion Layout', *Differences* 2 (Summer), 76–104.

Gross, Louis S. (1989) *Redefining American Gothic: From 'Wieland' to 'Day of the Dead'*, Ann Arbor and London: UMI Research Press.

Gunzenhäuser, Randi (1993) *Horror at Home: Genre, Gender und das Gothic Sublime*, Essen: Die Blaue Eule.

Gurevitch, Michael, Tony Bennett, James Curran and Janet Wollacott, eds (1982) *Culture, Society and the Media*, London: Routledge.

Gussow, Mel (1996) 'Alternate Personalities in Life and Art', *New York Times* (30 December), B1f.

Gussow, Mel (1997) 'The Alternate Personalities of Margaret Atwood', *International Herald Tribune* (7 January).

Haggard, H. Rider (1989) *She* [1887], London: Ian Deuchar.

Haggarty, George E. (1989) *Gothic Fiction/Gothic Form*. University Park and London: Pennsylvania State University Press.

Hanly, Charles (1988) 'Autobiography and Creativity: Alice Munro's Story "Fits"', in Stich, 163–74.

Haraway, Donna (1988) 'A Manifesto for Cyborgs: Science, Technology and Socialist Feminism in the 1980s', *Feminist Studies* 14, 575–99.

Harding, Sandra and Merrill B. Hintikka, eds (1983) *Discovering Reality: Feminist Perspectives on Epistemology, Metaphysics, Methodology, and Philosophy of Science*, Dordrecht: D. Reidel.

Hart, James D. (1976) *The Popular Book: A History of America's Literary Taste* [1950], Westport, CT: Greenwood.

Harwell, Thomas Meade, ed. (1986) *The English Gothic Novel: A Miscellany in Four Volumes*, Vol. I: *Contexts: Romantic Reassessment*, ed. James Hogg, Salzburg: Institut für Anglistik und Amerikanistik.

Hassan, Ihab (1982) *The Dismemberment of Orpheus; Toward a Postmodern Literature* [1971], New York: Oxford University Press.

Hassan Ihab (1987) *The Postmodern Turn: Essays in Postmodern Theory and Culture*, Columbus: Ohio State University Press.

Hawkes, Terence (1977) *Structuralism and Semiotics*, Berkeley: University of California Press.

Hazen, Helen (1983) *Endless Rapture: Rape, Romance, and the Female Imagination*, New York: Scribner's.

Hebdige, Dick (1993) *Subculture: The Meaning of Style* [1979], London: Routledge.

Hébèrt, Anne (1973) *Kamouraska*, New York: Crown Publishers.

Heble, Ajay (1994) *The Tumble of Reason: Alice Munro's Discourse of Absence*, Toronto: University of Toronto Press.

Hedges, Elaine (1982) 'The Nineteenth-Century Diarist and her Quilts', *Feminist Studies* 8:2 (Summer), 293–9.

Hedges, Elaine (1993) 'Stitches in Time: Sewing, Gender, and the Politics of Feminism at the Ends of Two Centuries', unpublished manuscript.

Hedges, Elaine and Ingrid Wendt (1980) *In Her Own Image: Women Working in the Arts*, New York: McGraw-Hill.

Heiland, Donna (1992) 'Postmodern Gothic: *Lady Oracle* and its Eighteenth-Century Antecedents', *Recherches Sémiotiques/Semiotic Inquiry* 12, 116–35.

Heilbrun, Carolyn (1985) 'Women's Autobiographical Writings: New Forms', *Prose Studies* 8:3, 14–28.

Heilman, Robert (1981) 'Charlotte Brontë's "New Gothic"', in Watt.

Heller, Agnes (1984) *Everyday Life*, trans. G. L. Campbell, London: Routledge & Kegan Paul.

Heller, Tamar (1992) *Dead Secrets: Wilkie Collins and the Female Gothic*, New

Haven, CT: Yale University Press.

Heller, Terry (1987) *The Delights of Terror: An Aesthetics of the Tale of Terror*, Urbana and Chicago: University of Illinois Press.

Hengen, Shannon (1993) *Margaret Atwood's Power: Mirrors, Reflections and Images in Select Fiction and Poetry*, Toronto: Second Story Press.

Hengen, Shannon (1995) 'Zenia's Foreignness', in York, 271–86.

Hill Rigney, Barbara (1987) *Margaret Atwood*, London: Macmillan Education.

Hilmes, Carola (1990) *Die Femme Fatale: Ein Weiblichkeitstypus in der nachromantischen Literatur*, Stuttgart: Metzler.

Hite, Molly (1989) *The Other Side of the Story: Structures and Strategies of Contemporary Feminist Narrative*, Ithaca, NY and London: Cornell University Press.

Hoffmann, Gerhard, ed. (1988) *Der zeitgenössische amerikanische Roman*, Munich: Fink.

Hoffmann, Gerhard, ed. (1989) *Making Sense: The Role of the Reader in Contemporary American Fiction*, Munich: Fink.

Hoffmann, Gerhard (1996) 'Waste and Meaning, the Labyrinth and the Void in Modern and Postmodern Fiction', in Hoffmann and Hornung, 115–94.

Hoffmann, Gerhard and Alfred Hornung, eds (1996) *Ethics and Aesthetics: The Moral Turn of Postmodernism*, Heidelberg: Winter.

Hoffmann, Gerhard and Alfred Hornung, eds (1997) *Emotion in Postmodernism*, Heidelberg: Winter.

Hogle, Jerrold E. (1980) 'The Restless Labyrinth: Cryptonomy in the Gothic Novel', *Arizona Quarterly* 36, 330–58.

Holland, Norman and Leona F. Sherman (1977) 'Gothic Possibilities', *New Literary History* 8, 279–94.

Hollander, Anne (1978) *Seeing Through Clothes*, New York: Viking.

Holmes, Frederick M. (1994) 'The Historical Imagination and the Victorian Past', *English Studies in Canada* 20:3 (September), 319–34.

Hong Kingston, Maxine (1976) *The Woman Warrior: Memoirs of a Childhood among Ghosts*, New York: Knopf.

Horne, Alan John (1974) *A Preliminary Checklist of Writings By and About Margaret Atwood*, Toronto: Canadian Library Association.

Hornung, Alfred (1985) 'The Autobiographical Mode in Contemporary American Fiction', *Prose Studies* 8:3, 69–83.

Hornung, Alfred (1989) 'Art over Life: Henry James's Autobiography', in Hoffmann, 198–219.

Hornung, Alfred (1992a) *Lexikon amerikanische Literatur*, Mannheim: Meyers Lexikonverlag.

Hornung, Alfred (1992b) 'Postmodern – Postmortem: Death and the Death of the Novel', in Versluys, 87–109.

Hornung, Alfred (1996) 'Ethnic Fiction and Survival Ethics: Toni Morrison, Louise Erdrich, David H. Hwang', in Hoffmann and Hornung, 209–20.

Hornung, Alfred (1997a) 'Postmoderne bis zur Gegenwart', in Hubert Zapf, ed., *Amerikanische Literatur Geschichte*, Stuttgart: Metzler.

Hornung, Alfred (1997b) 'The Witchcraft of Fiction/The Fiction of Witchcraft', in Hoffmann and Hornung, 309–20.

Howard, Jacqueline (1994) *Reading Gothic Fiction: A Bakhtinian Approach*, Oxford: Clarendon Press.

Howe, Florence, ed. (1991) *Tradition and the Talents of Women*, Urbana: University of Illinois Press.

Howells, Coral Ann (1978) *Love, Mystery, and Misery: Feeling in Gothic Fiction*, London: Athlone Press.

Howells, Coral Ann (1987) *Private and Fictional Words: Canadian Women Novelists of the 1970s and 1980s*, London and New York: Methuen.

Howells, Coral Ann (1989) 'The Pleasure of the Woman's Text: Ann Radcliffe's Subtle Transgressions', in Graham, 151–62.

Howells, Coral Ann, ed. (1991) *Narrative Strategies in Canadian Literature: Feminism and Postcolonialism*, Philadelphia and Milton Keynes: Open University Press.

Howells, Coral Ann (1996) *Margaret Atwood*, New York: St. Martin's Press.

Hoy, Helen (1980) '"Dull, Simple, Amazing and Unfathomable": Paradox and Double Vision in Alice Munro's Fiction', *Studies in Canadian Literature* 5, 100–15.

Hulme, Keri (1985) *The Bone People* [1983], London: Picador.

Hume, Kathryn (1984) *Fantasy and Mimesis: Responses to Reality in Western Literature*, New York and London: Methuen.

Hume, Robert D. (1969) 'Gothic vs. Romantic: A Revaluation of the Gothic Novel', *PMLA* 84 (March), 282–90.

Hume, Robert D. and Robert Platzner (1971) 'Gothic vs. Romantic: A Rejoinder', *PMLA* 86 (March), 266–74.

Humm, Maggie (1997) *Feminism and Film*, Edinburgh: Edinburgh University Press.

Hustvedt, Siri (1996) *The Enchantment of Lily Dahl*, New York: Holt.

Hutcheon, Linda (1980) 'From Poetic to Narrative Structures: The Novels of Margaret Atwood', in Grace, 17–32.

Hutcheon, Linda (1984) *Narcissistic Narrative: The Metafictional Paradox* [1980], New York and London: Methuen.

Hutcheon, Linda (1985) *A Theory of Parody: The Teachings of Twentieth-Century Art Forms*, New York and London: Methuen.

Hutcheon, Linda (1987) 'Metafictional Implications for Novelistic Reference', in Whiteside and Issacharoff, 1–13.

Hutcheon, Linda (1988a) *A Poetics of Postmodernism: History, Theory, Fiction*, London: Routledge.

Hutcheon, Linda (1988b) *The Canadian Postmodern: A Study of English-Canadian Fiction*, Toronto, New York and Oxford: Oxford University Press.

Hutcheon, Linda (1989) *The Politics of Postmodernism*, New York and London: Routledge.

Hutcheon, Linda (1990) *As Canadian as ... possible ... Under the Circumstances!*, Toronto: ECW Press and York University.

Hutcheon, Linda (1991) *Splitting Images: Contemporary Canadian Ironies*, Toronto, Oxford, New York: Oxford University Press.

Hutcheon, Linda (1992a) 'The Complex Functions of Irony', *Revista Canadiense de Estudios Hispanicos* 16:2 (Winter), 218–34.

Hutcheon, Linda, ed. (1992b) *Double Talking: Essays on Verbal and Visual Ironies in Canadian Contemporary Art and Literature*, Toronto: ECW Press.

Hutcheon, Linda (1994) *Irony's Edge: The Theory and Politics of Irony*, London and New York: Routledge.

Hutcheon, Linda and Marion Richmond, eds (1990) *Other Solitudes: Canadian Multicultural Fictons*, Toronto: Oxford University Press.

Hutchison, Don, ed. (1992) *Northern Frights*, Oakville: Mosaic Press.

Huyssen, Andreas (1986) *After the Great Divide: Modernism, Mass Culture, Postmodernism*. Bloomington: Indiana University Press.

Huyssen, Andreas and Klaus Scherpe, eds (1989) *Postmoderne: Zeichen eines kulturellen Wandels*, Reinbek: Rowohlt.

Inge, M. Thomas, ed. (1979) *Handbook of Popular Culture*, Westport, CT: Greenwood Press.

Irigaray, Luce (1981) 'And the One Doesn't Stir Without the Other', trans. H. Wenzel, *Signs* 7:1 , 60–67.

Irigaray, Luce (1985) *Speculum of the Other Woman* [1974], Ithaca, NY: Cornell University Press.

Irvine, Lorna (1981) 'Surfacing, Surviving, Surpassing: Canada's Women Writers', *Journal of Popular Culture* 15:3, 70–79.

Irvine, Lorna (1983) 'Changing Is the Word I Want', in MacKendrick, 99–111.

Irvine, Lorna (1986) *Sub/version: Canadian Fictions by Women*, Toronto: ECW Press.

Iyer, Pico (1993), 'The Empire Writes Back', *Time* (8 February), 50–55.

Jackson, Rosemary (1981) *Fantasy: The Literature of Subversion*, London: Methuen.

Jacobus, Mary (1986) 'The Buried Letter: Feminism and Romanticism in *Villette*', in Eagleton, 119–20.

Jakobson, Roman (1956) 'Two Aspects of Language and Two Types of Aphasic Disturbances', in Roman Jakobson and Morris Halle, eds, *Fundamentals of Language*, The Hague: Mouton, 69–96.

Jakobson, Roman (1960) 'Closing Statement: Linguistics and Poetics', in Thomas Sebeok, ed., *Style in Language*, Cambridge, MA: MIT Press, 350–77.

James, Henry (1988) *The Turn of the Screw* [1897], New York: Bantam.

Jameson, Fredric (1979) 'Reification and Utopia in Mass Culture', *Social Text* 1, 94–109.

Jameson, Fredric (1981) *The Political Unconscious: Narrative as a Socially Symbolic Act*, Ithaca, NY: Cornell University Press.

Janeway, Elizabeth (1972) *Man's World, Woman's Place: A Study in Social Mythology*, New York: Morrow.

Jardine, Alice (1985) *Gynesis: Configurations of Woman and Modernity*, Ithaca, NY: Cornell University Press.

Jena, Seema (1990) *Carving a Pattern Out of Chaos: Withdrawal, a Narrative Device in Women's Writings*, New Delhi: Ashish Publishing House.

Johnson, Barbara (1987a) *A World of Difference*, Baltimore, MD: Johns Hopkins University Press.

Johnson, Barbara (1987b) 'My Monster/My Self', *Diacritics* 12:2, 2–10.

Jones, Douglas G. (1970) *Butterfly on Rock: A Study of Themes and Images in Canadian Literature*, Toronto: University of Toronto Press.

Jong, Erica (1973) *Fear of Flying*, New York: Holt.

Just, Martin-Christoph (1997) *Visions of Evil: Origins of Violence in the English Gothic Novel*, Frankfurt: Lang.

Kahane, Claire (1980) 'Gothic Mirrors and Feminine Identity', *The Centennial Review* 24, 43–64.

Kahn, Coppelia (1982) 'Excavating those "Dim Minoan Regions": Maternal Subtexts in Patriarchal Literature', *Diacritics* 12:2, 32–41.

Kamboureli, Smaro (1986) 'It Was Not a Dark and Stormy Night', *Tessera* (March), 13–17.

Kamboureli, Smaro and Shirley Neumann, eds (1986) *A Mazing Space: Writing Canadian Women Writing*, Edmonton: Longspoon/NeWest Press.

Kaplan, E. Ann, ed. (1980) *Women in Film Noir* [1978], London: British Film Institute.

Kaplan, E. Ann (1983a) 'Is the Gaze Male?', in Ann Snitow, Christine Stansell and Sharon Thompson, eds, *Powers of Desire: The Politics of Sexuality*, New York: Monthly Review Press, 309–27.

Kaplan, E. Ann (1983b) *Women and Film: Both Sides of the Camera*, New York: Methuen.

Kappeler, Susanne (1986) *The Pornography of Representation*, Minneapolis: University of Minnesota Press.

Karrasch, Anke (1995) *Die Darstellung Kanadas im literarischen Werk von Margaret Atwood*, Trier: Wissenschaftlicher Verlag.

Keitel, Eveline (1984) 'Die gesellschaftlichen Funktionen feministischer Textproduktion', in Opitz 239–54.

Keitel, Eveline (1986) *Psychopathografien: Die Vermittlung psychotischer Phänomene durch Literatur*, Heidelberg: Winter.

Keith, W. J. (1982) 'Approaches to Atwood: Taste, Technique, Synthesis', *Essays on Canadian Writing* 23, 88–96.

Keith, W. J. (1985) *History of English-Canadian Literature*, Toronto: University of Toronto Press.

Keith, W. J. (1989) *Introducing Margaret Atwood's 'The Edible Woman': A Reader's Guide*, Toronto: ECW Press.

Kelley, Mary (1979) 'The Sentimentalists: Promise and Betrayal in the House', *Signs* 4, 434–51.

Kelly, Kathleen Coyne (1996) *A. S. Byatt*, New York: Twayne Publishers.

Kiely, Robert (1972) *The Romantic Novel in England*, Cambridge, MA: Harvard University Press.

King, Stephen (1974) *Carrie*, New York: Doubleday.

King, Stephen (1981) *Danse Macabre*, New York: Everest House.

King, Stephen (1983) *Pet Sematary*, Garden City: Doubleday.

King, Stephen (1988) *Bare Bones: Conversations on Terror with Stephen King*,

New York: McGraw-Hill.

Kirkwood, Hilda (1986) 'Travelling Woman', *The Canadian Forum* 66, 40–41.

Klein, Jürgen (1975) *Der gotische Roman und die Ästhetik des Bösen*, Darmstadt: Wissenschaftliche Buchgesellschaft.

Kolodny, Annette (1975) *The Lay of the Land: Metaphor as Experience and History in American Life and Letters*, Chapel Hill: University of North Carolina Press.

Kolodny, Annette (1985) 'Dancing through the Minefield. Some Observations on the Theory, Practice and Politics of a Feminist Literary Criticism', in Showalter, 144–68.

Kosofsky Segdwick, Eve (1986) *The Coherence of Gothic Conventions* [1976], New York and London: Methuen.

Kristeva, Julia (1981) 'Women's Time', trans. Alice Jardine, *Signs* 7:1, 13–35.

Kristeva, Julia (1982) *Powers of Horror: An Essay on Abjection* [1980], trans. Leon S. Roudiez, New York: Columbia University Press.

Kristeva, Julia (1984a) 'My Memory's Hyperbole', in Stanton, 219–36.

Kristeva, Julia (1984b) *Revolution in Poetic Language* [1974], New York: Columbia University Press.

Kristeva, Julia (1986) *The Kristeva Reader*, ed. Toril Moi, New York: Columbia University Press.

Kristeva, Julia (1987) *Tales of Love* [1983], trans Leon S. Roudiez, New York: Columbia University Press.

Kristeva, Julia (1988) *Étrangers à nous-mêmes*, Paris: Seuil.

Kroetsch, Robert (1989) *The Lovely Treachery of Words: Essays Selected and New*, Toronto, New York, Oxford: Oxford University Press.

Kuhn, Annette (1982) *Women's Pictures: Feminism and Cinema*, London and New York. Routledge & Kegan Paul.

Kuhn, Annette (1985) *The Power of the Image: Essays on Representation and Sexuality*, London and Boston: Routledge & Kegan Paul.

La Belle, Jenijoy (1988) *Herself Beheld: The Literature of the Looking Glass*, Ithaca, NY and London: Cornell University Press.

Lacey, Liam (1986) 'Gods of Literature Smile on van Herk', *Globe and Mail* (22 September), C11.

Laqueur, Thomas (1990) *Making Sex: Body and Gender from the Greeks to Freud*, Cambridge, MA: Harvard University Press.

Lecker, Robert (1981) 'Janus through the Looking Glass: Atwood's First Three Novels', in Davidson and Davidson, 177–203.

Lecker, Robert, Jack David and Ellen Quigley, eds (1985) *Canadian Writers and Their Works*, Toronto: ECW Press.

LeClair, Tom (1989) *The Art of Excess: Mastery in Contemporary American Fiction*, Urbana and Chicago: University of Illinois Press.

Lehmann-Haupt, Christopher (1976) 'It's All the Rage', *New York Times* (23 December).

Lennox, John (1984) 'Gothic Variations: De Gaspe's Les Anciens Canadiens and Cable's The Grandissimes', *Essays on Canadian Writing* 29, 128–41.

Lentricchia, Frank and Thomas McLaughlin, eds (1990) *Critical Terms for*

Literary Study, Chicago and London: University of Chicago Press.

Lernout, Geert (1992) 'Postmodernism and the Canadian Condition Canadienne', in D'haen and Bertens, 67–74.

Lessing, Doris (1962) *The Golden Notebook*, London: Michael Joseph.

Lewis, Paul (1980) 'Fearful Lessons. The Didacticism of the Early Gothic Novel', *CLA Journal* 4, 470–84.

Light, Alison (1991) *Forever England: Femininity, Literature, and Conservatism Between the Wars*, London: Routledge.

Light, Alison (1986) '"Returning to Manderley" – Romantic Fiction, Female Sexuality and Class', in Eagleton, 140–44.

Lloyd-Smith, Allan Gardner (1989) *Uncanny American Fiction: Medusa's Face*, London: Macmillan.

Lochhead, Liz (1982) *Blood and Ice*, Edinburgh: Salamander Press.

Lomax, Marion (1994) 'Gendered Writing and the Writer's Stylistic Identity', in Wales, 1–19

Lord, Michel (1985) *En Quête du roman gothique québécois, 1837–1860: Tradition littéraire et imaginaire romanesque*, Quebec: Centre de Recherche en Littérature Québécoise, Université Laval.

Lovecraft, H. P. (1973) *Supernatural Horror in Literature* [1927], New York: Dover Publications.

Löwenthal, Leo (1972) *Literatur und Gesellschaft: Das Buch in der Massenkultur* [1964], Neuwied: Luchterhand.

Lyotard, Jean-François (1984) *The Postmodern Condition: A Report on Knowledge* [1979], trans. Geoff Bennington and Brian Massumi, Minneapolis: University of Minnesota Press.

McAndrew, Elisabeth (1979) *The Gothic Tradition in Fiction*, New York: Columbia University Press.

McCaffery, Steve (1986) *North of Intention: Critical Writings, 1973–1986*, New York: Roof Books.

McCarthy, Mary (1973) *Can There Be a Gothic Literature?*, Amsterdam: Uitgeverji de Harmonie.

McClung, Nelly (1935) *Clearing in the West: My Own Story*, Toronto: T. Allen.

McCombs, Judith (1978) 'Atwood's Native Concepts. An Interview', *Waves* 7, 68–77.

McCombs, Judith, ed. (1988) *Critical Essays on Margaret Atwood*, Boston: G. K. Hall.

McCombs, Judith (1989) '"Up in the Air So Blue": Vampire and Victims, Great Mother Myth and Gothic Allegory in Margaret Atwood's First, Unpublished Novel', *The Centennial Review* 33:3, 251–7.

McCombs, Judith (1991) *Margaret Atwood: A Reference Guide*, Boston: G. K. Hall.

McGowan, John (1991) *Postmodernism and Its Critics*, Ithaca, NY and London: Cornell University Press.

McGregor, Gaile (1985) *The Wacousta Syndrome: Explorations in the Canadian Langscape*, Toronto: University of Toronto Press.

McHale, Brian (1987) *Postmodernist Fiction*, New York, London: Methuen.

McHale, Brian (1992) *Constructing Postmodernism*, London, New York: Routledge.

MacKendrick, Louis K., ed. (1983) *Probable Fictions: Alice Munro's Narrative Acts*. Downsview: ECW Press.

McKinstry, Susan Janet (1987) 'Living Literally by the Pen: The Self-Conceived and Self-Deceiving Heroine–Author in Margaret Atwood's *Lady Oracle*', in Mendez-Egle, 58–70.

MacLean, Susan (1980) '*Lady Oracle*: The Art of Reality and the Reality of Art', *Journal of Canadian Fiction* 28/29, 179–97.

McMillan, Ann (1988) 'The Transforming Eye: *Lady Oracle* and Gothic Tradition', in Van Spanckeren and Castro, 48–64.

Mallet, Gina (1981) 'A Good Time to be a Canadian Writer', *The Toronto Star* (20 October), F1, F3.

Mallinson, Jean (1984) *Margaret Atwood and Her Works*, Toronto: ECW Press.

Mandel, Eli (1977) 'Atwood Gothic', *Malahat Review* 41.

Manguel, Alberto, ed. (1990) *The Oxford Book of Canadian Ghost Stories*, Toronto: Oxford University Press.

Manske, Eva (1982) 'The Nightmare of Reality: Gothic Fantasies and Psychological Realism in the Fiction of Joyce Carol Oates', in Versluys, 131–43.

Marcus, Jana (1997) *In the Shadow of the Vampire: Reflections on the World of Anne Rice*, New York: Thunder's Mouth Press.

Markovits, Andrei S. (1992) '"Hey, hey, ho, ho, Western Culture's got to go!" Über Multikulturalismus und Political Correctness in den USA', *Blätter für deutsche und internationale Politik*. 36:8, 989–1001.

Marks, Elaine and Isabelle de Courtivron, eds (1981) New *French Feminisms: An Anthology*, New York: Schocken Books.

Marlatt, Daphne (1988) *Ana Historic*, Toronto: Coach House Press.

Marsbridge, Francis (1978) 'Search for Self in the Novels of Margaret Atwood', *Journal of Canadian Fiction* 22, 106–17.

Martens, Catherine (1984) 'Mother Figures in *Surfacing* and *Lady Oracle*: An Interview with Margaret Atwood', *American Studies in Scandinavia* 16:1, 45–55.

Martin, W. R. (1979) 'Alice Munro and James Joyce', *Journal of Canadian Fiction* 24, 120–26.

Martin, W. R. (1982) 'The Strange and Familiar in Alice Munro', *Studies in Canadian Literature* 7, 214–26.

Martin, W. R. (1987) *Alice Munro: Paradox and Parallel*, Edmonton: University of Alberta Press.

Massé, Michelle (1992) *In the Name of Love: Women, Masochism and the Gothic*, Ithaca, NY: Cornell University Press.

Mayberry, Katherine (1994) 'Narrative Strategies for Liberation in Alice Munro', *Studies in Canadian Literature* 19:2, 57–66.

Mendez-Egle, Beatrice, ed. (1987) *Margaret Atwood: Reflection and Reality*, Living Author Series No. 6, ed. James M. Haule, Edinburg, TX: Pan American University Print Shop.

Michael, Magali Cornier (1996) *Feminism and the Postmodern Impulse: Post-*

World War II Fiction, Albany: State University of New York Press.

Miller, J. Hillis (1978) 'Ariadne's Thread: Repetition and the Narrative Line', in Valdes and Miller, 148–66.

Miller, Judith, ed. (1984) *The Art of Alice Munro: Saying the Unsayable*. Waterloo: University of Waterloo Press.

Miller, Karl (1976) 'Orphans and Oracles: What Clara Knew', *New York Review of Books* 23 (8 October), 30–2.

Miller, Nancy K. (1980) *The Heroine's Text: Readings in the French and English Novel*, New York: Columbia University Press.

Miller, Nancy K. (1981) 'Emphasis Added: Plots and Plausibilities in Women's Fiction', *PMLA* 96:1, 36–48.

Miller, Nancy K., ed. (1986) *The Poetics of Gender*, New York: Columbia University Press.

Mills, John (1977) 'Recent Fiction', *Queen's Quarterly* 84, 103–4.

Miner, Madonna (1984) *Insatiable Appetites: 20th-Century American Women's Bestsellers*. Westport, CT: Greenwood Press.

Minudri, Ragina (1973) 'From Jane to Germaine with Love', *Library Journal* 98 (15 February), 658–9.

Mishra, Vijay (1994) *The Gothic Sublime*, Albany: State University of New York Press.

Mitchell, Juliet (1974) *Psychoanalysis and Feminism*, Harmondsworth: Penguin.

Miyoshi, Maseo (1969) *The Divided Self: A Perspective of the Literature of the Victorians*, New York: New York University Press.

Modleski, Tania (1982) *Loving with a Vengeance: Mass-Produced Fantasies for Women*, Hamden: Archon Books.

Modleski, Tania, ed. (1986) *Studies in Entertainment: Critical Approaches to Mass Culture*, Bloomington: University of Indiana Press.

Modleski, Tania (1991) *Feminism without Women: Culture and Criticism in a 'Postfeminist' Age*, New York and London: Routledge.

Moers, Ellen (1978) *Literary Women* [1976], London: Women's Press.

Moglen, Helene (1976) *Charlotte Brontë: The Self Conceived*, Madison: University of Wisconsin Press.

Mohr, Hans Ulrich (1990) 'The Beginnings of the Gothic Novel from a Functional and Sociohistorical Point of View', in Ahrends and Diller, 9–28.

Mohr, Hans Ulrich (1991) 'Terror, Horror, Violence in the Postmodern Context', unpublished paper given at the International Gothic Conference, University of East Anglia, Norwich.

Moi, Toril (1985) *Sexual/Textual Politics*, London: Methuen.

Moi, Toril (1989) 'Feminist, Female, Feminine', in Belsey and Moore, 117–32.

Moodie, Susanna (1976) *Life in the Clearings versus the Bush* [1853], Toronto: MacMillan.

Moodie, Susanna (1989) *Roughing it in the Bush, or, Forest Life in Canada* [1852], Toronto: McClelland & Stewart.

Moretti, Franco (1983) *Signs Taken For Wonders: Essays in the Sociology of Literary Forms*, London: Verso.

Moretti, Franco (1987) *The Way of the World: The 'Bildungsroman' in European*

Culture, London: Verso.

Morrison, Toni (1987) *Beloved*, London: Chatto & Windus.

Morrow, Bradford and Patrick McGrath, eds (1991) *The New Gothic: A Collection of Contemporary Gothic Fiction*, New York: Random House.

Moss, John (1977) 'Alice in the Looking Glass: Munro's *Lives of Girls and Women*', in *Sex and Violence in the Canadian Novel: The Ancestral Present*, Toronto: McClelland & Stewart, 54–68.

Moss, John, ed. (1978) *The Canadian Novel Here and Now*, Toronto: NC.

Mott, Frank L. (1947) *Golden Multitudes: The Story of Bestsellers in the United States*, New York: Macmillan.

Mulvey, Laura (1975) 'Visual Pleasure and Narrative Cinema', *Screen* 16, 6–18.

Mulvey, Laura (1989) *Visual and Other Pleasures*, London: Macmillan.

Munro, Alice (1974) 'Home', in David Helwig and Joan Harcourt, eds, *New Canadian Stories: 74*, Ottawa: Oberon, 133–53.

Munro, Alice (1982a) 'The Ferguson Girls Must Never Marry', *Grand Street* 1:3 (Spring), 27–64.

Munro, Alice (1982b) 'What is Real?', in John Metcalf, ed., *Making It New: Contemporary Canadian Studies*, Toronto: Methuen, 223–6.

Munro, Alice (1983) *Lives of Girls and Women* [1971], New York: Plume.

Munro, Alice (1986) The Alice Munro Papers, first accession: An Inventory of the Archive at the University of Calgary Libraries. Calgary: University of Calgary Press.

Munro, Alice (1987) *Who Do You Think You Are?*, Toronto: Macmillan (published in the USA as *The Beggar Maid: Stories of Flo and Rose*, New York: Knopf, 1989).

Munro, Alice (1990) 'Meneseteung', [1988], *Friend of My Youth*, New York: Knopf, 50–74.

Munro, Alice (1996a) 'The Love of a Good Woman', *The New Yorker*, 23 and 30 December, 102ff.

Munro, Alice (1996b) *Selected Stories*, London: Chatto & Windus.

Murphy, Georgeann (1993) 'The Art of Alice Munro: Memory, Identity and the Aesthetics of Connection', in Pearlman, 12–27.

Murray, Heather (1986) 'Women in the Wilderness', in Kamboureli and Neumann, 74–83.

Murray, Heather (1990) 'Connectedness', *Canadian Literature* 124/125, 362–3.

Mussell, Kay (1975) 'Beautiful and Damned: The Sexual Woman in Gothic Fiction', *Journal of Popular Culture* 9, 84–9.

Mussell, Kay (1979) 'Gothic Novels', *Handbook of Popular Culture*, in Inge, 153–69.

Mussell, Kay (1981) *Women's Gothic and Romantic Fiction: A Reference Guide*, Westport, CT: Greenwood Press.

Mussell, Kay (1983) '"But Why Do They Read Those Things?": The Female Audience and the Gothic Novel', in Fleenor, 57–68.

Mussell, Kay (1984) *Fantasy and Reconciliation: Contemporary Formulas of*

Women's Romance Fiction, Westport, CT and London: Greenwood Press.

Napier, Elizabeth (1987) *The Failure of Gothic: Problems of Disjunction in an Eighteenth-Century Literary Form*, New York and Oxford: Oxford University Press.

Natoli, Joseph and Linda Hutcheon, eds (1993) *A Postmodern Reader*, Albany: State University of New York Press.

Neuburg, Victor (1976) *Popular Literature: A History and Guide: From the Beginnings of Printing to the Year 1897*, Harmondsworth: Penguin.

Neuman, Shirley and Glennis Stephenson, eds (1993) *ReImagining Women: Representations of Women in Culture*, Toronto: University of Toronto Press.

Neumeier, Beate (1991) 'Past Lives in Present Drama: Feminist Theatre and Intertextuality', in Fischer-Seidel, 181–98.

Neumeier, Beate (1996) 'Postmodern Gothic: Desire and Reality in Angela Carter's Writing', in Sage and Smith, 141–51.

Neumeier, Beate (1997) 'Female Visions: The Fiction of A. S. Byatt', in Irmgard Maasen and Anna Maria Stuby, eds *(Sub)Versions of Realism – Recent Women's Fiction in Britain*, Heidelberg: Winter, 11–25.

Neumeier, Beate, ed. (forthcoming) *Engendering Realism and Postmodernism: Contemporary Women Writers in Britain*, Amsterdam: Editions Rodopi.

Newton, Judith (1988) 'Women, Power and Subversion: Social Strategies in British Fiction 1778–1860', *Cultural Critique* 9, 87–121.

Newton, Judith and Deborah Rosenfeldt, eds (1985) *Feminist Criticism and Social Change: Sex, Class, and Race in Literature and Culture*, New York and London: Methuen.

Nicholson, Colin, ed. (1994) *Margaret Atwood: Writing and Subjectivity. New Critical Essays*, New York: St. Martin's Press.

Nicholson, Linda, ed. (1990) *Feminism/Postmodernism*, New York: Routledge.

Nicholson, Linda (1997) 'Emotion in Postmodern Public Spaces', in Hoffmann and Hornung, 1–24.

Nietzsche, Friedrich (1988) *Die Geburt der Tragödie: Sämtliche Werke*, ed. Giorgio Colli, Munich: DTV.

Nischik, Reingard M. (1991) *Mentalstilistik: Ein Beitrag zu Stiltheorie und Narrativik, dargestellt am Erzählwerk Margaret Atwoods*, Tübingen: Narr.

Northey, Margot (1976) *The Haunted Wilderness: The Gothic and Grotesque in Canadian Fiction*, Toronto and Buffalo: University of Toronto Press.

Nye, Russell (1970) *The Unembarrassed Muse: The Popular Arts in America*, New York: Dial Press.

Oates, Joyce Carol (1978) 'A Conversation with Margaret Atwood', *Ontario Review* 9, 5–15.

Oates, Joyce Carol (1980) *Bellefleur*, New York: Dutton.

Oates, Joyce Carol (1988) *(Woman) Writer: Occasions and Opportunities*, New York: Dutton.

O'Connor, Flannery (1987) 'A Temple of the Holy Ghost' [1954], in *The Complete Stories*, New York: Farrar, Straus, & Giroux, 236–48.

Ohmann, Carol (1977) 'Historical Reality and "Divine Appointment" in Charlotte Brontë's Fiction', *Signs* 2:4, 757–78.

Olney, James, ed. (1988) *Studies in Autobiography*, New York and Oxford: Oxford University Press.

Opitz, Claudia (1984) *Weiblichkeit oder Feminismus: Beiträge zur Interdisziplinären Frauentagung. Konstanz 1983*, Weingarten: Drumlin.

Ortner, Sherry (1974) 'Is Female to Male as Nature is to Culture?', in Rosaldo and Lamphere, 67–87.

Osborne, Carol (1994) 'Constructing the Self through Memory: *Cat's Eye*', *Frontiers: A Journal of Women's Studies*. 14:3, 95–112.

Pace, Eric (1978) 'Pulp Feminists: Gothic Liberation', *Human Behaviour* 7 (February), 50.

Page, P. K. (Patricia Kathleen) (1973) *'The Sun and the Moon' and Other Fictions*, Toronto: Anansi.

Papp-Carrington, Ildiko de (1985) *Margaret Atwood and Her Works*. Downsview: ECW Press.

Papp-Carrington, Ildiko de (1989) *Controlling the Uncontrollable: The Fiction of Alice Munro*, DeKalb: Northern Illinois University Press.

Parker, Patricia L. (1987) *Literary Fat Ladies: Rhetoric, Gender, Property*, New York and London: Methuen.

Parsons, Ann (1986) 'The Self-Inventing Self: Women Who Lie and Pose in the Fiction of Margaret Atwood', in Judith Spector, ed., *Gender Studies: New Directions in Feminist Criticism*, Bowling Green, OH: State University Popular Press, 97–109.

Patterson, James T. (1983) *America in the Twentieth Century: A History*, San Diego: Harcourt Brace Jovanovich.

Pearlman, Mickey, ed. (1993) *Canadian Women Writing Fiction*, Jackson: University Press of Mississippi.

Peirce, Charles Sanders (1965) *Collected Papers of Charles Sanders Peirce*, Cambridge: Belknap Press/Harvard University Press.

Perrakis, Phyllis S. (1982) 'Portait of the Artist as a Young Girl: Alice Munro's *Lives of Girls and Women*', *Atlantis* 7:2, 61–7.

Peterson, M. Jeanne (1972) 'The Victorian Governess: Status Incongruence in Family and Society', in Vicinus.

Place, Janey (1980) 'Women in Film Noir', in Kaplan, 35–67.

Plath, Sylvia (1988) *The Bell Jar* [1963], New York: Bantam.

Poenicke, Klaus (1971) 'Schönheit im Schoße des Schreckens: Raumgefüge und Menschenbild im englischen Schauerroman', *Archiv* 207, 147–51.

Poenicke, Klaus (1972) *Dark Sublime: Raum und Selbst in der amerikanischen Romantik*, Beiheft zum Jahrbuch für Amerikastudien 36, Heidelberg: Winter.

Poenicke, Klaus (1989) 'Eine Geschichte der Angst? Appropriationen des Erhabenen in der englischen Ästhetik des 18. Jahrhunderts', in Pries, 75–90.

Poovey, Mary (1980) 'My Hideous Progeny: Mary Shelley and the Feminization of Romanticism', *PMLA* 95, 332–47.

Poovey, Mary (1984) *The Proper Lady and the Woman Writer: Ideology as Style in the Works of Mary Wollstonecraft, Mary Shelley, and Jane Austen*, Chicago and London: University of Chicago Press.

Porrmann, Maria (1985) 'Angst-Flucht-Hoffnung: Von der Gothic Novel zum utopischen Roman', in Gnüg and Möhrmann.

Potter, Russell A. (1992) 'Edward Schizohands: The Postmodern Gothic Body', *Postmodern Culture: An Electronic Journal of Interdisciplinary Criticism* 2:3, 30ff.

Praz, Mario (1970) *The Romantic Agony* [1933], trans. Angus Davidson, London: Oxford University Press.

Pries, Christine, ed. (1989) *Das Erhabene: Zwischen Grenzerfahrung und Größenwahn*, Weinheim: Acta Humaniora.

Propp, Vladimir (1968) *Morphology of the Folktale*, Austin: University of Texas Press.

Prose, Francine (1996) 'Death and the Maid', *New York Times* (29 December), 6.

Punter, David (1980) *The Literature of Terror: A History of Gothic Fictions from 1765 to the Present Day*, London and New York: Longman.

Pusch, Luise, ed. (1983) *Feminismus: Inspektion der Herrenkultur. Ein Handbuch*, Frankfurt: Suhrkamp.

Radcliffe, Ann (1970) *The Mysteries of Udolpho* [1794], Oxford and New York: Oxford University Press.

Radcliffe, Elsa J. (1979) *Gothic Novels of the 20th Century: An Annotated Bibliography*, London: Scarecrow.

Radway, Janice (1977) 'A Phenomenological Theory of Popular and Elite Literature', dissertation, University of Michigan.

Radway, Janice (1981) 'The Utopian Impulse in Popular Literature: Gothic Romances and "Feminist" Protest', *American Quarterly* 33, 140–161.

Radway, Janice (1984) *Reading the Romance: Women, Patriarchy and Popular Literature*, Chapel Hill: University of North Carolina Press.

Railo, Eino (1927) *The Haunted Castle: A Study of the Elements in English Romanticism*, New York: Dutton.

Rao, Eleonora (1993) *Strategies for Identity: The Fiction of Margaret Atwood*, New York: Lang.

Rasporich, Beverly J. (1990) *Dance of the Sexes: Art and Gender in the Fiction of Alice Munro*, Edmonton: University of Alberta Press.

Redden, Sister Mary Mauritius (1939) *The Gothic Fiction in the American Magazines 1765–1800*, Washington: University of America Press.

Redekop, Magdalene (1992) *Mothers and Other Clowns: The Stories of Alice Munro*, London and New York: Routledge.

Restuccia, Frances (1986) 'Female Gothic Writing: "Under Cover to Alice"', *Genre* XVIII (Fall), 245–66.

Rhys, Jean (1982) *Wide Sargasso Sea* [1966], London: Norton.

Rich, Adrienne (1973) 'Jane Eyre: Temptations of a Motherless Woman', *Ms.* 10, 68–72, 106–7.

Rich, Adrienne (1976a) *Of Woman Born: Motherhood as Experience and Institution*, New York: Norton.

Rich, Adrienne (1976b) *On Lies, Secrets and Silence: Selected Prose, 1966–1978*, New York: Norton.

Richardson, John (1967) *Wacousta: or, The Prophecy: A Tale of the Canadas* [1833], Toronto: McClelland & Stewart.

Richler, Mordecai (1992) *Oh Canada! Oh Québec! Requiem for a Divided Country*, Harmondsworth: Penguin.

Richter, David H. (1996) *The Progress of Romance: Literary Historiography and the Gothic Novel*, Columbus: Ohio State University Press.

Ricou, Laurence (1973) *Vertical Man/Horizontal World: Man and Landscape in Canadian Prairie Fiction*, Vancouver: University of British Columbia Press.

Riedel, Wolfgang and Thomas Stein, eds (1992) *A Decade of Discontent: British Fiction of the Eighties*, Anglistik and Englischunterricht, Heidelberg: Winter.

Rigney, Barbara Hill (1978) *Madness and Sexual Politics in the Feminist Novel: Studies in Brontë, Woolf, Lessing and Atwood*, Madison: University of Wisconsin Press.

Rigney, Barbara Hill (1987) *Margaret Atwood*, Totowa: Barnes & Noble Books.

Rimmon-Kennan, Shlomith (1983) *Narrative Fiction: Contemporary Poetics*, New York: Methuen.

Ringe, Donald (1982) *American Gothic. Imagination and Reason in Nineteenth-Century Fiction*, Kentucky: University of Kentucky Press.

Riviere, Joan (1966) 'Womanliness as a Masquerade', in Rvitenbeek.

Roberts, Bette (1980) *The Gothic Romance: Its Appeal to Women Writers and Readers in Late Eighteenth-Century England* [1975], New York: Arno Press.

Robinson, Lillian S. (1985) 'Treason our Text: Feminist Challenges to the Literary Canon', in Showalter, 105–21.

Robinson, Sally (1991) *Engendering the Subject: Gender and Self-Representation in Contemporary Women's Fiction*, Albany: State University of New York Press.

Rocard, Marcienne (1996) 'Approche Gothique du Paysage Canadien: "Death by Landscape" de Margaret Atwood', *Caliban* 33 (Toulouse), 147–56.

Rogan, Helen (1975) 'How to Write a Gothic Novel', *Harper's* 250 (May), 45–7.

Rogers, Robert (1970) *A Psychoanalytical Study of the Double in Literature*, Detroit: Wayne State University Press.

Ronald, Ann (1983) 'Terror Gothic: Nightmare and Dream in Ann Radcliffe and Charlotte Brontë', in Fleenor, 176–86.

Rosaldo, M. Z. and L. Lamphere, eds (1974) *Women, Culture, and Society*, Stanford, CA: Stanford University Press.

Rose, Jacqueline (1987) *Sexuality in the Field of Vision*, London: Verso.

Rosenberg, Jerome H. (1984) *Margaret Atwood*, Boston: Twayne Publishers.

Rosowski, Susan J. (1981) 'Margaret Atwood's *Lady Oracle*: Social Mythology and the Gothic Novel', *Research Studies* 49:2, 87–98.

Ross, Catherine Sheldrick (1979) 'Calling Back the Ghost of the Old-Time Heroine: Duncan, Montgomery, Atwood, Lawrence and Munro', *Studies in Canadian Literature* 4:1, 43–58.

Ross, Catherine Sheldrick (1980) '"Banished to this Other Place": Atwood's *Lady Oracle*', *English Studies in Canada* 5:4, 460–75.

Ross, Catherine Sheldrick (1992) *Alice Munro: A Double Life*, Toronto: ECW Press.

Rowe, Karen (1979) 'Feminism and Fairy Tales', *Women's Studies* 6, 237–57.

Roy, Arundhati (1997) *The God of Small Things*, London: HarperCollins.

Ruggiero, Josephine and Louise C. Weston (1977) 'Sex-Role Characterization of Women in "Modern Gothic" Novels', *Pacific Sociological Review* 20, 292–300.

Ruskin, John (1960) 'The Nature of Gothic', in *The Stones of Venice* [1853], New York: Hill & Wang, 157–90.

Russ, Joanna (1983a) *How to Suppress Women's Writing*, Austin: University of Texas Press.

Russ, Joanna (1983b) 'Somebody's Trying to Kill Me and I Think It's My Husband: The Modern Gothic', in Fleenor, 31–56.

Russo, Mary (1987) 'Female Grotesques: Carnival and Theory', in De Lauretis 1987b.

Rvitenbeek, Hendrik M., ed. (1966) *Psychoanalysis and Female Sexuality*, New Haven, CT: College and University Press.

Sadleir, Michael (1969) *The Northanger Novels: A Footnote to Jane Austen* [1927], Folcroft: The Folcroft Press.

Sage, Lorna (1980) 'Invasion from Outsiders', *Granta* 3, 131–6.

Sage, Lorna (1992) *Women in the House of Fiction: Post-War Women Novelists*, New York: Routledge.

Sage, Victor, ed. (1990) *The Gothick Novel. A Casebook*, London: Macmillan.

Sage, Victor and Allen Lloyd Smith, eds (1996) *Modern Gothic: A Reader*, Manchester: Manchester University Press.

St Andrews, Bonnie (1986) *Forbidden Fruit: On the Relationship between Women and Knowledge in Doris Lessing, Selma Lagerlöf, Kate Chopin and Margaret Atwood*, Troy: Whitston.

Sanchez, Victoria (1995) 'A. S. Byatt's *Possession*: A Fairytale Romance', *Southern Folklore* 52:1 (Spring), 33–52.

Sandler, Linda, ed. (1977) *Margaret Atwood: A Symposium*, *Malahat Review* 41, Victoria: University of Victoria Press.

Sauermann-Westwood, Doris (1978) 'Das Frauenbild im englischen Schauer-roman', dissertation, Marburg.

Sawai, Gloria (1986) 'The Day I Sat with Jesus on the Sundeck and a Wind Came Up and Blew My Kimono Open and He Saw My Breasts', in Atwood and Weaver, 243–54.

Schlaffer, Edith and Cheryl Benard (1985) *Viel erlebt und nichts begriffen*, Reinbek: Rowohlt.

Schöwerling, Rainer, Gunter Tiggesbaumer and Hartmut Steinecke, eds (1996) *Literatur und Erfahrungswandel 1789–1830*, Munich: Fink.

Screen (1992) *The Sexual Subject: A Screen Reader in Sexuality*, London: Routledge.

Sellers, Susan, ed. (1991) *Feminist Criticism: Theory and Practice*, Toronto and Buffalo: University of Toronto Press.

Shelley, Mary (1993) *Frankenstein, or: A Modern Prometheus* [1818], London: Pickering.

Sherman, Leona F. (1980) *Ann Radcliffe and the Gothic Romance: A Psycho-analytic Approach* [1975], New York: Arno Press.

Shields, Carol (1989) 'Afterword', in Moodie, 335–40.

Shields, Carol (1991) 'In Ontario', *London Review of Books* 7 (February), 22–3.

Shields, Carol (1994) *The Stone Diaries*, Harmondsworth: Penguin.

Shields, Carol (1997) *Larry's Party*, Harmondsworth: Penguin.

Shinn, Thelma (1995) 'What's in a Word? Possessing A. S. Byatt's Metonymic Novel', *Papers on Language and Literature* 31:2 (Spring), 164–83.

Shorten, Lynda (1990) 'Imagine a Romance that Begins Like This', in Van Herk, 307–17.

Showalter, Elaine (1977) *A Literature of Their Own: British Women Novelists from Brontë to Lessing*, Princeton: Princeton University Press.

Showalter, Elaine, ed. (1985) *The New Feminist Criticism: Essays on Women, Literature, Theory*, New York: Pantheon.

Showalter, Elaine, ed. (1989) *Speaking of Gender*, New York and London: Routledge.

Showalter, Elaine (1991) 'American Female Gothic', in *Sister's Choice: Tradition and Change in American Women's Writing*, Oxford: Clarendon Press, 127–44.

Showalter, Elaine (1997) *Hystories: Hysterical Epidemics and Modern Culture*, New York: Columbia University Press.

Silverman, Kaja (1983) *The Subject of Semiotics*, New York and Oxford: Oxford University Press.

Silverman, Kaja (1986) 'Fragments of a Fashionable Discourse', in Modleski, 139–52.

Silverman, Kaja (1988) *The Acoustic Mirror: The Female Voice in Psychoanalysis and Cinema*, Bloomington: Indiana University Press.

Silverman, Kaja (1992) *Male Subjectivity at the Margins*, New York and London: Routledge.

Singley, Carol J. and Susan Elizabeth Sweeney, eds (1993) *Anxious Power: Reading, Writing, and Ambivalence in Narrative by Women*, Albany: State University of New York Press.

Skow, John (1996) 'In Very Confused Blood', *Time* (16 December).

Smith, Henry Nash (1974) 'The Scribbling Women and the Cosmic Success Story', *Critical Inquiry* 1, 47–70.

Smythe, Karen (1992) *Figuring Grief: Gallant, Munro and the Poetics of Elegy*, Montreal: McGill-Queen's University Press.

Snitow, Ann Barr (1979) 'Mass Market Romance: Pornography for Women is Different', *Radical History Review* 20, 141–61.

Sontag, Susan (1977) *On Photography*, New York: Farrar, Straus, & Giroux.

Spacks, Patricia Meyer (1975) *The Female Imagination*, New York: Knopf.

Spender, Dale (1986) *Mothers of the Novel: 100 Good Women Writers Before Jane Austen*, London and New York: Pandora.

Spigel, Lynn (1985) 'Detours in the Search for Tomorrow: Tania Modleski's *Loving with a Vengeance*', *Camera Obscura* (Spring/Summer), 215–34.

Spivak, Gayatri Chakravorty (1989) 'Three Women's Texts and a Critique of Imperialism', in Belsey, 175–95.

Stade, George (1987) 'The Big Chiller', *The Nation* (28 February), 258–63.

Staels, Hilde (1995) *Margaret Atwood's Novels: A Study of Narrative Discourse*, Tübingen: Francke Verlag.

Staines, David, ed. (1977) *The Canadian Imagination*, Cambridge: Cambridge University Press.

Stanton, Domna C., ed. (1984) *The Female Autograph: Theory and Practice of Autobiography from the Tenth to the Twentieth Century*, Chicago and London: University of Chicago Press.

Steele, Valerie (1985) *Fashion and Eroticism: Ideals of Feminine Beauty from the Victorian Era to the Jazz Age*, New York: Oxford University Press.

Stein, Karen (1975) 'Reflections in a Jagged Mirror. Some Metaphors of Madness', *Aphra* 6:2, 2–12.

Stein, Karen (1983) 'Monsters and Madwomen: Changing Female Gothic', in Fleenor, 123–37.

Stich, K. P., ed. (1988) *Reflections: Autobiography and Canadian Literature*, Ottawa: University of Ottawa Press.

Stimpson, Catherine (1976) 'Don't Bother Me, I'm Dead', *Ms.* (October), 36–40.

Stovel, Nora Foster (1986) 'Reflections on Mirror Images: Doubles and Identity in the Novels of Margaret Atwood', *Essays on Canadian Writing* 33 (Fall), 50–67.

Strossen, Nadine (1995) *Defending Pornography: Free Speech, Sex, and the Fight for Women's Rights*, New York: Scribner.

Struthers, J. R. (Tim) (1975) 'Reality and Ordering: The Growth of a Young Artist in *Lives of Girls and Women*', *Essays on Canadian Writing* 3, 32–46.

Struthers, J. R. (Tim) (1977) 'An Interview with Margaret Atwood', *Essays on Canadian Writing* 6, 18–27.

Struthers, J. R. (Tim) (1978) 'Alice Munro and the American South', in Moss, 121–33.

Struthers, J. R. (Tim) (1981) 'Some Highly Subversive Activities: A Brief Polemic and a Checklist of Works on Alice Munro', *Studies in Canadian Literature* 6:1, 140–50.

Struthers, J. R. (Tim) (1983) 'The Real Material: An Interview with Alice Munro', in MacKendrick, 5-36.

Sukenick, Roland (1969) *The Death of the Novel and Other Stories*, New York: Dial Press.

Summers, Montague (1964) *The Gothic Quest* [1938], New York: Russell & Russell.

Swan, Susan (1993) *The Wives of Bath*, Toronto: Knopf.

Tautsky, Thomas E. (1986) '"What Happened to Marion?": Art and Reality in *Lives of Girls and Women*', *Studies in Canadian Literature* 11:1, 52–76.

Taylor, Mark C. and Esa Saarinen1994 *Imagologies: Media Philosophy*, London: Routledge.

Tefs, Wayne (1986) '*No Fixed Address*: Review', *Border Crossings* 5:4, 55–6.

Tessera (1990) *Auto-Graph(e)* 8 (Spring).

Tessera (1995) *Bodies, Vesture, Ornament* 19 (Winter).

Thacker, Robert (1983) '"Clear Jelly": Alice Munro's Narrative Dialectics', in

MacKendrick, 37–60.

Thacker, Robert (1988) '"So Shocking a Verdict in Real Life": Autobiography in Alice Munro's Stories', in Stich, 153–62.

Thacker, Robert (1989) *The Great Prairie: Fact and Literary Imagination*, Albuquerque: University of New Mexico Press.

Thomas, Audrey (1970) *Mrs. Blood*, New York: Bobbs-Merrill.

Thomas, Audrey Callahan (1984) *Intertidal Life: A Novel*, Don Mills: Stoddart.

Thomas, Audrey (1986) 'A Fine Romance, My Dear, This Is', *Room of One's Own* 10:3 (March).

Thomas, Clara (1981) '*Lady Oracle*: The Narrative of a Fool Heroine', in Davidson, 159–75.

Thompson, G. Richard, ed. (1974) *The Gothic Imagination: Essays in Dark Romanticism*, Pullman: Washington State University Press.

Thompson, G. Richard, ed. (1979a) *Romantic Gothic Tales, 1790–1840*, New York: Harper & Row.

Thompson, G. Richard (1979b) 'Introduction: Gothic Fiction and the Romantic Age: Context and Mode', in Thompson 1979a, 1–43.

Thompson, Lars (1990) *Companions to Literature: A Teacher's Guide for 'The Handmaid's Tale'*, Mississauga: S. B. F. Media.

Tillman, Lynne (1987) *Haunted Houses*, New York: Poseidon Press.

Tillman, Lynne (1991) *Motion Sickness*, New York: Poseidon Press.

Tillotson, Marcia (1983) '"A Forced Solitude": Mary Shelley and the Creation of Frankenstein's Monster', in Fleenor, 167–75.

Tinkler-Villani, Valeria and Peter Davidson, with Jane Stevenson, eds (1995) *Exhibited by Candlelight: Sources and Developments in the Gothic Tradition*, Amsterdam: Rodopi.

Todd, Janet, ed. (1980) *Gender and Literary Voice*, New York and London: Holmes & Meier, 128–48.

Todd, Janet, ed. (1983) *Women Writers Talking*, New York and London: Holmes & Meier.

Todd, Janet (1986) *Sensibility: An Introduction*, London, New York: Methuen.

Todd, Janet and Marilyn Butler, eds (1989) *The Works of Mary Wollstonecraft*, New York: New York University Press.

Todd, Richard (1997) *A. S. Byatt*, Plymouth: Northcote House Publishers.

Todorov, Tzvetan (1975) *The Fantastic: A Structural Approach to a Literary Genre* [1970], trans. Richard Howard. Ithaca, NY: Cornell University Press.

Todorov, Tzvetan (1976) 'The Origin of Genres', *New Literary History* 8, 159–70.

Todorov, Tzvetan (1977) *The Poetics of Prose* [1971], trans. Richard Howard, Ithaca, NY: Cornell University Press.

Tompkins, Jane, ed. (1970) *Twentieth-Century Interpretations of 'The Turn of the Screw', and Other Tales: A Collection of Critical Essays*, Englewood Cliffs: Prentice Hall.

Tompkins, Jane, ed. (1980) *Reader-Response Criticism: From Formalism to Post-structuralism*, Baltimore and London: Johns Hopkins University Press.

Tompkins, Jane (1985) *Sensational Designs: The Cultural Work of American*

Fiction, 1790–1860, New York: Oxford University Press.

Tompkins, J. M. S. (Joyce Marjorie Sanxter) (1976) *The Popular Novel in England 1770–1800* [1932], Westport, CT: Greenwood Press.

Trautwein, Wolfgang (1980) *Erlesene Angst: Schauerliteratur im 18. und 19. Jahrhundert*, Munich: Hanser.

Tucker, Lindsey (1994) *Textual Escap(e)ades: Mobility, Maternity, and Textuality in Contemporary Fiction by Women*, Westport, CT: Greenwood Press.

Tyler, Anne (1976) 'The Woman Who Fled From Her Self', *The National Observer* (9 October), 25.

Urquhart, Jane (1986) *The Whirlpool*, Toronto: McClelland & Stewart.

Urquhart, Jane (1990) *Changing Heaven*, Toronto: McClelland & Stewart.

Valdes, Mario J. and Owen J. Miller, eds (1978) *Interpretation of Narrative*, Toronto: University of Toronto Press.

Van Herk, Aritha (1978) *Judith*, Toronto: McClelland & Stewart.

Van Herk, Aritha (1981) *The Tent Peg: A Novel*, Toronto: McClelland & Stewart.

Van Herk, Aritha (1984a) 'Picaros and Priestesses: Repentent Rogues', *Humanities Association of Canada Newsletter* 7:1, 14–18.

Van Herk, Aritha (1984b) 'Women Writers and the Prairie: Spies in an Indifferent Landscape', *Kunapipi* 6:2, 15–25.

Van Herk, Aritha (1986a) 'Double Crossings: Booking the Lover', in Kamboureli and Neumann, 276–86.

Van Herk, Aritha (1986b) *No Fixed Address: An Amorous Journey*, Toronto: McClelland & Stewart.

Van Herk, Aritha (1987) *The Aritha van Herk Papers: First Accession: An Inventory of the Archive at the University of Calgary*, Calgary: University of Calgary Press.

Van Herk, Aritha (1990a) *Places Far from Ellesmere: A Geografictione: Explorations of Site*, Red Deer: Red Deer College Press.

Van Herk, Aritha, ed. (1990b) *Alberta Rebound: Thirty More Stories by Alberta Writers*. Edmonton: NeWest Press.

Van Herk, Aritha (1991) *In Visible Ink: Crypto-Frictions*, Edmonton: NeWest Press.

Van Herk, Aritha (1992) *A Frozen Tongue*. Sydney: Dangaroo Press.

Van Herk, Aritha, ed. (1993) *Boundless Alberta*. Edmonton: NeWest Press.

Van Herk, Aritha (1996) 'Pioneers and Settlers', in Bruce King, ed., *New National and Post-Colonial Literatures: An Introduction*, Oxford: Clarendon Press, 81–101.

Van Herk, Aritha and Rudy Wiebe, eds (1980) *More Stories from Western Canada*, Toronto: Macmillan of Canada.

Van Herk, Aritha, Leah Flater and Rudy Wiebe, eds (1983) *West of Fiction*, Edmonton: NeWest Press.

Van Herk, Aritha, Wayne Tefs and Geoffrey Ursell, eds (1996) *Due West: 30 Great Stories from Alberta, Saskatchewan, and Manitoba*, Edmonton: NeWest Press.

Van Leeuwen, Fredericke (1982) 'Female Gothic: The Discourse of the Other', *Revista Canaria de Estudios Ingleses* 14, 33–44.

Van Spanckeren, Kathryn and Jan Garden Castro, eds (1988) *Margaret Atwood: Vision and Forms*, Carbondale and Edwardsville: Southern Illinois University Press.

Van Varseveld, Gail (1975) 'Talking with Atwood', *Room of One's Own* 1:2, 68.

Varma, Devendra P. (1966) *The Gothic Flame, Being a History of the Gothic Novel in England: Its Origins, Efflorescence, Disintegration, and Residuary Influences* [1957], New York: Russell & Russell.

Verduyn, Christl (1985) 'From "The Word on Flesh" to "The Flesh Made Word": Women's Fiction in Canada', *The American Review of Canadian Studies* 15:4, 449–64.

Versluys, Kristiaan, ed. (1992) *Neo-Realism in Contemporary American Fiction*, Amsterdam: Rodopi.

Vespermann, Susanne (1995) *Margaret Atwood: Eine mythokritische Analyse ihrer Werke*, Augsburg: Dr Bernd Wißner.

Vicinus, Martha, ed. (1972) *Suffer and Be Still: Women in the Victorian Age*, Bloomington: Indiana University Press.

Vincent, Sybil Korff (1983) 'The Mirror and the Cameo: Margaret Atwood's Comic/Gothic Novel *Lady Oracle*', in Fleenor, 153–63.

Vinken, Barbara, ed. (1992) *Dekonstruktiver Feminismus: Literaturwissenschaft in Amerika*, Frankfurt: Suhrkamp.

Vinken, Barbara (1993a) 'Der Stoff, aus dem die Körper sind', in *Neue Rundschau: Den Körper neu denken. Gender Studies*, Frankfurt: S. Fischer, 9–22.

Vinken, Barbara (1993b) *Mode nach der Mode: Kleid und Geist am Ende des 20. Jahrhunderts*, Frankfurt: S. Fischer.

Vinken, Barbara, ed. (1997) *Die nackte Wahrheit: Zur Pornographie und zur Rolle des Obszönen in der Gegenwart*, Munich: DTV.

Von Dadelsen, Bernhard (1992) 'Romantik ist mir zu gefährlich. Jodie Foster: Ein Interview', *Aspekte extra*, ZDF television (5 February).

Von Dadelsen, Bernhard (1994) 'Frankensteins Erben? Hollywoods neue Horror-Welle', *Aspekte*, ZDF television (9 December).

Wajcman, Judy (1991) *Feminism Confronts Technology*, University Park: Pennsylvania State University Press.

Wales, Kate (1994) *Feminist Linguistics in Literary Criticism*, Cambridge: English Association.

Wallace, Bronwen (1978) 'Women's Lives: Alice Munro', in David Helwig, ed., *The Human Elements: Critical Essays*, Ottawa: Oberon, 52–67.

Walpole, Horace (1986) *The Castle of Otranto* [1764], in Peter Fairclough, ed., *Three Gothic Novels*, London: Penguin.

Warwick, Susan J. (1984) 'Growing Up: The Novels of Alice Munro', *Essays on Canadian Writing* 29, 204–25.

Watson, Sheila (1966) *The Double Hook*, Toronto: McClelland & Stewart.

Watt, Ian (1957) *The Rise of the Novel*, London: Winds.

Watt, Ian, ed. (1981) *The Victorian Novel: Modern Essays in Criticism*, London:

Winds.

Waugh, Patricia (1989) *Feminine Fictions: Revisiting the Postmodern*, London and New York: Routledge.

Weedon, Chris (1987) *Feminist Practice and Poststructuralist Theory*, New York: Basil Blackwell.

Weedon, Chris (1997) 'Race, Gender, Emotion and the Construction of Otherness', in Hoffmann and Hornung, 39–54.

Weigel, Sigrid (1987) *Die Stimme der Medusa: Schreibweisen in der Gegenwartsliteratur von Frauen*, Reinbek: Rowohlt.

Weinzweig, Helen (1980) *Basic Black with Pearls*, Toronto: Anansi.

Weissberg, Liliane (1996) 'Gothic Spaces: the Political Aesthetics of Toni Morrison's *Beloved*', in Sage and Smith, 104–20.

Weißmann-Orzlowski (1997) *Das Weibliche und die Unmöglichkeit seiner Integration: Eine Studie der Gothic Fiction nach C. G. Jung*, Frankfurt: Peter Lang.

Weldon, Fay (1983) *The Life and Loves of a She-Devil*, New York: Pantheon.

Weldon, Fay (1984) 'How to Be Feminist', *New Society* (31 May), 354.

Whiteside, Anna and Michael Issacharoff, eds (1987) *On Referring in Literature*, Bloomington: Indiana University Press.

Whitney, Phyllis (1967) 'Writing the Gothic Novel', *The Writer* 80 (February), 9–13, 42f.

Wiebe, Rudy (1989) *Playing Dead: A Contemplation Concerning the Arctic*, Edmonton: NeWest Press.

Williams, Anne (1995) *Art of Darkness: A Poetics of Gothic*, Chicago: University of Chicago Press.

Wilson, Sharon Rose (1993) *Margaret Atwood's Fairy-tale Sexual Politics*, Jackson: Mississippi University Press.

Wilt, Judith (1980) *Ghosts of the Gothic: Austen, Eliot and Lawrence*, Princeton, NJ: Princeton University Press.

Winter, Kari J. (1992) *Subjects of Slavery, Agents of Change: Women and Power in Gothic Novels and Slave Narratives, 1790–1865*, Athens: University of Georgia Press.

Wolf, Naomi (1991) *The Beauty Myth: How Images of Beauty Are Used Against Women*, New York: W. Morrow.

Wollstonecraft, Mary (1986) *Vindication of the Rights of Woman* [1792], Harmondsworth: Penguin.

Wollstonecraft, Mary (1989) *The Wrongs of Woman, or Maria* [1798], in Janet Todd and Marilyn Butler, eds, *The Works of Mary Wollstonecraft*, Vol. 1, New York: New York University Press.

Wolstenholme, Susan (1993) *Gothic (Re)Visions: Writing Women as Readers*, Albany: State University of New York Press.

Wood, Robin (1979) *American Nightmare: Essays on the Horror Film*, Toronto: Festival of Festivals.

Wood, Robin (1986) *Hollywood from Vietnam to Reagan*, New York: Columbia University Press.

Woodcock, George (1986) 'The Plots of Life: The Realism of Alice Munro',

Queen's Quarterly 93:2, 235–50.

Woolf, Virginia (1979) *Women and Writing* [1925], London: Women's Press.

Woolf, Virginia (1985) *A Room of One's Own* [1929], London: Panther.

Worthington, Kim L. (1996) *Self as Narrative: Subjectivity and Community in Contemporary Fiction*, Oxford: Clarendon Press.

Yelin, Louise (1992) 'Cultural Cartography: A. S. Byatt's *Possession* and the Politics of Victorian Studies', *Victorian Newsletter* 81 (Spring), 38–41.

York, Lorraine M. (1988) *'The Other Side of Dailiness': Photography in the Works of Alice Munro, Timothy Findley, Michael Ondaatje, and Margaret Laurence*, Downsview: ECW Press.

York, Lorraine, ed. (1995) *Various Atwoods: Essays on the Later Poems, Short Fiction, and Novels*, Toronto: Anansi.

Index